AF868952

Investor Relations That Work

Investor Relations That Work

ARTHUR R. ROALMAN

amacom

A Division of American Management Associations

Library of Congress Cataloging in Publication Data
Main entry under title:

Investor relations that work.

Includes index.
1. Corporations—Investor relations—Addresses, essays, lectures. I. Roalman, Arthur R.
HD59.I58 658.2'85 80-65707
ISBN 0-8144-5620-0

© 1980 AMACOM
A division of American Management Associations, New York.
All rights reserved. Printed in the United States of America.

This publication may not be reproduced, stored in a retrieval system, or transmitted in whole or in part, in any form or by any means, electronic, mechanical, photocopying, recording, or otherwise, without the prior written permission of AMACOM, 135 West 50th Street, New York, N.Y. 10020.

First Printing

Preface

The purpose of this book is to show investor relations at work. It answers such questions as:

What does a company do when it's attacked?

What are the realities (as opposed to the myths) of investor relations?

How do you make an annual report stand out from the millions printed annually?

How can a company recover its reputation after a long-term disaster?

What are the essentials of investor relations?

What's ahead for investor relations?

The editor turned to leading professionals who were asked to give detailed descriptions of major investor relations experiences they have lived through.

Michael Seely starts this book with a chapter concerning myths (there are thousands) about investor relations and the realities that puncture the myths. Because of the billions of dollars that can be affected by investor relations, it is remarkable that so many myths have been allowed to exist without being broadly challenged and destroyed. Seely, a long-time student of the profession's literature, sets the stage for the other chapters of the book by describing what can be believed—and what should not be.

Terry Wilson, who wrote Chapter 2, has directed for some years one of the more successful investor relations programs functioning today. For Borg-Warner, he has created a strategy and has utilized techniques that, in some instances, follow well-worn paths, but in other instances are completely original. Someone trying to create an investor relations program would do well to emulate much of what Wilson does.

In Chapter 3, William Dunk analyzes one of the fundamental investor relations tools: the annual report. He discusses how to approach an annual report, how to establish its purpose, how to organize the work that goes into the report, and how to make it cost-effective. Dunk selected one report and did an in-depth presentation of why that report was organized, designed, and written as it was. But in describing one report, he offers information useful in the construction of most others.

In the next chapter, Frank Allston describes in detail what many companies are trying to do: present an accurate description of themselves to the financial community. A variety of techniques—usable in some form by most companies—were employed by Allston and IC Industries to do the job they wanted done.

Marvin Krasnansky, in Chapter 5, shares with us his plan for his company's broad communications effort and its investor relations program. Here he gives us his program presentation to the rest of the Becton-Dickinson management. Anyone can become more professional by reading and studying this presentation.

Robert Gaertner writes about a special company—Medtronic—whose actions directly affect human life. What happens when something goes wrong with your product (as it always can when human endeavor is involved)? Read what Gaertner has to say about the problems his company encountered, and what it did under the most trying of circumstances.

The next chapter goes from Medtronic and human hearts to a company called Castle & Cooke, where the problems are different. Here, the company's job is to achieve recognition. What does a company do to achieve financial recognition when its brand names are famous but the company name is not? Or when certain of its products are even less well-known than the little-known corporate name? N. John Douglas, the company's Director of Investor Relations, gives a detailed discussion of that problem.

In Chapter 8, William Baker of FMC Corporation does a sound job of describing his company's well-rounded yet (in many ways) traditional investor relations program. Few companies would go wrong if they copied FMC's actions.

Gerald Parsons stepped into a difficult situation when he joined Evans Products in Oregon. The company had many problems. Only a professional of Parsons's stature could have done what needed to be done. He had to convince the rest of management that the fragile strategy he proposed was the right one. It was not a quick and easy fix he was offering to a management that ached for remedies; but what he did worked, as is shown in Chapter 9.

And then there is the last chapter by Charles Kuehner, who directs investor relations for American Telephone & Telegraph, the sophisticate of sophisticates when it comes to investor relations. Kuehner was asked what's ahead for investor relations, and this chapter is his response. Coming from a top person in the field, his ideas and projections are both stimulating and incisive.

This book contains a great deal of actual IR material from the corporations discussed here. For convenience's sake, these documents (fact sheets, annual reports, and so forth) are reprinted in the back of the appropriate chapters, following the text of the chapter itself.

Arthur R. Roalman

Contents

1 **Myth and Reality in Investor Relations** **1**
Michael Seely
President, Investor Access Corp.

2 **Investor Relations: The Need to Disclose** **5**
Terry Wilson
Investor Relations Director, Borg-Warner Corp.

3 **How to Excel with an Annual Report** **95**
William P. Dunk
President, Corpcom Services, Inc.

4 **IC Industries, Inc.** **135**
Frank J. Allston
Director, Financial Communications, IC Industries, Inc.

5 **Corporate Communications—A Comprehensive View** **179**
Marvin L. Krasnansky
Former Vice President, Corporate Communications, Becton Dickinson & Co.

6 **Investor Relations at Medtronic** **195**
Robert A. Gaertner
Director of Corporate Administration, Medtronic, Inc.

7 **What's a Castle & Cooke?** **211**
N. John Douglas
Director of Investor Relations, Castle & Cooke, Inc.

8 **Investor Relations at FMC Corporation** **231**
William R. Baker
Director of Investor Relations, FMC Corporation

9 **Investor Relations in an Adverse Environment** **263**
Gerald A. Parsons
Vice President, Corporate Relations, Evans Products Co.

10 **The Next Ten Years in Investor Relations** **269**
Charles D. Kuehner
Director, Investor Relations, American Telephone & Telegraph Co.

Index **275**

1

Myth and Reality in Investor Relations

Michael Seely

There's a situation we might call the "gun to the temple" scenario for investor relations managers.

It goes like this. The CEO calls you in and says, "Joe, the fourth quarter looks lousy—we'll probably come in 20 percent under the Street's forecasts. Our stock's gyrating and I don't see how we're going to get that secondary off in any size. The board meets Monday and I'm going to recommend a dividend hike and maybe a 10 percent stock dividend. If we defer all our scheduled R&D into next year and ship all the inventory, we can scratch out a 10 percent EPS increase.

"What really worries me is the short position that's built up. (What is it now—50,000 shares?) Oh, and by the way, we're not going to adopt that new accounting principle on segment reporting. It shows just how bad the widget division is doing. To hell with the analysts—they never understand this company anyway.

"Finally," our imaginary CEO says, "our stock wouldn't be acting this way if you hadn't gotten so many institutions into it. We need more *individual* investors—Aunt Janes don't sell when you get a little bad luck."

For "keepers of the multiple" today, there is clearly no shortage of problems. There is even a new gospel among portfolio managers—the efficient market theory—that raises questions about whether *anyone* can outperform the market, and whether investor relations even matters.

What is this efficient market idea, and can it help you deal with less melodramatic versions of the scenario I just recounted? Efficient market theory says that, at any given time, stock prices adjust quickly to new information, like an earnings announcement, and do so in an *unbiased* manner: that is, the new prices are as likely to be too high as too low. The credibility of this theory is reflected in today's index funds, which are simply an effort to buy the "market," rather than to seek undervalued companies.

First, let it be said that efficient market literature *can* help IR managers. The research underlying modern portfolio theory has developed compelling data

Michael Seely is President of Investor Access Corp.

about why stocks sometimes act as they do. It offers IR managers some useful information, objective data that would have helped Joe deal in an objective manner with his CEO's misconceptions.

The fiduciary task of any management is to make shareholders richer. The valuation process with which investor relations is concerned represents the final link in the elaborate process of procurement, production, marketing, and finance. This final link—the capitalization of the resulting earnings stream—is too often the subjective stepchild of these other activities. The result is much activity that is speculative, if not purposeless. This is shocking when one realizes what a very, very small margin of stock price in any way relates to how well the individual company is doing in conventional terms—earnings, sales, and so forth.

In a classic study conducted by Benjamin King, it was found that only 20 percent of the variation in price in individual stocks had anything to do with the company itself. It is this slender margin of valuation over which management exercises any influence at all; overall market influences account for about 31 percent, industry influences 12 percent (although this varies), and other influences confined to limited groups of stocks but including subgroups (lodging stocks with an interest in Atlantic City are one good example) account for the balance.

In defining risk, many retail firms use a "proxy" term, which they routinely offer to their customers—the Beta coefficient. Betas define the historical volatility of individual stocks or portfolios, i.e., how much they go up or down with market movement. They define "market risk." (It's interesting to observe that volatility has little to do with whether a company is institutionally held or is owned by individuals. Domestic oil companies, for example, all have a Beta of around one. Some firms are 10 percent owned by institutions; others, over 60 percent.)

There are other kinds of risk—business, financial, and a third kind, which we call credibility. Faith in how a business keeps its books is obviously an important part of this. Because they're obliged so often to reconcile the perceptions of management with the perceptions of investors *about* management, IR managers must sometimes deal with controversial accounting issues that affect their company's credibility.

Adherents of the efficient market theory contend that sophisticated traders preclude a company from influencing stock prices through the legitimate use of alternative accounting policies. Let me offer some evidence that this is true.

A case for the market's efficiency can be derived from the introduction of generally accepted accounting principles (GAAP) to stock life companies. Analysts and others had complained that the existing statutory accounting led to difficulties in comparing publicly held life insurance companies. A study showed, though, that investor evaluations (particularly of one company vs. another) were unchanged by the new standardized accounting treatment. Evidence like this can buttress the IR manager's efforts to reflect investors' needs in his company's disclosure policy. Such evidence would have helped Joe deal with his CEO.

With regard to another point that the CEO raised, stock dividends or splits are usually meaningless, according to academic research. There are only two situations where, in this writer's view, there may be any justification for them at all—first, where you can split a stock back to a price level that reflects the taste of logical buyers ($20 for retail brokers, for example), or where a reverse split can get it out of the $5 area where most brokers can't solicit orders for it or provide margin.

A firm's *cash* dividend policy can be an eloquent way for management to tell investors what it thinks of the firm's prospects. While academics debate the "indifference" of investors to cash dividends or appreciation, it is apparent that the market likes a high rate on reinvestment by companies in expanding industries. Such firms should thus consider paying only a nominal dividend, and then primarily to get on approved lists. Contrary to popular opinion, there is little evidence that yield can "floor" a stock price, except at impractically high levels, as in voluntary liquidation.

Because dividends may be an eloquent information device, it is important to fully utilize dividend announcements as an opportunity to convey information about the rationale behind a firm's policy and the target payout. If investors understand (as they clearly try to do) the firm's reinvestment opportunities, its marginal cost of capital, and other important factors, the firm will acquire the kind of shareholders appropriate to it. This is what the academics refer to as the "clientele effect."

The kind of shareholders you attract should and often does depend on their incremental tax rate: if your yield is high, you'll tend to attract lower-income investors and, I suppose, institutions enjoying the 85 percent dividend exclusion. Small growth companies with a nominal dividend will tend to attract affluent, sophisticated investors with high incremental tax rates. Thus, if your company contemplates changing its dividend policy, and the change is expected to be a long-term one, and you know who your shareholders are, the communications needs are easier to define. Similarly, this kind of information can guide you in deciding whom to present your company to, and how to present it.

Let me briefly cover some related topics on the mind of our mythical CEO—unusual events that often seem to affect short-term price action.

Does listing matter? Many companies on the over-the-counter market wonder today about whether they should list their stock. More and more are electing to stay over the counter and work harder at developing better dealer support, rather than list on the New York or American Stock Exchanges.

The evidence shows that between the announcement of a firm's intention to list and the actual event, its stock does experience abnormal gains—gains that do not, however, endure. Similarly, an investigation of stock price action two weeks before and after 300 meetings of the New York Society of Security Analysts demonstrated the same action—a small price increase before and a decline thereafter.

Does volume affect stock prices? In itself, volume offers no convincing predictive value as to subsequent price action. Many investor relations managers and others (like our mythical CEO) are apprehensive that institutions and other large traders cause severe price changes at the expense of individual shareholders. It is possible to look at some specific events that alter supply and demand—for example, block sales and secondary distributions.

Studies on block sales and secondary distributions have shown that prices declined an average 2.3 percent, most of it occurring in the first week of the offering. Interestingly, the size of the deal made very little difference: the price declined just as sharply if 30 percent of the company were sold, as if less than 20 percent were sold.

What happens when the company is the seller, as in a rights offering? It has been shown that more often than not, the seller acted after a period of relatively strong price action, the stock on average declined negligibly (about .3 percent) during the month of the issue, and the size had little to do with the decline.

Finally, let me touch on short selling. Many of us get apprehensive when we see this going up, and it's hard to derive much solace from Bernard Baruch's favorite adage—that the bears don't have houses on Fifth Avenue. But he was right. In individual stocks, there is no objective evidence of a relationship between the volume of short selling and price movement, even when a big movement to sell short develops.

Obviously, much of this material that seeks to explain why stocks act as they do focuses on big companies and suffers from what the academics refer to as "multiple colinearity"—or, as one of our clients put it, "who's doing what to whom when." With so many factors affecting the valuation of individual companies, it's difficult to isolate a single factor for investigation.

So, no handbook exists on how to maximize value. Nor is there an easy answer for a major problem that particularly hurts smaller companies—the fact that today's Wall Street research goes where the commissions are, rather than where the quality of management and return may be. Effective investor relations will always reflect a large measure of imagination and hard work, as well as financial acumen and communication skill.

But this information is designed to rebut a lot of folklore and offers compelling evidence about the importance of shareholder communications that depict the real economic nature of the company; how alternative financial policies *may* affect valuation; and why individual stocks *sometimes* act the way they do.

The market deals with what it knows, and management must exercise a great deal of initiative in communicating company information to investors, or it must accept a discount in stock price. We look at IR as helping management contribute to market efficiency in its company's securities. To us, this means assuring that investment decisions in the securities are made by the right investors for the right reasons. It also means interpreting those collective buy-sell decisions to management on a basis that contributes to corporate decisions, rather than simply reflecting the market's perceptions of those decisions.

This is a tough job, but not an impossible one, as the following successful case histories eloquently substantiate.

2

Investor Relations: The Need to Disclose

Terry Wilson

Companies have had investor relations since the first stock sale under the old buttonwood tree, although investor relations programs have until recently tended to be more reactive than initiative.

More than any other single factor, the advent of negotiated brokerage commission rates has probably been responsible for the growing realization that an aggressive investor relations program is an essential element in corporate stewardship. The wrenching contraction and realignment within the brokerage industry that came with negotiated rates has left most companies with reduced research coverage and some with virtually none at all. A Drexel Burnham study found that some 500 companies lost their regular Wall Street research following in 1977 alone.

Smart company managements have recognized the need to fill the information void created by fewer research reports through marketing programs that focus on explaining the attractiveness of their company's shares in the same way they long have marketed products or services. Of course, even the most effective financial communications program has a limit. Good communications will not substitute for good management, a proven record of results, or future potential. But other factors being equal, the stock of a company that has maintained dialog with the financial community generally is more highly valued than one that has not done so.

Acceptance of this has led to a new and more enlightened approach to investor relations. Not too long ago, managements and investor relations practitioners were more concerned about minimum disclosure requirements than they were about the long-term value of providing investors with the information and insight they needed to make informed investment decisions about a stock.

As a complex company serving diverse markets and one whose performance has been spotty (except for the last few years), Borg-Warner has always found it difficult to capture the attention and sustain the interest of busy security

Terry Wilson is Investor Relations Director of Borg-Warner Corp.

analysts. To do so, we have tried to provide the quality disclosure necessary to understand our company's present status and future prospects.

In the zeal to attract new investors, however, companies sometimes overlook the ones they already have, yet this is the very audience that has already expressed an interest in the company through financial commitment. They are a known quantity, relatively easy to reach, and eager for meaningful news that could affect the future of their investment. It is not necessary to clamor for their attention; it need only be nurtured.

Borg-Warner's program has long recognized this fact and is designed as a two-part effort—the care and feeding of current investors, and attracting new investors. Naturally, there is considerable overlap. The important thing is that the information needs of existing shareholders is not subordinate to the search for new ones.

A written investor relations and disclosure policy (one example is included here) governs Borg-Warner's program and spells out the disclosure guidelines that we follow. This policy statement has appeared in each company Investor Fact Book since 1975. It has been helpful to corporate management and to present as well as potential investors.

The original purpose in publishing this document was to provide a set of ground rules that analysts and investors could trust the Company to follow in dealing with them. We found that the policy was equally valuable to managers inside the Company who on occasion had reason to be in contact with investor audiences. Since investor contact is not a big or frequent part of their normal jobs, these managers welcomed a set of published guidelines they could rely on in helping to serve this important audience.

In addition to our commitment to openness and equal treatment covered in the policy, we believe that good investor relations involves appropriate disclosure. An important part of the practitioner's role is as counselor on what disclosure is important to an understanding of the Company. To be effective, the program must strike a balance between too much and too little information. The "give 'em everything and dare 'em to sort it out" approach is just as wrong as not providing enough information.

The objective of the investor relations program should be to provide information necessary to forewarn investors about possible surprises (negative or positive); to convince investors that management is prepared to cope with good times and bad; and, finally, to show how the company is planning for future growth.

A myriad of communication tools is available to do this job. In deciding how best to use them, it is critical for the company to have a clear understanding of who their investors are and what their investment objectives are. They should be compatible with the character of the company. If they aren't, one of the first investor relations priorities should be to attract the category of investor whose expectations the company will most likely be able to fulfill.

Here is how we have used some of these tools at Borg-Warner. The annual report is probably the single most important item in this arsenal. There are many approaches to an annual report. No single approach is right for all companies, and no single approach will serve any one company indefinitely.

Unfortunately, few companies make the most of it. Many annual reports are delivered but few are read.

The primary objective of the annual report should be to inform. Some companies assign additional tasks to this document—to impress, persuade, or build a constituency. Where it must do all of these, it usually fails to do any. I believe the annual report should concentrate on its primary objective.

It should inform investors on the four factors that, according to an SEC study, are most instrumental in investor decisions to buy, sell, or hold a stock:

1. The outlook for the industries served.
2. Product and market data.
3. The financial condition of the particular company.
4. The quality of management.

This is not to say that companies shouldn't work to motivate employees, and move products, and be active in social and political issues—these things are expected of enlightened corporations today. But other vehicles than the annual report are better suited for conveying these messages.

We have used several Borg-Warner annual reports as editorial opportunities to tell a story of special interest to the Company. The 1977 report dealt with attitudes toward work. The 1978 report took a different tack and returned to a more basic financial document, a trend that continued in the 1979 report reprinted here. (We have not included most of the financial data and have omitted some handsome color photographs that appeared in the original.)

To handle part of the communications load that the annual report had tried to carry, Borg-Warner also published a separate photo book designed to tell the story of the Company's markets and how it serves them. We think both publications will be more successful in doing their own communications jobs and will at the same time promote an easier and fuller understanding of Borg-Warner.

To be effective, the annual report must address those four subject areas investors would like to know more about. And it doesn't do much to build readership to discuss these issues only in terms of the past: too few annual reports talk about the future. Assuming that the content of the annual report should be confined to developments in the specific year covered is also a mistake; to be timely and helpful to investors, it should also be an annual update on the company's prospects.

A fact book is another supplemental publication that can help reduce the communications burden the annual report must otherwise carry. The primary objective of Borg-Warner's Investor Fact Book has been to provide a midyear update on the Company's operations plus information on selected aspects of the Company in more detail than is usually appropriate or possible in the annual report. The content is aimed at professional investors and others who have more than a casual interest in the Company. The 1979 fact book, which appears after the 1979 annual report at the end of this chapter, was originally intended for professional investors, but was also sent to more than 6,000 shareholders who asked for a copy. In all, about 30,000 copies are distributed during the year.

We have used the fact book as a forum to discuss subjects of importance to management and readers alike and to present the Company in an additional perspective. Our own surveys indicate that perhaps we have overdone the editorial approach. Future issues will probably include a larger proportion of statistical data in tabular form.

Crisp quarterly reports offer the best communications link with shareholders on a continuing basis, yet many companies have not worked to make them effective. Here again is an opportunity to expand on material that is not considered significant enough for treatment in the annual report. Our quarterly report (in the back of the chapter, we show the one that covers the third quarter of 1979) is enclosed with each dividend check. In that way, we know that at least it will be opened. There are some disadvantages to this approach, however. Because the dividend check must usually be mailed in a letter-sized envelope, the quarterly report must conform to the same packaging. This limits the bold use of photography and restricts overall size.

For more immediate, fast-breaking news items of significance, we mail a financial bulletin to specific audiences. This informal communication, which is issued irregularly but as often as seems advisable, provides timeliness, and its controlled distribution keeps costs to a minimum. In 1979, 12 financial bulletins were prepared and mailed.

Other written communications that we use in investor relations include special interim reports, cards, and national advertisements aimed at audiences not otherwise reached. In addition to written communications, there is a variety of tools the investor relations professional can use to build an effective program.

Appearances by top management before regular analyst society meetings or before smaller meetings sponsored by the particular company are an important aspect of any well-rounded program. Borg-Warner tries to schedule about eight such meetings each year in the United States. Key presentations are reprinted and mailed to stock analysts and others.

Society meetings are especially helpful in trying to build a new and larger following in that geographic area. The smaller, company-sponsored meeting is often more productive in satisfying the information needs of key analysts already following the company in that area.

We try to set a specific objective for each meeting we hold. We like to concentrate our presentation on a few points rather than touch all the bases. An overview can be effective, however, especially at society meetings where a large segment of the audience may be relatively unfamiliar with the specific company.

In recent years, our meeting program has been expanded in an effort to reach retail brokers and current shareholders as well. Tying an analyst luncheon meeting to a morning meeting for shareholders and an after-the-close-of-the-market meeting for registered representatives (with perhaps one or two personal office visits sandwiched in between) makes efficient use of your management's time in an out-of-town location. In addition to our financial meeting program in the United States, we meet with current and potential institutional shareholders in the financial capitals of Europe at least once a year.

The annual meeting of shareholders, viewed by some companies as a necessary evil, actually represents a significant opportunity to show off your company, its management, and your products. To allow a few vocal gadflies to deprive the company and its owners of the chance to get to know each other better is a cop-out. (A number of these shareholder activists, however, have actually made positive contributions to corporate/shareholder democracy, the present level of disclosure, and the annual meeting itself.)

In 1978, the Borg-Warner meeting was held in the evening for the first time. This change from the traditional morning sessions was a major factor in the threefold increase in attendance.

We also have held a number of regional shareholder information meetings during the last ten years to give owners living outside the headquarters city a chance to meet the Company's management team first hand. We have scheduled the meetings both in the morning and in the afternoon. Their format is more informal than that of the annual meeting, and the question period has proved a valuable two-way communications forum that has been as beneficial to Company managers as to owners. We have tried to keep prepared presentations to 20 minutes in length. This allows plenty of time for questions during the approximately one-hour meetings. At this point, we have visited eight different cities, mostly in the South and West; and we have met four times in two of these cities—New York and Los Angeles.

Another minor program touch that has paid handsome rewards in our effort to build shareholder loyalty was the appointment of a shareholder representative. Shareholders with questions about their accounts or about the business no longer need to call or write an impersonal corporate office; they have a friend there, and they can contact her by name, Ms. Dorothy Flynn. Soon they may be able to reach her direct via an "800" telephone line. Dorothy and her job have been highlighted in the last three annual reports and in quarterly newsletters. Her role as shareholder ombudsman is catching on. And if Dorothy herself doesn't know the answer to a question, she usually knows someone who does.

There are plenty of other things in the shareholder relations area that we'd like to be doing but aren't doing yet. The ideas come easy; putting them in place and making sure there is a follow-through are the tough jobs that require good people.

Borg-Warner's investor relations staff includes a director, a manager of financial communications, and two helpers who function as paraprofessionals. Dorothy Flynn is on the legal staff. The financial communications manager is responsible for increasing the Company's retail research coverage and for building a greater following among retail brokerage salespeople. In this job, he spends a good part of his time on the phone with security analysts and stockbrokers discussing the Company and answering their questions.

Borg-Warner's top management, including the chief executive and chief financial officer, has long taken an active and personal interest in the Company's investor relations program. Senior Vice President, Finance, James J. Gavin, Jr., says:

Not being one of the so-called "nifty 50" and not even close, we've had to work hard at investor relations by trying new approaches, spending more time, and making our people more accessible in explaining our Company and management philosophy. We owe this to those who have invested in the Company.

Because of Borg-Warner's complexity, we accepted the responsibility of trying to help analysts, and investors in general, understand its future through openness and candor in our communications and other investor relations programs.

There was a time when I found analysts' prying questions irritating and annoying. Finally, I realized that most of the questions were good ones—the kind we (management) should be asking ourselves.

About the best set, in my opinion, was used by a pair of Japanese analysts who visited us a few years ago. They asked these questions:

- What growth trend do you expect in the industries you serve compared with the nominal and real GNP growth you foresee?
- Our estimate is that average U.S. corporate profits will be up X percent this year. How will your company do relative to this?
- How does your company differ from others in your markets?
- What are your company's weak points, and what are your plans to resolve them?
- What are your company's strengths?
- Which of your present business areas would you like to expand most, and are there any new fields you would like to enter?

I think any company that knows the answers to these questions is probably a well-managed one.

And the company that is willing to discuss these questions in good times and bad has an investor relations program that will serve its own long-range best interests and those of its shareholders and potential investors alike.

Security analysts seem to agree with Jim Gavin. In a recent Opinion Research Corporation study that asked their views on corporate investor relations, the analysts and portfolio managers surveyed said that their ideal requirements for an effective investor relations program were candor, credibility, and an up-to-date, knowledgeable investor relations officer who could tell them honestly and promptly of both positive and negative developments in the company's operations without subjecting them to a pitch. At the same time, 9 out of 10 of the analysts and portfolio managers surveyed in the ORC study agreed that companies have strengthened their investor relations programs in recent years and have improved the quality of their annual reports and other written materials.

Of course, there remains room for improvement. We will be doing everything right when we have a compatible shareholder base composed of investors who no longer sell their stock because they don't understand the company or why they invested in it, because of poor communications, because they were surprised by poor earnings results, or because they didn't know what to expect in good times and bad. They will sell their stock only when their own investment objectives have changed.

Investor relations and disclosure policy

BORG WARNER

Objectives. Borg-Warner's investor relations program aims to provide the information investors, both personal and professional, need to make informed decisions. To that end, we release, widely and promptly, any information that can reasonably be expected to affect the market value of Borg-Warner stock, or investor's attitudes toward it. This is accomplished by news releases, annual and quarterly reports and the *Investor Fact Book;* through in-person meetings with shareholders, security analysts and the news media. We also answer reasonable questions of a non-material nature from the latter groups, within the limits of confidentiality. When we do answer such queries, we do not feel obliged to pass on the information to others who haven't specifically asked for it.

Spokesmen. Investors, analysts and reporters sometimes want to speak directly with our operating officers; and we make them available as schedules permit. To reduce the need for such contracts, however, we normally schedule several occasions a year when interested groups can meet company officers personally. Our officers appear only at meetings open to the press.

We've designated company contacts for the professional investment community, shareholders and the news media:

Financial Community
- William Valiant, 322-8700
- Terry Wilson, 322-8672
- James Gavin, 322-8517
- Jack Frisbie, 322-8674

Shareholders
- Russell Parsons, 322-8530
- Dorothy Flynn, 322-8568

News Media
- Robert Kelly, 322-8676
- Douglas Mueller, 322-8670
- Robert Morris, 322-8552

We suggest that analysts who don't regularly follow Borg-Warner first contact Terry Wilson, the manager of investor relations. Registered representatives should contact Jack Frisbie.

No other Borg-Warner employee is authorized to answer inquiries or discuss the financial or operating affairs of the corporation with members of the financial community without prior approval of one of the above named persons.

Projections. We don't regularly make earnings forecasts, but we will make earnings projections when we think it appropriate. We're most apt to do so when something happens that seems likely to materially affect results previously expected. We'll disseminate these projections widely and update them as needed in the affected period.

We will neither estimate our earnings nor comment on the estimates of others, though we may comment on the assumptions others have used in predicting our results if they differ markedly from our own. Except for such comments, however, our designated contacts won't confirm the accuracy of outside estimates either implicitly or explicitly.

Our schedule of quarterly earnings announcements is generally as follows:

First quarter—Annual Meeting, usually fourth Tuesday in April
Second quarter—July 20-25.
Third quarter—October 20-25.
Fourth quarter—February 5-10.

During the approximately three weeks before the announcement of each quarter's earnings, company contacts won't answer questions on specific units' performance, though they will answer those dealing with routine operational matters.

Limits. We'll try to answer your questions as fully and promptly as possible, but there are certain limits. We release earnings by product or service group only annually; we give only general information on the performance of separate divisions or plants. We review these limits periodically and change them as warranted or possible.

Publications. We routinely distribute the *Investor Fact Book*. Financial Bulletins, reprints of some speeches and other items of interest to security analysts. Shareholders may obtain copies of these documents from the manager of investor relations.

Borg-Warner

1979 Annual Report

Earnings up 16%; sales 17%

Margins slip slightly due to inflation impact

Return on equity tops 15%

Dividend rate up 15%; 4th increase in four years

The year in brief

Year ended December 31

Operations		1979	1978	Change
		(millions except per share data)		
	Net sales	**$2,717.4**	$2,326.0	+17%
	Net earnings	**155.6**	133.8	+16%
	Net earnings retained in business	**111.8**	94.5	+18%
Per share of common stock				
	Net earnings	**$ 7.25**	$ 6.24	+16%
	Dividends paid	**2.075**	1.85	+12%
Financial data				
	Shareholders' equity	**$1,076.9**	$ 966.1	+11%
	Return on average equity	**15.2%**	14.6%	
	Book value per share of common stock	**50.99**	45.64	+12%

Technology: testing, tribulation and triumph

***Short lengths of metal belt** are all they are, but they assume impressive stature. Quite the opposite of traditional transmission belts, this one transmits torque by compression; each precision element pushes the one ahead of it. Its design is one key to a fuel-saving, small-car automatic transmission being developed cooperatively by Van Doorne Transmissie in The Netherlands, Fiat and Borg-Warner. Perfecting the concept of a continuously variable transmission has long been a quest of automotive engineers. We don't have all the bugs out yet, but we're working on them.*

Borg-Warner's growth and success in the past half century have resulted directly from our dedication to innovation. Our developments have improved the mobility, comfort and convenience of millions of people. Now, however, not just success but survival itself will depend on innovation geared to tomorrow's needs.

That is why Borg-Warner is making a larger commitment than ever to innovative technology.

The following pages tell about some of our developments and research programs. Many are related to energy efficiency.

In our constant testing of new ideas, we have had triumphs, frustrations and failures. Some of the developments pictured in this report may never come to commercial fruition. But they demonstrate the breadth of our inquiry—out of which will come the seeds of our business future.

Inside this report

Financial and operating review	2
Management commentary	16
Inflation and its impact	20
Financial section	24-39
Officers and directors	40
The businesses of Borg-Warner	41

Borg-Warner's 1979 performance set records of all kinds—for the fourth year in a row

For the fourth consecutive year, Borg-Warner sales, earnings and earnings per share were the highest in the company's history. Return on shareholders' equity topped 15% for the first time since 1955. Profit margin, however, slipped slightly—the first decline in four years.

Net sales totaled $2.7 billion, up 17%. Earnings of $156 million were 16% ahead of 1978. Per-share earnings equaled $7.25, compared with $6.24 in the prior year. Each of the company's major business areas shared in the sales uplift, and all but the Air Conditioning group had higher earnings.

Performance was helped by a sharp jump in earnings from the financial and protective services companies and a much lower tax rate for the year.

While earnings from manufacturing operations rose 11%, earnings from service-related operations surged 52% ahead of 1978. Nearly 18% of Borg-Warner's total earnings in 1979 was derived from service businesses. Ten years ago, service businesses contributed only 5% of total earnings.

There were bright spots among the manufacturing operations with the Chemicals and Plastics group showing a 50% jump in earnings. The Transportation Equipment group managed a 9% earnings improvement despite the depressed auto market in the U.S., and the Industrial Products group maintained its string of uninterrupted growth for the ninth year with a 20% increase in earnings.

A significantly lower effective tax rate, which was 35% in 1979 and 43% in 1978, also helped net earnings. The lower rate resulted primarily from a 2% reduction in the U.S. statutory tax rate for corporations, a tax credit on inventories related to U.K. operations, and favorable tax settlements in cases involving operations disposed of in prior years. Overall, the difference in tax rates contributed 78 cents to 1979 earnings per share.

More than offsetting this tax gain was the negative impact of continuing severe inflation. The last-in, first-out (LIFO) method of inventory valuation used by Borg-Warner on a worldwide basis results in a downward adjustment to earnings during periods of rising prices to recognize the effect of inflation. The LIFO adjustment to earnings in 1979 was 90 cents per share more than in 1978.

Sales of consolidated units outside the U.S. were a record $794 million, up 25% from 1978, and nearly 30% of total sales for the company. Export sales from U.S. operations added another $268 million to non-U.S. business and were 26% higher than the previous record in 1978. Non-U.S. profit margins continue to improve but still trail the return earned on U.S. manufacturing operations in 1979.

Earnings from affiliates were up sharply in 1979, especially operations in Japan.

Borg-Warner's financial condition remains strong. During the year, Borg-Warner's invested capital

Net sales

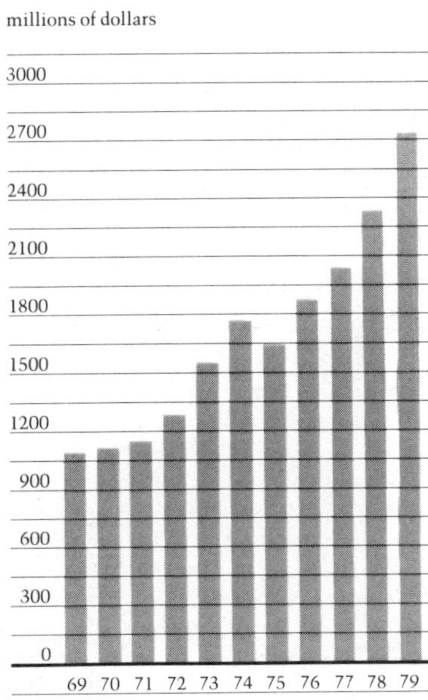

Net earnings

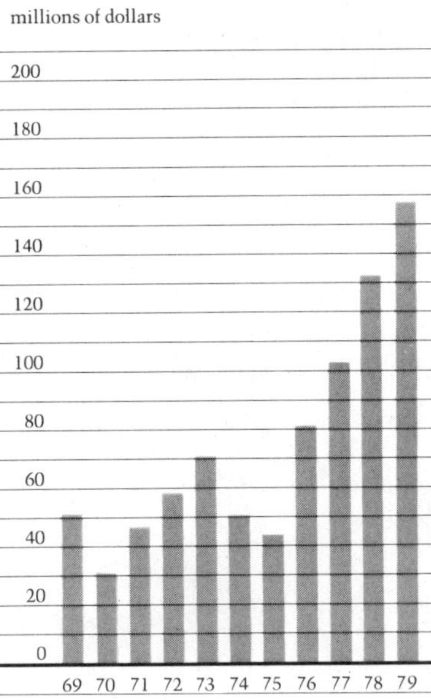

Earnings per share
Dividends per share

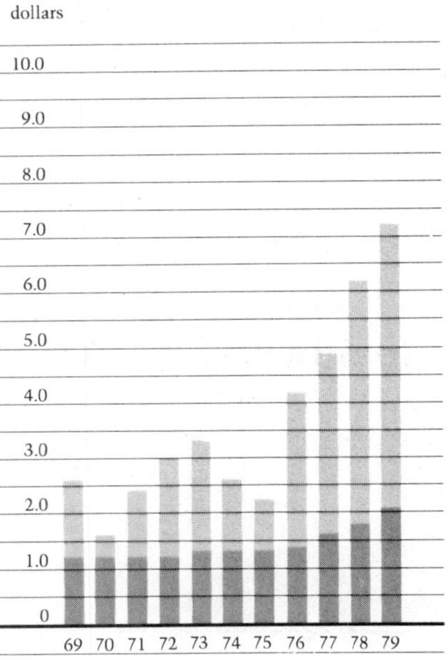

increased by $135 million—$111 million from equity growth and only $24 million from added debt. However, of the $111 million increase in equity, $104 million was required to support the higher level of capital spending, higher dividends paid to shareholders and increased investments and advances, largely the reinvestment of earnings in unconsolidated subsidiaries.

As a result, cash flow was a negative $49 million; and working capital declined by $9 million, in spite of record earnings. These factors caused the company's current ratio to drop below the 2-to-1 mark for the first time in recent history. At the same time, the company's debt-to-equity ratio was held at a conservative 20% level.

Borg-Warner has established adequate reserves to cover contingencies, including the announced closing of the Letchworth transmission plant in the U.K. during 1980.

Inventories at current value were up 20%, and receivables 21%—slightly above the gain in sales for the year. The real quantity increase in inventories was only 6%, with 14% due to inflation.

Interest expense rose 24% because of generally higher rates during the year and slightly higher debt.

Capital expenditures, including capitalized leases, totaled $131 million in 1979, compared with $115 million the year before. In 1980, Borg-Warner expects to invest about $125 million in new plants and equipment. It should be possible to finance this investment without the need for additional borrowing.

In addition to new facilities, Borg-Warner invested $56 million in research and development. This effort goes on at major divisions throughout the company and at the corporate research center near Chicago. Some of the technology and innovation that has resulted is featured photographically in this report.

Capital expenditures
Depreciation
millions of dollars

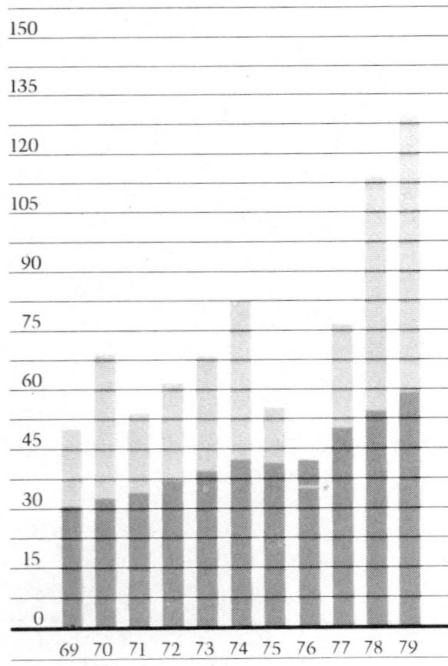

Shareholders' equity
Debt
millions of dollars

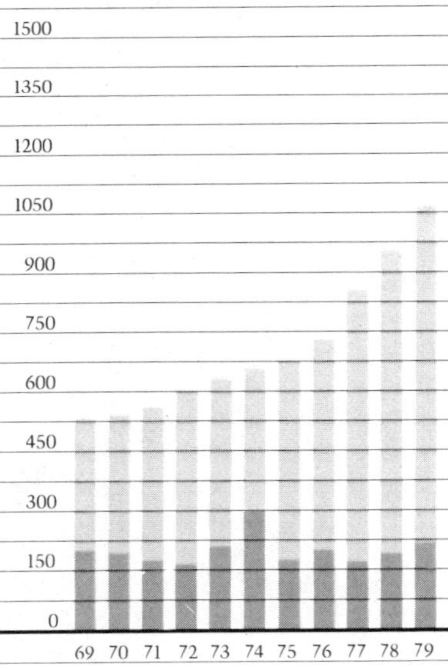

Return on average equity
percent

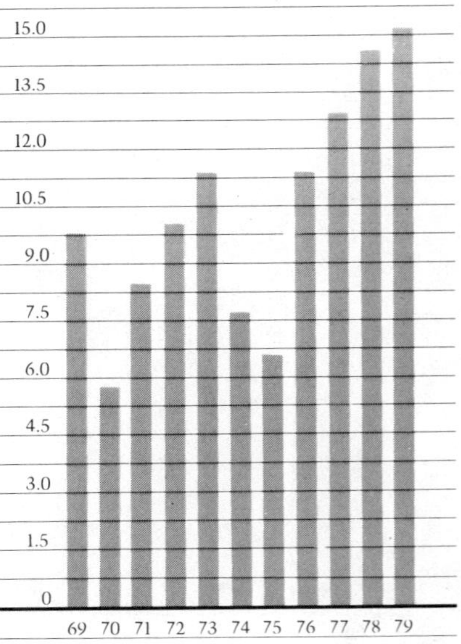

*Capital expenditures are $36 million in 1976.

Group results show improvement in all but one area

Sales and earnings by product or service area						
(millions of dollars)	**1979**	1978	1977	1976	1975	1974
Sales						
Air Conditioning	**$ 570.3**	$ 516.9	$ 439.2	$ 352.5	$ 313.1	$ 312.4
Chemicals & Plastics	**595.4**	472.1	421.8	399.1	278.9	345.1
Industrial Products	**552.3**	474.1	434.3	410.4	378.6	316.9
Transportation Equipment	**986.6**	844.5	718.5	652.4	582.5	614.4
Sales of present operations	**2,704.6**	2,307.6	2,013.8	1,814.4	1,553.1	1,588.8
Discontinued operations	**12.8**	18.4	18.1	48.0	85.9	179.0
	$2,717.4	$2,326.0	$2,031.9	$1,862.4	$1,639.0	$1,767.8
Net earnings						
Air Conditioning	**$ 12.1**	$ 19.6	$ 18.3	$ 9.7	$ 6.0	$ (1.0)
Chemicals & Plastics	**27.7**	18.5	6.6	13.2	(2.3)	8.6
Financial and Protective Services	**27.3**	18.0	12.8	10.6	8.1	8.0
Industrial Products	**41.7**	34.7	33.8	21.3	17.6	12.4
Transportation Equipment	**46.2**	42.4	32.0	26.5	14.3	17.2
Earnings of present operations	**155.0**	133.2	103.5	81.3	43.7	45.2
Discontinued operations	**.6**	.6	.5	.4	.8	5.6
	$ 155.6	$ 133.8	$ 104.0	$ 81.7	$ 44.5	$ 50.8*

**After accounting changes*

Transportation Equipment group had improved results despite downturn in auto sales

For the fourth year in a row, the units representing Borg-Warner's largest product area turned in improved sales and earnings. The 1979 performance was the toughest since it was achieved while U.S. auto production was falling to its lowest level in five years. Net earnings for the group in 1979 rose 9% on an increase of 17% in sales.

The diversification of the group within the broad transportation market was a big factor in 1979's strong performance. The group sells a variety of components not only to passenger car manufacturers around the world, but to the truck, off-highway, recreational, agricultural and marine industries as well. Replacement parts for vehicles of all kinds represent about 15% of the group's total business.

Contrary to what usually is assumed, components sold to new-car manufacturers (OEMs) in the U.S. make up less than one-quarter of the group's sales. Yet, these sales are important to its current and future success as more stringent fuel efficiency and environmental standards and the resulting capital requirements are forging closer relationships between OEMs and their suppliers. The ability to provide technology and innovation, as well as price and quality, will characterize the successful suppliers of the future.

New products for fuel economy

The key words in Detroit are "fuel economy." Each new product must be designed around that concept if it is to help OEMs meet the government's 27.5 mpg fuel efficiency mandate for 1985.

Borg-Warner products, recently introduced or in the advanced testing state, will contribute to this goal in two ways—through improved efficiency of the component and through reduced weight of the vehicle. On 1980 models are: a lockup torque converter clutch damper that

Transportation Equipment
Sales ■
Earnings ■
millions of dollars

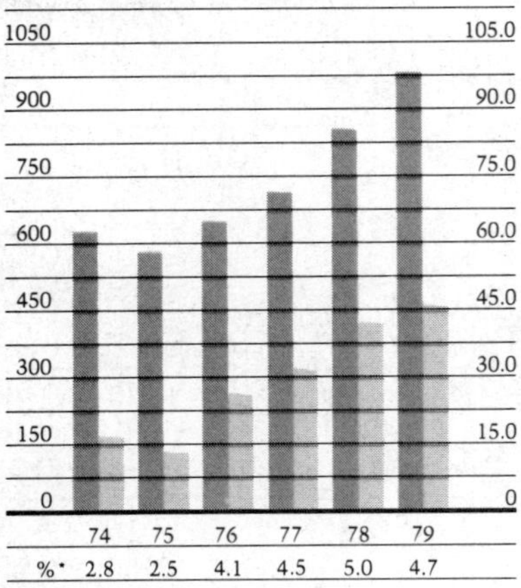

*Margin on sales

reduces fuel consumption with automatic transmissions, a fan clutch that both saves fuel and reduces noise on heavy-duty trucks, a transfer case for part-time four-wheel drive for light trucks, and a more efficient transmission for medium-weight diesel-powered trucks.

Other products designed to save weight and/or energy are in the development stage. A number of them could be ready for market within a short time. They include: self-locking hubs that will put convenience and economy back into four-wheel driving, aluminum radiators, a continuously variable transmission for small cars that could make automatic driving smoother and more efficient, and perhaps eventually an electronically controlled automatic transmission for the ultimate in fuel efficiency.

Non-U.S. markets strong

During 1979, 31% of the group's total sales came from non-U.S. operations, not including sales from unconsolidated units (primarily in Japan, where a record half million transmissions were sold, including a newly designed automatic with fuel-saving overdrive for Toyota).

And while the auto industry outside the U.S. will probably be down slightly in 1980, we do not expect the decline to be as severe as at home.

Transmission operations in the U.K. continue to be a nagging problem. After roughly break-even years in 1978 and 1979, and with the picture not much brighter for 1980, the group has announced the closing of its transmission plant at Letchworth. Manufacturing will be consolidated at the newer and larger plant in Kenfig, South Wales.

Outlook guarded

As 1980 began, new orders were down, production cutbacks and attendant layoffs were increasing, and a long strike at a major truck component customer were having a negative effect on early 1980 results.

New products and a positive model mix should help the group counter some of the decline in new-car sales. It is unlikely, however, that these factors will be enough to offset declines in both car and truck sales.

Chemicals group shows strength around the world

Chemicals & Plastics
Sales ■
Earnings ■
millions of dollars

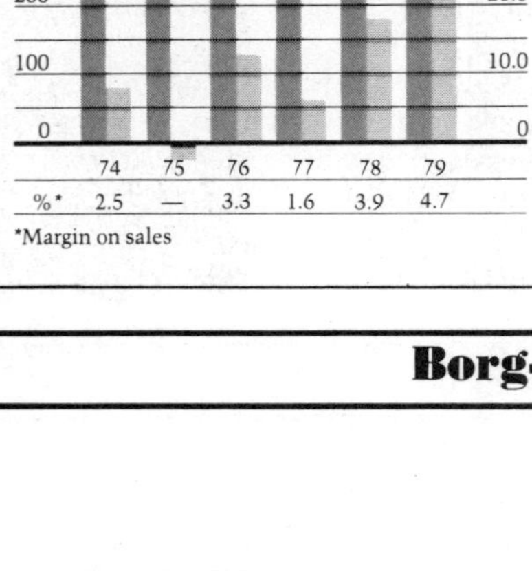

*Margin on sales

Despite skyrocketing raw material costs, the Chemicals and Plastics group set sales and earnings records in 1979. Leading the way were strong performance of the European business, steady demand for ABS plastics worldwide, new applications, and increased sales of petrochemicals.

Earnings for the group jumped 50% to $28 million while sales increased 26% to $595 million in 1979.

More than three-quarters of total group revenues come from sales of Cycolac® ABS, a versatile family of engineering thermoplastics used primarily in durable goods, automobiles and housing. Its success comes from the adaptability of its basic formulation, which can be varied to produce ABS resins in a number of grades for a variety of applications.

This versatility opens a constant stream of new uses and is the reason for our confidence in the continuing growth of ABS.

Perhaps the greatest growth potential is for applications requiring specialty high-performance materials. Two new grades of Cycoloy® brand ABS/polycarbonate alloy were successfully introduced in specialty markets for power tools, business machines and plumbing fixtures.

Another market gaining momentum in 1979 was ABS for refrigerator liners. All major U.S. manufacturers have approved Cycolac ABS for use in their units—a market growing five times the rate of the entire ABS industry and expected to reach 200 million pounds by 1981.

Capacity expansion continues

During 1979, Borg-Warner Chemicals added about 50 million pounds of ABS capacity to existing facilities in Illinois and California.

If this pattern pleases, it shouldn't surprise. Objects designed for function alone often have the visual appeal of artwork. Pictured is a corner section of a new Borg-Warner radiator made of wave upon wave of aluminum sheet. The radiator's metal components are bonded in a special oven in a patented brazing process. There is no soldering, no mechanical joining. What emerges is an aluminum radiator 30% lighter than current brass and copper units. A sophisticated anti-corrosion system with time-release rust inhibitors for years of protection can be incorporated into the radiator. Pilot production begins in late 1980 at Long Manufacturing division in Canada.

The group also announced construction of a $50 million ABS plant in Mississippi. When completed in late 1982, the 150-million-pound plant will bring the company's total U.S. capacity to about 800 million pounds, a 40% increase, and world capacity to 1.2 billion pounds.

In the specialty chemicals business, Borg-Warner increased penetration of Weston 618™ heat stabilizer for plastics into the food packaging market. Weston 618 is less expensive and offers characteristics not commonly available.

Borg-Warner strengthened its non-plastics business in Europe in 1979 with the opening of a new Blendex® BTA modifier facility located in Scotland. The plant is Borg-Warner's worldwide source for BTA products and should be operating at full capacity by mid-1980. BTA is in strong demand as an additive for PVC used primarily in plastic bottles and film.

Also being considered is a 70% expansion of styrene monomer capacity at a Louisiana plant owned in partnership with American Petrofina. Styrene, one of three ABS ingredients, comprises up to 50% of the end product. The present plant provides more than enough styrene to meet Borg-Warner's needs, and the sale of the excess on the open market has been a significant contributor to group earnings.

Squeeze on margins will continue

Rapidly escalating costs of raw materials and the resulting pressure on operating margins will continue to be a major problem in 1980.

During late 1979, U.S. consumer durables, automobiles and housing markets weakened. This condition is expected to continue into 1980. Since ABS sales are largely dependent upon these three markets, the group's outlook is tempered, although some offset is expected as a result of new applications.

Air Conditioning group hit by higher material costs, poor product mix

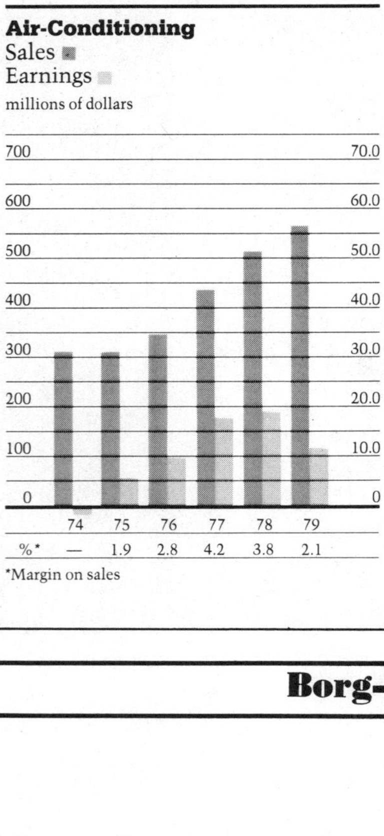

*Margin on sales

York® products fall into three broad categories of about equal sales volume: air conditioning and refrigeration equipment specially designed and engineered for large installations, unitary products of a standard design for cooling or heating homes and small to medium-sized commercial buildings, and compressors for vehicle air conditioning systems.

Although 1979 sales for the group were again a record, earnings dropped 38% from the record $20 million York earned in 1978.

Several factors were responsible for the poor 1979 performance. Most severe perhaps was a shift in product mix. With both the auto and housing markets in a state of decline through much of the year, York had unused capacity at the two plants producing for those markets.

At the same time, York's third major market, commercial and industrial construction, showed continued strength. York's backlog of orders for large systems to meet this demand already was swelled by a two-month strike at the end of 1978. It grew even larger as the year progressed, with York unable to keep pace with heavy incoming orders. The situation has improved. Recent shipments are at all-time highs, and York expects to make on-time delivery for most 1980 orders.

However, the shipment delays that occurred in 1979, as well as stiff cost increases (especially for aluminum and copper) that could not be fully recovered in the marketplace, cut deeply into York margins. This pressure on profitability will continue during 1980.

Another problem for York during 1979 was reduced orders for compressors from new-car makers and from the add-on market, where York was hurt by a severe drop in van and RV sales induced by the gasoline shortage. The planned introduction of a new, small rotary compressor is expected to increase York's market share. The compressor is targeted at the growing imported small-car market, which represents approximately 25% of the U.S. market available to York.

__Rare is the plastic__ that can stand up to a Bunsen burner's hot, blue flame. However, when heat sears this stick of plastic, bubbles form to create a protective layer of insulating foam between plastic and flame. A new chemical additive—developed and still under test at Borg-Warner's research center—has made the vital difference. Plastics containing this additive will not support combustion and give off substantially less smoke and fumes when exposed to flame. Potential applications include internal components for television and telephone equipment and mass transit interiors where nonconductive, flame-resistant materials are required for safety. Test marketing is planned for late 1980.

Non-U.S. business mixed

Export sales remained at high levels, up 16% from 1978. They are expected to hold steady in 1980 despite some softening of Middle East sales. Losses in Iran were minimal, but the situation there has resulted in lost business opportunities.

Non-U.S. sales were above 1978 levels in all areas, and especially in Mexico. Profitability of European operations, however, suffered due to labor unrest in the U.K., the costs of changing product offerings to meet shifts in demand and the strength of the pound sterling against the dollar.

Service business was again one of the bright spots in York operations. Record-high revenues and earnings were achieved in 1979.

Technology buoys York outlook

York's success in combining the cost-effective inverter, developed by Borg-Warner Electronics, with a sophisticated electronic control system that automatically and constantly matches air conditioning compressor speed to varying air conditioning load requirements can save energy and reduce commercial building operating costs. At test installations in operation for up to two years, energy consumption of the centrifugal chiller has been cut up to 30%.

The new Turbomodulator system can be installed in new or existing buildings whether they use York or competitive chillers. Production of retrofit units has begun. First deliveries of systems for new buildings are slated for the second quarter of 1980. Resulting energy savings should pay for the equipment within three to five years.

Start-up costs for the new product will be high through 1980, and sales of the product itself will not have much effect on Borg-Warner 1980 net earnings.

Industrial Products group margin, ROI are highest in the company

The Industrial Products group continued to lead all Borg-Warner operations in profitability on sales in 1979 with a margin of 7.6%, compared with a return of 4.7% for the company's manufacturing operations overall. Return on investment for this group is the highest in the company.

Earnings for the group were $42 million, up 20% from $35 million the year before on a sales gain of 16%. The major components of the Industrial Products group include the energy equipment units and Morse Chain division.

Despite loss of some business from Iran and the lack of a well-defined U.S. energy policy, the energy equipment units (Byron Jackson Pump; Centrilift, Inc.; Nuclear Valve; and Mechanical Seal) showed continued improvement in 1979. (In early 1980, Borg-Warner signed a letter of intent covering an exchange of Centrilift, Inc. assets for common stock in the Hughes Tool Company. See page 17.)

A variety of sophisticated products and product refinements was introduced in 1979. Centrilift introduced a new rotary gas separator, a high impedance transformer and a heat-resistant submersible pump cable, all used in oil production. The Mechanical Seal division introduced two types of improved seal systems to help users meet increasing EPA requirements.

New orders for nuclear power plant components have slowed but have not dried up completely—especially outside the U.S., where nuclear construction plans are being implemented. A backlog sufficient to maintain production at a healthy pace through '80 and '81 is holding firm.

Industrial Products
Sales ■
Earnings ■
millions of dollars

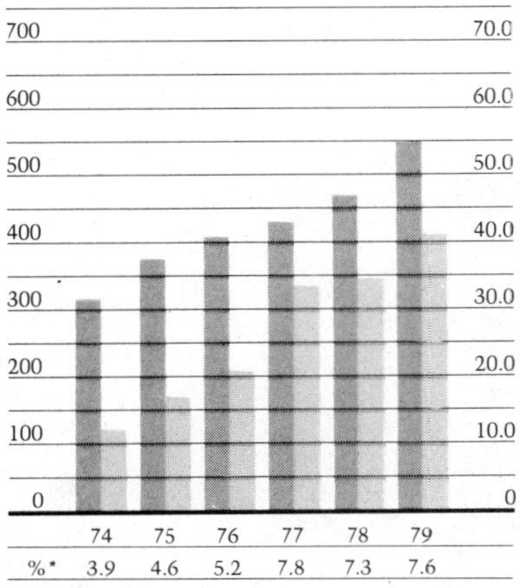

*Margin on sales

Petroleum involvement brightens future

The rush to find and extract oil around the world is a good sign for the energy equipment units. Expanded petroleum activities in Mexico, the Middle East and Continental Europe will more than offset business lost in Iran during 1980.

No tarantula this. *It's a busy little gate driver with a key role to play in a new, energy-saving air conditioning system from our York division. The driver gets its instructions from an electronic brain at the heart of York's variable speed control system. The brain senses the cooling required; the inverter provides variability, permitting the air conditioning compressor to run slower when the load is lighter. Speed and need are precisely and automatically matched. With the chiller motor no longer churning constantly at full speed, energy saving is considerable—up to 30% of normal energy consumption for centrifugal chillers, which represent a large part of the total system.*

Expanded service activities in Europe, the Middle East, Canada, Mexico and particularly in the U.S. will provide increased sales and earnings in 1980 and beyond. The growth in U.S. pump aftermarket sales is expected to increase in excess of 20% per year over the next five years.

U.S. and Canadian "synfuel" programs could result in major contract awards during 1980 for Byron Jackson Pump.

Morse Chain continues record pace

Morse Chain division, the second major component of the Industrial Products group, enjoyed another record year in 1979. Sales of both automotive and industrial products were strong for the first three quarters, tapering off in the fourth quarter.

The backlog of orders for Morse Chain was up 26% over 1978. A significant portion of the increase in backlog was attributable to the expansion of the OEM industrial roller chain business.

The successful introduction of General Motors' energy-efficient "X-body" cars has meant increased sales for Morse's Hy-Vo® drive chain, which is used on those cars as well as on GM's larger, front-wheel-drive and four-wheel-drive models. By 1985, a large percentage of U.S.-built cars will be front-wheel-drive vehicles.

Morse Chain will begin marketing a family of alternating current inverters for electric motors during 1980. Combining microcomputer technology with a power transistor, these inverters provide substantial energy savings in a wide variety of applications.

Continued strong growth, near 30%, is expected for the Hy-Vo chain line in 1980. Otherwise, it appears that sales for Morse's automotive and industrial products will be flat during most of the year with some rebound expected in the fourth quarter. Sales of the new inverter are expected to build gradually during the year with momentum building into the 1980s.

Ingersoll Products recorded the best year in its history, and incoming orders for 1980 thus far indicate a repeat performance.

Were they petals *of delicate flowers, these strands of copper conductors couldn't be protected and pampered more. Viewed here in cutaway, the conductors are wrapped in a tough cocoon of insulation, tape and braid and sheathed in shiny armor. Yet, with all this protection, they can still "breathe" and thereby withstand the 250°F heat in oil wells. Developed by Centrilift, Inc. and the Borg-Warner research center, this heat-resistant power cable eases problems of oil recovery from new and secondary wells by feeding power to pumping units far below the earth's surface.*

Financial Services records 14th year of steady growth

The pace quickened for the Financial Services group in 1979 with net earnings increasing 31% to a record $21 million. In face of the highest interest rates in U.S. history, the group reported its 14th year of uninterrupted earnings improvement. Earnings increased dramatically with only an 8% gain in employment.

At year-end, the group's gross receivables totaled $1.7 billion, up 25% from the prior year. With at least 50% of the group's finance receivables geared to prime rate and more than 70% of its receivables maturing in any 12-month period (compared with only 30-40% for most finance companies), the group probably weathered rising interest rates better than many of its competitors.

Factors contributing to record results were the penetration of new markets in the U.S. and good growth in Canada and Australia. The group's international business continued strong in 1979 with receivables acquired up 26% over 1978.

The largest segment of the group is Borg-Warner Acceptance Corporation (BWAC), specializing in four business areas: inventory financing, insurance, retail financing and commercial/industrial leasing. Inventory financing is the major BWAC service with about 50% of its revenues generated in this area.

BWAC provides inventory credit for manufacturers, distributors and dealers in industries such as home electronics, recreational vehicles, appliances and agricultural equipment. In 1979, this business grew by 27%; and a special division was set up to handle marine financing.

Each major segment of the group had improved performance in 1979 with the exception of leasing. The latter was off substantially due to increased credit losses and higher interest rates which could not be

Financial Services
Total finance income
Net earnings
millions of dollars

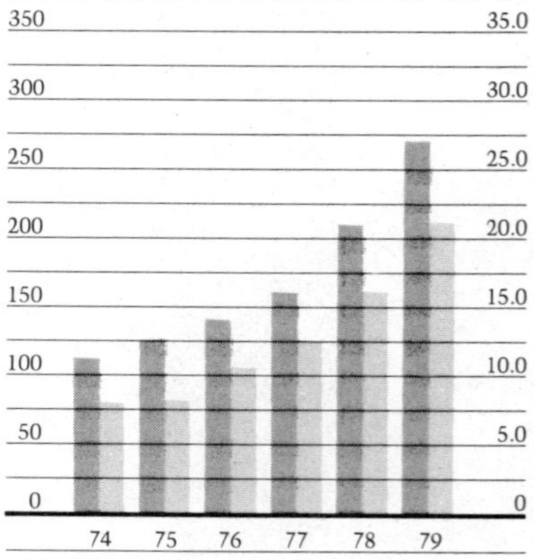

%*	7.1	6.3	7.5	7.9	7.6	7.8

*Margin on total finance income

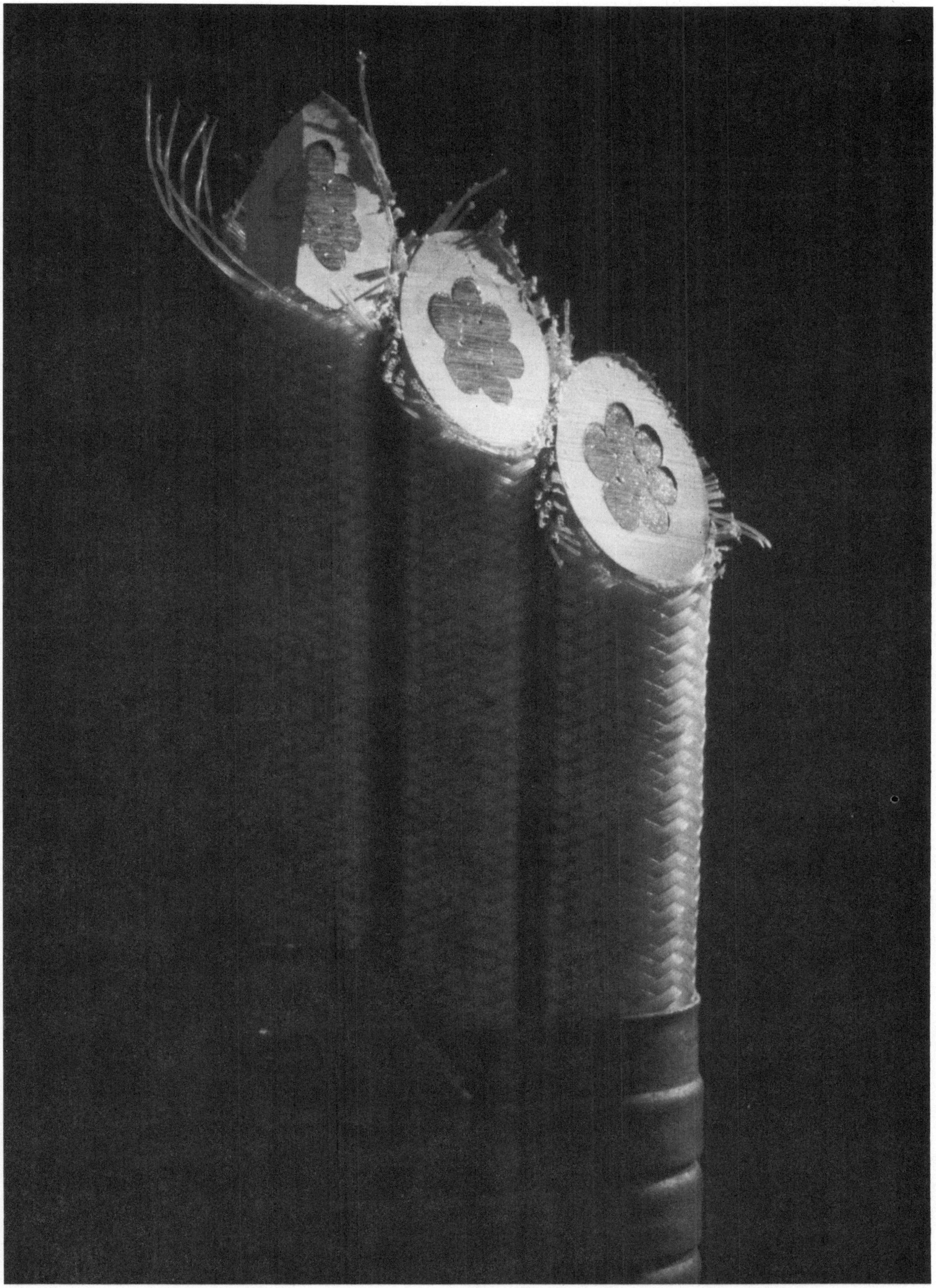

compensated for on longer-term contracts—characteristic of the leasing business. The insurance unit, smallest but fastest growing unit within the group, had a record year.

During late 1979, the Financial Services group was reorganized to consolidate reporting responsibilities. The reorganization strengthens BWAC's operations and makes it easier to add new businesses.

Interest rates will probably remain high in 1980, which could have a further negative effect on equipment leasing earnings and several less significant businesses. Even though higher interest rates could also increase collection problems, BWAC continues to maintain an above-average collection record in the industry.

All other businesses look strong for BWAC in 1980. Continued growth in Europe and Canada in the inventory financing area for appliances and recreational vehicles is expected. The credit life insurance business should also grow substantially. Overall, the Financial Services group should report its 15th straight year of record earnings in 1980.

Protective Services' business rebounds in second year

Baker Industries—acquired in 1977—experienced good growth in 1979 with revenues increasing 13% and net income 226%. The improvement comes after a year that was below management expectations, partially due to costs related to a plant closing.

Baker, comprising the protective services companies, recorded earnings of $6.2 million, compared with $1.9 million in 1978. Revenues totaled $236 million in 1979 versus $210 million the year before.

The company's Wells Fargo alarm, armored and guard operations grew 22% in revenues and 14% in earnings in 1979. Revenues for the Pony Express Courier division—a unit that delivers time-critical business materials—grew impressively in 1979 with a 25% revenue increase.

The year was marked by new product development, greater market penetration, a major acquisition and the moderate easing of a problem in the residential smoke detector industry.

New production innovation

The alarm division of Wells Fargo shipped its first multiplex computerized security system during the year. Expected to become a major factor in the alarm business, the sophisticated system offers customers increased security and efficiency not found in competitive systems. With the new multiplex system, customers can program in constantly changing security instructions to match their particular needs.

With the acquisition of the Burns International central station and local alarm business, Wells Fargo now has the second largest alarm network in the U.S. providing service to 30 major metropolitan centers.

Residential smoke detectors still a trouble spot

Though the residential smoke detector business continued to decline in 1979, the drop was not as steep as the previous year. Excessive inventories and depressed prices continue to plague the industry. During the year, Baker initiated various cost-cutting measures, including the closing of one manufacturing plant to streamline its smoke detector operation. This part of the business has not been profitable.

Baker provides the widest selection of protective services of any company in the U.S. As a result, it has a solid position in the marketplace. During the coming year, integration of the Burns International alarm business into Wells Fargo should be completed; and a strong demand for multiplex system installations is expected.

With exception of residential smoke detectors, all of Baker's businesses have good growth potential for 1980. Demand brought on by crime, fire and insurance company pressures should mean continued improvement for the group.

Ill wind or no, *the client needs to know—right now—if its manufacturing operations should ever exceed (or even threaten to violate) pollution control standards. Quick, corrective action can save a fine—and our environment. Borg-Warner's Kemron Environmental Services, with a master computer and a network of on-site "Kemputers," can measure the quality of the environment, document it quickly and graphically, and warn of trouble—sometimes even before it breaks out. This eye-catching overlay illustrates the point. Software packages are tailored to meet each client's needs.*

Strategic planning brings progress toward five-year plan goals

(An interview of chief executive officer James F. Beré, February 26, 1980)

How did Borg-Warner's performance through 1979 measure up to the objectives set five years ago as part of the company's strategic long-range plan?

We have made considerable progress since initiating our five-year plan, and for that I am grateful to our employees throughout the company. Even so, our progress hasn't been sufficient to meet some of the tough goals we set five years ago.

There were two basic thrusts to our long-range planning. First was to reduce the cyclicality of our business by expanding into the faster-growing service sector of our economy. As a result of the acquisition of Baker Industries and the continuing growth of our Financial Services companies, 18% of our earnings are now derived from service operations, compared with only 5% ten years ago.

The second emphasis of our strategic planning was to improve the efficiency and profitability of our current businesses. We concentrated on two key indexes of operating efficiency—asset management and profit margins on sales.

We more than achieved our goal of making our assets work harder by increasing our capital turnover rate from 1.6 to 2.3 times annually.

Improving margins has been more difficult. As a consequence, we may not achieve our key objective of reaching the *FORTUNE 500* median return on equity for 1979 when rankings are announced in May. High inflation has made it an even more difficult task, but that is where we will concentrate our efforts under our new five-year plan.

What are your margin goals, and what can you do differently in the coming five years to achieve them?

Our 1984 goal is to increase our margin on sales from manufacturing operations from 4.7% to at least 6% on sales of $5 billion.

To get there we must hold to our gain in asset turnover while improving the effectiveness of our operating functions. And that's where Jerry Dempsey, our new chief operating officer, has a job to do.

Do you agree that inflation is the major problem we face today; and, if so, is there a remedy?

I don't think there is any question that inflation is the most obstinate economic problem we face today and one that is getting worse. Perhaps if we could agree on the causes of inflation, a solution would be more likely. One of the causes is the automatic inflation adjustments we continue to build into our economic system. They do nothing but make an eventual cure more painful for everyone.

We must convince our political leaders that inflation is a blight we are serious about eradicating and that we are willing to sacrifice to achieve its demise. The trick will be to develop a plan to even out the sacrifices. A clear mandate from the electorate is needed to prod officials into action toward this end.

(A special story on inflation and its impact begins on page 20.)

Energy would seem to be critical to several of your product areas. What effect is the current situation and the outlook likely to have on these businesses?

I'm basically optimistic—primarily because of what I believe is the ability of the American people to assess negative situations and turn them into positive ones.

While we would rather the problem did not exist, it has presented real opportunities for Borg-Warner.

The energy shortage is creating revolutionary changes in the automobile industry and the way Americans view their car. Rather than spelling the industry's demise, I believe it will bring a needed revitalization. And through technology and innovation, I see supplier companies like ours emerging as a bigger part of the finished product.

The energy situation may change the type of dwellings we live in, the cars we drive, and the way our communities are structured, but it will not stop our economy from finding new paths for growth.

The inverter advances announced by Borg-Warner could mean significant energy savings. What do these product developments mean to the company?

Long range, I feel the inverter—and more important, its application in a number of our product areas—will have a very positive impact on our results. In its first year, however, it won't be much.

We believe the potential market is huge, and we continue to uncover applications we hadn't thought of initially. The difficulty will be to convince builders of homes and owners of large buildings that they should spend more for a product just because it saves energy when the savings in operating costs will accrue to the eventual owner or tenant.

Robert O. Bass and James F. Beré

Why did you decide to exchange Centrilift, Inc. for shares in Hughes Tool Company?

A bit of background might help explain our reason. Borg-Warner already owned 3.75 million shares of Hughes' common stock issued in exchange for our oil well service operations in 1974. This has proved to be a very successful transaction for both companies. Because the sharply focused nature of Hughes Tool closely matched that of the unit we sold them, that unit has grown and prospered to a greater degree as part of Hughes than would probably have been the case had it remained part of Borg-Warner. In exchange, our investment in the form of Hughes stock has proved a very satisfactory one for Borg-Warner shareholders. We expect the same will be true in the case of Centrilift. The additional 1.2 million shares of Hughes Tool common stock we would receive would give Borg-Warner slightly more than 20% of Hughes Tool's common stock outstanding. This would permit us to include that share of Hughes' profits in our future earnings. Because of the future growth we expect for both Centrilift and Hughes, we believe the transaction will allow Borg-Warner shareholders to participate more fully in the vital energy market.

What happened to the proposed merger with Firestone, and what is your current acquisition posture?

The Firestone merger proposal was aborted for one simple reason: they decided to ask for more money than called for in the initial agreement. It was our feeling that the risks and potential rewards to our stockholders did not merit an increase. Looking back, I'm not too unhappy about the way it turned out.

I would describe our present acquisition posture as active. We still would like to find a well-managed, service-related organization to expand our participation in this segment of our economy. We are also looking at opportunities to strengthen our current businesses.

What do you see ahead for the economy and for Borg-Warner in 1980?

I look for the economy to be relatively strong in the first quarter with some slowdown beginning thereafter. A recession could be deeper and longer than many expect, and my real concern is with 1981 prospects.

Right now, I feel Borg-Warner will have a good year; but it would be folly to make a prediction. At the same time, I do believe we have the capability to outperform the economy overall.

Borg-Warner: yesterday, today...

Dear Borg-Warner investors and friends,

There are a number of things I would like to talk with you about in this—my last letter reporting to you as chief operating officer.

I'm confident that Jerry Dempsey, who succeeds me in that job, has the ability and experience to continue the record of improved operating results we have achieved at Borg-Warner during the last several years.

I've always felt one of the most important responsibilities of leadership is to ensure there are opportunities and challenges for qualified younger people within the organization. A balance of young managers with fresh ideas and "old salts" with the wisdom gained through hands-on experience is a necessary ingredient of any ongoing management team. Jerry's election as chief operating officer provides that balance at Borg-Warner and will help ensure our continued progress and vitality.

At the small company I came from the key problem was always money. When I joined Borg-Warner through an acquisition, I soon found the key concern here (and I think probably in most large companies) was not money, but people. Our ability to grow and prosper depends on our ability to attract, motivate and keep good people.

In the more than twenty years that I have been part of this company, this situation has not changed. What has changed is that most of our management now recognizes this fact. We've stopped just talking about it and started at least a few programs I think will help us deal with the problem. Doing so has changed the entire tone of our company.

The larger the company, the more difficult it is to solve this people problem. Part of the solution, therefore, is to run each part of our big company as if it were a small one. Let the big company worry about the money, and the small one about the people.

Easier said than done. But at Borg-Warner I believe we've made progress. Our so-called "strategic management" system has divided Borg-Warner into more than 100 small businesses. Each one serves its own markets, and each has access to the capital needed to dominate those markets.

While this system has moved us more toward central control of strategic planning and allocation of resources, it has kept the day-to-day operating responsibility with people at the local level.

In this environment, people can better know each other; and motivation and initiative are strengthened among employees at all levels. The company can afford to encourage prudent risk taking and the intelligent mistakes that come with it in building a cadre of experienced young managers.

I'm convinced the key to making our system work is the development of meaningful, two-way communication throughout our organization. And, I'm not referring to management broadcasting, which we've always done. I'm talking about creating an environment where a person doing a job cares enough to raise a fuss when something is going wrong, where the boss cares enough to listen, decide if there is anything to the complaint, and do something about it quickly if there is. That is two-way communication.

The best way I know of to really increase productivity is to work toward a common goal agreed to by everyone. Productivity does not result from management exhortations to work harder. It comes from a mutual understanding about the tools, the systems, the incentives and the environment needed to make production easier, more efficient and more rewarding for all who participate in the process.

It's simply a common interest philosophy. That's what the changes at Borg-Warner are meant to achieve. We're not there yet, not by a long way. But because of our traditional decentralized philosophy, we perhaps have a better chance of eventually carrying it off than many other large companies.

Not only has there been change within our company, but the environment in which we operate as a company has changed. Our relationships and responsibilities to people other than customers, employees and shareholders have expanded. In the list we must now include: government, special interest groups and our plant communities. But this has not altered our basic reason for being: to produce goods and services at a fair profit, which results in the creation of jobs and contributes to a better life for more people.

If you've read this far, you might reasonably be asking: "Why have you been telling me all this? I'm an investor, not an employee."

I think there is a good reason, assuming my philosophy is correct. Our development into a better company—and a better investment—depends on our ability to create a "common interest" environment among *all* our employees, regardless of collar color.

If, in fact, Borg-Warner can build an environment which will encourage and permit employees to contribute to the extent of their ability; then, as has oft been said: "You ain't seen nothing yet." We are committed to try.

Robert O. Bass
Vice Chairman

February 25, 1980

...and tomorrow

Jerry E. Dempsey

Jerry E. Dempsey, Borg-Warner's newly elected chief operating officer, talks about his challenges:

"Much of my energies will be devoted to improving margins, a task which is absolutely essential in the face of raging inflation.

"While we have accomplished a great deal over the past five years through sound asset management, our future rests on improving our operating results. Among other priorities, that means building the common interest philosophy Bob Bass refers to, reducing costs and putting additional muscle into our technology development and creative marketing.

"Our marketing efforts must feature a growing role for research and development. Technology is the key to developing products that command high margins. I am particularly encouraged by our progress in applying intelligent electronics to a variety of our products. Certainly the energy shortage has brought problems and hardship, but it also carries the seeds of opportunity.

"Finally, we face a philosophical challenge—to encourage our operating managers to think long range. In a recessionary environment, operating people are tempted, understandably, to make cut-backs in critical areas to provide a quick fix on their bottom line. By doing this, however, we risk mortgaging the future for the sake of making this month's objective. I plan to encourage our managers to invest in areas that have long-range potential, even if the immediate economic outlook is less than inspiring. We're in business for the long haul, and the managers who help prepare us for it will share in the rewards."

Inflation—we must do more than worry about it!

by James J. Gavin, senior vice president—finance

We hardly noticed inflation when it was only 2% or less per year. Nobody got hurt much. In fact, some economists contend that a little inflation is necessary to lubricate a healthy economy. But with inflation (based on the consumer price level) averaging better than 7% over the last decade, and in double digits during the last year, everyone is hurt.

Most dictionaries define inflation in purely economic terms. It is explained basically as the relationship between the supply of money and the supply of goods and services. I think Conference Board chief economist Albert Sommers is on track in suggesting the cause of inflation is as much social as economic.

The increasing demands placed on the economy by the public and private sectors have exceeded our available resources to respond to those demands. The fact that the public sector has grown so much faster than the private sector has contributed enormously to the problem.

But, whether inflation is in fact caused by an excessively fast expansion of the money supply or whether expansion of the money supply is caused by swelling demands is not the concern of the retiree, the wage-earner, or the businessman. All they know is that their money won't buy as much as it would last year. They've lost, and they can feel it. The question is: "Who has gained?"

The question might better be: "Who has lost least?" Certainly those who *owe* money lose less than those who *own* it in inflationary times. Certainly those who find themselves sheltered by pension or compensation programs that are indexed to consumer prices lose less than those who do not.

It is popular to look for inflation scapegoats. They are not hard to find. In fact, each of us has contributed to it: the federal government, which will have piled up a deficit of $116 billion in the three fiscal years ending in 1980; the business community, which has worried more about passing on higher costs through higher prices than it has about reducing costs and improving efficiency; the worker, who has supported calls for wage increases that are indexed for inflation and greater than productivity improvement; and also the consumer, who has gone on an extended credit buying binge to hedge against inflation.

The real problem is that we, collectively as a nation, have been living substantially beyond our means for a long time. This condition cannot go on indefinitely. Something must give. We must cool the overheated demand in the private sector and slow the programs that contribute to federal deficits in the public sector. We must establish programs to reduce overall growth in the economy and restore a healthier flow of capital for the supply side of the economic equation. If we don't, the self-perpetuating momentum of the inflationary spiral will continue until the only thing left running is the government printing press.

But enough on the problem of inflation in general. What about inflation's impact on Borg-Warner and its shareholders?

The data on the opposite page give us an indication. The lighter number in each column in the first table shows the actual dollar amount for that item as reported for that year. The bold number is the same data adjusted for inflation (or changing prices as the accountants refer to it) in terms of current 1979 dollars. For example: Reported Borg-Warner sales in 1976 were $1.9 billion. Those same sales today would equal $2.4 billion in 1979 dollars.

The basis for adjusting prior year numbers to 1979 dollars is the Consumer Price Index (CPI). This index is the last line in the table. It is only one of several measures of inflation we could have used, but we believe it shows inflation on a "worst-case" basis. This index grew by 47.2% over the period—a compound annual increase of 8%.

The bold numbers in the right-hand column show the extent to which Borg-Warner was able to keep pace with the rate of inflation in real values during the last five years.

How did we do? While reported sales grew at an average annual rate of 9% between 1974 and 1979, the

Comparison of selected data adjusted for effect of changing prices

(millions of dollars except share data)	As reported / **Adjusted (1979 dollars)** 1979	1978	1977	1976	1975	1974	Average annual rate of change
Sales	$2,717.4	$2,326.0	$2,031.9	$1,862.4	$1,639.0	$1,767.8	9.0%
	2,717.4	**2,587.9**	**2,433.8**	**2,374.7**	**2,210.4**	**2,602.0**	**.9**
Net earnings	155.6	133.8	104.0	81.7	44.5	50.8	25.1
	155.6	**148.9**	**124.6**	**104.2**	**60.0**	**74.8**	**15.8**
Earnings per share	7.25	6.24	4.93	4.21	2.31	2.66	22.2
	7.25	**6.94**	**5.91**	**5.37**	**3.12**	**3.92**	**13.1**
Common stock dividend	2.08	1.85	1.65	1.41	1.35	1.35	9.0
	2.08	**2.06**	**1.98**	**1.80**	**1.83**	**1.99**	**.8**
Book value per common share	50.99	45.64	41.10	38.36	35.51	34.63	8.0
	50.99	**50.78**	**49.23**	**48.91**	**47.89**	**50.97**	—
Market value per share	35.88	28.38	27.88	30.50	20.00	13.38	21.8
	35.88	**31.63**	**33.38**	**38.88**	**27.00**	**19.69**	**12.8**
Capital expenditures	130.7	115.3	77.0	36.0	55.9	83.0	9.5
	130.7	**128.3**	**92.2**	**45.9**	**75.4**	**122.2**	**1.4**
Depreciation	59.6	55.2	50.9	43.4	42.8	43.1	6.7
	88.6	**86.0**	**81.8**	**77.5**	**83.6**	**88.8**	—
Net earnings adjusted for constant dollar depreciation	**126.6**	**124.2**	**103.7**	**82.0**	**34.1**	**49.4**	**20.7**
Consumer price index urban yearly average (base year: 1967)							

Impact of changing prices on operating margins

	Operating margin (FIFO)		Operating margin (LIFO)		Operating margin current cost*	
	1979	1978	**1979**	1978	**1979**	1978
Air Conditioning	**7.5%**	9.3%	**4.3%**	8.2%	**3.6%**	7.7%
Chemicals & Plastics	**12.6**	10.0	**9.5**	9.2	**8.2**	7.5
Industrial Products	**16.6**	16.2	**14.4**	15.1	**13.7**	14.1
Transportation Equipment	**10.2**	12.1	**8.3**	10.6	**7.0**	9.7
Total	**11.5%**	11.9%	**9.0%**	10.7%	**7.9%**	9.7%

FIFO, or first-in, first-out, values inventories at current cost. LIFO, or last-in, first-out, values inventories at historic cost.

*Operating margin on a LIFO basis, excluding the excess of current cost over historical cost depreciation.

real growth, when reduced by inflation during the same period, was less than 1%.

The pattern looks much better for net earnings. Reported earnings increased at an average annual rate of 25% over the five years. Real growth has been lower—but at nearly 16%, a darn good performance.

Our real growth in earnings was significantly higher than growth in sales for several reasons. First, Borg-Warner earnings in our base year of 1974 were depressed by our change to the LIFO method of inventory valuation and the recession that began that year. In addition, we have since made substantial improvement in our return on sales from manufacturing operations and have added to our service business base through excellent internal growth and acquisition.

Per-share earnings increased at a slightly lower rate because we issued two million new shares of common stock to Robert Bosch GmbH in 1977.

The next category hits shareholders closer to home. Common stock dividends have risen 9% per year in current year dollars but have barely stayed even in real terms over the period. In spite of increases in each of the last four years, our dividend payout did not keep pace with our earnings increase. Our dividend policy is to pay out about 40% of prior year's earnings, averaged over the long term. We would like to continue that pattern of annual dividend increases, even if we have a flat or down year in a recession.

Another figure that should have great significance for our shareholders is the book value calculation. The light numbers in reported dollars indicate a compounded growth of 8% per year. In other words, we were able to reinvest after dividends an average of 8% of our equity over the last five years. The darker inflation-adjusted numbers indicate that book value in real terms did not grow at all.

This comparison points up the essence of the problem of inflation for a business entity: How can we finance both inflation and real growth and at the same time protect the shareholders' capital from erosion?

The fact is, inflation must be financed just as real growth must be financed. It is very difficult to achieve real growth in equity in a double-digit inflationary environment.

Fortunately, Borg-Warner has a strong equity base; and we have been able to use our resources more efficiently in the last five years through better working capital management and reallocation of capital to more productive areas.

For the last five years, we have been able to avoid an erosion of our shareholders' equity in real terms. We should point out that our book value is conservatively stated since our inventories at LIFO are $195.5 million less than replacement cost, and our investment in the Hughes Tool Company was carried at a value $150 million less than the market value at year-end.

The Borg-Warner market value comparison indicates that our share value increased in real terms at an average rate of 12.8% for each of the last five years. This, however, is from a very low value at the end of 1974, and is still less than the previous high of $39.50 achieved in 1968.

We have also presented inflation-adjusted comparisons for capital expenditures and depreciation. Capital spending in real terms has grown only 1.4%, in line with real sales growth. Reported depreciation grew by 6.7%. However, constant dollar depreciation adjusted to 1979 dollars has been flat for the reporting period. During the recession period (1975-76), capital expenditures were less than depreciation expense in 1979 dollars because we did not replace our plants or equipment as fast as they were wearing out. That unhealthy situation has been corrected.

Net earnings adjusted for constant dollar depreciation have been estimated for each of the years shown. There is no question that historical cost depreciation understates the true economic cost of the wear and tear on assets that must be replaced at substantially higher future values, and our earnings are overstated to this extent. Since we pay federal income taxes on this overstatement, there is a loss of capital in real terms.

We have concluded that the key to coping with inflation in Borg-Warner is to improve our operating margins. The table on the bottom of page 21 shows the impact of changing prices on operating margins. It compares 1978 and 1979 for our manufacturing groups on a FIFO basis, a LIFO basis and a current cost basis which deducts replacement cost depreciation from the LIFO basis.

This comparison dramatically illustrates the erosion of margins caused by inflation. Since Borg-Warner values inventories worldwide on a LIFO basis, our segment figures in this report correspond with the center column. Note, however, that if we had clung to FIFO reporting, as some companies do, our overall operating margin would have been 2.5% higher in 1979.

Our reported operating margins did show a worrisome decline of 1.7% in 1979 from 1978. This decline is directly traceable to the fact that inflation in 1979 was the worst since 1974.

It is unfortunate that the impact of increased inflation is to decrease margins while the obvious goal of management to finance inflation and preserve capital is to increase margins.

Seeking to increase margins is not a new goal for Borg-Warner. The problem of inflation merely intensifies the need. We cannot afford to remain in product areas that tie up capital with little or no promise of generating margins required to finance inflation and real growth. We must continue to work diligently to reduce costs and improve productivity, and we must accelerate our efforts to combine our technology and proprietary know-how with market needs to bring new products and services to the market place.

During the last round of double-digit inflation in 1974, there was an upsurge of interest in accounting for inflation. I was convinced then that by the time the accountants came to some agreement on how to account for inflation, it would have ceased to be a problem.

I was mistaken. I grossly underestimated the degree to which the federal government could abort the curative process set in motion with the recession of 1974-75. In their frantic efforts to restore the economy to a growth mode, they set the stage for the current inflation, which is significantly more severe.

We think it is constructive to probe the various approaches to reporting inflation's impact on our business. Our research and study in this area already has contributed to a better understanding of the dynamics of inflation and its effect on our company.

Let us hope the full disclosure of the serious impact of inflation on the private enterprise system will strengthen the will of our leadership in Washington to stick with the fiscal and monetary restraints required to cool excess demand, dispel inflation psychology and restore confidence to our capital markets.

Summary of accounting policies

The following paragraphs briefly describe the company's significant accounting policies. Certain amounts in the 1978 financial statements have been reclassified to conform to the 1979 presentation.

Principles of consolidation
The consolidated financial statements include all subsidiaries except those in Mexico and South America, which are carried at cost due to political and economic uncertainty, and the financial and protective services companies. Investments in the financial and protective services companies and in affiliated companies, at least 20% owned by Borg-Warner, are carried at equity in underlying net assets.

Marketable securities
Marketable securities are valued at cost, which approximates market.

Inventories
Inventories are valued at the lower of cost or market. Cost of substantially all inventories worldwide is determined by the last-in, first-out (LIFO) method.

Property, plant and equipment and depreciation
Property, plant and equipment is valued at cost less accumulated depreciation. Expenditures for maintenance, repairs and renewals of relatively minor items are generally charged to earnings as incurred. Renewals of significant items are capitalized.

Depreciation is computed generally on a straight-line basis over the estimated useful lives of related assets. For income tax purposes, accelerated methods of depreciation are generally used.

Income taxes
For financial accounting purposes, investment tax credits are used to reduce income tax provisions over a seven-year period. For federal income tax purposes, investment tax credits are recognized currently.

Taxes have not been provided on undistributed net earnings of subsidiaries and affiliates to the extent these earnings are intended to be reinvested in those companies.

Deferred taxes have been provided on timing differences in reporting certain transactions for financial accounting and tax purposes.

Earnings per share
Earnings per common share are based on average outstanding common shares and common share equivalents. Common share equivalents recognize the dilutive effects of common shares which may be issued in the future upon conversion of preferred stock and upon exercise of certain stock options.

Retirement benefit plans
All eligible Borg-Warner domestic employees participate in non-contributory pension plans and substantially all non-U.S. employees participate in contributory or non-contributory pension plans. In addition, a number of employees are covered by non-contributory retirement benefit plans providing life insurance and medical benefits. The related expenses are based on independent actuarial valuations and substantially all are funded currently. Expenses include amortization of prior service costs over periods not exceeding 40 years.

Responsibility for financial statements

To our shareholders:

Borg-Warner Corporation has in place long-standing reporting guidelines and policies designed to ensure that the statements and other information in this report present a fair and accurate financial picture of the company. In fulfilling this responsibility, management must make informed judgments and estimates conforming with generally accepted accounting principles.

The company's comprehensive system of internal accounting controls provides reasonable assurance that assets are protected from improper use, that material errors are prevented or detected within a timely period, and that records are sufficient to produce reliable financial reports. Formal corporate policies demanding high standards of ethical and financial integrity are part of this system, which is subject to frequent review by an internal audit staff and the corporation's independent public accountants.

An Audit Committee composed entirely of Borg-Warner directors who are not employees of the company meets at least twice a year with the company's management and independent public accountants. They review financial results and procedures, internal financial controls and internal and external audit plans and recommendations. To guarantee independence, the Audit Committee and the independent public accountants have unrestricted access to each other with or without the presence of management representatives.

James F. Beré
Chairman and Chief Executive Officer

James J. Gavin, Jr.
Senior Vice President and Chief Financial Officer

Management's discussion and analysis of the summary of earnings and financial position

In 1979, net sales were $2.7 billion, a 17% increase from 1978 sales of $2.3 billion. Net income of $156 million ($7.25 per share) in 1979 represents a 16% increase over 1978 net income of $134 million ($6.24 per share). The 1978 sales were 14% above the 1977 level while 1978 net income was 29% over the $104 million ($4.93 per share) earned in 1977.

The summary of earnings for the years 1975 through 1979 is included in the eleven-year comparative financial summary on pages 38 and 39 of this annual report. The accompanying operating and financial review on pages 2 through 14 provides additional information regarding the company's operations and financial performance.

Manufacturing Operations

Chemicals and Plastics sales increased 26% from 1978 reflecting improvements worldwide with especially strong performance in Europe. The Transportation Equipment group sales increased 17% in both 1979 and 1978. All business areas within the group reflected increases from 1978 with the most significant improvement coming from the non-passenger vehicle and off-highway areas. 1979 Air Conditioning sales increased 10% from 1978, and 1978 sales were 18% over the 1977 level due to new and expanded product lines which minimize energy consumption.

Other income, which includes dividends from unconsolidated subsidiaries and other investments, earnings from affiliated companies and interest, was down 6% in 1979. A breakdown of this item is on page 30. The increase in interest income is due principally to increased earnings rates on investments in short-term securities. This increase, coupled with improved earnings from affiliated companies, was not sufficient to offset the decline in dividend income. Other income in 1978 was up 5% from 1977 with increased dividend income and equity in earnings of affiliates more than offsetting the decline in interest income resulting from lower investment in short-term securities.

The 20% increase in cost of sales in 1979 outpaced the increase in sales. This is a direct result of inflation's impact. With substantially all inventories valued using the last-in, first-out (LIFO) method, the current recognition of higher costs reduced 1979 earnings $33.4 million ($1.56 per share) as compared to $14.0 million ($.66 per share) in 1978 and $8.8 million ($.42 per share) in 1977.

Research and development expenditures increased to $56 million in 1979 compared with 1978 expenditures of $49 million and 1977 expenditures of $45 million. These increases reflect the expansion of the company's research efforts. Depreciation increased 8% in 1979 and 1978 over the respective previous year.

Total debt including capitalized leases increased during 1979 to $219 million at year-end, from $195 million at December 31, 1978. Interest expense and other financial charges increased 24% in 1979 to $33 million from $27 million in 1978 reflecting increased short-term borrowing rates.

The provision for income taxes in 1979 was 35% of earnings from manufacturing operations, compared with an effective tax rate of 43% in 1978 and 44% in 1977. The lower rate resulted primarily from a 2% reduction in U. S. corporate taxes, tax credits on inventories related to our U. K. operations and favorable tax settlements in cases involving operations disposed of in prior years.

All manufacturing groups showed an increase in earnings in 1979 with the exception of Air Conditioning. This group was affected by an out-of-balance product mix, reduced orders for automobile compressors and dramatic copper price increases.

Sales by Borg-Warner consolidated units outside the U. S. were $794 million, up 25% from $633 million in 1978. This follows the 1978 increase of 18% over the 1977 sales level. Net earnings from these units were $33 million in 1979, compared with $24 million in 1978 and $5 million in 1977. Both the increased sales and improved earnings reflect continued improved economic conditions in the geographic areas in which we operate.

Services Earnings

Earnings from the Financials Services companies increased 31% in 1979, following a 26% increase in 1978. Contributing to the improvement in both years were higher inventory financing volumes, increased commercial financing income and increased net investment income from insurance companies.

Protective Services companies contributed $6 million in 1979 as compared to $2 million in 1978. The poor 1978 performance was due to a depressed residential smoke detector market and provisions to close one of two plants manufacturing these products. Protective Services had no impact on 1977 results since the acquisition of Baker Industries, Inc. was treated as a purchase effective at the close of business, December 31, 1977.

Financial Position

Borg-Warner's current ratio decreased to 1.87 to 1 in 1979 from 2.04 to 1 in 1978. Valuing inventories under the last-in, first-out (LIFO) method is the cause for this decline. Had inventories been valued at current cost, this ratio would have been 2.31 to 1 in 1979 and 2.37 to 1 in 1978.

The debt to equity ratio increased slightly to 20.3% in 1979 compared to 20.1% in 1978, indicating the company's ability to internally finance the majority of its increased capital spending program in 1979.

Officers

Robert O. Bass
Vice Chairman
46 years service

James F. Beré
Chairman and Chief Executive Officer
19 years service

Donald W. Collier
Senior Vice President Corporate Strategy
19 years service

Jerry E. Dempsey
President and Chief Operating Officer*
24 years service

James R. Deters
Vice President and Controller
10 years service

James J. Gavin, Jr.
Senior Vice President Finance
11 years service

Clarence E. Johnson
Vice President Human Resources
27 years service

Frederic C. Kautz
Assistant Treasurer
14 years service

Robert E. LaRoche
Vice President (Financial and Protective Services)
24 years service

James R. Lidman
Assistant Secretary
13 years service

Robert A. Morris
Vice President Communications
3 years service

Mark F. Ogan
Assistant Treasurer
10 years service

Russell J. Parsons
Senior Vice President, General Counsel and Secretary
33 years service

Frank E. Pilling
Vice President (Transportation Equipment)
30 years service

Elmer D. Robinson
Executive Vice President (Air Conditioning, Industrial Products)
24 years service

John P. Rozinsky
Assistant Controller
14 years service

Jeannette E. Terris
Assistant Secretary
31 years service

Donald C. Trauscht
Vice President Business Development and Acquisitions
12 years service

William M. Valiant
Vice President and Treasurer
32 years service

Peter C. Valli
Vice President (Energy Equipment)
21 years service

William H. Weltyk
Vice President Engineering and Development
20 years service

Jack L. Wentz
Assistant Secretary
17 years service

Management Committees

Policy and Planning Committee
James F. Beré, Chairman
Robert O. Bass
Donald W. Collier
Jerry E. Dempsey
James J. Gavin, Jr.
Clarence E. Johnson
Russell J. Parsons
Elmer D. Robinson

Operations Committee
*Jerry E. Dempsey, Chairman
James R. Deters
Leonard A. Harvey
Robert E. LaRoche
Frank E. Pilling
Elmer D. Robinson
Peter C. Valli

*Elected to post on 1/8/80.

Directors

Hans Bacher
Member, Board of Management
Robert Bosch GmbH
Stuttgart, West Germany
Director since 1977

Robert O. Bass
Vice Chairman
Borg-Warner Corporation
Director since 1973

James F. Beré
Chairman and Chief Executive Officer
Borg-Warner Corporation
Director since 1968

Weston R. Christopherson
President and Chief Executive Officer
Jewel Companies, Inc.
Chicago, Illinois
Director since 1973

Jerry E. Dempsey
President and Chief Operating Officer
Borg-Warner Corporation
(Elected a director in Jan. 1980)

Gaylord Donnelley
Chairman of the Executive Committee
R. R. Donnelley & Sons Company
Chicago, Illinois
Director since 1966

Gaylord Freeman
Honorary Chairman
First Chicago Corporation and The First National Bank of Chicago
Director since 1957

James J. Gavin, Jr.
Senior Vice President—Finance
Borg-Warner Corporation
Director since 1969

William B. Graham
Chairman and Chief Executive Officer
Baxter Travenol Laboratories, Inc.
Deerfield, Illinois
Director since 1971

Raymond M. Holliday
Chairman of the Board
Hughes Tool Company
Houston, Texas
Director since 1975

Robert S. Ingersoll
Deputy Chairman, Board of Trustees
The University of Chicago
Director since 1976 and 1955-72

William G. Karnes
Retired Chairman of the Board
Beatrice Foods Co.
Chicago, Illinois
Director since 1959

Hans L. Merkle
Chairman of the Board of Management
Robert Bosch GmbH
Stuttgart, West Germany
Director since 1977

James J. O'Connor
President
Commonwealth Edison Company
Chicago, Illinois
Director since 1978

James E. Olson
Vice Chairman of the Board
American Telephone & Telegraph Company
New York, New York
Director since 1974

Thomas C. Theobald
Executive Vice President
Citibank, N.A.
New York, New York
Director since 1977

Committees of the Board

Executive Committee
James F. Beré, Chairman
Robert O. Bass
James J. Gavin, Jr.
William B. Graham
William G. Karnes

Compensation Committee
Gaylord Freeman, Chairman
James E. Olson, Vice Chairman
Weston R. Christopherson
Gaylord Donnelley

Finance Committee
William G. Karnes, Chairman
William B. Graham
Raymond M. Holliday
Robert S. Ingersoll
James J. O'Connor
Thomas C. Theobald

Audit Committee
Weston R. Christopherson, Chairman
Gaylord Donnelley
Robert S. Ingersoll
James J. O'Connor

Nominating Committee
William B. Graham, Chairman
Weston R. Christopherson
James E. Olson
Thomas C. Theobald

The businesses of Borg-Warner

Originally rooted in the auto industry, Borg-Warner now is a diversified manufacturing company involved in eight markets basic to the world's economy: transportation, construction, consumer products, machinery, agribusiness, energy, and financial and protective services.

Our products largely are durable goods. Few reach individual consumers with our name on them. More often, they are components in products made by others.

Millions of telephones, for example, are molded of Borg-Warner's Cycolac® ABS thermoplastic. Thousands of motorists drive cars equipped with Borg-Warner transmissions, while hundreds of the world's large buildings are cooled with equipment from York®.

Borg-Warner has some 50 major divisions with operations in 20 countries on 6 continents. These operating units are organized into five product and service groups based on similarity of products or technology, and not necessarily the markets served. The five groups are:

Air Conditioning
The York division is a major manufacturer of engineered air conditioning systems for large buildings and industrial refrigeration equipment for the petrochemicals, food and other process industries. It also produces commercial air conditioning equipment for smaller office buildings, schools, hotels, factories and apartment buildings.

A growing part of York's business is residential air conditioning systems, heat pumps and furnaces. In addition, it makes automotive air conditioning compressors.

Chemicals and Plastics
Cycolac brand ABS is the trade name for a wide range of tough, engineering thermoplastics produced and marketed around the world by Borg-Warner Chemicals. In addition, the group manufactures and markets a full line of Blendex® impact modifiers used for upgrading the physical properties and processing characteristics of PVC and other plastics.

Borg-Warner Chemicals also is in the fine chemicals business with a growing line of intermediates, additives and alkylphenols. The group produces styrene monomers for Cycolac ABS and for sale on the open market.

Financial and Protective Services
The 1977 acquisition of Baker Industries, with its well-known Wells Fargo protective services units, brings added excitement to this group. Baker's six divisions provide the broadest range of protective services and products in the security field.

Borg-Warner Acceptance Corporation remains the group's major services unit. Today, it offers these financial services: wholesale, retail and receivables financing; consumer financing; credit life, disability and property insurance; and vehicle and equipment leasing.

Industrial Products
This is the most diversified of the five product and service areas. Major products of this group are: centrifugal pumps for power plants, pipelines and water plants; precision seals for pumps and compressors; valves; chains, bearings and power transmission products.

Other products include: agricultural discs, hospital furniture and audio-visual educational systems.

Transportation Equipment
As the leading independent producer of automatic transmissions, the group supplies automatics to major car and light-truck manufacturers outside the U.S. The company's five-speed manual transmission with overdrive was the first mass-produced in the U.S.

In addition to transmissions, other components include: clutches, four-wheel-drive units, spin-resistant differentials, axle assemblies, locking hubs for four-wheel-drive vehicles, propeller shafts, carburetion and ignition equipment, radiators and other heat exchangers.

Borg-Warner also supplies replacement parts for passenger cars, trucks, off-highway and farm equipment, boats, aircraft, recreational vehicles and industrial machines.

Information and publications

The following publications can be obtained by writing: Director of Investor Relations, Borg-Warner Corp., 200 S. Michigan Ave., Chicago, IL 60604.

- Form 10-K Annual Report to the Securities and Exchange Commission
- Investor Fact Book
- The First Fifty Years (History of the company)
- Information Directory (Listing products and facilities)
- Description of principal pension plan

For answers to questions about shareholder accounts, dividends and dividend reinvestment, contact shareholder representative Dorothy Flynn at the address above, or phone 312-322-8563.

Transfer agents/registrars for Borg-Warner stock:

- The Continental Illinois National Bank and Trust, Chicago
- Citibank, N.A., New York

The annual meeting of shareholders will take place on Tuesday, April 22, beginning at 9:30 a.m. in the First Chicago Center at Dearborn and Madison Streets.

Dial 800-621-5445 for Borg-Warner NEWS

You can get a quick, recorded update on recent Borg-Warner news developments by calling 800-621-5445. There is no charge to you for "800" line calls.

If you live in Illinois, phone 312-322-8600.

Printed in U.S.A. by Heritage Press, Dallas
Design by Boller/Coates/Robert, Chicago
Photography by Erich Hartmann, Magnum, New York

Borg-Warner

1979 Investor Fact Book

1979 will be 4th record year in a row

Dividend raised 15%; 70% since 1975

Energy-saving motor speed control to debut in early 1980

Contents

New inverter technology sparks Borg-Warner drive in electronics	1
A view from inside: Condensed remarks by key company executives at a recent seminar for financial analysts	2
Recent performance measures up when compared with top-rated companies	10
Capital expenditure and depreciation review	12
On the way to a better business mix	13
A breakdown of sales by market	14
Fifteen-year financial summary (deflated data)	15
Fifteen-year financial summary	16
The management team: key executive biographies	18
The businesses of Borg-Warner	20
Investor relations and corporate disclosure policies	21

Foreword:

To members of the financial community:

I hope this edition of the Investor Fact Book will help you better know our company and judge its potential.

As always, we welcome your comments on this or other of our communications and your suggestions on how we could better serve your information needs.

James F. Beré

James F. Beré
Chairman and
Chief Executive Officer

November 1, 1979

New inverter technology sparks Borg-Warner drive in electronics

Borg-Warner's new line of microcomputer-controlled variable speed motor drives promises to make "a significant contribution to our nation's drive toward energy conservation," according to James F. Beré, chairman and chief executive officer.

It also promises some exciting business opportunities for two Borg-Warner divisions—Morse Chain and York. Morse will offer a line of microcomputer-controlled alternating current (AC) inverters for use with 1-20 horsepower motors in the first quarter of 1980, and will expand the line to up to 50 horsepower by the end of the year.

The use of power transistors has enabled Morse to cut the cost of the inverter by 50%, making it competitive in cost with direct current controls, the type most commonly used by industry.

York has incorporated an energy-saving inverter control package into a new line of residential heat pumps, and has also packaged a unit for controlling the centrifugal chiller component of the commercial air conditioning system. Both systems will be available in early 1980.

The development also moves Borg-Warner toward a major objective—making good on opportunities to marry its experience in mechanical and hydraulic devices with its emerging skill in electronics.

Broad industrial application

Basically, an inverter adjusts the power coming from a given electrical line so it matches the power needed by the motor it is feeding. Most motors in the United States run at fixed speed, and must be mechanically throttled if their speed is to be reduced. The throttling process results in energy losses.

Borg-Warner, based on work in its Research Center, has been in the inverter business for over 20 years. Until now, however, the inverter's high cost has limited its use. The use of proven electronics in its new products, Borg-Warner says, has driven down the cost and increased reliability.

According to Clarence E. (Red) Johnson, president and general manager of Morse,* "the energy saved by using adjustable speed control in industry could be as high as one-third, depending on the application." Johnson cited fans, pumps and blowers as holding the greatest potential for energy savings.

*Now Borg-Warner vice president—human resources

Morse's inverter line, named the CF-1100, has use in a wide variety of other applications, including material handling, extruders, food and pharmaceutical packaging, drilling, textile machinery, printing, machine tools, paper converting and metal working equipment.

Johnson pointed out that the inverter could lead to further strides to keep pace with the increasing sophistication in manufacturing technology. One possibility is speed control for an entire plant. "We envision tying a number of speed controls to motors throughout a total system, and through a directly coupled central computer, controlling the overall process," he said.

"Estimates peg the market for adjustable speed controls for 1-50 horsepower motors at an annual growth rate of about 22% through the mid-eighties," Johnson noted.

Commercial, residential air conditioning markets

For York, which was concerned with 'life cycle' air conditioning and heating costs long before energy was a national concern, the inverter control package is the latest in a series of product developments aimed at energy efficiency.

Over two years of testing show that the package, when applied to the centrifugal chiller of a commercial air conditioning unit, can save up to 30% of the energy consumed by the chiller. In addition to being offered as part of York's new commercial systems, the inverter control package will be provided on a retrofit basis for York or competitive equipment in existing buildings.

Beré noted that while York has only applied the inverter to the centrifugal chiller, which consumes around 30% of the energy used by the entire system, the division is working on control of the motors for blowers and recirculating pumps, which account for the remaining energy consumed.

Beré said that an inverter-controlled commercial system maintaining a building's temperature at 72 degrees could save more energy than a conventional commercial system operating at the 78-degree level mandated by the federal government as a summer standard for all office buildings.

With this in mind, Beré feels the new technology could spell relief "for those of us who spent our office time in shirt-sleeves this summer," if government action is taken to grant users of energy-saving technologies an exemption from the 78-degree standard.

While York is optimistic about the inverter's performance in the new commercial building market, Jack W. Kennedy, York's president, sees the biggest market initially in retrofit installations. Kennedy estimates that the new technology could be applicable to as many as 30,000 existing buildings. Depending on the building, payback periods would range from three to seven years.

On the residential side, the application of the inverter to York's own line of energy efficient three-ton capacity heat pumps can save up to 17% of energy consumed. Kennedy noted that residential marketing efforts will be focused on the custom-built end of the home construction market.

Energy savings immediately

Noting reports of other work being done in inverter technology, chairman Beré stressed that the company has set concrete dates for product availability. "We're talking about energy savings that can be realized almost immediately, not at some uncertain future date," he added.

Borg-Warner stressed that the technology was generated internally, and said that the company would not need any outside assistance to market or manufacture the products. The inverter and electronic controls for both York and Morse products will be manufactured by Borg-Warner Electronics, a collaboration between the two divisions, formed in 1977.

Thomas C. Jednacz, general manager of Borg-Warner Electronics and a key person on the inverter project since its inception in 1965, said that opportunities for the inverter don't end here. "We're looking at ways in which this technology can be applied in other areas of Borg-Warner," he said.

A view of Borg-Warner—from the inside

(Based on comments to security analysts at a meeting in Chicago earlier this year.)

The following is an update on Borg-Warner's businesses from both the corporate and operational points of view. It covers Borg-Warner's progress in reaching strategic planning goals, describes the company's planning process at work and reviews some key financial yardsticks. In addition, it contains in-depth remarks from the people who make the company tick —the presidents of key operating groups.

Depending on which economist you talk to, we're either heading for a recession, or are already there. Borg-Warner chairman James F. Beré is quick to point out the fundamental differences between the Borg-Warner of today and the company which dropped 38% in net earnings during the last recession.

Beré: "We've been very aggressively pursuing what we call our 'honing and divestment' program. The primary thrust of this program is to optimize our efforts in operating units that have high-growth potential. This has involved divesting of assets in marginal operations and targeting our capital allocations in those areas which promise the greatest rate of return."

Beré also points to the company's increasing emphasis on service businesses:

Beré: "We purchased Baker Industries two years ago, giving us a prominent position in a broad range of protective service markets. This acquisition, coupled with the continued success of our financial services subsidiary, Borg-Warner Acceptance Corporation, has had a strong effect on our profit picture."

Beré evaluates the opportunities posed by the current energy situation. In transportation:

Beré: "The redesign of cars to meet federally mandated fleet economy requirements provides us with enormous opportunities. Companies like Borg-Warner that can approach Detroit with sophistication in both marketing and product development will stand to gain in this type of environment."

A sign of this sophisticated approach in his own company, Beré feels, is Borg-Warner's relationship with Robert Bosch GmbH, the German high-technology firm. How does Borg-Warner's relationship with Bosch fit into this scenario?

Beré: "Many of us are convinced that the next major change in the transportation industry will involve the marriage of mechanical engineering with electronics. We believe there are opportunities to work together that could benefit both our companies and consumers, too."

What has happened since Bosch assumed a 10% equity position in Borg-Warner?

Beré: "So far, we have spent most of our time learning about each other's products and markets. In addition, we have a permanent task force charged with determining areas of compatibility, which we feel are many. We *have* jointly purchased a share in American Microsystems, Inc., a California-based manufacturer of solid-state chips. We're now exploring ways their technology can improve a number of products."

Beré also sees further opportunity in air conditioning:

Beré: "York was designing systems for energy efficiency long before any real demand for this efficiency surfaced. As a result, for many purchasers, both residential and commercial, a York® system has traditionally been 'overdesigned.' The escalating cost of energy, however, has virtually played into York's hands, as consumers, consulting engineers and owners of commercial buildings are all thinking about how they can minimize energy consumption."

Beré also discussed growth opportunities associated with Hughes Tool, a company in which Borg-Warner holds an 18% equity interest:

Beré: "Our interest in Hughes was acquired in 1974 when we sold Hughes our own oilfield services operation, Byron Jackson, Inc. So, we continue to share in that growing part of the energy market through Hughes."

Is there another Firestone in Borg-Warner's future?

Beré: "Well, I can safely say that we are not actively *seeking* another Firestone. That was a special situation, one that we felt we had to pursue. Our *ideal* acquisition candidate would be in the service area, also, but it might be any company with a strong market position that would strengthen our present business areas. We would look for a company with a strong leadership position in its particular field, with management willing to stay and prosper under the Borg-Warner banner."

Robert O. Bass, the company's vice chairman, provides a description of the strategic planning system, established in 1975:

Bass: "First, we aimed at improvement of our existing businesses, emphasizing margins. Second, by analyzing strategic business units—SBU's as we call them—we would select the portions of our existing businesses which seemed to have better earnings and sales growth potential than the corporate average. These businesses would then be given a priority on capital resources. Third, we would plant the seeds for future high-growth businesses by acquiring or generating technology in these business areas. Finally, we would consider making a select number of acquisitions that would improve our 'business mix.'"

Bass elaborates on the second strategy—identification of high-growth businesses:

Bass: "...it is here where our people have really

gotten into the act. You see, the system dictates that the strategic planning process begin at the operating level. While we at corporate headquarters are analyzing in a broad sense what businesses we should be in, our divisional people are responsible for dividing their own operations into strategic business units. So, it's operations people who really begin the process of defining growth areas."

Bass claims that this process has helped build the character of Borg-Warner's operating managers:

Bass: "I know from years of experience that it's really rough to give up on a product or market strategy that you've nursed from conception. But that's what many of our managers had to do—sacrifice one part of their operation to nurture other, more profitable parts."

The trauma, however, was outweighed by the benefits:

Bass: "On the up side, our managers became more sensitive to market opportunities and have been quick to identify where investment in people, capital or technology could enable us to take advantage of these opportunities."

What about the prognosis on achieving the goal of reaching the median return of the *Fortune* "500"?

James Deters, *Vice president & controller:* "... this is a moving target, and whether we will break through the median by the end of the year is still a question. High inflation is putting Borg-Warner and other LIFO companies at a growing disadvantage by comparison as ROE measures are inflated by inventory profits. By reporting on LIFO, our relative position in ROE rankings suffers accordingly."

How has the company's rise from 471 in 1975 to 266 in the *Fortune* median return on equity rankings been accomplished?

Deters: "Better asset management has been our primary focus. Since 1971, we have divested operating assets equal to slightly more than $200 million. Our working capital position has been further strengthened by our success in speeding up inventory turnover. Since 1970, we have increased turns from three to nearly four times, annually. We have substantially improved our receivables picture. Receivables were reduced from 65 days in 1970 to 55 days in 1975. We cut this further to 51 days by the end of last year. And that's about what we're averaging now. This performance is substantially better than our five-year plan goal, which was initially set at 55 days."

What kind of progress has been made on another long-range Borg-Warner goal, margin improvement?

Deters: "Improving operating margins has been a gnawing problem for Borg-Warner and one that grows more acute during periods of high inflation. But here, too, we have made good progress. For 1978, our return on sales equalled 5.8%, a full point better than the median for the '500' industrials. Our improvement in this category has significantly outpaced the '500' since 1975; and last year, our 5% return on manufacturing operations alone exceeded the *Fortune* median for the first time in this decade."

William M. Valiant, Borg-Warner's vice president and treasurer, cites some other numbers that confirm Deters' assessment of the company's financial strength. Valiant is particularly proud of Borg-Warner's 20% debt-to-equity ratio, which is well within the company's self-imposed guideline of 35%.

Valiant: "We could raise an additional $144 million through debt financing and still remain within that guideline. We project that we'll be able to exceed the $200 million plus capital investment program over the next two years without increasing our debt."

But capital budgets are certainly not the only area in which Borg-Warner is showing its aggressiveness. Research and development is a vital factor in meeting strategic goals, as it provides the technological basis for penetration into growth market areas. William H. Weltyk, Borg-Warner's vice president of engineering and development, describes the ways that R&D dovetails with the four-part strategy outlined earlier by Bob Bass.

Cutting manufacturing costs is a major role for R&D—and a good way of improving the performance of present businesses, the first part of the plan:

Weltyk: "This can be done by finding less costly substitutes for present materials and by increasing the value-added of our products so they command higher prices without significantly higher production costs."

Weltyk points out that the second part of Borg-Warner's strategy, dividing operations into discreet units, gives R&D a basis for channeling time and dollars to the right places:

Weltyk: "This activity demands internal generation of technology in areas of promise and licensing of technologies in areas where we lack expertise. And, our research and development capability influences our acquisition strategy. Because our technological base is so broad, we may be able to enhance the R&D effort of a narrow-based acquisition candidate."

Weltyk feels that a good example of this seed planting program is Kemron Environmental Services. Kemron's major business is the monitoring of air quality at remote locations through a device known as a Kemputer™—a field-based data system:

Weltyk: "The development of the Kemputer was through a marriage of an acquired technological expertise and Borg-Warner's financial resources. With

"ABS is not one plastic, but a family of plastics... each tailored to meet a specific need." Harvey

the proliferation of Environmental Protection Agency regulations, the monitoring business has grown dramatically during the 1970s. Kemron, despite its short life as a distinct entity, enjoys a technological leadership position in this market. The technology developed through Kemron will lead us into other growth opportunities."

Until now, we've heard from a number of corporate officials on the plans and aspirations they have for Borg-Warner. But the people charged with turning those aspirations into reality are the operating managers. Their thoughts follow.

First, Frank E. Pilling, corporate vice president (Transportation Equipment group—TEG), describes Borg-Warner's largest business segment:

Pilling: "Our 30 operating units, in some 44 worldwide locations, accounted for 37% of Borg-Warner's total sales and earnings for 1978. As a separate entity, the Transportation Equipment group would rank in the top 300 of the *Fortune* '500', with sales exceeding $860 million..."

Pilling also points out that the group is far less dependent on the automotive industry than it is generally perceived to be:

Pilling: "While sales to automobile manufacturers are important to TEG, these sales represent only 41% of our total sales, and 35% of our total income."

The rest of the group's sales are evenly divided among manufacturers of trucks, off-highway and construction equipment, agricultural equipment, replacement parts and a category which includes recreational vehicles and marine equipment. Pilling notes the strong growth rate of the group's aftermarket business, which provides a counterbalance for his group's cyclical markets. The TEG chief expects aftermarket sales to double by 1982, using 1977 as a base year:

Pilling: "Our strength in the aftermarket centers on our worldwide distribution network which handles over 20,000 parts for nearly 3000 accounts in some 70 countries."

Pilling discusses research and development, where the emphasis is on fuel economy:

Pilling: "We have successfully introduced a new fan drive for medium- and heavy-duty trucks which uses a patented variable clutch. This unit is currently being tested on off-highway vehicles. The fan only operates when the engine requires cooling, which, on a truck, is usually less than 5% of the time... We've just started production on a new part-time four-wheel-drive transfer case for Ford light trucks. The unit weighs only 80 pounds, complete with lubricant; and the part-time feature means increased fuel economy. We have a new automatic locking hub that is scheduled for standard equipment for late in the model year 1980 for a major manufacturer."

Pilling finds a good deal to be encouraged about with the group's unconsolidated operations overseas. The Japanese operation is beginning production of a new line of automatic transmissions for a major Japanese auto manufacturer. The transmission, which has an overdrive device, outperformed competing models. Pilling is particularly optimistic about a new clutch that the group's Brazilian plant will be producing for General Motors' new "J" car, the automotive giant's new entry into the world car market:

Pilling: "We are projecting strong sales for the new unit and feel the potential exists for supplying clutches to North and South America from that facility."

The group's United Kingdom transmission facility turned a profit in 1978 for the first time since 1971; West German operations and the Japanese joint ventures are also doing well. What about Mexico?

Pilling: "Recent fiscal policy changes by the Mexican government, an improved balance of payments situation, large oil and gas reserves and Mexico's proximity to the United States combine to make it an attractive expansion site. Several opportunities are under discussion."

Another topic Pilling likes to discuss is cost control, an area he feels might have been the main reason for increased earnings and a more favorable return on investment in 1978:

Pilling: "In 1978, the savings realized from cost reduction programs increased 32% from the previous year."

In its chemicals business, Borg-Warner has a manager whose pursuit of new market opportunities often has been as easy as A-B-S. The initials stand for acrylonitrile-butadiene-styrene, a versatile thermoplastic compound used in literally hundreds of applications. Leonard A. Harvey, president of Borg-Warner Chemicals-Americas, describes his company's market position:

Harvey: "In the U.S., ABS volume surpasses 1.1 billion pounds a year; and Borg-Warner supplies 40% of that volume."

He points out that not all ABS material is alike:

Harvey: "...ABS is not one plastic...it is a family of plastics. Borg-Warner has manufactured about 80 grades of ABS over the years, each tailored to meet a specific need."

Harvey points to three good reasons why his company is focusing its marketing efforts on specialty grades of ABS:

Harvey: "First, specialty materials yield margins two to three times higher than general purpose grades. Second, the use of special grades is growing faster than general purpose grades—for some ABS products, 20% a year. And third, plastics with the performance and economic benefits of Cycolac® ABS have only a small part of those markets currently."

Harvey assesses ABS' major markets. First, the automotive industry:

Harvey: "ABS has been used in automotive applications such as grilles and instrument clusters for many years. The trend to lighter, smaller cars will lead to a 330-million-pound-a-year market for ABS in Detroit by 1983."

Next is pipe, long a staple ABS market:

Harvey: "ABS applications in pipe now stand at some 300 million pounds a year."

Harvey estimates the refrigeration market will grow to 200 million pounds of ABS a year by the early 1980s:

Harvey: "These are big numbers for a material that sells for 50 to 80 cents a pound."

He evaluates Chemicals' position now as compared with its position during the last recession:

Harvey: "Our product mix is such that we are more strongly positioned in the higher margin, high-growth potential markets. This was not the case in 1975. It is true that to a large extent as the durable goods, automotive and construction indicators go, so go plastics. But we think our penetration in specialty areas provides a buffer."

How does the raw material situation look?

Harvey: "In terms of supply, we feel we're in much better shape than we were at the time of the last downturn. ... the competition between gasoline and petrochemicals demand is the cause of the current benzene shortage. It's also the reason that benzene prices have nearly doubled since the end of last year."

What about styrene?

Harvey: "Our styrene production is protected by a joint venture for styrene production with American Petrofina. The venture capacity there is over 1.3 billion pounds a year. This allows us not only to supply our own requirements for ABS (100% in the U.S. and Canada), but also allows us to satisfy some of our requirements in Europe, and to sell styrene to the merchant market."

The international situation looks much better than 1975, when the chemicals operation was saddled with overcapacity and cutthroat pricing competition:

Harvey: "Last year, Europe accounted for a $4 million operating profit, as opposed to a $5 million loss in 1977. That's a $9 million turnabout—and a significant part of that came through internal cost reductions. This year, we project even higher operating income, despite heavy startup costs incurred at our new Scotland plant, where we manufacture modifier resins for the PVC market."

Japanese and Australian operations are also looking very good, Harvey notes:

Harvey: "Our joint venture in Japan, Ube Cycon, is now making a good return on investment, as is our Australian operation. In fact, we announced at the end of May that we had bought out our Australian partner there, Nylex, Ltd."

On the domestic front, Harvey noted that his group would be building a $50 million ABS plant in Port Bienville, Miss. The new plant, plus additions at five existing plants, will increase the group's domestic capacity 40% by 1982.

Through its York division, Borg-Warner is a leader in providing air conditioning and heating systems for residential, commercial, and industrial markets and in the manufacture of air conditioning compressors for automobiles and in commercial refrigeration equipment.

Jack W. Kennedy, *President of York division:* "Our equipment has been installed in systems in the World Trade Center in New York City, the Hilton Hotel in Hong Kong... Our products are making people comfortable while they check their bags at Orly or De Gaulle airports in Paris or attending a performance of the opera at Milan."

York products also keep a large number of Washington, D.C., regulators and legislators from getting too hot under the collar or overly chilled from the climate of public opinion. In fact, Kennedy claims that over 70% of all office buildings constructed in Washington over the past 15 years have York systems.

Kennedy comments on York's share in each of its major markets:

Kennedy: "In unitary air conditioning, we're number five, to Carrier's number one position, and GE is number two. In commercial air conditioning, we are number three, to Trane's number one, and Carrier is in second place. We are an industry leader in industrial refrigeration, in the highly technical applications for the chemical and petrochemical market, and we are the world's largest independent producer of automotive air conditioning compressors."

Much of York's reputation as a top-of-the-line manufacturer has been earned overseas, as 40% of York's production is for the international market. Of that 40%, 20% is exported from the U.S. Kennedy remarks that it is all part of the plan:

Kennedy: "Our marketing strategy has been

"In 1976, only 18% of our system sales were applied to energy-efficient applications. Now it's 50%." Kennedy

put together so that we do have good export business production in the United States, which helps on any kind of a downturn that is U.S. economy oriented."

He points out, however, that exportation is only one part of a total international organization:

Kennedy: "The three major facets of York Europe are our operations in Basildon, England; in Nantes, France; and our joint venture with Brown-Broveri in Mannheim, Germany. In further support of the European operations we have plants in Durango and Monterrey, Mexico. The Monterrey plant is being replaced with a new plant scheduled for completion and production in the first quarter of 1980. And last, we have a facility in St. Jerome, Quebec."

He points to York's exceptionally strong European reputation:

Kennedy: "In Europe, we developed energy-saving systems that offset higher first costs with substantially lower operating costs; and we sold our customers on the concept of 'life cycle costing' while U.S. buyers were still basing their buying decisions on first cost."

Kennedy notes that U.S. buyers are now coming around to this concept:

Kennedy: "This is evidenced by the fact that in 1976, only 18% of our total system sales were applied to energy-efficient applications, where in 1978, this has grown to 50%."

Kennedy sees energy efficiency having a greater role in the company's maintenance and service operations, which influenced the development of a separate energy and maintenance division two years ago:

Kennedy: "We now obtain contracts that are based solely on increasing the equipment's operating efficiency, where in the past, the purpose of most maintenance contracts was to prevent breakdown and extend equipment life. In addition, we're now obtaining contracts to retrofit existing systems with more energy-efficient components, with the associated costs to the owner being offset by energy savings."

The industrial segment of Borg-Warner's business is primarily made up of the Morse Chain division and the Energy Equipment group. Morse Chain, which supplies industrial and automotive markets with a variety of power transmission products, sees continued growth despite the maturing of its markets:

C. E. Johnson, *President of Morse Chain**: "While profitability relates to the economic cycle, our industrial line does not react as sharply on the down side due to the moderating effect of our strong distribution base. Whereas equipment manufacturing declines, industry continues to allocate funds for maintaining existing equipment and machinery. Although this in-plant activity does not totally offset capital spending slowdowns, it certainly tempers an overall business decline."

Johnson adds that Morse's strategy of emphasizing distributor business over original equipment manufacturers has lent further stability to the division's growth picture:

Johnson: "The emphasis on developing a strong distributor program has had the planned effect of shifting our sales mix from 45% distributor and 55% OEM in 1978 to 60% distributor and 40% OEM in 1979."

Morse now has 974 stocking distributors in the United States, a leadership position in the industrial products area. This is bound to have a positive effect on market share, as Johnson notes:

Johnson: "The served market share by our industrial SBU was approximately 13% in 1978, and we are forecasting an increase in share to 17.5% by 1983."

In the automotive market, Morse's big news is its Hy-Vo® chain, as Johnson notes:

Johnson: "Our Hy-Vo business has been given added thrust by the recent upgrading of Hy-Vo as part of our continuing product development programs. 'Hy-Vo® Lite,' as we call it, has approximately 40% more loading capacity than earlier designs and is well covered by U.S. and foreign patents. Hy-Vo Lite has enabled us to use narrower chain in transmission and transfer cases, thereby helping to reduce size and weight and making a valuable contribution to fuel economy."

While sales of four-wheel-drive vehicles has suffered during the latest gasoline crisis, Johnson projects a solid future for these vehicles:

Johnson: "Manufacturers feel that when the government's energy policy has been established, and the situation stabilized, the long-term outlook will be bright."

Front-wheel drive, which used to be a novelty in the American automobile industry, is coming of age, as Johnson points out:

Johnson: "The front-wheel-drive market has just entered a dramatic growth stage with the recent introduction of the General Motors X-car line. Early response for the new cars has been excellent and has created significant demand for our Hy-Vo Lite chain. ...it has been estimated that by the late 1980s, over 75% of the cars that General Motors produces will be front-wheel-drive."

The other major component of the industrial products business is the Energy Equipment group, which designs, manufactures and markets pumps,

*Now Borg-Warner vice president—human resources

valves, actuators and mechanical seals for the petroleum and power generation industries.

The largest of the four divisions in this group is Byron Jackson Pump. Borg-Warner believes this division is the largest centrifugal pump manufacturer in the world:

Peter C. Valli, *corporate vice president (Energy Equipment):* "We definitely have more primary coolant pumps in service than any other producer at this time. We have enjoyed a market share in primaries of about 60% of the available market."

The Nuclear Valve division, as the name implies, provides valves actuated by electric, pneumatic or hydraulic means for the nuclear industry. The Mechanical Seal division, an offshoot of Byron Jackson, makes products which mechanically prevent leakage at the rotating shafts of pumps and compressors. Finally, the Centrilift subsidiary makes submersible pumps used in the enhanced recovery of oil. Valli breaks down his group's major markets:

Valli: "Our products and services are dedicated to three major markets: petroleum, power generation and what we refer to as commercial... Petroleum represents the largest market for our products—51%. We serve the market subsegments of production, refinery, pipeline and petrochemicals."

What about power generation?

Valli: "The power market represents approximately 24%, which includes both fossil—that is, coal, gas and petroleum-fired plants—and nuclear power plants."

Valli notes that half of this market is in the United States, while the remainder is spread out overseas. He contends that the group has a very strong market position in the Far East and Canada, as well as the United States:

Valli: "Our third major market area, commercial, represents a tremendous potential market consisting primarily of agricultural, waterworks, general industry and other segments. About $200 million of this market is in the United States, where Environmental Protection Agency regulations and clean water laws are having a positive impact on demand."

He claims that existing product lines represent a $2 billion market, with real growth of 6 to 7% projected over the next five years. He further points out that while the group's major markets are cyclical, they tend to run in counter cycles, contributing to a consistent overall growth rate.

A good example of how different market segments offset each other is the power generation market:

Valli: "In spite of all the controversy, we believe the electrical utility market in the United States will have to grow at a 4 to 4-1/2% rate through the year 2000. Unless you buy the notion of a 'no-growth' economy, we'll need the additional capacity."

Valli notes that his group's sales to electric utilities should continue steady improvement, as strength in the fossil fuel market will offset any roadblocks in the way of nuclear plant construction:

Valli: "The dollar value of business available in every nuclear plant is larger for us than in a fossil plant, but many more fossil plants will be built if nuclear construction continues to be impeded."

He sees the group barrelling along in the petroleum market, as well:

Valli: "Our present market share averages about 14 to 15%. We see the U.S. markets we serve as growing at about 8%... Mexico, incidentally, where we have an excellent position, will grow at a 12% level."

In the commercial area, he mentions some new things in the works:

Valli: "Commercial markets offer exceptional opportunities for us. Nineteen percent of our sales go to these markets, where we have a 12% share. Present activity includes a major reorganization, and plans for the construction of a new facility to produce pre-engineered pump products for commercial and utility markets in the United States and elsewhere."

Borg-Warner's service businesses, a growing element in the company's earnings picture, include Borg-Warner Acceptance Corporation (BWAC), a financial services subsidiary, and Baker Industries, a diversified supplier of protection services. Richard J. Doyle, BWAC president, describes the scope of his company's operations:

Doyle: "We do business with more than 1000 manufacturers and 35,000 retailers in the United States, Canada, Puerto Rico, Australia and Europe from over 350 locally managed offices."

Doyle comments on 1978, BWAC's 13th consecutive year of growth:

Doyle: "Our net earnings, $15.3 million, were 10 times our earnings just 10 years ago. And our gross finance receivables, $1.3 billion, were almost nine times greater last year than they were in 1968. As a result, our annual compounded growth in earnings since 1968 is 26.1%. That's almost four times greater than the average growth in earnings of 10 major non-captive finance companies from 1967 to 1977."

According to Doyle, two principles guide all BWAC activities:

Doyle: "First, we develop a strategic plan for each area of business for each year from the bottom up. Second, we provide prompt, efficient and intelligent

"One in every five TVs, stereos, or home appliances sold in the U.S. is financed by BWAC." Doyle

local service to our customers."

Doyle believes that BWAC's involvement in financing television sets is a good example of how the company conducts its business in its oldest activity, inventory financing:

Doyle: "In the early 1960s, expensive color televisions presented a much greater sales risk to the retailer—and to BWAC. We measured our capabilities and the market's potential. We offered a distributor local service throughout his market area, which his bank couldn't provide. As an independent company, not a captive, we would serve all of the industry's manufacturers. We're now the industry leader in television floor planning; and one in every five televisions, stereos or home appliances sold in the United States is financed by BWAC at some time on its way from the factory to your home, or to mine."

Doyle assesses BWAC's ability to enter other markets and expand into other forms of financing:

Doyle: "Our leasing division established its first office in 1969. Our first international branch office opened in 1969, and we entered the agricultural equipment market in 1975. Each of those three areas of business today makes more profit for BWAC than the entire company did in any of its first 15 years."

He analyzes the future prospects for each of BWAC's four divisions. First, inventory financing:

Doyle: "We expect continued growth in all our inventory financing markets, from home entertainment equipment, to white goods, to agricultural. And we expect continued diversity. Just 10 years ago, for example, two-thirds of our branch offices were serving the inventory financing needs of just one manufacturer. Today, exclusive of Borg-Warner, less than one-twentieth of our total financing portfolio is represented by any one manufacturer."

How about insurance?

Doyle: "In insurance, the volume of insurance premiums we financed increased 72% last year, 118% in 1977. We anticipate more growth, though not at the same rates of gain, as more businesses look to the cash flow benefits of financing their insurance premiums. The continuing demand for consumer credit, which has doubled since 1973, will require a supporting growth in credit life, disability and property insurance —three of the insurance services we provide."

In retail financing?

Doyle: "We've just entered the marine industry, projected to become a $9 billion industry by 1980. We plan to be serving at least 15 of our country's major markets for large sailboats and cabin cruisers through local offices by the end of this year."

In the leasing area, Doyle cites new programs:

Doyle: "The increasingly high cost of farm implements and other equipment frequently reaches or exceeds the lending limits of small- and medium-sized banks. Losing that opportunity to a larger bank can cost a small bank a customer and his basic business. Through a BWAC participating leasing program, one of BWAC's newest services, the bank can serve and keep its customer by lending up to its limit, then placing the remainder with us."

Now for an assessment of opportunities for Borg-Warner's newest major acquisition—Baker Industries. First, an analysis of the competition in several major markets and how Baker stacks up:

Malcolm Baker, *President of Baker Industries:* "Pinkerton is the largest guard organization in the United States and serves over 100 markets. Wells Fargo serves some 50 markets. American District Telegraph, the largest alarm company in the United States, is in over 100 communities—we are in 20. Purolator, the largest courier company in the United States, has revenues of over $200 million. We have courier revenues of some $15-20 million. So you see, there's plenty of room for growth."

What is Baker's verdict on the residential smoke detector market, a market burdened over the past two years with overcapacity and a surplus of competition?

Baker: "The timing and severity of the shakeout in the marketplace was far more severe than initially anticipated. It is our intent to participate in this market only on an economically viable basis. At some point in the future, we believe the substantial inventories at the retail level will dissipate and pricing will stabilize."

He points to legislation as providing hope for this market:

Baker: "Twenty-three states and the District of Columbia have adopted statewide mandatory smoke detector laws for new residential construction. Six states and the District of Columbia also require smoke detectors in existing residential structures under selected conditions."

And on the municipal level:

Baker: "Los Angeles, Atlanta, Boston and St. Louis are examples of larger cities that require smoke detectors in new or renovated residential structures."

Overall, Baker believes his company will grow at a faster rate than the industry. He cites recent history to back up his prediction:

Baker: "Specifically, in the courier business, the two largest factors have grown at an average rate of 18% and 12% in revenues over the past four years. Our courier business has had an average growth in this segment of 25%. Pinkerton, Wackenhut, and Burns, our largest competitors in contract security guard work, have an average revenue growth in this area of only 6 to 8%. Ours has been 25%. In the alarm segment, the major competition has grown at a 9% rate. We've grown at 11%."

What of the future?

Baker: "The future includes serious consideration of complementary services such as executive protection, investigative services and a broad-based expansion of our courier services into general commodities."

Baker also mentioned acquisition as a means of enhancing his present services. Shortly after these remarks, he made good on those words by announcing the planned acquisition of Burns Electronic Security Systems, Inc., the domestic central station subsidiary of Burns International. The acquisition ties in with an area that Baker views with enthusiasm—the expansion of the role of central station operations:

Baker: "Rather than viewing this operation merely as a burglar and fire alarm service, one could and should view this operation as a 24-hour monitoring center with installation and service capability. Energy conservation and industrial process supervision are certainly areas of opportunity when you view a central station in this manner."

Now that the major operating groups have been covered, we'll close with an evaluation of the company's prospects within the overall business environment. First, what are some of the negative factors that could affect performance?

James J. Gavin, *senior vice president—finance:* "One is the disturbing escalation of industrial raw material prices, which has placed serious pressure on margins. These prices are also reflected on our bottom line in another manner—through our 'last-in, first-out' method of valuing inventories."

Another negative is what Gavin calls a crisis in consumer confidence:

Gavin: "One convincing piece of evidence for this crisis in consumer confidence is the declining housing market. We are predicting that housing starts will reach only 1.6 million units for the whole of 1979—almost a 20% downturn from the year before. The housing market, of course, has a ripple effect throughout other sectors of the economy."

On the plus side, there's capital spending, which is on the rise:

Gavin: "We see real growth in capital spending of 6 to 8% in 1979. While the pace should slow for 1980, we're still projecting real growth in the neighborhood of 2 to 3% next year."

Another plus is the continuing strength of economies outside the United States:

Gavin: "A major difference between the last recession and the one we appear to be entering is that this one is presently confined to the United States. Foreign economies, most notably Europe and Australia, have continued to look strong. Our overseas operations stand to prosper if this trend holds through 1980."

Gavin also cites the service sector as an area where Borg-Warner is gathering strength:

Gavin: "Baker showed overall improvement in the third quarter on a year-to-year basis and should be up for the year as a whole."

Recent performance compares favorably with other top-rated companies

These charts compare Borg-Warner's relative performance since 1970 in nine key financial ratios with that of about 100 other companies whose debt is rated "A" by Moody's and Standard & Poor's and about 70 companies rated "AA" by these agencies. Borg-Warner itself has a split rating—"double A minus" by S&P, and "A" by Moody's. The charts also show the performance of the S&P 400 industrials during the same period.

In most of the charts, it would appear that Borg-Warner had down operating years in both 1974 and 1975. The sharp 1975 decline did result from the broad economic recession, but the dip in 1974 was due to our change to LIFO inventory accounting that year.

Net income as a percent of sales for Borg-Warner has shown steady improvement since the 1975 recession and now compares favorably with the other top-rated U.S. companies.

Return on equity has shown the same trend and is now at the highest level in more than 20 years. For the 12-month period ending September 30, 1979, Borg-Warner's return-on-average equity reached 15.4%.

Because of its low-debt position, Borg-Warner shows up much better, in relative terms, when measuring return based on average total assets. Return on this basis has more than doubled since 1975, and 1979 will show continued improvement.

Borg-Warner's performance is made more impressive when considering our low debt-to-equity ratio, which has been almost consistently below the average for top-rated companies. Current debt is about 22% of total equity. This leaves plenty of flexibility for acquisition opportunities.

The reinvestment rate has attracted increasing attention from analysts. As an indicator of its ability to sustain future growth, Borg-Warner now compares favorably when measured against other top-rated companies.

Borg-Warner's dividend policy is to pay out an average of about 40% of our earnings in the form of cash dividends. Since 1970, our payout has averaged 40.7%, although there have been some wide swings on a year-to-year basis.

In addition to maintaining a roughly 40% payout ratio, the company's dividend policy also calls for more regular and frequent dividend increases, as has been the case during the last four years.

The dividend was increased to 57½ cents per share effective November 15, 1979. And since 1975, the dividend rate has risen 70%—from $1.35 per share to the present $2.30.

This dividend policy has resulted in a yield to Borg-Warner investors that over the years has been consistently above that of the average of both "A" and "AA" companies, and the S&P 400.

Unfortunately, the price/earnings ratio chart shows exactly the opposite picture. Borg-Warner's p/e has continued to be below that of the other top-rated companies. Perhaps Borg-Warner has deserved to sell at a discount in view of its cyclical performance and below-average return on equity of *earlier* years. Apparently, investors aren't yet convinced of the basic changes in our company.

The real test of our planning will come with the next economic downturn, which some economists say already has begun. But whatever shape a recession may take, we expect to come through it in a much better way than we did in 1974-75.

10

Net income as a percent of sales 1970-1978

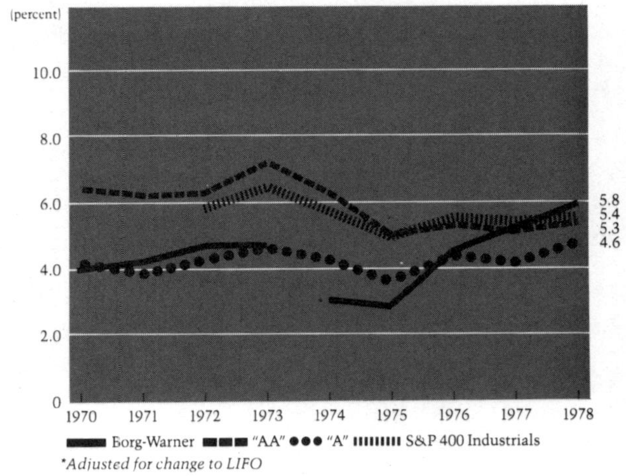

Return on equity 1970-1978

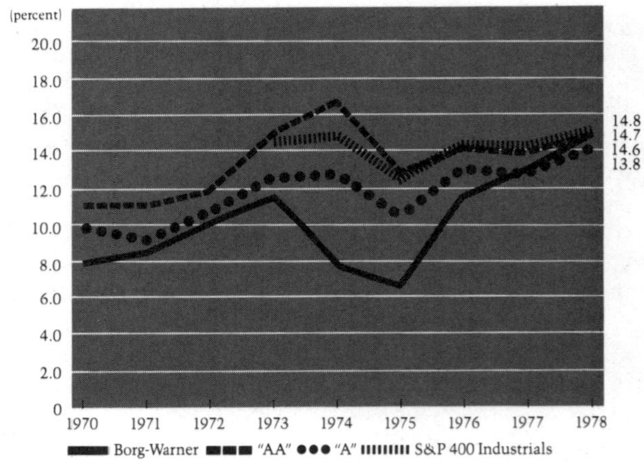

Return on average total assets 1970-1978

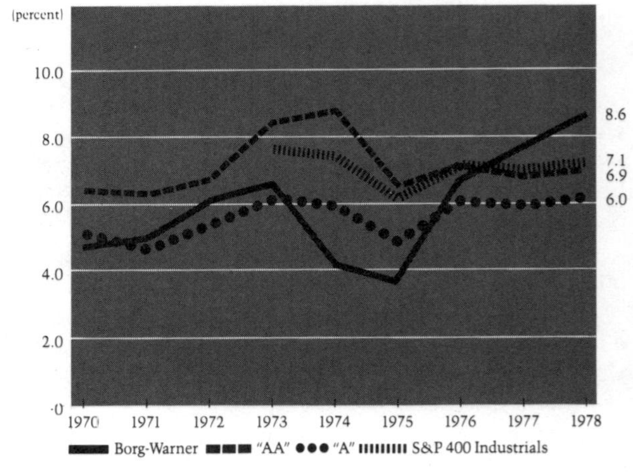

Debt/equity ratio 1971-1978

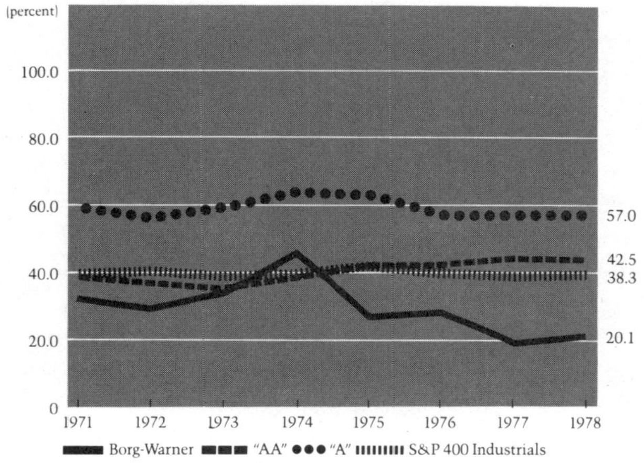

Dividend payout 1970-1978
(As a percent of prior year earnings)

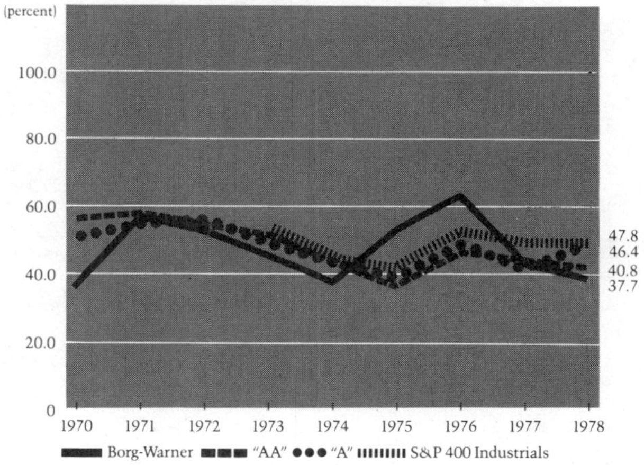

Reinvestment rate 1970-1978

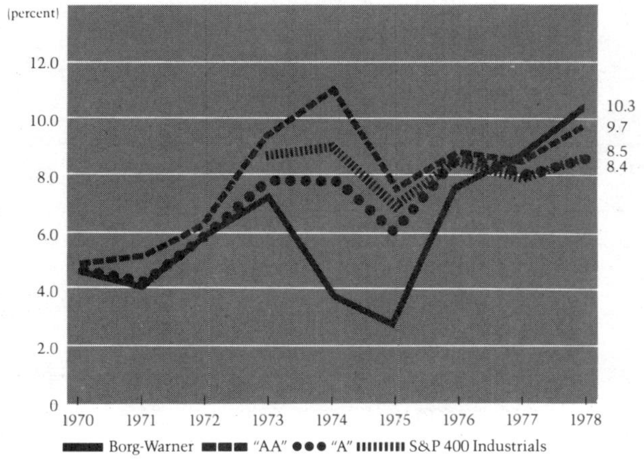

Price/earnings ratio 1970-1978

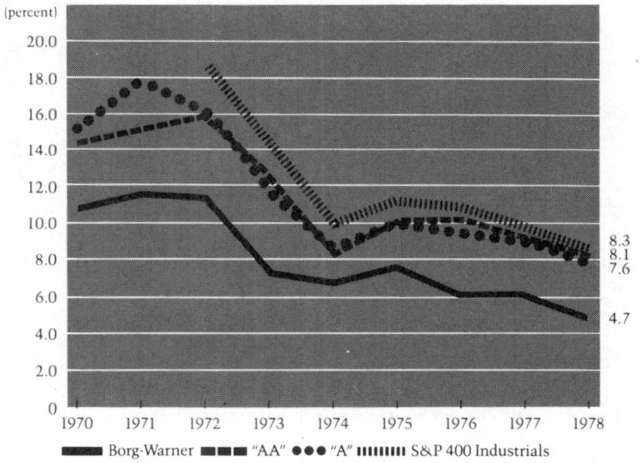

Dividend yield *1970-1978

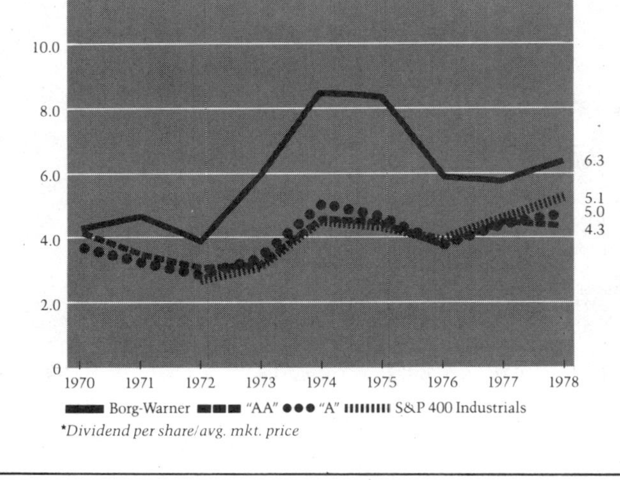

**Dividend per share/avg. mkt. price*

Market price/book value 1970-1978

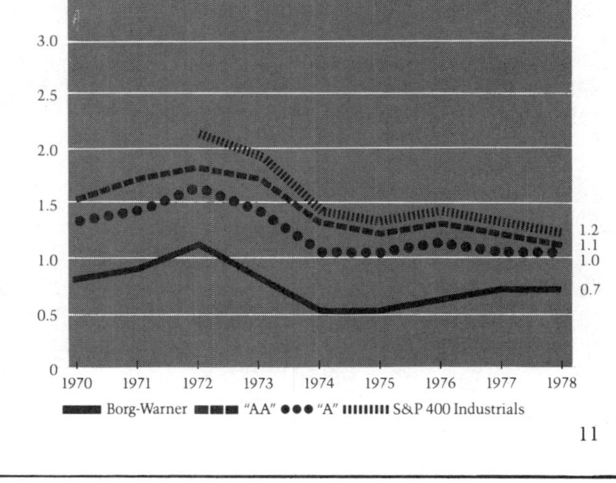

Capital expenditures review

(millions)	Capital Expenditures 1974-1978 Amount	%	1979 Forecast Amount	%	Depreciation 1974-78 Amount	Ratio
Groups						
Air Conditioning	$ 36.8	10%	$ 11.4	9%	$ 25.8	1.4
Chemicals and Plastics	109.7	30	31.1	24	59.8	1.8
Industrial Products	77.2	21	33.9	26	41.0	1.9
Transportation Equipment	122.5	33	51.0	39	100.0	1.2
Corporate	21.0	6	2.6	2	8.8	2.4
Total Expenditures	$367.2	100%	$130.0	100%	$235.4	1.6
Geographic Breakdown						
United States	$251.9	69%	$ 91.0	70%		
Europe	72.3	20	22.0	17		
Australia	19.8	5	10.3	8		
Canada	15.0	4	4.7	4		
Other Foreign	8.2	2	2.0	1		
Total	$367.2	100%	$130.0	100%		
Type of Project						
Renewal & Replacement	$ 79.9	22%	$ 30.4	24%		
Cost Reduction	25.4	7	14.7	11		
Other*	47.0	13	12.1	9		
Total Standard	152.3	42	57.2	44		
Expansion	214.9	58	72.8	56		
Total	$367.2	100%	$130.0	100%		
Type of Assets						
Land	$ 3.1	1%	$ 2.0	1%		
Buildings & Land Improvements	92.8	25	28.0	22		
Machinery & Equipment	271.3	74	100.0	77		
Total	$367.2	100%	$130.0	100%		

*Primarily environmental and comfort/convenience items

Borg-Warner Corporation sales, after tax earnings & capital expenditures by geographic segment 1971, 1974, 1978

	Sales			After-tax earnings			Capital expenditures		
(millions)	1978	1974	1971	1978	1974	1971	1978	1974	1971
Australia	$ 143	$ 133	$ 78	$ 6.5	$ 4.0	$ 2.0	$ 5.8	$ 5.9	$11.8
Canada	107	90	45	4.4	5.7	2.1	2.9	2.8	.8
Europe	355	231	129	13.5	.7	2.7	35.7	16.5	14.5
Other	28	33	26	4.6	2.4	.7	.5	1.5	2.7
Total Non-U.S.	633	487	278	29.0	12.8	7.5	44.9	26.7	29.8
U.S.	1693	1281	870	104.8	38.0	39.9	70.4	56.3	25.4
Total	$2326	$1768	$1148	$133.8	$50.8	$47.4	$115.3	$83.0	$55.2

12

A better business mix

Business mix, a much-discussed concept, has particular significance for Borg-Warner.

Borg-Warner sales and earnings historically have varied with fluctuations both in the overall economy and in specific markets, notably automotive. But expanding our stake in service businesses, which are affected by economic cycles to a lesser degree and by differently timed variables, establishes a "counter-cyclical" pattern that moderates the impact of business cycles. In addition, this expansion reduces our dependence upon the strength of the transportation market.

Our first such diversification was, into the financial area. Borg-Warner Acceptance Corporation, the flagship of our Financial Services group, was formed in 1953 and is now one of the 15 largest independent finance companies in the U.S. Last year was the 13th in succession of improved earnings for the group. At year end 1978, its receivables totaled $1.4 billion—up 25% from the prior year. In the 10 years ended in 1977, the group's average annual compound earnings growth was 26%.

Baker Industries, whose acquisition was consummated in January, 1978, represents a significant enlargement of our service business. Baker, whose Pony Express corporate symbol enjoys wide recognition, has a robust balance sheet, a good earnings history and an able management team. And, as a supplier of guard, courier and armored-vehicle services as well as smoke and fire detection equipment and fire extinguishers, it has a strong position in markets whose cycles differ from those of our existing manufacturing businesses.

We are projecting that Financial Services and Baker, combined, will account for more than 15% of our 1979 net earnings. They will represent a smaller percentage of revenues, however, because margins are normally wider in services than in capital goods (service businesses have lower fixed costs). This solid position in services should afford us a buffer against economic downturns of the type that have hurt us in the past.

Major Markets 1978 Sales

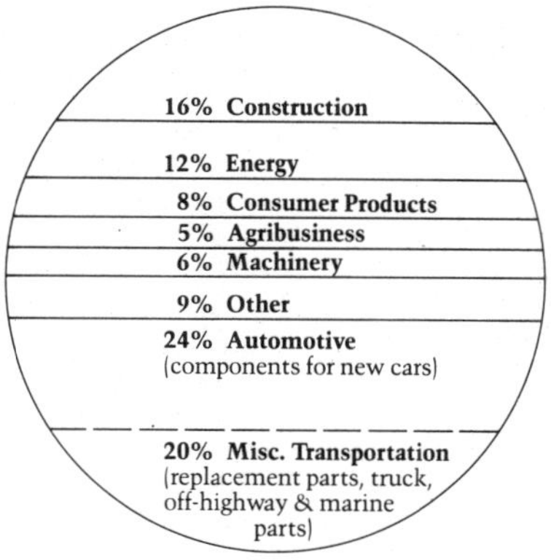

Borg-Warner Net earnings

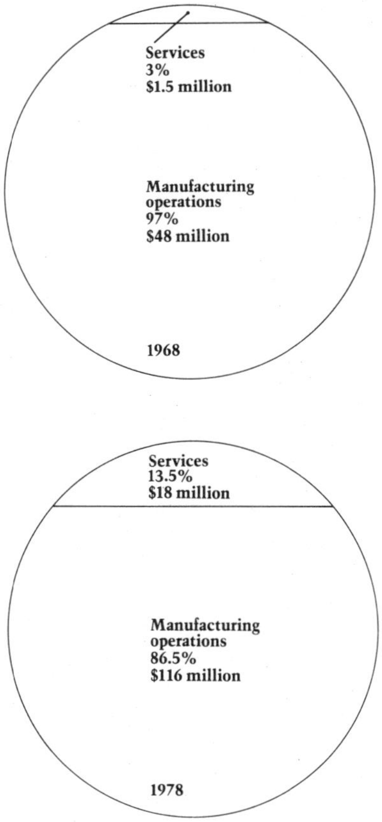

Borg-Warner manufactures products and components that serve the needs of 6 essential markets: automotive, construction, energy, consumer products, agribusiness and machinery.

Even though the broad automotive market continues to be the company's largest, Borg-Warner sales to automobile manufacturers for passenger car production account for less than one-quarter of total company sales. And in 1978, less than 20% of total sales were components for U.S. passenger car production.

This market breakdown does not include the company's growing revenues from financial and protective service operations which add to Borg-Warner's diversity.

One of Borg-Warner's major objectives is to increase its participation in the service sector of the economy as a means of reducing the impact of economic cycles on its performance.

Since 1968, the contribution to earnings of Borg-Warner's service businesses has grown from 3% to 13.5%, equal to $18 million in 1978. In 1979, earnings from existing service operations will exceed $25 million.

Through continued internal growth and further acquisition, the long-term objective is to derive about one-third of total company earnings from service operations.

Sales by market

Borg-Warner sales by market

(millions)	1978		1977		1976	
Automobiles	$ 553	23.8%	$ 483	23.8%	$ 447	24.0%
Energy & Petrochemicals	271	11.6	253	12.5	238	12.8
Trucks & Off Highway	271	11.6	197	9.7	123	6.6
Consumer Products	193	8.3	157	7.7	148	8.0
Construction (industrial & commercial)	185	8.0	144	7.1	110	5.9
Housing	179	7.7	162	8.0	151	8.1
Replacement Parts	154	6.6	133	6.5	151	8.1
Machinery	134	5.8	126	6.2	107	5.7
Agribusiness (farm equipment & food processing)	124	5.3	142	7.0	141	7.6
Government Defense & Aerospace	71	3.1	62	3.1	60	3.2
Other	191	8.2	172	8.4	154	8.3
Discontinued Operations	—	—	1	—	32	1.7
Net Sales	$2326	100.0%	$2032	100.0%	$1862	100.0%

Air Conditioning group

	Total		U.S.		Non-U.S.	
(millions)	1978	1977	1978	1977	1978	1977
Housing	$144	$119	$135	$111	$ 9	$ 8
Construction—Commercial	131	92	85	69	46	23
Automobiles	93	69	93	69	—	—
Construction—Industrial	42	43	12	12	30	31
Government & Defense	28	21	25	19	3	2
Energy—Petrochemical	15	20	12	15	3	5
Energy—Petroleum	13	15	10	14	3	1
Trucks	7	10	7	10	—	—
Agribusiness—Food Handling & Processing	5	10	2	4	3	6
Marine	5	10	5	5	—	5
Other	34	30	34	30	—	—
Total	$517	$439	$420	$358	$ 97	$ 81

Chemicals & Plastics group

	Total		U.S.		Non-U.S.	
(millions)	1978	1977	1978	1977	1978	1977
Consumer Products	$186	$157	$ 88	$ 77	$ 98	$ 80
Automobiles	77	67	70	59	7	8
Energy—Petrochemical	39	39	39	37	—	2
Housing	35	41	25	30	10	11
Off-Highway Equipment	19	15	—	—	19	15
Agribusiness—Food Handling & Processing	16	17	2	5	14	12
Recreational Vehicles	9	8	8	7	1	1
Construction—Industrial	6	5	1	1	5	4
Agribusiness—Agricultural Equipment	3	4	3	4	—	—
Other	82	69	75	62	7	7
Total	$472	$422	$311	$282	$161	$140

14

Sales by market

Industrial Products group

(millions)	Total 1978	Total 1977	U.S. 1978	U.S. 1977	Non-U.S. 1978	Non-U.S. 1977
Machinery	$114	$106	$ 84	$ 75	$ 30	$ 31
Energy—Electric Utilities	96	68	77	57	19	11
Energy—Petroleum	87	86	62	70	25	16
Agribusiness—Agricultural Equipment	35	38	34	36	1	2
Automobiles	21	24	18	18	3	6
Energy—Petrochemical	17	21	7	5	10	16
Government & Defense	17	12	16	12	1	—
Aerospace	15	18	15	18	—	—
Replacement Parts	12	12	10	10	2	2
Off-Highway Equipment	9	3	1	1	8	2
Other	51	46	48	41	3	5
Total	$474	$434	$372	$343	$102	$ 91

Transportation Equipment group

(millions)	Total 1978	Total 1977	U.S. 1978	U.S. 1977	Non-U.S. 1978	Non-U.S. 1977
Automobiles	$362	$323	$178	$154	$184	$169
Replacement Parts	142	122	126	108	16	14
Off-Highway Equipment	127	80	89	68	38	12
Trucks	107	85	102	80	5	5
Agribusiness—Agricultural Equipment	58	67	46	56	12	11
Machinery	20	20	14	18	6	2
Recreational Vehicles	17	4	16	4	1	—
Government & Defense	6	6	6	6	—	—
Aerospace	6	4	5	4	1	—
Marine	5	16	—	9	5	7
Other	13	9	9	2	4	7
Total	$863	$736	$591	$509	$272	$227

15-Year financial summary

Deflated data *(1965 constant dollars)*

	Trailing 12 mos. 6/30/79	78	77	76	75	74	73	72	71	70	69	68	67	66	65
Net sales	$1151	1135	1064	1034	964	1126	1082	950	890	907	929	926	898	886	815
Net earnings	$ 66.9	65.3	54.5	45.4	26.2	32.4	49.9	44.1	36.7	25.9	44.4	44.6	40.8	45.8	45.4
Earnings per share	$ 3.12	3.04	2.58	2.33	1.36	1.69	2.59	2.24	1.90	1.34	2.26	2.24	2.17	2.42	2.47
GNP deflator index	$ 2.20	2.05	1.91	1.80	1.70	1.57	1.43	1.35	1.29	1.23	1.17	1.11	1.06	1.03	1.00

15-Year financial summary

	Trailing 12 mos. 6/30/79	1978	1977	1976	1975
	(millions except per share; individuals in thousands)				
Net sales	$2533	$2326	$2032	$1862	$1639
U.S.	1840	1693	1497	1336	1161
Non-U.S.	693	633	535	526	478
Net earnings	147.2	133.8	104.0	81.7	44.5
U.S.	118.5	109.9	99.2	78.4	38.2
Non-U.S.	28.7	23.9	4.8	3.3	6.3
Net earnings per share	6.87	6.24	4.93	4.21	2.31
Return on sales (net)	5.8%	5.8%	5.1%	4.4%	2.7%
U.S.	6.4%	6.5%	6.6%	5.9%	3.3%
Non-U.S.	4.1%	3.8%	0.9%	0.6%	1.3%
Return on capital (debt plus equity)	13.3%	12.9%	11.1%	9.9%	6.2%
Return on average equity	15.3%	14.6%	12.9%	11.4%	6.6%
Reinvested earnings as % of equity·	10.4%	9.8%	8.0%	7.3%	2.6%
Shareholders' equity	1011	966	872	742	689
Total debt	161	195	171	206	181
Short-term	67	31	24	36	18
Long-term	94	164	147	170	163
Debt-to-equity ratio	16%	20%	20%	28%	26%
Total debt to total capital	14.2%	16.8%	16.4%	21.7%	20.8%
Current assets	849	789	649	688	590
Current liabilities	433	388	315	319	244
Net working capital	416	401	333	370	346
Working capital turns	6.1	5.8	6.1	5.0	4.7
Current ratio	1.96	2.03	2.06	2.16	2.42
Capital expenditures	110	115	77	36	56
Depreciation	56	55	51	43	43
Capital expenditures times depreciation	2.0	2.1	1.5	.8	1.3
Interest and finance charges	29.6	26.7	25.8	26.0	36.4
Interest coverage	12.6	13.3	13.5	9.3	3.7
Effective tax rate	42.4%	43.2%	43.9%	48.5%	36.5%
Inventory	370	369	335	339	337
Inventory turns	4.1	3.9	3.7	3.6	3.4
Receivables	381	296	259	210	183
Days' sales in receivables	50	51	50	50	55
Stock price					
High	34-3/8	34-3/8	33-7/8	30-3/8	21-3/8
Low	26	26	25-1/4	19-7/8	13-1/8
Price earnings ratio (average)	4.3	4.7	5.7	6.7	7.7
Yield (average)	6.6%	6.3%	5.9%	5.0%	7.6%
Book value per share	47.91	45.64	41.10	38.36	35.51
Shares outstanding (average, fully diluted)	21.4	21.4	21.1	19.4	19.3
Dividends per share (paid)	1.95	1.85	1.65	1.41	1.35
Dividend payment ratio	.28	.30	.33	.33	.58
Shareholders (year end)	54.2	55.9	57.0	58.6	63.3
Employees (average)	55.4	47.0	38.9	38.9	39.6

#After extraordinary items, net of income tax, of $260 thousand or one cent per share of common stock. ‡Interest, net.

16

1974	1973	1972	1971	1970	1969	1968	1967	1966	1965
$1768	$1547	$1283	$1148	$1115	$1087	$1028	$ 952	$ 913	$ 815
1281	1143	971	870	890	890	874	834	846	758
487	404	312	278	225	197	154	118	67	57
50.8	71.3	59.5#	47.4	31.8*	52.0	49.5	43.2	47.2	45.4
38.0	59.6	51.1	39.9	27.0	46.1	44.2	40.7	44.0	42.1
12.8	11.7	8.2	7.5	4.8	5.9	5.3	2.5	3.2	3.3
2.66	3.70	3.03#	2.45	1.65*	2.65	2.49	2.30	2.50	2.41
2.9%	4.6%	4.6%#	4.1%	2.9%*	4.8%	4.8%	4.5%	5.2%	5.6%
2.9%	5.2%	5.3%	4.6%	3.0%	5.2%	5.1%	4.9%	5.2%	5.6%
2.6%	3.0%	2.6%	2.7%	2.1%	3.0%	3.4%	2.1%	4.8%	5.8%
7.3%	9.8%	8.6%	7.2%	5.3%	8.1%	8.4%	—	—	—
7.7%	11.4%	10.0%#	8.4%	5.8%*	9.8%	9.6%	9.1%	10.3%	10.4%
3.7%	7.0%	5.7%	4.0%	2.4%	5.0%	4.3%	4.5%	4.5%	5.5%
670	642	610	575	553	544	528	484	467	447
302	215	174	183	207	208	147	131	68	29
55	79	33	34	63	67	52	44	63	24
247	136	141	149	144	141	95	87	5	5
45%	33%	29%	32%	37%	38%	28%	27%	14%	6%
31.0%	25.0%	22.2%	24.2%	27.2%	27.7%	21.7%	—	—	—
688	642	528	502	522	537	468	450	413	384
264	291	188	169	195	221	171	164	189	134
423	351	340	333	327	316	296	286	224	251
4.2	4.4	3.8	3.4	3.4	3.4	3.5	—	—	—
2.60	2.20	2.81	2.98	2.68	2.43	2.73	2.74	2.18	2.88
83	70	63	55	70	52	45	62	66	45
43	41	37	35	33	31	29	25	22	22
1.9	1.7	1.7	1.6	2.1	1.7	1.6	2.5	3.0	2.0
38.1	21.7	17.1	17.4	19.6	9.1‡	6.7‡	6.1‡	2.7‡	1.8‡
3.4	8.9	9.5	7.6	5.6	9.9	10.7	—	—	—
33.8%	48.8%	47.0%	45.9%	53.8%	49.5%	46.2%	44.9%	45.6%	43.7%
443	372	298	289	297	282	240	236	225	196
3.0	3.6	3.4	3.2	3.1	3.5	3.5	3.3	3.4	3.4
200	221	189	179	176	206	170	168	153	137
55	59	61	62	65	60	58	63	58	58
22-5/8	36-5/8	38-5/8	32-1/4	29-5/8	36-1/8	39-1/2	30-3/8†	25†	27-1/8†
12-1/2	17-1/8	29-1/4	23-3/4	18-1/8	22-1/2	25-7/8	18-7/8†	18-3/8†	22-3/4†
6.4	6.7	11.2	11.6	14.1	10.9	12.6	12.0	8.6	10.3
7.8%	5.5%	3.7%	4.4%	5.4%	4.3%	4.0%	4.0%	5.1%	4.4%
34.63	33.47	30.93	29.40	28.20	27.49	26.10	25.84	24.68	23.55
19.1	19.3	19.6	19.3	19.3	19.6	19.9	18.8	18.8	18.7
1.35	1.35	1.25	1.25	1.25	1.25	1.25	1.10	1.10	1.10
.51	.36	.41	.51	.76	.47	.50	.48	.44	.46
63.7	61.6	60.8	64.3	67.0	65.7	66.7	67.9	69.9	65.3
46.5	46.3	42.9	41.4	43.4	41.6	39.6	38.9	38.2	35.9

*After extraordinary items, net of income tax, of $11.7 million or 60 cents per share of common stock. †Adjusted for 2-for-1 stock split.

The Borg-Warner management team

(Background data on the Borg-Warner executives financial analysts are most likely to meet.)

James F. Beré
Chairman and
Chief Executive Officer

His business experience particularly suits Jim Beré to his present post; he's twice headed manufacturing operations.

Before joining Borg-Warner in 1961 as president and general manager of the Borg & Beck division, Jim was president of U.S. Industries' Axelson Manufacturing division. Elected Borg-Warner president and a director in 1968, he assumed the CEO post in 1972 and the chairmanship in 1975.

Jim's directorships include Abbott Laboratories; Continental Illinois National Bank and Trust Company of Chicago, and its parent company; Hughes Tool Company; Northwest Industries; Time, Inc.; and Illinois Bell Telephone Company.

He is a native Chicagoan and holds a bachelor's degree in industrial engineering (1946) and a master's in business administration (1950) from Northwestern University.

Robert O. Bass
Vice Chairman and
Chief Operating Officer

Bob Bass' Borg-Warner career might be said to date from his first summer job with a Denver machine shop. By the time that company, Eberhardt-Denver, was acquired by Borg-Warner's Morse Chain division in 1956, he was a principal owner and became Morse's president in 1958.

He was elected a group vice president in 1966, executive vice president-industrial equipment in 1968, executive vice president of the Transportation Equipment group in 1973 and the latter's president in 1974. In 1975 he was named president and chief operating officer, and was elected to the newly-created vice chairmanship in 1979. He has been a director of the corporation since 1973, and is a director of SCM Corporation and The Raymond Corporation.

Bob received a bachelor's degree in business administration from the University of Denver in 1941.

Jerry E. Dempsey
President

Elected president in 1979, Jerry Dempsey oversees operations of the Chemicals and Plastics and Transportation Equipment groups.

Jerry started with the York division in 1956 as a student engineer and has spent most of his Borg-Warner career with York. He also has served as executive assistant to chairman Jim Beré, as vice president in charge of the Chemicals and Plastics group. He was named executive vice president in 1978.

Jerry holds a bachelor's degree in mechanical engineering from Clemson University (1954). He later attended the University of Chicago and Georgia State College, where he received a MBA degree in 1968.

He is a director of Ube Cycon and Cos-Mar, both Borg-Warner joint ventures, and of the National Association of Manufacturers.

James J. Gavin, Jr.
Sr. Vice President-Finance

Jim Gavin has been Borg-Warner's top financial officer since he joined the company in 1968 as vice president-finance. He has been a director since 1969.

Jim is a director of Arkwright-Boston Insurance and a member of its Midwest Advisory Board. He is also a director of BW Steel, Inc. and of Chicago Economic Development Corporation (CEDCO). He serves as board chairman of the latter's affiliate, CEDCO Capital, which provides venture capital to small, especially minority-owned, businesses.

After World War II service, Jim attended the Wharton School of Finance of the University of Pennsylvania, which awarded him a bachelor's degree in 1949. He completed the Harvard Business School's Advanced Management Program in 1961.

Donald W. Collier
Sr. Vice President-Corporate Strategy

By both education and work experience, Don Collier is consummately equipped to coordinate Borg-Warner's technological planning. He was named to his current position in 1978, having been vice president-technology.

He joined the company in 1960. His present responsibilities include counseling Borg-Warner's top management on matters of technology, strategic planning and corporate development.

Before joining Borg-Warner, Don was president of McGraw-Edison Company's Thomas Edison Research Laboratory and, earlier, a chemical engineer and research chemist for Sharples Corporation. He worked on the Manhattan Project in 1944-45.

Don holds an undergraduate degree from Catholic University in Washington, DC, and a master's degree in chemical engineering and a PhD in physical chemistry, both from Princeton.

Russell J. Parsons
Sr. Vice President,
General Counsel and Secretary

Russ Parsons' professional life has been spent with Borg-Warner. After a wartime stint (1942-46) with the U.S. Marine Corps Reserve, he joined the company's legal department in 1946. He was named to his present position in 1976.

He holds memberships in several business and professional organizations, including the American, Illinois and Chicago Bar Associations, the Legal Club of Chicago and the Law Club of Chicago. He has served as vice president, director and Chicago chapter president of the American Society of Corporate Secretaries.

Russ earned a bachelor's degree (1940) and a law degree (1942) from the University of Chicago.

Elmer D. Robinson
Executive Vice President

Robbie Robinson's charge is group officer for the Morse Chain division of the Industrial Products group and the Air Conditioning group.

Robbie's association with Morse Chain goes back to his beginnings with Borg-Warner; he joined the company in 1955. He was made a Borg-Warner vice president in 1975.

He is a director of Applied Electronics Corporation, a joint venture of Borg-Warner and Robert Bosch North America; and of American Microsystems, Inc. Robbie holds a bachelor's degree in business administration from Rutgers.

Robert E. LaRoche
Vice President,
Chairman, Borg-Warner
Acceptance Corporation

Bob has steered the Financial and Protective Services group into an exciting era with its 1978 acquisition of Baker Industries. He has been with Borg-Warner Acceptance Corporation (BWAC), the largest unit in the group, almost since its 1953 inception.

He came to BWAC as its first branch manager in 1955. He was named BWAC chairman in 1971 and a vice president of Borg-Warner in 1975.

Bob attended Washington University in St. Louis.

Frank E. Pilling
Vice President,
President,
Transportation Equipment group

As operating head of the Transportation Equipment group, Bud Pilling is very much in the spotlight. His group's sales are the largest among Borg-Warner segments, and its products are those for which the company is best known worldwide. He has been a Borg-Warner vice president since 1974 and president of the Transportation Equipment group since 1975.

Currently, Bud is a director of the Wagner Castings Company and the Motor Equipment Manufacturers Association, and a trustee of Milliken University.

Bud received a bachelor's degree in mechanical engineering from California State Polytechnic College in 1950.

Peter C. Valli
Vice President

Peter Valli heads the Industrial Products group divisions that sell directly to the energy market. These are Byron Jackson Pump, Nuclear Valve and Mechanical Seal.

Peter's Borg-Warner career began in 1959 at what is now the Nuclear Valve division. Appointed assistant to the president of Borg-Warner in 1968, he was made vice president-management services in 1972 and assumed his present post in 1975.

Trained as an attorney, Peter is a member of the Massachusetts Bar Association.

Following World War II Navy service, Peter attended Colby College in Waterville, Maine, and later received a juris doctor degree from Boston University Law School.

James R. Deters
Vice President and Controller

As former controller of Borg-Warner's Automotive Equipment and Industrial Products groups, Jim Deters is sensitive to the need for maintaining line management's decision-making latitude without sacrificing corporate-wide control.

He's been the corporation's controller since 1975, and has held financial positions with The Procter and Gamble, Boise Cascade, and Trans Union Corporations. He is a frequent lecturer for the American Management Association. He is a member of the Financial Executives Institute's financial accounting and reporting committee.

Jim was educated at Ohio University (bachelor's degree in finance and business, 1959) and Ohio State University (master's in business administration, 1963).

William M. Valiant
Vice President and Treasurer

Bill Valiant has made Borg-Warner his career; 1979 marks his 31st year with the company. He arrived as a junior accountant in 1948, and became treasurer in 1968, and a vice president in 1978.

Valiant, in managing the worldwide "bank" of the corporation, is responsible for assessing Borg-Warner's financial needs and arranging appropriate capital to meet those needs.

He holds a bachelor's degree in accounting from the Walton School of Commerce and also attended Northwestern University.

William H. Weltyk
Vice President—Engineering & Development

Bill Weltyk has been a Borg-Warner vice president since 1974. He was given responsibility for corporate engineering and product development in mid-1978.

He began his Borg-Warner career in 1959 as a sales engineer for the Borg & Beck division in Michigan. Bill received a bachelor's degree in mechanical engineering from Wayne State University in 1956.

Other key officers:

C. E. (Red) Johnson
Vice President—Human Resources

Robert A. Morris
Vice President—Communications

Donald C. Trauscht
Vice President—Business Development and Acquisitions

The average Borg-Warner service among this group of executives is 21 years.

Management Committees

Policy and Planning Committee

James F. Beré, Chairman
Robert O. Bass
Donald W. Collier
James J. Gavin, Jr.
C. E. Johnson
Russell J. Parsons
Elmer D. Robinson

Operations Committee

Robert O. Bass, Chairman
Jerry E. Dempsey
James R. Deters
Robert E. LaRoche
Frank E. Pilling
Elmer D. Robinson
Peter C. Valli

The businesses of Borg-Warner

Most Borg-Warner products are components used in items manufactured and sold by other companies.

Millions of telephones, for example, are molded of Borg-Warner's Cycolac® ABS thermoplastic. Thousands of motorists drive cars equipped with Borg-Warner transmissions. And hundreds of the world's large buildings are cooled with equipment from York®.

Borg-Warner has some 50 major divisions with operations in 20 countries on 6 continents. These operating units are organized into five product and service groups based on similarity of products or technology, and not necessarily the markets served. The five groups include:

Air Conditioning

The York division is a major manufacturer of engineered air conditioning systems for large buildings and industrial refrigeration equipment for the petrochemicals, food and other process industries. It also produces commercial air-conditioning equipment for smaller office buildings, schools, hotels, factories, and apartment buildings.

A growing part of York's business is in central residential air-conditioning systems. In addition, it manufactures residential furnaces and automotive air-conditioning compressors.

Chemicals and Plastics

Cycolac® brand ABS is the trade name for a wide range of tough, engineering thermoplastics produced and marketed around the world by Borg-Warner Chemicals. The group also manufactures and markets a full line of Blendex® impact modifiers used for upgrading the physical properties and processing characteristics of PVC and other plastics.

Borg-Warner Chemicals also is in the fine chemicals business with a growing line of intermediates, additives and alkyl phenols.

Financial and Protective Services

The 1978 acquisition of Baker Industries, with its well-known Wells Fargo protective-services unit, brings added excitement to this group. Baker's six divisions provide the broadest range of protective services and products in the security field.

Borg-Warner Acceptance Corporation remains the group's major services unit. Today, it offers these financial services: wholesale, retail and receivables financing; personal loans; credit life, disability and property insurance; and vehicle and equipment leasing.

Industrial Products

This is the most diversified of the five product and service areas. Major products of this group are: centrifugal pumps for power plants, pipelines and water plants; submersible oil well pumps; precision seals for pumps and compressors; valves; chains, bearings and power transmission products.

Other products include: agricultural discs, hospital furniture, and audio-visual educational systems.

Transportation Equipment

The leading independent producer of automatic transmissions, supplies automatics to major car and light truck manufacturers outside the U.S. The company's five-speed manual transmission with overdrive was the first mass-produced in the U.S.

In addition to transmissions, other components include clutches, four-wheel-drive units, spin-resistant differentials, axle assemblies, propeller shafts, carburetion and ignition equipment, radiators and other heat exchangers.

A broad range of other equipment comes from Borg-Warner, including clutches, four-wheel-drive units, radiators, and replacement parts in passenger cars, trucks, off-highway and farm equipment, boats, aircraft, recreational vehicles and industrial machines.

Markets served by each major product or service area

	Automobile	Commercial construction & housing	Consumer products	Energy	Agribusiness	Government & defense	Industrial machinery	Wholesale, commercial, consumer & lease financing	Armored car, guard & alarm services
Transportation Equipment	●				●	●	●		
Air Conditioning	●	●		●	●	●			
Chemicals and Plastics	●	●	●	●	●				
Industrial Products	●			●	●	●	●		
Financial & Protective Services								●	●

20

Investor relations and disclosure policy

Objectives. Borg-Warner's investor relations program aims to provide the information investors, both personal and professional, need to make informed decisions. To that end, we release, widely and promptly, any information that can reasonably be expected to affect the market value of Borg-Warner stock, or investor's attitudes toward it. This is accomplished by news releases, annual and quarterly reports and the *Investor Fact Book*; through in-person meetings with shareholders, security analysts and the news media. We also answer reasonable questions of a non-material nature from the latter groups, within the limits of confidentiality. When we do answer such queries, we do not feel obliged to pass on the information to others who haven't specifically asked for it.

Spokesmen. Investors, analysts and reporters sometimes want to speak directly with our operating officers; and we make them available as schedules permit. To reduce the need for such contacts, however, we normally schedule several occasions a year when interested groups can meet company officers personally. Our officers appear only at meetings open to the press.

We've designated company contacts for the professional investment community, shareholders and the news media:

Financial Community
- William Valiant, 322-8700
- Terry Wilson, 322-8672
- James Gavin, 322-8517
- Daniel Stepanek, 322-8674

Shareholders
- Dorothy Flynn, 322-8563
- Russell Parsons, 322-8530

News Media
- Harlan Teller, 322-8676
- Patricia Brozowski, 322-8677
- Terry Wilson, 322-8672

We suggest that analysts who don't regularly follow Borg-Warner first contact Terry Wilson, the director of investor relations. Registered representatives should contact Daniel Stepanek.

No other Borg-Warner employee is authorized to answer inquiries or discuss the financial or operating affairs of the corporation with members of the financial community without prior approval of one of the above named persons.

Projections. We don't regularly make earnings forecasts, but we will make earnings projections when we think it appropriate. We're most apt to do so when something happens that seems likely to materially affect results previously expected. We'll disseminate these projections widely and update them as needed in the affected period.

We will neither estimate our earnings nor comment on the estimates of others, though we may comment on the assumptions others have used in predicting our results if they differ markedly from our own. Except for such comments, however, our designated contacts won't confirm the accuracy of outside estimates either implicitly or explicitly.

Our schedule of quarterly earnings announcements is generally as follows:

First quarter—Annual Meeting, usually fourth Tuesday in April.
Second quarter—July 20-25.
Third quarter—October 20-25.
Fourth quarter—February 5-10.

During the approximately three weeks before the announcement of each quarter's earnings, company contacts won't answer questions on specific units' performance, though they will answer those dealing with routine operational matters.

Limits. We'll try to answer your questions as fully and promptly as possible, but there are certain limits. We release earnings by product or service group only annually; we give only general information on the performance of separate divisions or plants. We review these limits periodically and change them as warranted or possible.

Publications. We routinely distribute the *Investor Fact Book*, Financial Bulletins, reprints of some speeches and other items of interest to security analysts. Shareholders may obtain copies of these documents from the manager of investor relations, Daniel Stepanek.

Dial 800-621-5445 for Borg-Warner NEWS

For a quick news update on Borg-Warner, call 800-621-5445. In Illinois, call 312-322-8600.

This taped message will be changed on the first Friday of each month or more often if developments warrant.

Borg-Warner's main telephone number is 312-322-8500.

Printed in U.S.A. by Rohner Printing
November 1979
Design by Francois Robert Associates

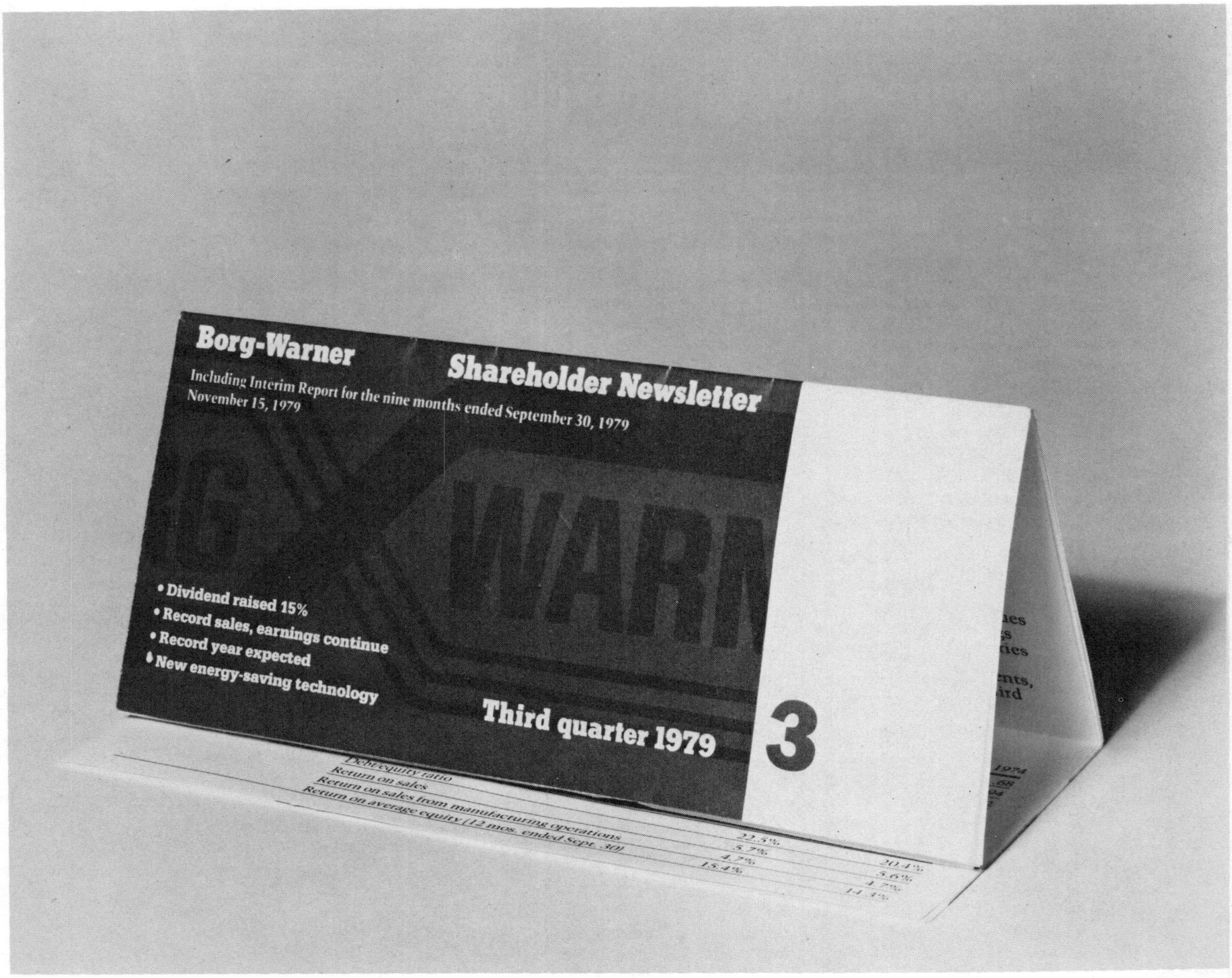

Highlights *(millions except share data)*

	Three months ended Sept. 30			Nine months ended Sept. 30		
	1979	1978	Change	1979	1978	Change
Net sales	$660.5	$572.1	+15%	$2,001.2	$1,706.3	+17%
Net earnings	$ 35.5	$ 30.8	+15%	$ 113.6	$ 95.5	+19%
Net earnings per common share	$ 1.65	$ 1.43	+15%	$ 5.30	$ 4.45	+19%
Average shares outstanding (fully diluted)				21,410,000	21,455,000	
Sales by major product area						
Air Conditioning	$133.6	$129.7	+ 3%	$ 412.0	$ 386.1	+ 7%
Chemicals & Plastics	157.7	114.6	+38%	438.6	344.9	+27%
Industrial Products	129.3	120.6	+ 7%	396.2	347.2	+14%
Transportation Equipment	232.7	203.0	+15%	741.6	614.6	+21%
Discontinued Operations	7.2	4.2	+71%	12.8	13.5	−5%
	$660.5	$572.1	+15%	$2,001.2	$1,706.3	+17%

Dividend increased 15% to 57-1/2 cents per common share

The dividend on Borg-Warner common stock has been raised for the fourth straight year effective with the November dividend. The increase was approved by directors at their September meeting.

Since 1975, the dividend rate paid to investors has risen by more than 70%. This equals an average annual increase of 14% during the last 4 year period. During the same time, U.S. inflation (based on the Consumer Price Index) has averaged 8% annually.

The company's dividend policy is to pay shareholders a long-term average of 40% of net earnings in the form of dividends through annual increases that are consistent with the company's current performance and outlook.

The higher dividend continues Borg-Warner's commitment that its owners share in higher earnings.

Dividends Up Again in 1979

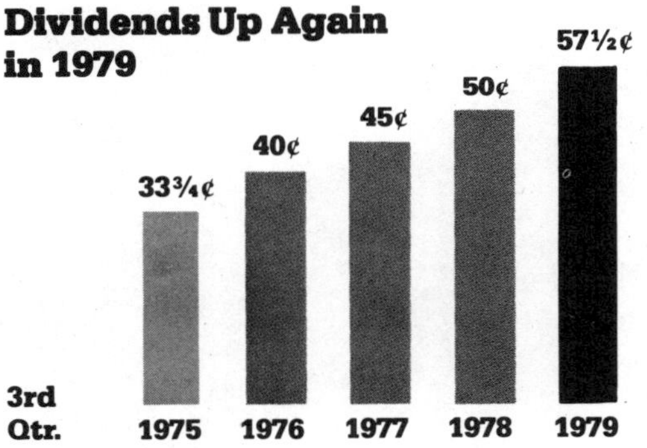

Borg-Warner's third quarter up; sales, earnings climb 15%

Your company's third quarter performance marks the 17th consecutive quarter that sales, earnings and earnings per share have been higher than in the year earlier period.

Sales of $660.5 million were up more than 15%, while net earnings of $35.5 million also represented a 15% increase. Earnings per share were $1.65 compared with $1.43 for the third quarter last year.

After-tax margins were about equal to those of last year for both the quarter and nine months.

Profit on sales *(percent)*	Third Qtr.		Nine Months	
	1979	1978	1979	1978
Manufacturing	4.3	4.5	4.7	4.7
All operations	5.4	5.4	5.7	5.6

Our overall earnings gain was boosted by a tax credit on inventories related to our United Kingdom operations. The gain—essentially a one-time credit covering price increases on inventories on hand from 1973-1975—raised earnings by 16 cents per share.

At the same time, inflation continues to have a large impact on our earnings picture. Accounting for our inventories on a LIFO (last-in, first-out) basis reduced per-share earnings by 24 cents, as opposed to seven cents in the third quarter of 1978.

Quarterly per share earnings

Quarter	1979	1978	1977	1976	1975	1974
First	$1.65	$1.22	$ .95	$ .88	$ .20	$ .68
Second	2.00	1.80	1.35	1.26	.60	.94
Third	1.65	1.43	1.15	.95	.66	.62
Fourth		1.79	1.48	1.12	.85	.42
Year		$6.24	S4.93	$4.21	$2.31	$2.66

Financial data

	Sept. 30, 1979	Sept. 30, 1978
Current ratio	2.0 to 1	2.2 to 1
Debt/equity ratio	22.5%	20.4%
Return on sales	5.7%	5.6%
Return on sales from manufacturing operations	4.7%	4.7%
Return on average equity (12 mos. ended Sept. 30)	15.4%	14.3%

Sales up in all areas

Sales gains were registered by each of the company's product segments, and earnings were up in all areas except the Air Conditioning group. In air conditioning, the York division has been unable to recover major cost increases for copper and aluminum raw materials. York, however, reports that orders for large, engineered systems remain steady; but that the higher backlog than at the same time last year is in itself causing some manufacturing and scheduling problems.

The Chemicals and Plastics group performed particularly well, capitalizing on strong demand worldwide, but especially in Europe. While this segment is experiencing some margin erosion due to increased material costs, it recently moved to ease the situation by announcing a two-cents-per-pound price increase on ABS for most applications, effective November 1.

While third quarter sales and earnings for the Industrial Products group were relatively flat compared with the year earlier period, the group's return on sales and return on investment continue to be the best in the company.

Transportation Equipment chalked up a slight earnings gain, as its strength in replacement parts, agricultural and off-highway markets overcame cutbacks in domestic passenger car component sales.

Financial and Protective Services also performed well, as Borg-Warner Acceptance Corporation (BWAC) continues to show improved results despite rapidly increasing interest costs.

We hold to our expectations of a fourth consecutive record year, even though some of our markets are beginning to show signs of the recession that long has been anticipated by the financial community. These warning signs also have clouded our outlook for 1980.

Long-range outlook bright

However, for the long term, we can point to some positive signs for your company. First, there is our emphasis on strategic planning and the resulting steps which have lessened our cyclicality.

Second, we enter a possible recession in a very satisfactory financial condition.

Finally, we are reaching the marketplace with a number of exciting new products. One major development, a line of microcomputer-controlled alternating current inverters, is discussed elsewhere in this report. This development confirms our commitment to meld our expertise in mechanics with our emerging strength in power electronics. This is an area in which your company holds great hope for the future.

James F. Beré
CHAIRMAN

November 9, 1979

Cash dividends

Payment date	Per share
Aug. 15, 1978	$ .45
Nov. 15, 1978	.50
Feb. 15, 1979	.50
May 15, 1979	.50
Aug. 15, 1979	.50
Nov. 15, 1979	.57½

Stock Price

	High	Low
2nd Qtr. '78	33	27½
3rd Qtr. '78	34⅜	27¾
4th Qtr. '78	34⅛	26
1st Qtr. '79	29⅝	26¾
2nd Qtr. '79	32	27⅜
3rd Qtr. '79	34½	30½

Borg-Warner units announce energy-saving technology

Borg-Warner will soon introduce a line of microcomputer-controlled inverters for generating variable voltage and frequency alternating current that could make a significant contribution to our nation's drive to save energy.

The new line of microcomputer-controlled inverters designed for use with industrial motors will be marketed early next year by the company's Morse Chain division. The use of power transistors has enabled Morse to cut the costs of the inverter by 50%, making it competitive in cost with direct current (DC) controls, the type most commonly used by industry.

The principle of the inverter itself is not new, and Borg-Warner has been making and selling them for 20 years. During this time, much of the pioneering design and engineering work on these products was done at the Borg-Warner Research Center.

Morse breakthrough has wide application

"The new, lower-cost alternating current models represent the 'state of the art' in speed control technology, which reinforces our belief that our new inverter line will have an impact which will be felt throughout American industry," said chairman James F. Beré in unveiling the breakthrough.

Morse will introduce microcomputer-controlled inverters for motors from 1 through 20 horsepower in the first quarter of 1980, and will expand the line to accommodate motors through 50 horsepower during the fourth quarter of that year. "For some applications, the amount of energy saved could be as high as one-third," according to Beré. Fans, pumps and blowers in industrial plants were cited as examples of where significant energy savings could be realized.

York application in air conditioning/heating

In addition, Beré said tests conducted by the company's York division, a major air conditioning and heating equipment manufacturer, show that the new alternating current inverter, when applied to the centrifugal chiller of a commercial air conditioning unit, can save up to 30% of the energy consumed by the chiller. In addition to being offered as part of York's new commercial systems, the inverter control package will be provided as an add-on for York or competitive equipment in existing buildings.

Beré noted that while York has applied the inverter only to the centrifugal chiller, which consumes about 30% of the energy used by the entire system, the division is working on control of the motors for blowers and recirculating pumps, which account for the remaining energy consumed.

An inverter control package incorporated into a new line of York division's residential heat pumps can save up to 17% of energy used to cool and heat homes, Beré said.

Products for both commercial and residential air conditioning applications will be available in early 1980.

Beré stressed that the technology was generated internally, and said that the company would not need any outside assistance to market or manufacture the products.

The inverter and electronic controls for both York and Morse products will be manufactured by Borg-Warner Electronics, formed in 1977.

Richard C. Barnett (left), executive vice president—unitary products for Borg-Warner's York division, discusses the model of York's new heat pump modulator (background) with Jenny Kahn, new products editor for HOUSING magazine at a recent press conference in Chicago. Tests show the computer-controlled modulator could result in an average 17 percent energy savings in home heating/cooling. The products will be ready for the market in early 1980.

Condensed balance sheet (Unaudited)

Borg-Warner Corporation and consolidated subsidiaries

(millions of dollars)

		September 30 1979	September 30 1978
Assets	**Current assets:**		
	Cash & marketable securities	$ 37.0	$ 43.1
	Receivables	346.9	280.5
	Inventories	392.1	349.3
	Other current assets	44.5	37.3
	Total current assets	820.5	710.2
	Other assets	404.2	354.6
	Property, plant, and equipment	528.2	471.6
		$1,752.9	$1,536.4
Liabilities and shareholders' equity	**Current liabilities:**		
	Notes payable	$ 69.0	$ 32.0
	Accounts payable	157.5	146.6
	Other liabilities and accrued expenses	175.8	149.6
	Total current liabilities	402.3	328.2
	Long-term debt	163.8	157.2
	Other long-term liabilities	152.8	122.9
	Shareholders' equity	1,034.0	928.1
		$1,752.9	$1,536.4

Statement of earnings (Unaudited)

Borg-Warner Corporation and consolidated subsidiaries

(millions of dollars except per share data)

		Three months ended September 30 1979	Three months ended September 30 1978	Nine months ended September 30 1979	Nine months ended September 30 1978
Earnings	**Sales and other income:**				
	Net sales	$660.5	$572.1	$2,001.2	$1,706.3
	Other income	3.8	4.5	12.6	10.1
		664.3	576.6	2,013.8	1,716.4
	Costs and expenses:				
	Cost of sales	527.7	439.0	1,572.8	1,307.0
	Depreciation	13.9	13.0	41.7	40.0
	Selling, general and administrative expenses	73.4	70.8	222.5	200.9
	Interest and other financial charges	7.8	7.5	23.1	19.9
	Minority interests	.7	.6	2.1	1.7
	Provision for income taxes	12.3	19.7	58.5	67.6
		635.8	550.6	1,920.7	1,637.1
	Earnings from manufacturing operations	28.5	26.0	93.1	79.3
	Net earnings from financial services companies	5.4	3.8	16.3	10.9
	Net earnings from protective services companies	1.6	1.0	4.2	5.3
	Net earnings	$ 35.5	$ 30.8	$ 113.6	$ 95.5
Per common share	**Net earnings**	$ 1.65	$ 1.43	$ 5.30	$ 4.45

Condensed statement of changes in financial position (Unaudited)

Borg-Warner Corporation and consolidated subsidiaries

(millions of dollars)

		September 30 1979	1978
Operations	Earnings from manufacturing operations	$93.1	$79.3
	Earnings from financial services companies	16.3	10.9
	Earnings from protective services companies	4.2	5.3
	Net earnings	113.6	95.5
	Non-fund charges (credits) to earnings: Depreciation	41.7	40.0
	Earnings of financial and protective services companies reinvested	(19.1)	(14.1)
	Total from earnings	136.2	121.4
	Funds used for short-term assets and liabilities	(108.7)	(45.3)
	Funds provided by long-term assets and liabilities	17.1	6.2
	Net funds provided by operations	44.6	82.3
Dividends	**Dividends declared**	(43.9)	(39.3)
Investments	Capital expenditures	(83.4)	(77.0)
	Retirements of fixed assets	6.6	9.3
	Net increase (decrease) in investments & advances	(15.0)	17.7
	Net funds used in investments	(91.8)	(50.0)
Financing	Net increase in notes payable	38.6	14.7
	Net increase (decrease) in long-term debt	(.4)	9.7
	Net decrease in treasury stock	.2	.8
	Net funds provided by financing	38.4	25.2
	Net increase (decrease) in cash & short-term securities	$(52.7)	$18.2

Victor J. Danilov (left), president and director of the Museum of Science and Industry, and Donald F. Hoeg (center), director of the Borg-Warner Research Center, discuss the Borg-Warner Vintage Car of the Future (background) with Rowland Emett, its creator, at the October 18 dedication of the Museum's Artscience Gallery.

News Notes

Regional meetings held for shareholders in Los Angeles, San Diego, New York City

A total of about 150 Borg-Warner shareholders attended informal information meetings in Los Angeles on October 23 and San Diego on the following day. Company officers, including the chairman, president and chief financial officer, reported on Borg-Warner's progress and prospects and answered shareholder questions.

A similar meeting took place in New York City on November 8.

As an added feature, those present saw a new 14-minute film showing the diversity of Borg-Warner's involvement in everyday life.

Houston meeting upcoming

Borg-Warner will be one of four firms taking part in an investors fair sponsored by the National Association of Investment Clubs at the Shamrock Hilton in Houston on Saturday, February 9, 1980. The Borg-Warner presentation will begin at 10:45 a.m. followed by lunch. Advance reservations are required, but if you are a registered shareholder in the Houston area you will receive an invitation.

Los Angeles area shareholders hear chairman James F. Beré report on third quarter results and the outlook at regional information meeting.

Show investor support for dividend reinvestment bill

A 15-cent investment could pay handsome dividends. That sum represents the cost of mailing letters to your federal legislators indicating support for the dividend reinvestment bill currently in the U.S. House of Representatives.

Introduced by Rep. J. J. Pickle (D-Austin, Texas), H.R. 654 would allow dividends reinvested in original-issue stock through qualified programs to be treated as stock-paid dividends. Reinvested dividends are now treated as cash-paid dividends, and thus are subject to shareholder individual income tax.

Under the proposed legislation, reinvested dividends would be exempt from shareholder income tax and subject only to a capital gains tax when sold. Shareholders could exclude up to $1500 annually in dividend income; the limit would be $3000 for joint filers.

No effect on Borg-Warner dividends reinvested

Since Borg-Warner's dividend reinvestment plan does not involve newly issued shares, reinvested dividends would not qualify for the favorable tax treatment under the proposed legislation. But the bill immediately would benefit shareholders with stock in companies (primarily utilities at this time) that have reinvestment programs based on newly issued shares. In addition, such legislation will help our economy by increasing capital formation for businesses and by in part reducing double taxation of dividends reinvested.

You can register your support for the Pickle bill simply by writing to your senators at the U.S. Senate, Washington, D.C. 20510, and to your congressman at the U.S. House of Representatives, Washington, D.C. 20515. We urge you to do so now.

Annual report for 1978 judged one of top five

There are numerous annual report competitions—most sponsored by paper companies, designers, printers or trade magazines.

One of the most meaningful, the Nicholson Awards, is conducted by none of the above but by the National Association of Investment Clubs. It is open to all publicly owned companies, and reports are judged from the viewpoint of the individual investor. And that's what annual reports should be about anyway.

The 1979 contest winners were just recently announced, and the Borg-Warner 1978 report was named one of the five best overall in the U.S. The four other annual reports so honored were those of Detroit Edison, Hercules, National Detroit and Textron. Other annual reports were selected as best in specific industries.

Borg-Warner grant creates museum home for 'Vintage Car'

After thousands of miles on the exhibition circuit in Europe and the United States since its 1972 debut, the Borg-Warner Vintage Car of the Future has rolled to a new destination: the new Artscience Gallery at Chicago's Museum of Science and Industry.

The only permanent museum gallery displaying works "marrying" scientific and artistic concepts, the Artscience Gallery was made possible by a grant from Borg-Warner. It features works by prominent artists including Alexander Calder, in addition to the car. Billed as an "engineering marvel" combining the best in automotive equipment, the car flashes its lights, spins its wheels, strums a harp, barbecues sausages, but goes nowhere under its own power.

Created by English inventor-cartoonist Rowland Emett, the car's components satirize real automotive technology. They include the "Solarmatic" infinitely variable automatic sun-and-planet transmission, and the world's only power-plant fueled by after-shave lotion.

Investor Fact Book for 1979 available free to shareholders

The 1979 edition of the Borg-Warner Investor Fact Book has just been printed. Shareholders who would like a personal copy should complete and return the enclosed post-paid card. Delivery will be in two to four weeks.

The 20-page book, written primarily for the professional investor, contains condensed comments from company managers during a seminar for financial analysts in Chicago earlier this year.

It also compares Borg-Warner performance as measured by nine key ratios with that of other top-rated U.S. companies, provides a breakdown of sales by market and offers other financial data, along with short biographical sketches of key officers.

If you are not a Borg-Warner shareholder but are interested in more information on the company and would like a copy of the Investor Fact Book, write to:

Terry Wilson
Borg-Warner Corporation
200 S. Michigan Avenue
Chicago, IL 60604

Johnson tapped for new VP post

Borg-Warner's election of Clarence E. (Red) Johnson to the new post of vice president—human resources "will allow us to concentrate our effort to tap the full potential of all our employees," according to chairman James F. Beré.

Johnson will supervise all facets of personnel administration activities, including pensions, benefits, development and quality of work life programs. The appointment marks the culmination of a plan to give increased direction to four areas of company activity: finance, planning, communications and human resources. It also underscores the expanded role of human resources in the company's planning during the Eighties.

Johnson, 53, had been president and general manager of the company's Morse Chain division since 1975. He joined the company's Marvel-Schebler/Tillotson division in 1953.

For your information and file

Financial Bulletin

BORG WARNER

February 7, 1979

BORG-WARNER POSTS 1978, 4TH PERIOD HIGHS:

PER SHARE EARNINGS ARE $6.24 FOR YEAR

Borg-Warner Corporation set sales and earnings records for the fourth quarter of 1978 and the year, with earnings per share topping $6.00 for the first time in the company's 51-year history, it was announced today. Margins also showed substantial gains for both periods.

In the quarter, Borg-Warner earned $38.3 million, or $1.79 per share, up 22% from the $31.5 million, or $1.48 a share earned in the same 1977 period. Fourth quarter sales were $619.7 million, up 13% from $546.2 million in the previous year's quarter.

Per share earnings for 1978 were $6.24, up 27% from $4.93 a year earlier, when about 300,000 fewer shares were outstanding. Earnings for the year rose 29% to $133.8 million, from $104 million in 1977. Sales for the year reached $2.3 billion, up 14% from $2.0 billion in 1977.

The company's after-tax return on sales for the year was 5.8%, compared with 5.1% the year before. Margins for the company's manufacturing businesses were 5.0%, up from 4.5% in 1977. Borg-Warner Chairman James F. Bere' said the margin gains "are largely the result of steady improvements in our operating efficiency and increased sales volumes during the year."

Each of the operating groups turned in improved sales for the quarter and year, with Chemicals and Plastics, and Transporation Equipment reporting biggest gains. The Financial Services group turned in improved results for the 13th consecutive year, posting an earnings gain of about 26%.

Bere' noted that fourth quarter and year-end results were adversely affected by strikes at units of the company's air conditioning, pump and auto components operations. These strikes have been settled. Baker Industries, which was seriously impacted by the depressed residential smoke detector market, suffered a loss for the quarter. The other segments of Baker Industries--primarily service-oriented--performed well in 1978.

Quarter Ended Dec. 31	1978	1977	CHANGE
Sales	$ 619,700,000	$ 546,200,000	+13%
Net Income	38,300,000	31,500,000	+22%
Share Earnings Net Income	1.79	1.48	+21%
Year Ended Dec. 31			
Sales	$2,326,000,000	$2,031,900,000	+14%
Net Income	133,800,000	104,000,000	+29%
Share Earnings Net Income	6.24	4.93	+27%
Average Shares Outstanding (fully diluted)	21,416,000	21,093,000	

From Investor Relations Dept., Borg-Warner Corporation, 200 S. Michigan Ave., Chicago, IL 60604
Contacts: Jack M. Frisbie 312/322-8674 or Terry W. Wilson 312/322-8672

A report to
Borg-Warner shareholders
Who owns
Borg-Warner
and
what do they
think about it?
Based on a survey of
present and former
individual shareholders
February, 1978

Highlights
of this special report...

Who owns the company.
Individual shareholders account for 95% of all Borg-Warner stockholders of record, but these 55,777 individuals owned slightly less than half of the nearly 19.5 million shares outstanding at the time of the survey. About half of Borg-Warner individual shareholders own between 100–499 shares. Only 7% own 500 shares or more. The others own less than 100 shares each.

Shareholder goals.
More than half of the company's current owners say they purchased Borg-Warner hoping for maximum growth over a long period of time. Dividend income was the primary investment goal cited by most other Borg-Warner holders. More than 8 out of 10 current shareholders view their Borg-Warner investment as either "highly" or "fairly" successful. About 14% have been disappointed.

What they like most/least.
Shareholders said they liked Borg-Warner's diversification, stability, quality products and dividend. Cited as negative factors were the company's perceived dependence on the auto industry, low dividend and cyclicality.

Change in attitudes.
Some 4 in 10 current shareholders said their opinion of Borg-Warner as an investment had improved since they acquired their shares. One-third said their attitudes were unchanged and 12% were less favorable.

Former shareholders.
People who recently sold their Borg-Warner stock did so to realize a profit, to make other investments or because they wanted money for non-investment purposes. More than half said they would recommend Borg-Warner as an investment and nearly 2 out of 3 former stockholders said they had reached their investment goals as a Borg-Warner owner.

Foreword

At our request, an independent opinion research firm conducted a survey of our current and former shareholders. We were anxious to learn more about their attitudes toward the company and the information we were providing them, so we could better respond to their needs as owners. The sample selected by the research firm was designed to project an accurate picture of our total shareholder family. We felt that all Borg-Warner owners would be interested in what the shareholders who responded to the survey told us and so this report.

If there were an "average" Borg-Warner shareholder, she (that's right, we have more women than men shareholders) would be about 63 years old; the owner of 11 stocks in addition to Borg-Warner. She would live in one of five states (Illinois, New York, California, Pennsylvania, Florida) and would have owned Borg-Warner stock for at least ten years.

1

According to our survey, she owns about 100 shares that were most likely acquired for long-term dividend income. If for some reason she was forced to sell part of her portfolio, Borg-Warner would be one of the last stocks to go. Her attitude about the company today is slightly more favorable than when the stock was first purchased, and in general she is reasonably satisfied with her Borg-Warner investment.

Although the survey showed she probably was not completely satisfied with the level of her dividend, there has since been a 12.5 percent increase in our dividend payout. (The quarterly common stock dividend was raised from 40¢ to 45¢ effective Nov. 15, 1977.) The current return to Borg-Warner shareholders is more than 6.5 percent—well above the average for all listed stocks.

Incidentally, if the description of our "average" shareholder fits you, please drop me a note. We'd like to know you. It doesn't matter whether you were one of those shareholders actually surveyed.

Our thanks to those shareholders and former shareholders who took time to give us their opinions.

Russell J. Parsons
Senior vice president,
and secretary

February 1, 1978

2

Shareholder survey report

How did we do it?

Surveys can be misleading, especially when the target universe is as large and diverse as our Borg-Warner shareholder population. The dangers lie in unscientific sample selection and inaccurate analysis. For that reason, surveys must be conducted by professional researchers who, through scientific techniques, can select a small sample that will yield highly accurate results.

The professional researchers* who conducted our shareholder survey did just that. We believe the result is a clear picture of our shareholder population.

Questionnaires were mailed to 2,265 current and 747 former shareholders. The response rate was 54%. This is considered high for a mail questionnaire that was relatively long and complex.

Why did we do it?

Borg-Warner wanted to make sure its communications program with shareholders was tuned to the needs of these individuals as the owners of the business. To do so, we were anxious to learn more about current patterns of ownership of Borg-Warner common stock and the personal investment characteristics of

*The attitudes reported here are based on survey data tabulated and interpreted by Financial Marketing Services Corporation of Parsippany, N.J., from responding Borg-Warner shareholders.

3

our shareholders as well as their attitudes toward the company as an investment opportunity. This information will help guide the direction and scope of future communications with shareholders.

Who owns Borg-Warner?

At the time of the survey Borg-Warner's 58,567 shareholders of record included 55,777 individual, or retail shareholders. While they represent 95% of all stockholders of record, they accounted for slightly under half of the nearly 19.5 million shares of Borg-Warner then outstanding. (Somewhat more than half of Borg-Warner stock is held in trust or custody for beneficial owners by banks and brokers or is owned by non-profit foundations, corporations, and other non-individuals. These shareholders were not surveyed.) Borg-Warner's individual holders include more women than men, but the men hold slightly more shares.

The "average" owner of BOR** shares is 63, lives in the Midwest on an annual household income of $25,000, and owns between 100 and 500 shares of BOR common. The stock was purchased 10 years ago primarily for income as part of a portfolio with shares in 11 or more other companies. The shareholder's stock portfolio is worth about $50,000.

**BOR is the ticker tape symbol for Borg-Warner common stock. As used in this report, it is an abbreviation referring to the company.

4

How many shares—by whom?

Nearly 50% of Borg-Warner's retail shareholders hold between 100 and 499 shares, and 7% own 500 shares or more. The remaining 43% hold fewer than 100 shares each. Nearly half of our shareholders are at least 65 years old; only 14% are under 45; the men average a few years younger than women, and holders of odd-lots (less than 100 shares) are 58 years old, on the average.

Among our individual shareholders there are as many retired persons as persons employed full time (41%). Another 15% are housewives and 2% are students.

The largest number of our employed shareholders have professional occupations (31%), skilled and semi-skilled occupations were reported by 17% of those responding, and general management positions were held by 15% of those shareholders holding full-time jobs.

The largest group of BOR owners lives in the Midwest, followed by Mid-Atlantic and Pacific regions. Specifically, more than half of all individual owners reside in Illinois, New York, California, Pennsylvania and Florida.

How . . . Why?

The highest percentage of shareholders said they made the decision to purchase BOR after conducting their own research and stock analysis. Factors that most influenced others were: broker recommendation, advice of a friend or relative,

5

reading brokerage firm research reports, liked company products, and through reading the Borg-Warner annual report.

Some shares were acquired under still different circumstances, such as gifts and inheritances, in exchange for other stock (acquired company), or through employment with Borg-Warner. (At least 6.5% of Borg-Warner stock is owned by employees who are members of company sponsored investment plans.)

What were shareholders' goals?

More than half of the surveyed shareholders said that, when they first acquired their BOR shares, their initial goals were to hold the shares for long periods of time to get maximum growth. A large number said they mainly were interested in income from dividends. Only a few said they originally had planned to sell the stock within a year for a quick profit, and even fewer said they hoped to sell in two to three years.

What do shareholders think of us?

When we asked our shareholders to rate Borg-Warner against other companies familiar to them, they were favorable in their opinions on the outlook for BOR's price level and ability to maintain adequate profitability during recessions. Those surveyed were not, however, as complimentary about Borg-Warner's dividend payout.

We received generally high marks on the adequacy of information furnished stockholders.

6

Opinions of the annual report were lukewarm, with the largest group calling it average and next largest saying it was above average. New shareholders and those with the most shares liked it best.

Nearly half regard Borg-Warner's cash dividend as about average and the remaining respondents were about evenly split between "below average" and "above average." (Since the survey was completed, the dividend has been raised by 12.5%).

What do shareholders think we are?

This was a multiple choice question, to which two out of three accurately saw Borg-Warner as a "Diversified manufacturer of transportation equipment, air conditioning, chemicals and plastics and industrial products." A minority described us as "supplier of parts to the auto industry." A few said we are simply a "conglomerate."

What do shareholders like most/least about us?

When asked, one of every three Borg-Warner shareholders didn't list anything they especially liked about the company. On the other hand, three out of four couldn't think of a feature about Borg-Warner they didn't particularly like.

Those who did mention likes and dislikes about the company mentioned the following characteristics most frequently:

7

Liked	Disliked
Diversification	Dependence on auto industry
Stable company	Inadequate dividend
Quality products	Cyclicality
Growth record	Conservative management
Good dividend	Stock volatility
Progressive management	Low growth
Stock undervalued	

Attitudes--then and now

Better than 4 in 10 shareholders said their opinions of BOR as an investment opportunity were more favorable now (at the time of the survey) than they were when they first acquired their shares. About one-third said their attitude toward the company was unchanged, and 12% indicated their present attitude was less favorable.

The most frequently mentioned reasons for the increase in esteem for BOR were: made good progress, increase in dividend, promising outlook, improved management.

Where attitudes were less favorable, the causes cited included: growth potential not good, inadequate dividend, erratic performance, outlook for Borg-Warner and the stock market in general was not bright.

One in four current shareholders regard their investment in Borg-Warner as "highly successful," 59% responded "fairly successful," and 14% were disappointed.

We asked shareholders to react to a hypothetical question: If you had to sell stock from your portfolio for some reason, would BOR be one of the first or last to go? Nearly half said

8

Borg-Warner would be one of the last stocks they sold, one-third weren't sure, and 13% said BOR would be one of the first.

To speak out or not

Asked if the company should "speak out" on social and economic issues that affect them as investors, taxpayers, or simply as citizens, three out of four shareholders said "yes." One in seven said "no."

Those in favor of a speak out program said they would be most interested in the company's views on: double taxation of dividends, the free enterprise economy, energy conservation, and environmental concerns. Most of those opposed said management "should concentrate on running the company."

Survey includes former owners

We also wanted to talk with some of the people who had recently sold their Borg-Warner stock to find out why. Among their reasons were: to buy other securities, 32%; to realize a profit, 31%; needed cash for non-investment purposes, 24%.

Even though they sold, more than half of these former owners said they would recommend BOR as a good investment opportunity. About 20% said they would not do so. Nearly two out of three former shareholders said they had achieved the investment goals they had set when buying their BOR stock. About one-third of this group had held their Borg-Warner stock for ten or more years when they sold.

9

Questions and answers

We invited those who returned the questionnaires to ask questions of special interest to them. About 200 did so.*** Those who included their names have received individual replies. Here are examples of some of the most frequently asked questions and condensed versions of our answers.

Q. *We wanted to buy a York central air conditioner for my house. We could not find a qualified dealer in our city.*

A. York has dealers and distributors in most metropolitan areas. If you can't find one in the Yellow Pages, write to: Mr. Todd L. Owens, York Division, Borg-Warner Corp., P. O. Box 1592, York, PA 17304. Tell him you are a shareholder.

Q. *Why not say more to remove the impression that Borg-Warner is an automotive company?*

A. Good idea and we've been trying to do so. Although that is our largest single market, more than half of our total sales are of products serving non-automotive markets. They include construction, energy, consumer products, agri-business, and machinery. In addition, about 13% of our earnings come from services pro-

***To protect the confidentiality of respondents, Borg-Warner did not at any time have access to the survey questionnaires. We received only a separate list of questions from the survey firm.

10

vided by our Financial Services group. (With the acquisition of Baker Industries, income derived from service related businesses will jump to more than 20%.)

Q. *I am interested in more information on the future impact of Borg-Warner's investment in Hughes Tool and Bosch's investment in Borg-Warner.*

A. Our investment in Hughes Tool Company was designed to provide Borg-Warner broader participation in what we see as an exciting and growing future for the oil services industry. As you may recall, we sold our BJ Services unit to Hughes for preferred stock convertible into 2.5 million shares of Hughes common. This is equal to about an 18% equity interest. This asset is carried on our books at substantially less than the current market value of the stock, and we view it as a sound investment.

We believe the roughly 10% equity interest in our company purchased earlier last year by Robert Bosch GmbH of Germany likewise offers exciting potential for both our companies. The product revolution taking place in the auto industry will likely result in a marriage of mechanical and electronic technology. Bosch is a recognized leader in the electronics field, and we think Borg-Warner does quite well in the mechanical side. We see a natural synergism between our two companies in bringing these technologies together. The growing importance of electronics goes far beyond the auto industry, and we hope to explore possibilities in products throughout Borg-Warner. While we have no definite agreements with Bosch at this time (other than the combined ownership of a 25%

11

interest in American Microsystems, a firm that makes metal-oxide-silicon integrated circuits), we are jointly exploring opportunities that could lead to cooperative manufacturing and marketing ventures.

Q. *What are the company's long-range prospects?*

A. We think they're good. Of course, no one can be certain about the future. But we have taken a number of steps we believe will improve what has been a lackluster performance in the recent past. We have divested more than $100 million in marginal assets. Our balance sheet has been returned to its traditionally strong position, and we have eliminated most of the inflation profits from our reported earnings by switching to more conservative last-in, first-out (LIFO) inventory accounting. We also have improved our return on sales in line with our key five-year objective. And we are placing greater emphasis on strategic long-range planning which includes a desire to make some changes in our business mix to reduce the cyclical impact of many of our current operations. Together, these measures put us in position to make the most of some exciting opportunities we see ahead in the markets we serve.

Q. *What areas of expansion are planned?*

A. A somewhat disproportionate share of our near-term expansion will be in the chemicals and plastics area. Of course, the other segments of our businesses also will be expanded as market conditions warrant.

12

A larger percentage of this expansion will be in the U.S. than has been the case in the recent past. Also, a large percentage of this investment will be spent to modernize and update our facilities for improved productivity rather than for adding new capacity.

We spent about $75,000,000 on new capital projects during 1977 and our budget for 1978 is approximately $100,000,000.

Q. *Why doesn't the company make some worthwhile acquisitions rather than buying back shares of its own stock?*

A. Our objective is to pursue acquisition opportunities that would improve our return on investment to shareholders. We have no intention of rushing into a deal simply to create the appearance of action. (The acquisition of Baker Industries which took place subsequent to this reply is consistent with our objective of balancing our traditional manufacturing lines with a greater proportion of services business. They are a strong, well-managed company with a good record of past performance and promising future in our view.)

Q. *Why should I keep Borg-Warner stock?*

A. Not knowing why you purchased it originally, that's an impossible question to answer. It depends on your investment objectives. Based on current market price, the yield on Borg-Warner stock exceeds 6.5%, and we believe the company has some significant opportunities for growth in the future. Your best bet is to check with your broker. They can suggest a course of

13

action that best meets your particular investment needs.

Q. *Can I invest in Borg-Warner shares without going through a broker?*

A. We know of no way to accomplish this initially. However, once you become a Borg-Warner shareholder it is possible to add to your investment through the Dividend Reinvestment Plan cash investment option.

If you decide to participate, after your first dividend has been reinvested, you are then eligible to purchase up to $1,000 per month in additional Borg-Warner common stock through the plan. Although at this time you still must pay a brokerage commission, it is usually less than if you were purchasing the same amount of shares individually.

Q. *Tell me why some of our directors own only 200 shares or less? With so little at stake, what incentive do they have?*

A. There are at least three schools of thought on this question. The first is representative of your view which says company directors should own substantial stock in the companies they serve. The second school is the antithesis. It argues that directors who hold few shares are not tempted to make decisions for their own short-term benefit and perhaps not in the long-term interests of all shareholders. The third school says the overriding consideration in selecting directors should be the individual's qualifications which should add depth and/or new perspective to the board's ability to rep-

14

resent all shareholders. It is the latter school to which we subscribe.

Q. *Why doesn't the company declare a stock dividend once in a while? I think they are more desirable than an increase in cash dividends.*

A. One of the initial effects of a stock dividend is to lower the price of the stock in proportion to the number of new shares issued. We have not felt that the general price level of Borg-Warner stock in recent years was conducive to this approach.

In addition, the declaration of a stock dividend as opposed to a cash dividend, is usually more costly in terms of distribution and maintenance.

Q. *What is Borg-Warner doing to promote energy and material conservation in the products it sells?*

A. Two of our largest markets are energy users — vehicles and air conditioning. In both areas we are contributing toward more energy efficient products. In the auto and related fields we have developed a gas recirculation cooler that saves fuel and reduces emissions. Another new product, this one for big trucks, is a variable-speed fan clutch that can cut fuel usage by 5-10% and reduce noise pollution. Less weight means less fuel, and our ABS plastics are helping to achieve this goal.

Several York developments also contribute to energy savings. They include the heat pump for residential use, a demand limiter that can cut energy costs in large buildings significantly, and

15

a rotary auto air conditioning compressor designed for smaller cars. In the service field, an air sampling system recently introduced monitors industrial emissions to help industry stay within government environmental standards.

In addition, Borg-Warner's own manufacturing operations have been working to cut the energy used in our plants. Between 1972-76, our U.S. plants reduced their energy consumption per sales dollar by 9.2%. In 1976 alone, this effort saved $2,175,000, and similar savings were expected for 1977.

Q. *What is your dividend policy?*

A. Ideally, we would like to provide shareholders about a 40% payout and have a dividend increase every year. We've more than met our payout objective over the last ten years, but we are just starting to build a record regarding annual increases. At a minimum we want to provide our shareholders parity with inflation.

16

BORG WARNER®

Borg-Warner sets record third quarter, 1978

Sales/Earnings

(millions except share data)

	Three months ended Sept. 30			Nine months ended Sept. 30		
	1978	1977	Change	1978	1977	Change
Net sales	$572.1	$498.4	+15%	$1,706.3	$1,485.7	+15%
Net earnings	$ 30.8	$ 24.5	+26%	$ 95.5	$ 72.5	+32%
Net earnings per common share	$ 1.43	$ 1.15	+24%	$ 4.45	$ 3.45	+29%
Average share outstanding (fully diluted)				21,455,000	21,018,000	

NYSE — **BOR**

Misc. data	Sept. 30, 1978	
Return on sales		5.6%
*Return on avg. equity		14.3%
*Reinvested earnings as a % of equity		9.4%
Current		2.2 to 1
Debt-to-equity ratio		20.4%
Book Value		$43.74
Dividend (annual, per share)		$2.00
Yield		6.2%
Stock price	High	Low
12 mos. 1977	33⅞	25¼
9 mos. 1978	34⅜	25⅜
Price/earnings ratio		5.7X
Avg. shares outstanding (fully diluted)		21.4 million
Shareholders		57,000
Employees		54,000

*12 months ended Sept. 30, 1978

Sales and earnings by major business (millions)	Sales 9 months 1978	Earnings 12 months 1977
Air Conditioning	$386.1	$18.3
Chemicals & Plastics,	$344.9	$ 6.6
Industrial Products	$347.2	$33.8
Transportation Equip.	$628.1	$32.7
Financial Services	N/A	$12.8

Borg-Warner Management Quotes

- Each of the company's six operating groups posted gains, with biggest improvements coming from chemicals and plastics operations, York air conditioning, and transportation equipment. Borg-Warner's chemicals and plastics business outside the U.S. has turned around more quickly than expected from the depressed market conditions of a year ago and expects continued improvement in the fourth quarter and in 1979.
- The company's return on sales has improved this year as a result of a continuing effort to control operating costs. Margins for the third quarter were 5.4 percent, compared with 4.9 percent in the same period last year. Margins for the first nine months were 5.6 percent, up from 4.9 percent for the first nine months of 1977.

Jack M. Frisbie, Borg-Warner Corp., (312) 322-8674
200 South Michigan Avenue, Chicago, IL 60604

Borg-Warner announces something better than its 50th anniversary (its best year yet).

For the 50th time, we're announcing our year-end results. And we really know how to mark an anniversary.

Sales and earnings in 1977 were the highest in our history. In fact, sales topped $2 billion and net earnings were above $100 million for the first time. Profit margins, an indicator of operating efficiency, also rose. And we entered 1978 with a good head of steam, thanks to record results in the fourth quarter as well.

Back in 1928, four automotive parts suppliers formed Borg-Warner. Their goal was to provide better service to the then young but vital vehicle market.

Today, transportation equipment remains our largest single market, but more than 60% of our earnings last year came from our other businesses, such as air conditioning, chemicals and plastics, financial services, and energy and industrial equipment.

And we plan more changes to build a stronger company to serve our employees, shareholders and customers.

For example, Baker Industries. We acquired this strong, well-managed company for about $120 million in cash. Baker Industries is a leader in the growing protective security and smoke detector markets. It's part of Borg-Warner's long-range objective to derive 30% or more of our earnings from service business.

Our first venture into the service area, Borg-Warner Acceptance Corporation (BWAC), turned in its 12th straight year of higher earnings in 1977. They have more than $1 billion in receivables and are one of the 15 largest independent finance companies in the U.S.

Sales in all major product areas were up, with air conditioning and transportation equipment providing the largest gains. We had our problems, mainly in Europe, where unused plant capacity made our chemicals and plastics and automatic transmission operations unprofitable. In 1978, we will be working hard to turn these situations around, and we are optimistic about what can be accomplished.

We also had another year of improved operating efficiency, as evidenced by an increase in profit margins to 5.1% from 4.4% in 1976.

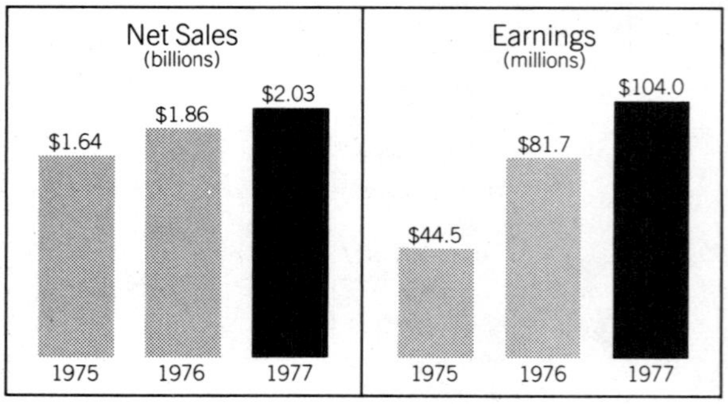

Finally, our shareowners continued to be profit sharers, too. We raised the common stock dividend again in November to an annual rate of $1.80. That provides a return of about 7%, based on recent stock prices. Not only is this return above the average for listed stocks, but we have paid dividends in each of the 50 years since our founding.

For more information on our record year and the outlook for 1978, write for a copy of our 1977 Annual Report to Terry Wilson, Investor Relations Manager, Borg-Warner Corporation, 200 S. Michigan Avenue, Chicago, Illinois 60604.

BORG WARNER®

Everything's coming up records at Borg-Warner.

Record sales. Record earnings. Record earnings per share. The best quarter and six months in Borg-Warner history.

Net Earnings (Millions of Dollars)

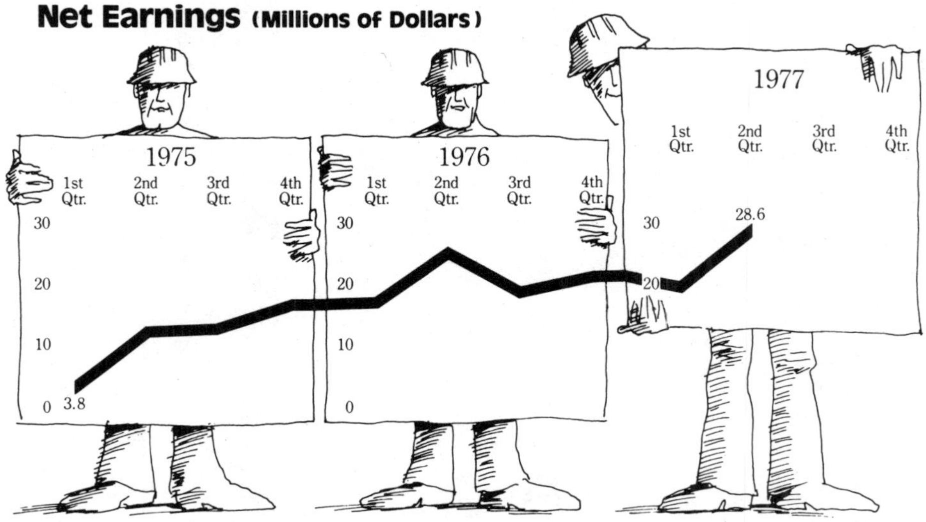

"I'm confident our second half improvement will be even stronger." James F. Beré, Chairman and Chief Executive Officer.

Here are details of the record second quarter and first half.

Sales

Second quarter and first half sales were the highest for any three-month and first half period in Borg-Warner's history. Sales for each of our major product areas were higher than for the corresponding periods of 1976, with air conditioning and transportation equipment leading the improvement. For financial services, gross receivables passed the billion dollar mark for the first time.

Earnings

Earnings for the second quarter also set a three-month record, and so did earnings for the first six months. For the quarter, net earnings increased 16.7 percent to $28.6 million on a 5.3 percent increase in sales. For the six months, earnings were up 15.7 percent on a 6.8 percent sales increase. Financial services net income rose 18 percent for the second quarter and 7 percent for the half-year period, compared with the 1976 periods.

For both periods, earnings per share were a Borg-Warner record despite a substantial increase in shares outstanding.

The Outlook

We expect sales for the full year 1977 to exceed $2 billion for the first time. Sales in 1976 were $1.86 billion. Net earnings also are expected to set a new record for the year. And at a higher rate of increase than the 15.7 percent gain of the first half.

The Reasons

This confidence in the outlook for the balance of 1977 is based largely on the following:

- The continuing strength we see ahead for the U.S. economy. Business spending for non-defense capital goods rose at a 19 percent rate in the second quarter, indicating a strong second half for capital spending.
- Borg-Warner's backlog of unfilled orders has been increasing, and is above the 1976 level at this time. Over a third of the backlog is in our growing energy equipment divisions.
- We expect 1977 auto sales to compare favorably with the strong sales of 1976, and our production schedules for the rest of the year continue at a high rate.
- New housing starts in the second half of 1977 should be substantially above those of 1976 for the same period.

The Full Story

We've shown you only the tip of the iceberg. For the complete record of our record-shattering quarter and half—and more of the Borg-Warner story—send for our quarterly report. Terry W. Wilson, Manager, Investor Relations, Borg-Warner Corporation, 200 S. Michigan Ave., Chicago, Ill. 60604.

BORG WARNER

BORG WARNER
Presentation to
The New York Society
of Security Analysts
By
James F. Beré,
Chairman and Chief Executive
and
James J. Gavin, Jr.,
Senior Vice President-Finance
Borg-Warner Corporation
October 27, 1978

Comments by James F. Beré
Chairman and Chief Executive Officer
Borg-Warner Corporation

JAMES F. BERÉ

We appreciate the opportunity to meet with you to discuss our performance and our outlook. Some of you might be surprised by the extent to which our company and our products touch the lives of people here and everywhere. I know I usually am.

Our major markets

Borg-Warner has grown from an amalgamation of four auto parts suppliers, fifty years ago, into a broadly based company serving several diverse and basic markets with sales of more than $2 billion.

Passenger car components, sold to automobile manufacturers in the U.S., in Europe, Japan and Australia, is our largest single market. Our products serving this market include a wide array of drive-line assemblies and sub-assemblies, automatic and manual transmissions, clutches, air conditioning com-

1

Borg-Warner Corporation

Headquartered in Chicago, Borg-Warner Corporation has grown from four auto parts suppliers fifty years ago into a broadly-based company serving several diverse and basic markets with 1977 sales of more than $2 billion worldwide. Based on sales, the company placed 127th in the FORTUNE "500" in 1977.

Components sold to vehicle manufacturers in the United States, Canada, Europe, Japan, Australia, South America and South Africa, represent the company's largest single market. Products serving this sector include a wide array of driveline assemblies and subassemblies, automatic and manual transmissions, clutches, air conditioning compressors, and plastic resins for automobile exteriors and interiors.

Other major markets are construction, where York air conditioning and refrigeration products and Cycolac ABS plastic resins are widely used and energy, for which the company makes submersible oilwell pumps, nuclear coolant pumps and equipment for refining. Consumer products, machinery, and agribusiness markets each account for between six and eight percent of the company's sales total.

Borg-Warner is comprised of six operating groups employing some 54,000 persons at about 110 plants and offices in the United States and 21 foreign countries.

As of September 30, 1978, Borg-Warner's assets totaled $1.5 billion. Shareholder equity was $928 million and long-term debt was $157 million. Listed on the New York, Midwest and Pacific stock exchanges with the symbol BOR, the company has an average 21,500,000 common shares outstanding.

Financial information contacts:

	Telephone Number
William M. Valiant	(312) 322-8700
Jack M. Frisbie	(312) 322-8674
Terry W. Wilson	(312) 322-8672
James J. Gavin, Jr.	(312) 322-8517

pressors, and plastic resins for both interior and exterior auto parts. The passenger car market accounts for roughly 24% of our total sales. Replacement parts for the auto market account for an additional 8% of our sales. In addition, components for trucks, off-highway and recreational vehicles, and marine equipment contribute to our participation in the broad transportation market which in total, represents about 42% of our sales.

Major Markets—1977 Sales

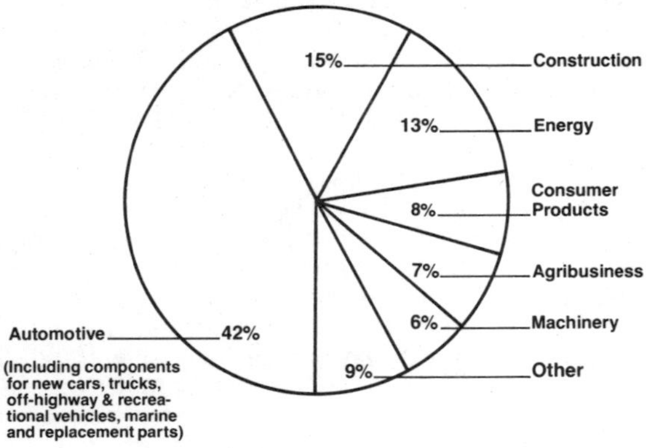

Construction—residential, industrial, and commercial—is another large market for Borg-Warner. In addition to York air conditioning equipment, our ABS plastic resins are widely used for pipe and other home construction items.

Another important and growing market for our company is energy. This market contributed 13% of our total sales in 1977. Our products here include: pumps for the extraction and pipelining of oil and gas; power generation pumps for both conventional and atomic power plants; gas compressors and other refrigeration equipment for refining.

Other markets served by Borg-Warner include: consumer products, agribusiness and machinery. Each of these accounts for between 6 and 8% of our sales total.

About one quarter of our sales are outside the U.S. Our major non-U.S. investments are in the U.K., Australia, Canada, Europe and Japan.

2

Nine-month results signal record year

So much for background, which, of course, is not your primary purpose in joining us here today. So let's talk about performance.
As I hope most of you are aware, Borg-Warner is well on the way to another record year—one that should be the best ever for our company in terms of sales, earnings and earnings per share.

A few days ago we announced our results for the three months just ended. It was the best third quarter in our history. I will cover some of the highlights of our third quarter. Net earnings were $1.43 per share compared with $1.15 per share a year ago—an increase of 24% on a per share basis and equal to a 26% jump in net earnings. This earnings improvement was on a sales gain of about 15% in the same three months.

Across-the-board improvement

All of our major business areas shared in this uplift, but we have been most encouraged by the continued improvement we have been able to make on our margins. This has been one of our key strategic planning objectives. In the third quarter, income as a percent of sales rose to 5.4% compared with 4.9% in the third quarter last year. While our third quarter earnings gain does represent some slowdown in the rate of progress we had achieved during the first half of 1978, this pattern had been anticipated. What about the balance of the year?

At this point, there is no doubt in our minds that 1978 will be a record year for Borg-Warner—our third in a row. And we are confident that we will exceed the $4.93 per share we earned in 1977 by a substantial margin. In fact, it is quite likely that our earnings for the year will top the $6 per share mark.

What about 1979?

Of course, the big question then becomes

3

—what about 1979? In spite of what we all are hearing from some well-respected economists at Borg-Warner, we are—with some reservations—optimistic both about the future of our company and of our economy. Although we don't believe a general recession is in the cards next year, we do see the generally slower growth patterns we are experiencing in the last half of 1978 continuing into 1979 with downturns in several important sectors of the economy.

The three segments of the economy that most significantly affect our performance are auto sales, housing and capital spending. We expect slight downturns in both the auto and housing markets next year. However, we believe the declines will be relatively modest —about 5% in terms of passenger car sales and perhaps a 10% drop in new housing starts. Offsetting this will be real growth of between 6-8% in capital spending, which we see as one of the strong segments of our economy in 1979.

About the only thing that could blunt our optimism would be the 1979 labor picture where we see hard bargaining ahead in a number of industries where major contracts will be expiring. Wage and price restraints could make the situation even more difficult and contribute to an eventual recession.

Our own labor situation should be quite healthy during the coming year; but we could be adversely affected if lengthy work stoppages take place in the trucking, rubber, or automotive industries.

Reasons for optimism

You are entitled to know the reasons for our optimism in view of the softness we see for at least two of our major markets. Our optimism is based on three factors. First, is several energy-related products we have recently introduced. In fact, I should point out that despite the problems the energy situation has caused in this country and around the world, the drive to conserve energy is on balance having a positive impact on our performance and

4

our outlook. This is especially so in the auto industry, where original equipment makers face almost total redesign of their product to meet federal energy and emission standards and the changing tastes of consumers. This fact, coupled with the massive capital commitment it entails, spells real opportunity for supplier firms such as Borg-Warner.

For example, our patented Morse Hy-Vo chain is an important component in front-wheel drive assemblies; and we are convinced the trend to this design configuration in the U.S. will accelerate. Another new product developed by Borg-Warner will improve the fuel efficiency of automatic transmissions by eliminating slippage between the torque converter and the transmission at highway speeds. We see great potential for this lock-up device and for Hy-Vo chain. Both will begin appearing on 1979 models in large numbers.

The air conditioning industry, on a smaller scale, is going through the same process of product redesign to improve energy efficiency as is the auto industry. As a result, our York division is selling as many of its energy-efficient heat pumps for residential and small commercial applications as it can manufacture. The modification of existing air conditioning systems in large building installations to achieve significant energy cost savings also is made possible using York control components recently introduced. In addition, the worldwide search to increase oil production means increased business for our Byron Jackson and Centrilift pump units.

Changes for the better

The second reason for our optimism about the year ahead is the changes we have made in the basic nature of our company. Ten years ago, earnings from our Transportation Equipment group accounted for more than half our total earnings. Last year, earnings from this group contributed less than one-third of the total with more than two-thirds coming from faster growing business areas.

5

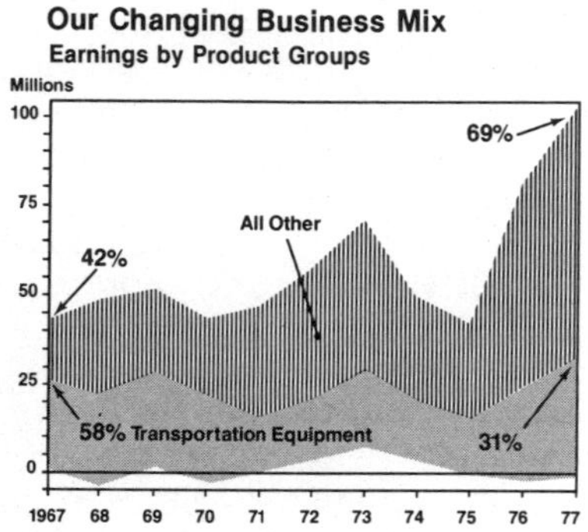

Still, in total, we have not been happy about the cyclical nature of our major markets; and I know this had bothered investors, too. Because of this, a major thrust of our strategic planning has been to improve this earnings pattern by expanding our involvement in service businesses.

This sector of the economy has grown faster than our traditional manufacturing operations and has tended to be less cyclical. In 1977, about 12% of our earnings resulted from the financial services operations of Borg-Warner Acceptance Corporation. With the acquisition of Baker Industries, our *1978* earnings from

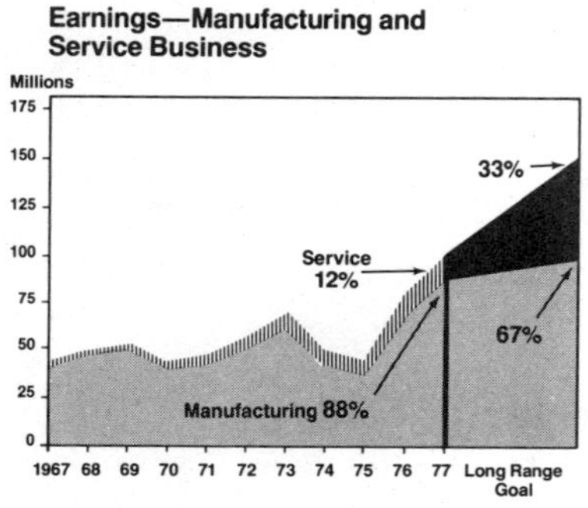

service related businesses will be between 15-20% of the total. Our long-term goal is to boost this percentage contribution even further, so eventually as much as one-third of our total earnings will derive from service businesses.

6

Strategic planning: a stronger company

But we've not forgotten the basic nature of Borg-Warner and that it is still subject to the fluctuations of the general economy. We have, however, made great strides in strengthening our company since the 1975 recession. And the lessons we learned then have not been forgotten. I'm not saying we will never have a down quarter. But I am convinced we've moved closer to our goal of smoothing our earnings pattern and building a base for continued earnings growth.

This brings us to the third and perhaps the most important reason for our optimism about 1979; that is, the progress we have made in following the strategy put together in 1975. This greater attention to strategic planning, strict goals, and emphasis on cost reduction is showing results. I'm going to ask Jim Gavin to review with you some charts we presented to our directors at their last meeting.

7

Comments by James J. Gavin, Jr.
Senior Vice President-Finance
Borg-Warner Corporation

JAMES J. GAVIN, JR.

We have compared Borg-Warner's performance in a number of key financial measurements against that of the average of all "double A" and "single A" bond rated companies in the U.S. Borg-Warner itself has a split rating—"single A" from Moody's and "double A minus" by Standard and Poors.

Net income as a percent of sales has shown steady improvement since the 1975 recession and now compares favorably with other top-rated U.S. companies. By the end of this year, this ratio should be closer to 6% for Borg-Warner.

In most of the charts, it would appear that Borg-Warner had down operating years in both

Net Income as a % of Sales 1970-1978

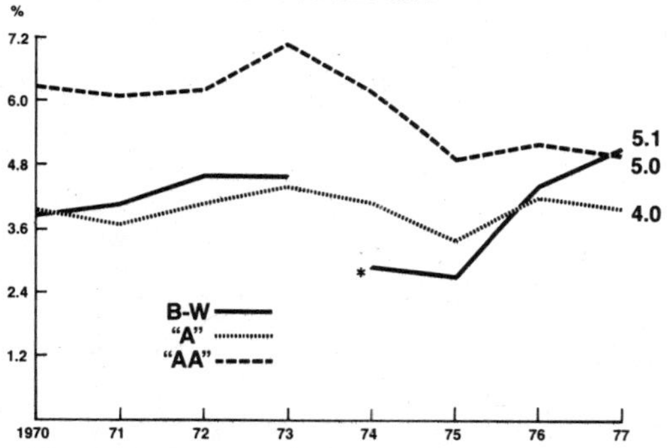

* Adjusted for change to LIFO

1974 and 1975. Let me remind you that while the sharp 1975 decline did result from the broad economic recession, the dip in 1974 was due to our change to LIFO inventory accounting that year.

Return on Equity 1970-1978

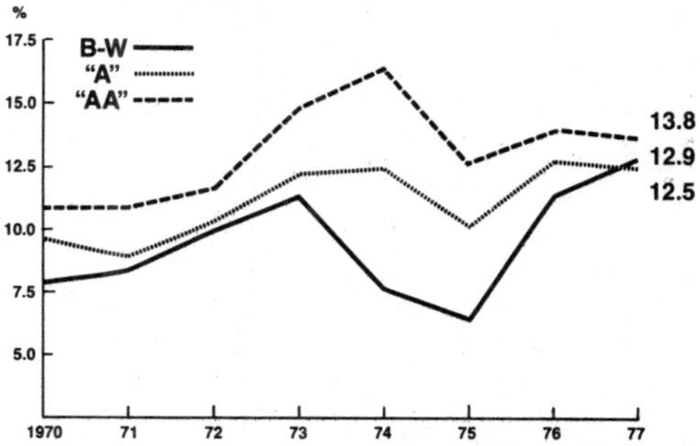

Our return on equity has shown the same trend and is now at the highest level in more than 20 years. Our return-on-average equity, over a twelve-month period ending September 30, was 14%.

Debt/Equity Ratio 1971-1978

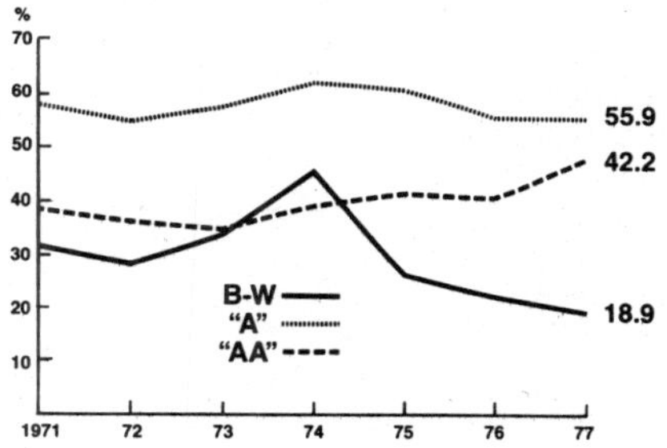

Again, our performance is better than it might at first appear because of our low debt-to-equity ratio, which has been almost consistently below that of the average for top-rated companies. Our current debt is about 20% of total equity. This leaves plenty of flexibility to take advantage of acquisition opportunities.

Return on Average Total Assets 1970-1978

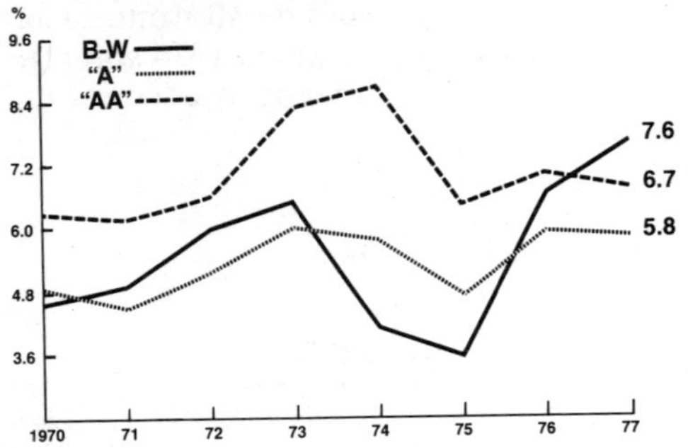

Because of our low-debt position, Borg-Warner shows up much better, relatively speaking, when measuring return based on average total assets. Our return on this basis has more than doubled since 1975, and 1978 will show continued improvement.

Reinvestment Rate* 1970-1978

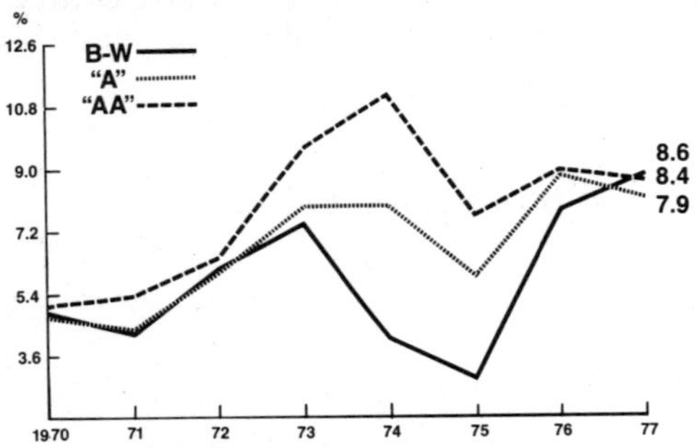

*Net Income—Dividends ÷ Equity

The reinvestment rate is one ratio we see analysts paying more attention to recently. As an indicator of our ability to sustain future growth, Borg-Warner now compares favorably when measured against other top-rated companies.

Our dividend policy, as stated on previous occasions, is to pay out an average of about 40% of our earnings in the form of cash dividends. Since 1970, our payout has averaged 38.5%, although there have been more wide swings on a year-to-year basis.

Dividend Payout 1970-1978
(As a % of Prior Years Earnings)

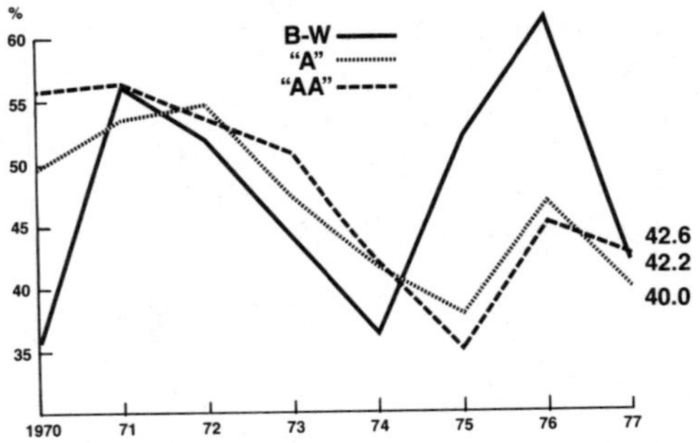

We are working to increase dividends on a more regular and frequent basis, as we *have done* during the last three years, while at the same time maintaining a roughly 40% payout rate. This dividend policy has resulted in a yield to our investors that over the years has been consistently above that of the average of both "A" and "AA" companies.

Dividend Yield* 1970-1978

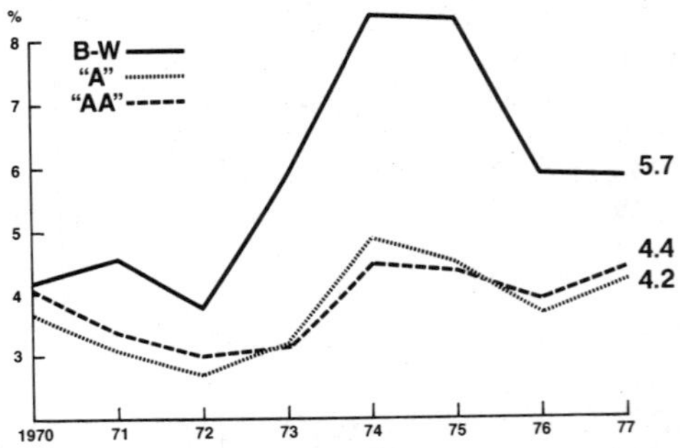

*Dividend per Share/Average Market Price

Unfortunately, our price/earnings ratio shows exactly the opposite picture. As you can see, our p/e has continued to lag that of the other top-rated companies. And I'll be the first to admit that perhaps Borg-Warner has deserved to sell at a discount in view of our cyclical performance and below-average return on equity of *earlier* years. And yet, if you look at Borg-Warner's earnings per share performance over the last 15 years, measured against that of the 30 companies that make up the Dow Jones Industrial Average, our earnings pattern closely parallels that of the Dow.

Price/Earnings Ratio 1970-1978

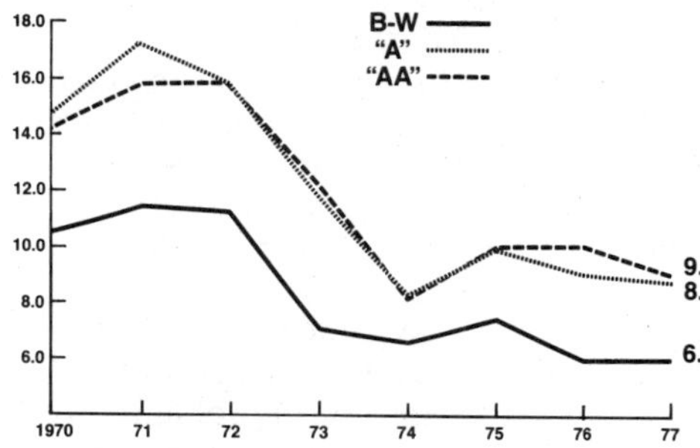

Cumulative Compounded Annual Investment Rates of Return Since 1963 (Appreciation and Dividends)

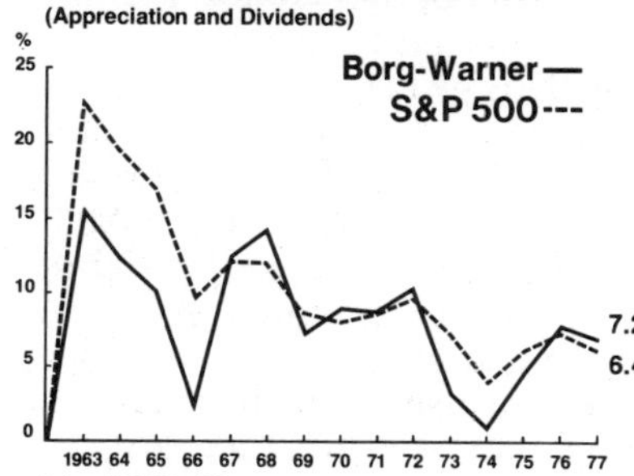

Index: 12/31/62 = 100

The exception was the severe recession of 1975. Our rebound in earnings since then, however, has significantly outpaced the Dow.

I'm convinced we're *now* a better company. The test of this, that will determine whether the changes we have made are real or simply wishful thinking, will come with the next economic downturn—whenever it takes place. We think we are up to that challenge.

Until that time, I'd ask you to keep in mind this final picture. Although the trend over the last 15 years has been a sad one for American business in general, it does show

12

that *Borg-Warner's* total return to investors, on a cumulative compound annual basis, is slightly better than that of the average of the S&P 500.

We've had our turn. Now it's yours. Who has the first question?

13

Question Session
New York Society of Security Analysts

Q. *If you want to reduce the cyclicality of your business, how does that fit with making an increased effort to get more business from the automobile companies? Could you quantify for us, roughly, how much new auto business means to you, either in 1979 or perhaps over a little less definite time period?*

A. (James F. Beré) The business cycle is going to be with us forever, and I think any company that believes it can insulate itself completely from this cycle is naive. Our aim is to moderate our cyclicality. While we don't expect to increase our auto-related sales as a percent of our total company, we do believe we will continue to grow in this business. We're very comfortable with the auto industry and its large role in our company. We have generations of people trained in how to react effectively to this market; we're very nimble, we understand the personalities of the O.E.M.'s and the other supplier firms. We don't want to destroy or minimize this asset. Our hope is, that by entering other businesses and by growing faster in those businesses, we can moderate our cyclicality.

14

In answer to the last part of your question, our new auto component business in '79 could be between $60-100 million. We are losing some '79 model clutch business to Ford which irks me, because of our leadership position on this product.

Q. *The dynamics of the whole ABS business has changed, not only in the supply side but also from the finance side. Markets have come and gone. Whether they've been knocked out by the EPA or whatever, I'm just wondering, on a long-term basis, how do you view this business? Do you see it a greater part of Borg-Warner three or four years from now?*

A. (Beré) I have to acknowledge that the chemicals/plastics business (in fact our business in general) is loaded with problems we did not foresee when we put together our five-year plan. A few examples of what I mean are: the oil embargo, floating rates, double-digit inflation, and the impact of the environmentalists.

Our ABS business has been growing about 10-12% a year. This growth hasn't been as steady as we once thought it would be, and it probably will not continue to grow at that rate. However, I believe the future for ABS is a good one. Automakers must find lighter materials to respond to regulatory requirements on fuel consumption. That fact, along with the increasing use of ABS by appliance manufacturers, indicates to me a positive long-term outlook for our chemicals/plastics business. There is no question in my mind that there will be increasing applications for plastics. They may not be ABS, but we are not frozen in one limited area.

Q. *Do you intend to broaden your base in plastics and chemicals?*

A. (Beré) Yes, we do. Our Weston Chemicals operation produces a variety of additives. They have been growing, but not as fast as we had anticipated. Perhaps the fault is ours in putting Weston under the jurisdiction of our plastics organization which naturally tends to think

15

"plastics" first. We remain excited about the future of the chemicals side of our business and we intend to participate in it. For example, our new plant now coming into production in Scotland, is a non-ABS plant. It will make additives for other plastics, primarily PVC. At this point, however, chemicals is a small part of our business.

Q. *Were there any divisions caught with their prices down on October 24?*

A. (Beré) The President's program was well rumored prior to his announcement of it three days ago. Based on what we understand will be required, I think we can live with it. Realistically, there aren't many markets we serve where we could go out and raise prices much above 5¾% anyway. The day of the automatic pass through is fast coming to a close—as it should. The challenge we face, and I'm speaking of business in general, is to find ways of increasing productivity. We must do more than simply pass on cost increases to the consumer if we are to beat inflation.

Q. *How will the next downturn affect Borg-Warner?*

A. (Beré) A lot depends on when it comes, but we feel confident we're better prepared than in 1974-75 because of the lessons we learned then. I'm optimistic at this time, assuming a downturn comes soon. When we went into the recession last time, we had an inventory turn of approximately 3.0. It's now running at 3.8 - 3.9. That's just one example of how we're now in better shape. Same story in receivables, which were something like 65 days when the last recession began, and shot all the way up to 80 before it was over. Our people have since done a superb job, and now receivables equal no more than 50 days sales. I'm convinced that, with the prime rate going up, we will have some very clever people out there trying to use our money. Finally, I think we have less risk of margins going down dramatically, but for us to think our margins will not be depressed somewhat in time of recession is unrealistic.

16

Q. *Since you said you were improving considerably overseas, can you give us rough numbers as to how much sales and earnings will be up this year?*

A. (James J. Gavin, Jr.) Our earnings improvement overseas is about double the rate of improvement overall. Our sales increase is about equal domestically and overseas.

Q. *The margins continue to be less overseas than they are domestically?*

A. (Gavin) Yes, we haven't gotten up to the level of domestic margins as yet.

Q. *Since you've identified service companies as an area of considerable potential interest, could you tell us which kind of service companies would be of interest to you, distinguishing for example, between vehicle leasing companies, industrial distribution companies, market research companies and so on.*

A. (Beré) We want to be a little cautious going into service businesses because they tend to be more labor intensive than those we're accustomed to as managers. We were interested in an insurance company but because they happened to be in vogue, we found we couldn't afford the prices the good ones were commanding. I would like to see us make an aggressive movement into the automotive aftermarket business. I think it is a terrific service business in our country. Within the next ten years, gasoline stations will not do any repair work because they all will be self-service stations. Market research or consulting companies are examples of service businesses we are not interested in.

Q. *Under what circumstances would you repurchase your own shares?*

A. (Beré) Well, I have an opinion and Jim Gavin has an opinion. Why don't we give Jim an opportunity first.

17

(Gavin) It always looks attractive to buy your own shares when they are selling at a 30% or 40% discount on book value. I don't particularly like that approach. If we looked at the many problems facing business today, one of the most significant is insuring adequate equity capital to support normal growth plus inflation. Regardless of how cheaply you may think you are buying your stock, you're reducing your capital base when you do so. I am not in favor of doing that, despite the fact that you can improve your earnings per share in this manner.

(Beré) I would agree that anytime a stock is over book value, or say within 10%, I would strongly support what Jim has said. It must be very obvious that we are even supporting him now, because we are not purchasing our stock.There is one exception. We are purchasing in the open market, enough shares to offset those being reserved for Borg-Warner employees under company benefit plans so there is no dilution for shareholders. Where I differ with Jim (he calls me the "book value kid") is when I see our stock selling at $30.00 with a book value of $48.00. That's when I get tempted.

Q. *Can you give us a definition of technology in your company?*

A. (Beré) I like the word "innovation". And, one of the present shortcomings of Borg-Warner (and many other U.S. companies as well) is a severe problem with the infusion of technology. In the '60s, we all built beautiful research centers, hired the best scientists from our fine schools, created "ideal" work environments, and thought great things would come as a result. The results have been disappointing. I think our technology efforts were too far removed from the marketplace. Of course, if we move too close to the market, we become myopic and can't see over the hill. To try to deal with this situation at Borg-Warner, we are, as part of our strategic planning process, beginning to evaluate innovation in the same way we do margin performance.

18

There are other reasons why I think innovation has been lagging in this country, and one of the big ones is the massive regulation we face. It's not so bad for the very large companies; we have the resources to deal with it, even though it is by-and-large wasteful and non-productive. But for the small company—the entrepeneur—where much of our innovation has emanated, it is stifling. Even if he manages to get an idea and then the capital to develop it, he then faces a multitude of inspectors at his door asking for information about smoke stacks, stair steps, employees, prices, and on and on . I don't argue that some of these regulations are necessary and even deserved. It's just too bad they can't be written for the 99% of business people who are honest, instead of for the 1% who aren't. The whole process has become a barrier to technology. The sad thing is that increased innovation could be one of our biggest weapons in fighting inflation.

At Borg-Warner, each of our decentralized units is responsible for its own technology for five years out. Beyond that time, we are setting up advance groups at our central research center. In addition, we have established a venture capital group. That's a fancy word for trying to plant seeds that might sprout innovation in areas we are not now in—hoping they will have an impact over a long period.

19

3

How to Excel with an Annual Report

William P. Dunk

What makes for excellence in an annual report?

What are the qualities that can make it stand out from the crowd and get notices—to bring deserved recognition to the issuing corporation?

Just suppose that you could turn out a report that would (a) attract the attention of both individual shareholders and professional investors; (b) tell them where your company is today and where it is going tomorrow in terms of growth areas and profitability; (c) do this in concise, easily understood exposition; and (d) at the same time satisfy the requirements of the Securities and Exchange Commission and other regulatory bodies. That would do it nicely. That would make for excellence.

And that is precisely what St. Joe Minerals Corp. accomplished with its 1976 annual report, reprinted in full at the end of this chapter.

To fully appreciate the effectiveness of the St. Joe report, it is important to understand the type of company it is, how it is changing, and what its needs are for communications and investor relations.

The Company used to be St. Joe Lead, and it produced lead and zinc. But in recent years, it has branched out into coal, oil, and natural gas businesses. It operates 34 coal mines. It has oil and natural gas interests in the United States, Canada, the North Sea, the Gulf of Mexico, and the Gulf of Suez. It has acquired overseas mining interests. It is also involved in energy research. So, St. Joe Lead Co. has diversified into a growing natural resources and energy company, called St. Joe Minerals Corp. It is admirably positioned for rapid expansion and profitability. It is a growth company.

The objective of the Company's investor communications program—and especially of the annual report—has been to project this new dynamic portrait of the Company.

The manner in which this objective was achieved in the Company's 1976 annual report was deceptively simple. The report was, in essence, a combination of candor, dramatic design, and clear, concise writing.

William P. Dunk is President of Corpcom Services, Inc., the parent company of Corporate Annual Reports.

According to surveys, the average investor spends one to two minutes on an annual report. This is hardly enough to register a true impression of a company. So, to enhance the chances of getting 15 to 20 minutes or more of a reader's time, it is necessary to do something different and dramatic. The St. Joe 1976 report dramatized itself with six compelling, creative full-page photographs.

One of the six was the cover, which cleverly told the story of diversification. The Company's name is cast in a bar of metal, and around it are samples of coal, oil, and mineral ore as well as pieces of a mineral core sample, which speaks for exploration and *growth.* The only lettering that appears on the cover is the year: "1976." Thus, the Company is clearly identified and its business is displayed. And this is done in a manner that draws the reader into the report.

As the reader turns the pages, he comes to one after another of the remaining five full-page pictures, each of which picks up an element from the cover. Each picture has with it a concise report about expansion and exploration projects of the Company for a specific year, starting with the present year and projecting five years ahead. And for each year, the projects are spelled out for each segment of the Company's business: oil and gas, or coal and minerals.

In a few words, the reader—whether he is a casual shareholder or a serious security analyst—gets a clear picture of exactly where the management expects to take the Company over the next five years.

The full-page photographs face pages of text and graphs that, one by one, show sales and profit for five products: coal, lead, zinc, oil and gas, and iron pellets. At the same time, a full-page chart presents capital expenditures by product groups for the previous four years, compared with expenditures projected for the next four years. Another full-page chart reveals the Company's profit, product by product, in the current year, compared with the previous year.

Thus, in dynamic photographs, charts, and a few words, the reader has already obtained a clear insight into the kinds of business the Company is engaged in, how it has fared in the recent past, and its prospects for the future.

If so inclined, the reader may then easily follow up on the details by dipping into the adjacent text. And a page of "Production and Financial Statistics" is simply arranged to spell out the details of sales, profit, and tonnage of the five products mined, produced, and sold, each year for five years.

Those are the major features of the report, and the main attributes that spell out its excellence. Among lesser, yet significant, features is the income statement. It compresses into a single table the usual income statement and the statistics required by the SEC. It makes a single tabulation do the work of two. Also, it presents two columns which most reports do not have, and which show actual increases or decreases in the figures in the income statement from 1974 to 1975 and from 1975 to 1976. The financial notes are positioned as closely as possible to the financial tables to which they refer. And throughout the notes, charts are inserted to greatly improve the clarity. It is most unusual to see these conveniences provided in the notes of an annual report.

Finally, the annual report was allowed to set the pace for St. Joe's investor relations program for the whole year. Some of the same or similar photographs were used in the interim reports, as well as in corporate advertising during the following months. This was not only economical; it also established a continuity in shareholder information. Readers could recognize the artwork and design from the annual report and the impression of the report itself was thus carried on through the other communications.

But how did it all happen? How did this report begin? And how did it develop? It was generated from the concepts of the chairman, John C. Duncan; his director of corporate communications, the late Robert W. Peckham; the outside designer, Len Fury; and the account executive, Warren Bimblick. The photographs were taken by Phil Marco.

Duncan wanted to emulate other companies in presenting the new look of St. Joe and its aspirations for the future as a growth company in the natural resources and energy fields. Then Peckham took up the idea and worked with Fury.

"Since we wanted to talk about future years," said Fury, "we couldn't use photographs of equipment and plants and mines that were not yet in operation. So we had to go back to the basics—the lump of coal, the drops of oil, the lead ingot and, to represent prospecting for the future, the mineral core sample.

"In the business St. Joe Minerals is in, they have to plan ahead. So, to the traditional review of operations we added the concept of the five-year forward 'calendar' in an attempt to bring it all together."

Added Peckham: "The main thing the report got across was that we were looking for a balance between the three main segments of the business by 1980 or 1981. The design of the report and the charts gave credibility to the fact that we were going to spend the money necessary to become a company that is one third base minerals, one third coal, and one third oil and gas.

"What brought it home to the reader was that we separated the story year by year, like an index, spread out through the review of operations. We made it apparent to the reader.

"The cover brought it all together. It expressed everything, including our diversification, which we had been trying to get across. Altogether it was a superlative design job. One thing that helps with this particular design firm is that on every project we get a designer and a project manager—the account executive—who pulls together all the details and makes it a lot easier to tackle an innovative annual report, which is what we have here."

However, the report did not come off completely without a hitch. In fact, at one point, when it was about ready to be printed, the whole concept was in jeopardy, because legal counsel pointed out that it might be hazardous to be so specific in dating completion times for projects that were not even planned to be started until some time in the future.

After a strategy meeting involving legal counsel, the chairman, the president, and the corporate secretary, it was agreed to insert a paragraph explaining that the projects "might be modified, delayed, or even terminated as a result of adverse geological or mining results or changes in prices, costs, operating conditions, or governmental regulations. Despite this degree of uncertainty," the paragraph added, "we believe that the inclusion of a step-by-step description of these mining projects will give shareholders a greater appreciation of the Corporation's activities and its present plans for these projects."

Another problem was the timing, according to Peckham: "You need to have a schedule and to stick to it."

Work on the report had begun during the previous August, when Peckham sat down with Fury, Bimblick, and senior executives of the corporation. The theme was worked out early enough so that there would be time for the necessary photography.

The dummy was set by the second week in December. Meanwhile, a first draft of the report had been written by Peckham, and was then submitted to the chairman, the president, legal counsel, the controller's department, and the heads of the various subsidiary companies. The color separations were done in January and the report came together at the printer's in late February.

Although St. Joe has 20,000 shareholders, 65,000 copies of the 1976 annual report were printed. Copies were distributed to employees, the investment community, the trade and business press, customers, corporate lists, and new shareholders through the year. Also, all corporate ads that were run each week in *The Wall Street Journal* and in various business publications carried a line inviting people to write for copies of the annual report. These ads brought in more than 50 requests a day.

"The annual report is the best selling document we have," said Peckham. "The better the report is—from graphics right on through the charts and the writing—the more useful it is going to be in getting your story across. You don't get many shots at the investor. So you might as well do the best you can. It's a great selling document for many different audiences. For that reason, it is worth doing a first-class job."

That it was a first-class job is affirmed by the wide recognition it received. It won the Silver Oscar of Industry from *Financial World* for the best annual report among all natural resource companies. It was judged the best nonferrous metals annual report by *Institutional Investor* magazine. It was included in both corporate and design categories in the Mead Library of Ideas. It was among exhibits in the New York Art Directors' Show. And it was featured in the Swiss magazine *Photographis* and in the publication "Creativity VII."

1976

CONTENTS

1 Financial Highlights
2 Letter to Shareholders
5 Operations Review
7 Project Timetable
16 Production and Financial Statistics
18 Financial Review
31 Auditors' Opinion
32 Corporate Data

ST. JOE MINERALS CORPORATION

St. Joe Minerals Corporation is a growing natural resources and energy company. As the annual report cover implies, St. Joe has diversified and expanded its interests to include coal, oil and natural gas as well as the traditional lead and zinc businesses. At the center of St. Joe's growth is exploration, exemplified by the mineral core samples.

St. Joe is a major producer of lead and zinc, and operates the largest lead and zinc smelters in the United States. Through A. T. Massey Coal Co., Inc., St. Joe operates 34 coal mines and 14 cleaning plants, and through CanDel Oil Ltd. and St. Joe Petroleum, St. Joe has oil and natural gas interests in the United States, Canada, the North Sea, the Gulf of Mexico and the Gulf of Suez. St. Joe's domestic oil and natural gas capacity should be expanded by the proposed acquisition of Coquina Oil Corporation. St. Joe also operates an iron pellet production facility, has overseas mining interests and is involved in energy research.

This 1976 annual report focuses on the plans and commitments St. Joe is making toward its growth and development over the next five years.

FINANCIAL HIGHLIGHTS

	1976	1975*	% Change
Net sales	**$778,331,000**	$762,645,000	+ 2.1
Income taxes	**$ 38,762,000**	$ 55,263,000	− 29.9
Net income	**$ 68,748,000**	$ 89,185,000	− 22.9
Dividends	**$ 26,594,000**	$ 23,979,000	+10.9
Net income per share	**$3.25**	$4.23	− 23.2
Dividends per share	**$1.27½**	$1.17½	+ 8.5
Shares of common stock outstanding December 31	**21,206,000**	21,128,000	+ 0.4
Number of shareholders	**19,851**	20,882	− 4.9
Shareholders' equity	**$415,773,000**	$372,502,000	+11.6
Shareholders' equity per share	**$19.61**	$17.63	+11.2

**1975 is restated for pooling-of-interests.*

TO THE SHAREHOLDERS

The year 1976 was one of mixed results for St. Joe but one that emphasized the importance of diversification. Coal earnings were down sharply, but the lead and zinc businesses recovered from the depressed levels of 1975.

Earnings in 1976 totaled $68.7 million, or $3.25 per share, compared with $89.2 million, or $4.23 per share, in 1975, a decline of 23.2%. Sales increased slightly (2%) to $778.3 million, compared with $762.6 million in 1975.

STRONG NEW ACQUISITIONS

St. Joe's stake in the energy field was strengthened further by acquisitions in the past year. In February, St. Joe purchased TCH Coal Company and in August completed the acquisition of Tennessee Consolidated Coal Company.

By year-end 1976, the Boards of St. Joe and Coquina Oil Corporation had approved the exchange of approximately 1.1 million shares of St. Joe common stock for 100% of Coquina. Coquina is an oil and gas exploration and development company operating in nine states with headquarters in Midland, Texas. The objectives of this proposed acquisition are to provide the Corporation with additional management to operate its domestic reserves of oil and gas and to utilize Coquina's successful drilling operations in expanding St. Joe's search for domestic oil and gas.

SUMMARY OF OPERATIONS

The results of our 1976 operations are detailed in the body of this annual report. Briefly to summarize these results: Our own coal tonnage increased by 4%, although profits declined because of lower prices and higher costs. Oil and gas earnings from operations increased, as did total reserves. Lead tonnage sold increased 30%, and profits went up by an even larger percentage. Zinc sales also increased early in the year but declined sharply in the fourth quarter because of weakening markets and a high level of imports; iron pellet production and profits declined; and earnings from South American operations increased substantially.

St. Joe's earnings for the fourth quarter were $18.3 million, or 87¢ per share, compared with $20 million, or 95¢ per share, for the corresponding 1975 period, a drop of 8.4%. The quarterly results include $4.9 million in pretax dividends from unconsolidated foreign operations. The prospect for further foreign subsidiary dividends is favorable in 1977.

Operating cash flow of $116.4 million was sufficient to enable St. Joe to meet its 1976 capital investment and exploration targets without adding appreciably to long-term debt, which increased by $4.6 million, principally for pollution control financing at our smelters.

CAPITAL EXPENDITURES — A RECORD

The capital investment program reached a new high of $104 million in 1976. About $52 million went to expanding and modernizing coal operations, while $38 million was invested in oil and gas exploration and in further development of existing oil and gas projects in the United States and abroad. The remaining $14 million was largely devoted to environmental expenditures and the upgrading of mining and smelting facilities.

Capital expenditures will climb even higher in 1977, to $138 million. Through capital investments in attractive projects we expect to bring a steadily improving return to shareholders in the form of higher dividends and earnings per share. Allocation of 1977 capital spending is 34% to coal, 34% to oil and gas, and 32% to metals.

The $210 million modernization and expansion program begun at A. T. Massey Coal Company in 1974 is presently at mid-stream and should boost coal production to approximately 16 million tons by 1981.

On January 28, 1977, Massey signed an option agreement with a subsidiary of one of the largest Austrian corporations for the sale of either 50% or 100% of the new Virginia Crews 750,000-ton-per-year preparation plant and mining properties.

It was felt that this option, if exercised, would help ensure the salability of this mid-volatile metallurgical coal and give the Corporation an entrée into an important Austrian market.

Prospective expenditures for oil and gas for 1977 include approximately $15 million for St. Joe and CanDel to develop the Buchan Field in the North Sea, in which our combined interest is approximately 28%. In addition, significant discoveries of oil and gas in the continental United States and Canada will require development expenditures to bring these wells into production as rapidly as possible.

In 1977, St. Joe's oil program should show its first profit after three years of exploration expenditures. With the acquisition of Coquina, we expect to realize our goal of establishing within St. Joe a viable domestic oil and gas exploration program upon which we can build for the future.

A major step toward increasing metals resources was taken in January of this year, when subsidiaries of St. Joe and Phelps Dodge Corporation concluded an agreement with a subsidiary of Australian Mining & Smelting Ltd. to develop jointly the Woodlawn zinc-lead-copper-silver deposit in Australia. Government approvals have been received and mining operations should begin in late 1978. Total capital investment by all parties will be approximately U.S. $88 million, of which St. Joe's share will be about U.S. $22 million.

ST. JOE'S CORPORATE STRATEGY

In this year's annual report, we portray a Corporation that five years ago set itself on a new course, a course we characterized as one of diversification into other basic raw materials, particularly energy-related. We believe this decision was correct and that there will be a continuing high level of demand for basic natural resources. A company with the ability to develop them efficiently will be in a position to prosper and benefit both its shareholders and society. We shall pursue this objective steadily through the coming years.

We hope that a better spirit of cooperation among government, business, and labor may develop under the new administration in Washington. It is essential that a national strategy be undertaken toward the development not only of energy resources but also of all basic raw materials.

AREAS OF CONCERN

Several aspects of government-business relations particularly concern us.

One of American business's greatest areas of frustration is government regulation—the multiplicity of regulations issued by government at all levels on many subjects, ranging from pollution control to tax assessment to safety. The objectives are desirable, but the end result is often not accomplished. If it is, the cost may prove to be out of proportion to the gain.

The area that vitally affects St. Joe is environmental regulation. We must deal with numerous governmental agencies at the federal and state levels, which often involves duplication of effort and can engender conflicts. We find ourselves aiming at a moving target. We live up to one regulation and then it is changed—so we must regroup and take aim again. This is wasteful, because it prevents systematic planning as to the proper allocation of resources.

For example, at our zinc smelter near Monaca, Pennsylvania, we have operated an efficient acid plant that removes 98% of the sulfur contained in the gases from zinc concentrate roasting. Under new state requirements we are now obliged to expend close to $10 million to install treatment facilities that will improve the sulfur removal by only an additional 1.5%. In addition to this cost, we will have to purchase elemental sulfur in order to make the system work efficiently. Costs of pollution control for the zinc smelter to date, together with projected expenditures in the next few years, may total $50 million in a plant representing present invested capital of about $92 million.

What we are concerned about is that few

Sales
(millions)

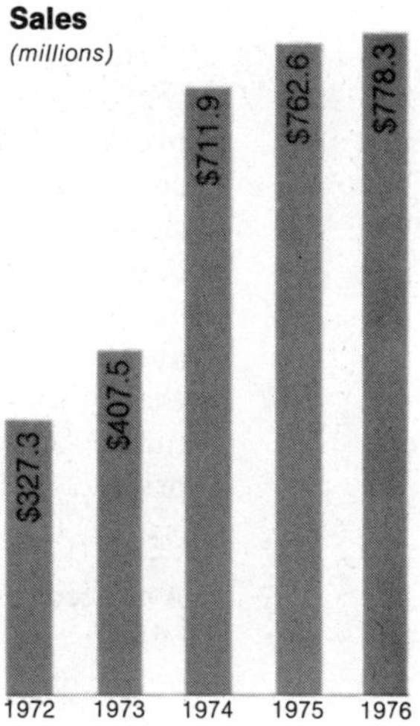

Earnings Per Share

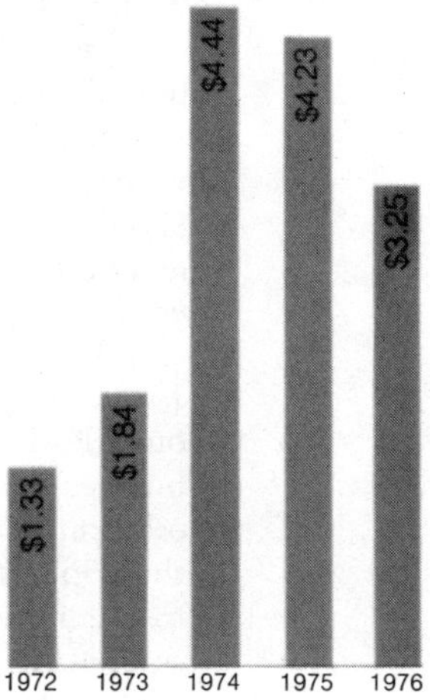

Funds Provided From Operations
(millions)

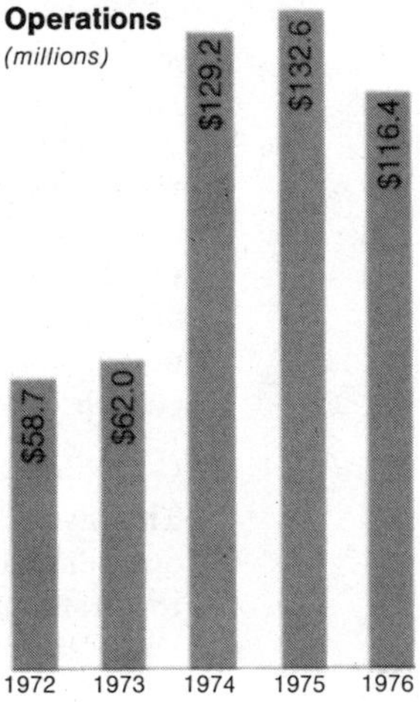

in Congress and in the agencies that promulgate these regulations seem to think about their cost and the inflationary pressures that result from these increased costs. The basic industries upon which the standard of living of our society depends, such as energy, automotive, steel, nonferrous metals, paper and chemicals, are bearing a disproportionate share of these environmental costs. This in turn limits our ability to increase vitally needed productive capacity in those industries.

NEED TO MAINTAIN PROFITS

A related concern is the widespread lack of awareness in government and among the public of the need to maintain corporate profits at a level sufficient to encourage continuing investment and expansion of basic industries.

We also believe that the double taxation of dividends—first as corporate profits, then as shareholder income—penalizes earnings and individual savings which should be channeled into capital investment creating much-needed additional employment.

A third subject of concern to us at St. Joe is the drive by some—in Congress and outside of it—to break up certain types of businesses, particularly the drive to force oil companies to divest essential aspects of their operations. As a small participant in the oil industry, we believe it is highly competitive and has established a record of service and efficient operation that is equaled by few other industries.

Furthermore, we are certain that, once such a campaign is successful in an industry such as oil, it may well spread to other industries. In the complex modern world, fragmentation of basic units of production results in higher costs, an inability to attain environmental goals, and a decline in the scientific and technological advance so essential to today's complex society.

CASH DIVIDEND INCREASE

The cash dividend paid during the second quarter of 1976 exceeded by more than 8% the first quarter payment, the fifth increase since November of 1973. The present annual dividend rate of $1.30 per share compares with 75¢ per share in 1972.

EXECUTIVE CHANGES

It is with deep sorrow that I report the passing of Andrew Fletcher, honorary chairman, who devoted most of his life to the development of St. Joe and the mining industry.

In May 1976, James L. Broadhead, Corporate Secretary, was elected Vice President —Development. He is responsible for coordinating the Corporation's research, exploration, and acquisition activities. In April, Robert P. Koenig retired at the age of 72 from the Board of Trustees. His wise and informed counsel has continued to be available through his role as a consultant.

FUTURE OUTLOOK

To some extent, the year 1976 was a disappointment for industries in our field in that the sharp recovery of the first six months did not continue for the entire year. However, the slower rate of recovery in late 1976 may signify that the business cycle will function in a more orderly manner during 1977 and 1978. For our industry, one of the unknowns is the state of international business, particularly in basic commodities and the effect on domestic markets of an increased tendency toward imports of these commodities.

Despite the uncertainties in the international and national scene, we look forward to the future with confidence and expect that the investments made over the past three years will produce substantially higher quantities of needed basic raw materials, which will in turn produce higher profits for the owners of St. Joe.

John C. Duncan
President

February 15, 1977

CAPITAL EXPENDITURES
(millions)

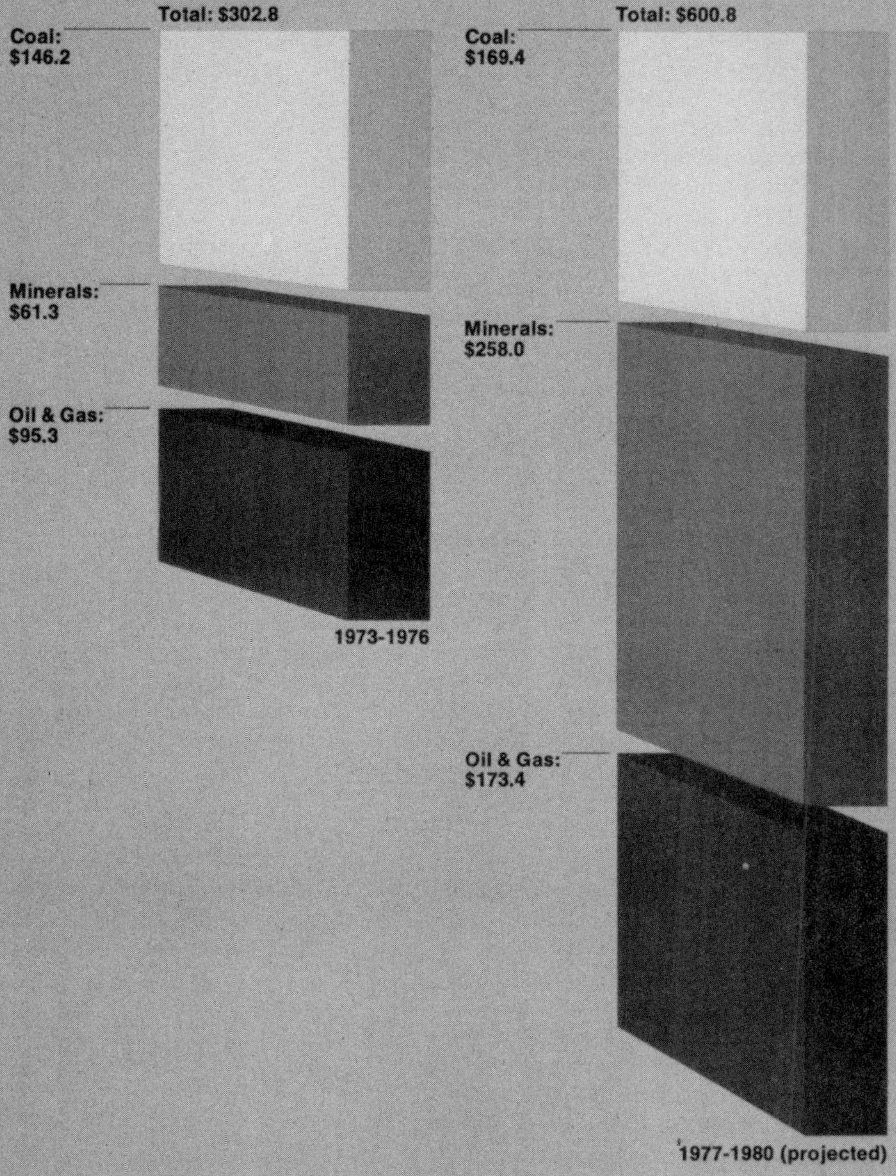

Included in the operations review is a project timetable which summarizes the Corporation's present plans for certain projects over the next four years. The timetable shows the many steps involved in bringing a mining project from the prospect stage to production. Each succeeding step is based on the assumptions that exploration and development activities will continue to yield positive results and that there will be no materially adverse change in other matters affecting the viability of the project. Thus, shareholders should keep in mind that the projects described may be modified, delayed, or even terminated as a result of adverse geological or mining results or changes in prices, costs, operating conditions or governmental regulations. Despite this degree of uncertainty, we believe that the inclusion of a step by step description of these mining projects will give shareholders a greater appreciation of the Corporation's activities and its present plans for these projects.

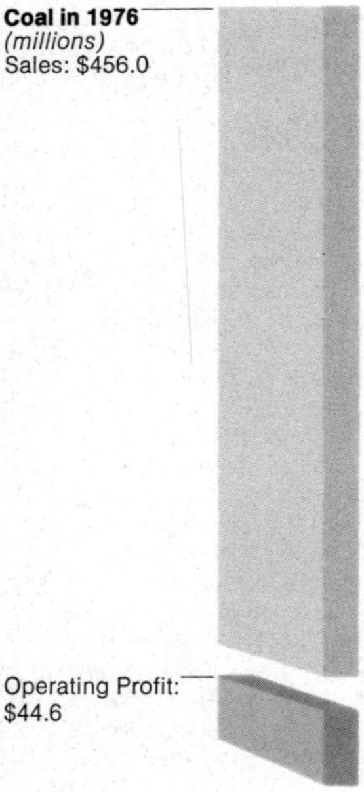

COAL PRODUCTION

A. T. Massey Coal Company, Inc. and Tennessee Consolidated Coal Company, St. Joe's principal coal subsidiaries, produce and process metallurgical and steam-grade bituminous coal from 34 mines and 14 preparation plants in West Virginia, Kentucky, Tennessee and Virginia. Massey also acts as a broker for significant additional tonnages of coal, both in the United States and abroad. In 1976, approximately 38% of the coal produced by Massey and 69% of the brokered coal was metallurgical grade, with the balance being steam grade.

Earnings from Massey's operations were substantially lower in 1976 than in 1975 because of lower prices and higher costs. However, Massey produced 10.5 million tons of coal in 1976 compared with 10 million tons in 1975. Brokered coal was 5 million tons compared with 5.5 million tons in 1975.

Long-term strength in our coal picture was enhanced during the year by development projects and acquisitions that will add to present and future production and to overall reserves.

One new development completed late in 1976 was Virginia Crews, a metallurgical coal mining complex that includes a preparation plant with a capacity of 750,000 tons per year. It is located in McDowell County, West Virginia, and is part of a $210 million expansion program that will bring Massey's production to about 16 million tons by 1981. Scheduled for completion in the spring of 1977 is the Sprouse Creek metallurgical coal mining complex, including a preparation plant with capacity of 1.5 million tons. It is on the border of West Virginia and Kentucky. Finally, construction of a new steam coal mine and preparation plant, with an annual capacity of 3.5 million tons, will begin in 1977. This facility will be located in Mingo County, West Virginia, and should be in operation in 1979. Long-term sales contracts have been signed for the major portion of the production from the Sprouse Creek and Mingo County plants.

Two acquisitions were completed in 1976. In February, TCH Coal Company was purchased for cash and notes. Tennessee Consolidated Coal Company, a high-volatile metallurgical coal producer located in Tennessee, was acquired in August in exchange for 971,300 shares of St. Joe common stock, an acquisition which was treated as a pooling of interests. TCH Coal has an annual production capability of 350,000 tons; in 1977, a fine-coal treatment circuit will be added to the existing plant to upgrade coal quality. Tennessee Consolidated Coal Company operates underground mines and has a modern preparation plant with a capacity of 1.2 million tons of washed coal.

Massey contributed $456.0 million to St. Joe sales in 1976, or 59% of the total, compared with $506.1 million, or 66%, in 1975. Operating profit from coal in 1976 was $44.6 million, or 39% of the total, while in 1975 it was $94.5 million, or 65%.

Although coal's contribution to St. Joe earnings fell in 1976, the long-term prospects remain attractive. Any long-term energy program that the United States develops must have as one of its basic ingredients the country's most plentiful fuel, coal. Production levels in 1977 are expected to exceed 11.5 million tons, with another 5 million tons brokered.

LEAD MINING

St. Joe owns and operates four underground lead mines and milling complexes in the New Lead Belt in southeast Missouri. Aggregate daily capacity is more than 20,000 tons of ore per day. Concentrates generated from these facilities are treated at our smelter in Herculaneum, Missouri. St. Joe's operations in the New Lead Belt have been described as "a showcase of modern mining and milling technology" by the editors of *Engineering & Mining Journal.*

During 1976, the move from the Old Lead Belt to Viburnum, in the New Lead Belt, was completed. St. Joe donated 8,500 acres of its land in the Old Lead Belt to the

1976

Coal and oil businesses expanded.

Oil and Gas

St. Joe announced plans to acquire in early 1977 Coquina Oil Corporation. Significant gas discovery made in Mississippi, and continued drilling in Kansas with 29 gas wells ready for marketing in 1977. In the Gulf of Mexico, St. Joe made two additional gas discoveries offshore Texas; offshore Louisiana a platform was positioned for up to 3 development wells. In Oklahoma, St. Joe acquired and drilled 11 oil and 17 gas wells.

In the North Sea, St. Joe continued drilling in the U.K. sector to delineate the Buchan Field on Block 21/1.

CanDel Oil Ltd. continued its Canadian expansion program, resulting in 58 gas and 10 oil wells.

Coal

Coal capacity was raised 1.2 million tons by acquisition and expansion, bringing total annual capacity to 11.5 million tons. TCH and TCC acquisitions completed.

The Virginia Crews preparation plant was completed and three existing preparation plants were upgraded.

Minerals

St. Joe's move to the New Lead Belt was completed with opening of central office at Viburnum, Missouri. Joint venture launched with Freeport Minerals Company to explore and develop zinc property in Carthage, Tennessee. Capital feasibility study completed on Pachon, Argentina, porphyry copper project. At Woodlawn, N.S.W., Australia, a co-venture agreement was reached in principle between St. Joe, Phelps Dodge Corporation and Australian Mining & Smelting Ltd. for development of this copper, lead, zinc and silver find.

Canadaka silver mill rebuilt after fire, and St. Joe acquired interests in gold mining properties in California and Chile plus alluvial diamond exploration rights in Brazil.

Lead in 1976
(millions)
Sales: $115.9

Operating Profit:
$39.5

State of Missouri for use as a state park. This park will be the second largest facility in the State's system.

Our mines operated at full production during the year. Concentrate production was 316,570 tons, which contained 221,404 tons of lead, compared with 284,200 tons of concentrates and 201,434 tons of lead produced in 1975. The mines also produced 17,936 tons of zinc in concentrates and 3,169 tons of copper in concentrates.

St. Joe has been able to maintain high productivity in its lead mining operations because of the higher grade ore in the New Lead Belt, extensive use of underground trackless mining equipment, and highly automated mills. Tons produced per man-shift worked underground range from a low of 30 tons to a high of 55 tons.

LEAD SMELTING

St. Joe's smelter and refinery at Herculaneum, Missouri, is the largest in the United States, with a rated capacity of 230,000 tons of refined lead per year. Reflecting strong demand, the plant operated at close to capacity for the entire year. Production of lead and lead alloys totaled 222,483 tons, up 20% from the 185,889 tons produced in 1975. Lead metal sold totaled 237,177 tons against 182,340 tons sold in 1975. Smelter inventories ended the year at a very low level.

The strength in lead demand caused an increase in posted lead prices. St. Joe's price began 1976 at the 19¢ per pound level, was raised to 21¢ per pound in March, to 23¢ in April, to 25¢ in July, and finally, to 26¢ in September. Additional increases to 29¢ per pound were announced early in 1977. Consequently, lead made a sizable contribution to St. Joe's sales and gross profits. Lead accounted for $115.9 million, or 15% of total sales, compared with $84.3 million, or 11%, in 1975. It contributed $39.5 million, or 34%, to operating profit, up from $20.3 million, or 14%, in 1975.

Lead demand was tied to the upsurge in demand for starting, lighting and ignition batteries because of the improved market for new autos and a strong replacement market. This demand should continue during 1977. Another factor was the Environmental Protection Agency's decision to delay the phase-down of lead in gasoline until 1979. The maintenance-free battery that utilizes calcium, lead-tin alloys continues to play an expanding role in overall battery production. By 1980, most new cars will be equipped with this type of battery.

In order to meet the more stringent proposed EPA and OSHA standards, St. Joe may face an additional investment of as much as $15 million at Herculaneum. Almost $7 million has previously been expended for environmental purposes.

ZINC MINING

St. Joe owns and operates a zinc mining and milling complex in the Balmat-Edwards mining district in northern New York State. The mine complex consists of four mines and two mills. Balmat-Edwards is the largest zinc mine complex in the United States and supplied 18% of the total U.S. mine production of zinc during 1976. One mill is located at Edwards and has a capacity of 600 tons of ore per day; the other, a highly-automated new mill at Balmat, has a capacity of approximately 4,300 tons per day. In 1976, the zinc content of concentrates produced was 77,409 tons, down from 80,034 tons in 1975. The decline in production resulted from the mining of slightly lower grade ore. Concentrate feed to our zinc smelter from St. Joe-owned mines in New York and Missouri can supply only a portion of the total feed required. The balance of concentrates and secondary feed material is purchased from other U.S. and foreign suppliers.

Achieving greater self-sufficiency in zinc concentrates is an important goal of the Corporation. In June 1976, a significant step was taken in this direction through the formation of a joint venture with a subsidiary of Freeport Minerals Company to define further and, if warranted,

1977

St. Joe's coal and oil operations continue to expand.

Oil and Gas

St. Joe to drill 2 development wells at Greens Creek gas field in Mississippi. South Timbalier Field offshore Louisiana to go into production as are 29 wells at Kansas/Bradshaw property. A 20-well oil development program to begin at Frio County, Texas. Offshore Texas, drilling to follow up 3 gas discoveries and 22 wells to be drilled in Oklahoma.

In the North Sea, an appraisal well is scheduled for recompletion in the Buchan Field on Block 21/1, and additional exploratory and development drilling are contemplated at locations in the U.K. and Netherlands sectors. CanDel plans to participate in drilling 60 wells in Alberta and British Columbia.

Coquina acquisition should be completed and a $44.5 million oil and gas program launched. Coquina to assume management of all St. Joe domestic programs and reserves.

Coal

Coal capacity is raised 1.1 million tons, bringing annual capacity to 12.6 million tons. Denver office begins western coal evaluation. Sprouse Creek plant to be completed and production to begin here and at Virginia Crews.

Minerals

Exploratory shaft to be completed at Carthage, Tennessee zinc property. Grading for permanent road to be completed at Pachon; initiate negotiations with Argentine government and others concerning development of the copper project. Mine and mill construction to continue at Woodlawn. Evaluation of deposit to continue at San Juan, California, gold property. Bulk sampling and drilling to continue on Chilean El Indio prospect.

eventually develop a property with zinc mineralization near Carthage, Tennessee. Preliminary planning on this project involves a three-year, $5 million exploration and development program that, after additional investment, could yield 50,000 to 75,000 tons per year of zinc in concentrates by 1981.

ZINC SMELTING

St. Joe's zinc smelter and refinery at Monaca, Pennsylvania, has a capacity of 250,000 tons per year and is the largest such facility in the United States. All zinc concentrates from the Balmat-Edwards mines are treated at the smelter. In 1976, St. Joe-mined concentrates supplied 48.3% of the feed used at Monaca. The balance was obtained from domestic and foreign suppliers. In 1976, demand for zinc improved over the 1975 depressed levels and production rose to 164,870 tons of zinc metal, up 57% from the 104,715 tons produced in 1975. Zinc oxide production rose to 52,246 tons, 11% over the 46,914 tons produced in 1975.

St. Joe's price for Prime Western zinc fluctuated in 1976, dropping from 39¢ per pound to 37¢ per pound in the first quarter, then rising in August to 40¢ per pound and dropping again in October to 37¢ per pound. St. Joe's prices for all grades of zinc oxide were raised in July by 3¢ per pound and reduced in October by 2¢ per pound.

Zinc accounted for $158.4 million, or 20%, of total sales, compared with $125.1 million, or 16%, in 1975. It contributed $15.9 million, or 14%, to operating profit, compared with $14.6 million, or 10%, in 1975.

Zinc sales improved largely during the first three quarters. Demand declined substantially in the last three months of 1976 because of lagging sales to the steel and heavy construction industries. These two industries use large quantities of galvanized products—steel coated with zinc to control corrosion—and constitute St. Joe's largest zinc market.

In addition, domestic zinc sales were adversely affected by unusually large imports of zinc sold in the U.S. market at "distress" prices.

We expect an improvement in zinc product sales in 1977 as the economy grows and as the capital goods and heavy construction industries participate in this growth to a larger extent than in 1976. To improve product mix, St. Joe is building a zinc dust facility at Monaca, which will have an initial capacity of 6,000 tons per year. This product is used in zinc-rich coatings employed by the auto industry to prevent corrosion.

In order to meet expected EPA and OSHA standards, St. Joe may have to invest as much as $32 million at the zinc smelter during the next four years.

OIL & GAS PRODUCTION

In 1976, sales of oil and gas amounted to $25.2 million, or 3% of the Corporation's total sales. Corresponding 1975 totals were $19.0 million, or 2% of sales. The contribution to operating profit was $10.9 million, or 9% of the total, compared with $6.0 million, or 4%, in 1975. The 1975 results included a gain of $4.1 million from sale of assets in Canada by CanDel Oil Ltd., a 94.6% owned Canadian subsidiary.

The operation produced 1,008,600 bbls. of oil and gas liquids in 1976 and 15,909,000 mcf of natural gas. Canada provided 91% of oil production and 87% of gas production, with the balance coming from U.S. sources.

St. Joe Petroleum and CanDel participated in drilling 129 wells in 1976. Of this total, 92 were successfully completed as oil or gas producers. 59 wells were drilled in the United States, 64 in the Canadian provinces of Alberta and British Columbia, three in the U.K. sector of the North Sea, two in the Netherlands sector, and one in the Egyptian sector of the Gulf of Suez.

Delineation of the Buchan Field situated on Block 21/1 in the U.K. sector of the North Sea continued. The fourth well

1978

Increased flow of oil and gas from North American properties

Oil and Gas
Texas offshore properties expected to begin producing, as well as a second location offshore Louisiana. Greens Creek gas field to start production.

Development drilling to continue in the Netherlands and U.K. sectors of the North Sea. CanDel to increase well participation from 1977 level and a substantial portion of effort to concentrate in deeper basin areas of Central Alberta. Coquina program continues.

Coal
The addition of 1.3 million tons of capacity from Virginia Crews, Sprouse Creek, TCC and TCH should bring annual capacity to 13.9 million tons. The completion of a preparation plant expansion at TCC alone would add 500,000 tons to capacity.

Minerals
Initial mine development for delineation of reserves scheduled for completion at Carthage zinc property. If sufficient reserves are found, St. Joe will continue to invest in the program. The Woodlawn development program scheduled to be completed this year. Assuming favorable negotiations with the Argentine government, and financing arrangements a decision to develop the Pachon copper project may be taken and detailed engineering design commenced.

Feasibility studies will determine whether to proceed at San Juan gold prospect in California and El Indio in Chile.

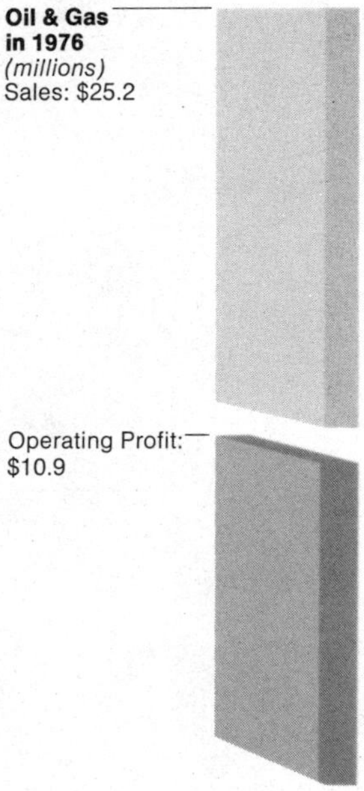

drilled on Block 21/1 was commenced in August and encountered the hydrocarbon reservoir some 300 feet higher than anticipated. Unusually high pressures were present, which led to suspension of the well for the winter months pending possible future re-entry. An exploration well on the border of Blocks 21/1 and 20/5 was drilled in the last quarter of the year and abandoned after producing a minor show of oil.

In the Netherlands sector of the North Sea on Block P/6, a gas extension well tested 27 million mcf per day. St. Joe's and CanDel's combined interest on Block P/6 is 12.5%. In the Gulf of Suez concession, a second well was abandoned after testing noncommercial amounts of gas and oil. A seismic program was implemented late in the year and will be evaluated in 1977.

Highlighting exploration activities was a significant natural gas discovery in Jefferson Davis County, Mississippi, where a well tested gas from two production zones at a combined rate of 9 million cubic feet per day. St. Joe has a 25% interest in the 4,000-acre block on which the discovery is located. In Kansas, 29 out of 33 wells drilled have been completed as gas producers and sales are expected to commence in mid-1977. St. Joe's interest in some 55,000 acres varies from 15% to 29%.

Two additional gas discoveries were made in 1976 in the Gulf of Mexico. Development of the South Timbalier 148 is in progress with a production platform in place. Two wells are to be drilled in the future. St. Joe's and CanDel's combined interest is 15.6%. Further oil and gas discoveries were made during the course of the year in the Anadarko Basin in Oklahoma; in Southeast Ohio; and in Frio and Starr Counties, Texas.

Incentives to explore for oil and natural gas in the United States were increased during 1976 through an improvement in pricing and the lifting of some controls by the Federal Government. St. Joe's and CanDel's average wellhead price for oil produced during 1976 in the U.S. was $11.93 per bbl., and their average selling price for gas produced was $1.44. Prices also improved in Canada during the year. CanDel's 1976 average price for Canadian oil was $8.14 per bbl. and its average price for natural gas was $1.03 per mcf.

St. Joe expects an expanding contribution to sales and profits from oil and gas in 1977. The overall expenditure for oil and gas exploration and development during 1976 was $38.3 million, and the anticipated investment for this purpose in 1977 is $44.5 million.

ENERGY RESEARCH CORPORATION

Energy Research Corporation's sales in 1976 were 75% higher than those in 1975. The company entered 1977 with an order backlog twice that of 1976. The bulk of 1976 sales were to three U.S. government agencies: the Department of Defense, the Energy Research & Development Administration and the National Aeronautics & Space Administration.

During 1976, ERC began new research and development contracts with ERDA on energy storage and conversion. Projects initiated involve a nickel-oxide/zinc battery for electric vehicle propulsion and a high-temperature fuel cell for central station electric power generation.

ERC also received Navy contracts totaling $1 million to manufacture specialty batteries and, in the fuel cell area, contracts from the U. S. Army to build two prototype portable power plants.

IRON PELLETS PRODUCTION

Meramec Mining Company, St. Joe's joint-venture with Bethlehem Steel, operates a large underground iron mine and pelletizing plant near Sullivan, Missouri. The plant produces a 67+% iron pellet for use as a direct reduction feed and also as a feed in steel blast furnaces.

In 1976, St. Joe continued to market its share of the production independently under long-term contracts with domestic steel producers. For the year, our share of pellets decreased to 670,206 long tons from

1979

St. Joe scheduled to receive first significant production from North Sea oil and Woodlawn projects.

Oil and Gas

Buchan Field wells scheduled to begin producing. Development proceeds in Netherlands sector properties.

CanDel to continue developing existing Canadian sites at Brewster, Cessford, Donalda, Pembina and Rainbow.

Coquina's oil and gas exploration program continues.

Coal

Some 400,000 tons of capacity to be added, bringing total capacity to 14.3 million tons per year.

Plans call for Marrowbone preparation plant to be completed. Sprouse Creek and TCH mines scheduled to reach full production.

Minerals

In zinc, an additional $5 million will be allocated for Carthage project if sufficient reserves are found. A second shaft will then be sunk and surface plant and mill begun.

Scheduled commencement of mining of 3,000 tons of ore per day to produce zinc, copper, silver and lead concentrates at the Woodlawn mill. If warranted, development of the Pachon copper project in Argentina may proceed.

Assuming positive evaluation results, mine development and construction to begin at El Indio gold site in Chile.

756,133 long tons produced in 1975, a decline of 11%. Sales for the year for St. Joe amounted to $21.4 million, compared with $27.4 million generated in 1975. Operating profit was $4.7 million, or 4%. This compares with the 1975 total of $9.9 million, or 7%. Two major factors contributed to this decline in profitability. The grade of ore and the resulting production of pellets were down from 1975 levels, adding to the cost of production; the steel industry operated at a lower rate than expected, particularly in the latter half of the year.

WORLDWIDE METALS MINING AND EXPLORATION

St. Joe subsidiaries are engaged in extensive exploration, development and production activities in Australia, Argentina, Peru and Brazil. In 1976, St. Joe's expenditures for worldwide metals exploration and development were $8.9 million compared with $7 million in 1975.

In January 1977, subsidiaries of St. Joe and Phelps Dodge Corporation concluded an agreement with a subsidiary of Australian Mining & Smelting Ltd. for a joint venture to develop a zinc-lead-silver-copper deposit at Woodlawn in New South Wales. Each co-venturer will have a one-third interest. The deposit is estimated to contain 10 million tons of ore, averaging 9.1% zinc, 3.5% lead, 1.8% copper and 1.8 ounces of silver per ton. This $88 million mine-mill facility is planned to come into production during 1978.

In Argentina, Compania Minera Aguilar, S.A., a St. Joe 99.9%-owned subsidiary, completed a capital cost feasibility study on the Pachon mine-mill-smelter complex. Pachon is a 790-million ton porphyry copper deposit discovered by Aguilar in the 1960s. Construction of an improved access road to the property is underway, and negotiations with the Argentine government should be initiated in 1977. In 1976, Aguilar's existing operations produced 89,287 tons of zinc concentrates, compared with 82,379 tons in 1975; 46,582 tons of lead concentrates containing 1,749,952 troy ounces of silver, compared with 41,353 tons of lead concentrates containing 1,764,200 troy ounces of silver in 1975.

Production from Compania Minerales Santander, Inc., our subsidiary operating in Peru, decreased in 1976. Production of zinc concentrates was 44,089 tons, compared with 49,103 tons in 1975; 3,159 tons of lead concentrates were produced, compared with 3,842 in 1975; and 2,008 tons of copper concentrates were produced, compared with 2,870 in 1975. Ores mined in Peru are sold in world markets, while those from Argentina are sold within that country. Dividends from these unconsolidated subsidiaries amounted to $7.9 million in 1976, compared with $2 million received in 1975. The prospects for continued dividends in 1977 remain favorable.

St. Joseph Explorations Ltd., a wholly-owned subsidiary, continued its program of exploration for base and precious metals in Canada. St. Joseph Explorations' subsidiary, Canadaka Mines Ltd., completed the construction of a new mill to replace one destroyed by fire in May 1975.

St. Joe continues to put emphasis on its exploration program in the United States. In northeast Arizona, a potentially commercial potash property has been partially delineated with additional drilling and metallurgical testing planned for the future. At Fountain Run, Kentucky, a low-grade zinc ore zone has been enlarged, though further drilling and, if warranted, an exploration shaft will be needed to assess the deposit's commercial value. Additionally, the Corporation has budgeted $1 million in 1977 for domestic uranium exploration.

St. Joe's subsidiary, Placer Service Corp., completed negotiations for leasing approximately 2,200 acres of a tertiary gravel deposit in California. The deposit is considered to be one of the largest known gold reserves in the United States. During 1977, a more complete evaluation of these reserves will be undertaken to determine if this property can be mined economically.

1980

Expanded coal production; flow from North Sea gas wells to begin.

Oil and Gas
Blocks P/6 and Q/7 in the Netherlands sector of the North Sea scheduled to begin production. Construction of waterflood facilities to increase oil production and reserves planned by CanDel at Cessford and Pembina.

Coquina continues its development and expansion program.

Coal
Plans call for additional production capacity of 700,000 tons to bring annual capacity to 15 million tons, an increase of over 30% from 1976 levels.

The construction and development phase is scheduled to be completed at Marrowbone.

Minerals
Development of the Pachon copper project should be proceeding with a view toward production at a rate of 100,000 metric tons of refined copper per year. Total investment by an international consortium projected at over $940 million.

Underground development and surface construction to continue at Carthage zinc property, assuming previous decision to continue. Project should be completed in 1981 and yield 50,000-75,000 tons of zinc in concentrates per year.

PRODUCTION AND FINANCIAL STATISTICS

LEAD	Tons Concentrate Mined	Tons Metal Produced	Tons Metal Sold	Net Sales[2]	Operating Profit (Loss)[3]
1972	312,662	207,877	223,230	$ 73,703 (In thousands)	$25,010
1973	283,602	215,012	284,018	97,543	28,811
1974	339,976	230,873	281,424	127,316	47,369
1975	284,200	185,889	182,340	84,278	20,357
1976	316,570	222,483	237,177	115,882	39,539

ZINC	Tons Concentrate Mined	Tons Metal Equivalent Produced	Tons Metal Equivalent Sold	Net Sales[2]	Operating Profit (Loss)[3]
1972	142,129	235,647	284,294	$111,744	$10,252
1973	180,502[1]	231,085	281,657	132,723	18,044
1974	221,436[1]	223,968	245,603	201,633	52,681
1975	169,885	142,406	137,009	125,059	14,573
1976	161,647	206,844	186,431	158,435	15,922

IRON	Long Tons Iron Pellets Produced	Long Tons Iron Pellets Sold	Net Sales[2]	Operating Profit (Loss)[3]
1972	839,520	876,664	$ 13,412	$ 2,739
1973	814,796	813,405	13,320	1,593
1974	563,457	567,278	11,468	(2,686)
1975	756,133	779,009	27,410	9,901
1976	670,206	604,964	21,395	4,706

COAL	Tons Produced Coal Sold	Tons Purchased Coal Sold	Net Sales	Operating Profit (Loss)[3]
1972	5,782,672	6,939,466	$122,225	$ 2,534
1973	7,871,603	5,159,419	153,117	9,058
1974	8,924,342	4,639,264	357,009	54,490
1975	10,037,405	5,530,353	506,099	94,495
1976	10,457,336	5,034,598	456,037	44,549

OIL & GAS[4]	MCF Gas Sold	Bbls Oil & Gas Liquids Sold	Net Sales	Operating Profit (Loss)[3]
1972	24,687,000	2,096,300	$ 6,183	$ 1,110
1973	24,644,000	1,988,500	10,782	3,560
1974	22,095,000	1,309,600	14,050	4,584
1975	18,207,000	945,600	19,017	5,991
1976	15,909,000	1,008,600	25,214	10,884

OTHER	Net Sales	Operating Profit (Loss)[3]
1972	$ -0-	$ -0-
1973	-0-	-0-
1974	420	(713)
1975	782	1,008[5]
1976	1,368	(428)

1. Includes 11,996 tons in 1973 and 8,072 tons in 1974 derived from purchased ore.
2. Net Sales includes by-products.
3. Defined, in accordance with Statement No. 14 of the Financial Accounting Standards Board, as Net Sales plus/minus all items of income/expense directly associated with the line of business. Income taxes, interest, exploration and that portion of corporate overhead expense not product-associated were not included.
4. Because of higher effective tax rates, oil & gas does not contribute as heavily to the Corporation's Net Income After Taxes as it does to Operating Profits.
5. Includes non-recurring adjustment to income.

OPERATING PROFIT
(millions)

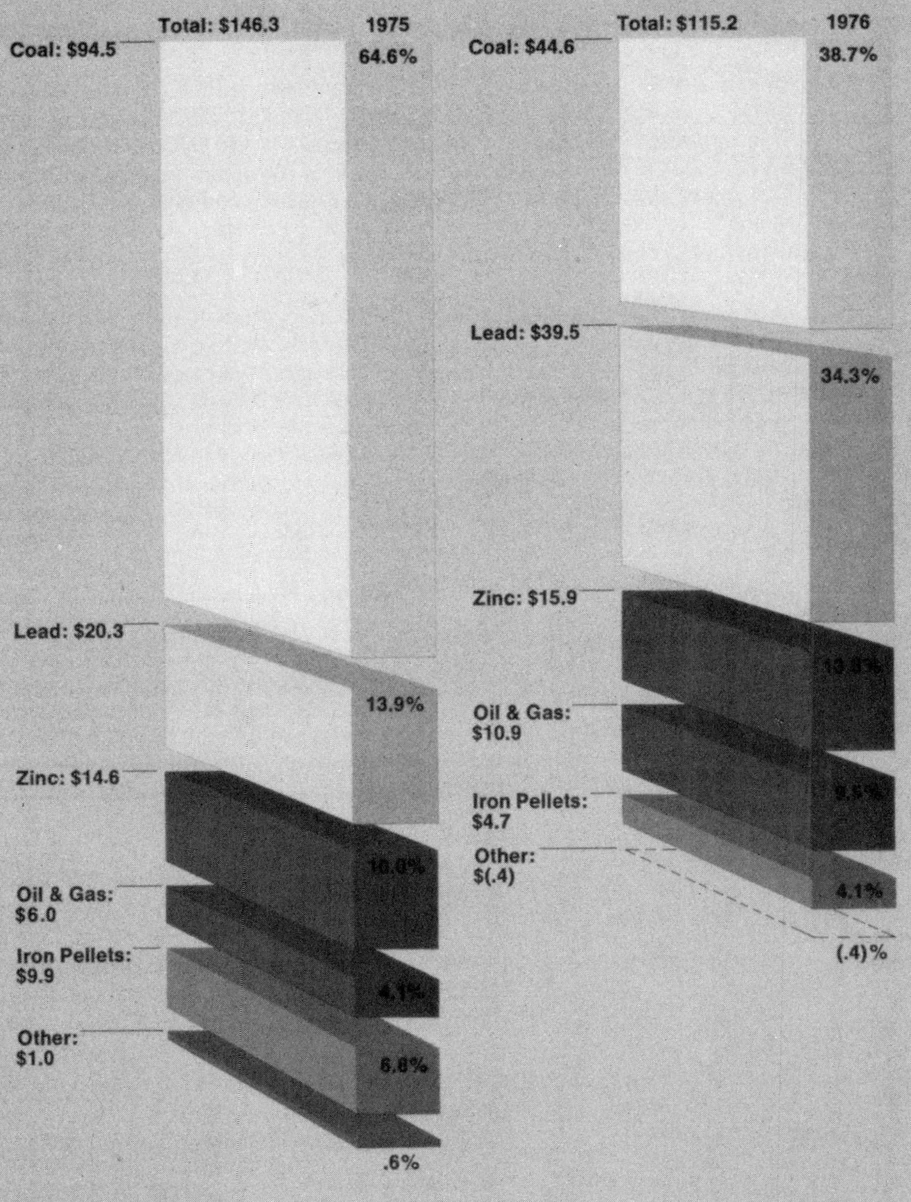

For the five years ended December 31, 1976	1976	1976 vs 1975 Increase (Decrease)	1975*	1975 vs 1974 Increase (Decrease)	1974*†	1973*†	1972*†
			(In thousands except per share data)				
Net Sales	**$778,331**	$ 15,686	$762,645	$ 50,749	$711,896	$407,485	$327,267
Costs and Expenses:							
Cost of sales	**611,759**	39,940	571,819	52,624	519,195	320,501	265,686
Depletion, depreciation and amortization	**38,391**	5,815	32,576	6,881	25,695	18,595	13,364
Administrative and selling	**21,246**	2,815	18,431	2,973	15,458	11,042	9,850
Research	**3,049**	(231)	3,280	131	3,149	1,954	1,306
Exploration	**5,869**	2,133	3,736	1,416	2,320	2,336	2,246
Interest	**5,151**	1,512	3,639	(971)	4,610	3,933	3,028
Amortization of goodwill	**1,552**	50	1,502	(97)	1,599	1,039	735
Total Costs and Expenses	**687,017**	52,034	634,983	62,957	572,026	359,400	296,215
Income From Operations	**91,314**	(36,348)	127,662	(12,208)	139,870	48,085	31,052
Other Income:							
Dividends from unconsolidated subsidiaries	**7,952**	5,952	2,000	2,000	—	4,697	4,174
Gain on sale of assets	—	(6,504)	6,504	6,504	—	—	—
Interest, royalties, etc.	**8,244**	(38)	8,282	1,958	6,324	5,025	3,360
Income Before Income Taxes and Extraordinary Items	**107,510**	(36,938)	144,448	(1,746)	146,194	57,807	38,586
Income Taxes (A)	**38,762**	(16,501)	55,263	2,674	52,589	19,654	12,122
Income Before Extraordinary Items	**68,748**	(20,437)	89,185	(4,420)	93,605	38,153	26,464
Extraordinary Items (net of related income taxes)	—	—	—	—	—	—	1,229
Net Income	**$ 68,748**	$(20,437)	$ 89,185	$ (4,420)	$ 93,605	$ 38,153	$ 27,693
Per Share of Common Stock:							
Income before extraordinary items	**$3.25**		$4.23		$4.44	$1.84	$1.27
Net income	**$3.25**		$4.23		$4.44	$1.84	$1.33
Cash dividends	**$1.27½**		$1.17½		$ .97½	$ .76¼	$ .75
Average Number of Shares of Common Stock Outstanding	**21,173**		21,000		21,068	20,776	20,766

(A) Income Taxes:
A reconciliation between the statutory Federal income tax rate of 48% and the Corporation's income taxes follows:

	1976	1975	1974	1973	1972
48% of income before income taxes	**$ 51,605**	$ 69,335	$ 70,173	$ 27,747	$ 18,521
Statutory depletion	**(16,013)**	(17,003)	(16,223)	(5,842)	(4,240)
Investment tax credits	**(3,819)**	(2,953)	(2,117)	(1,969)	(1,467)
DISC	**3,456**	(622)	(1,798)	(577)	(459)
State income taxes	**3,089**	2,867	1,445	545	507
Other-net	**444**	3,639	1,109	(250)	(740)
Income taxes	**$ 38,762**	$ 55,263	$ 52,589	$ 19,654	$ 12,122
Effective income tax rate	**36%**	38%	36%	34%	31%

*†Not covered by Auditors' Opinion. *Restated for pooling-of-interests.*
Pages 21, 23 and 25 to 30 are an integral part of these financial statements.

Sales

Sales in 1976 increased 2% over the 1975 level. The 1976 mix, however, was somewhat different from the previous year, as coal declined 9.9% (from $506.1 million to $456.0 million) on lower prices while metals increased 25.1% (from $237.5 million to $297.1 million) due, principally, to improved lead and zinc volumes and to a higher lead price. Lead sales volume increased from 182,340 tons to 237,177 tons while zinc increased from 137,009 tons to 186,431 tons. Zinc prices, however, were lower than the 1975 level and iron pellet volume was down from the prior year. Oil sales increased by $6.2 million or 33% over 1975.

1975's sales were 7.1% over those of 1974. Substantially higher coal sales more than offset a significant decline experienced in metals. Coal sales increased from $357.0 million to $506.1 million as metals dropped from $340.8 million to $237.5 million. Coal sales reflected higher prices ($33.00 per ton versus $26.00 per ton) and a 14.8% or 2.0 million ton volume increase over 1974 while metal sales declined due to lower sales volume of lead (down 99,084 tons or 35.2%) and zinc (down 108,594 tons or 44.2%) and a lower lead sales price. Iron sales increased from $11.5 million to $27.4 million on substantial volume and price increases.

Net Sales—Product Line
($ millions)

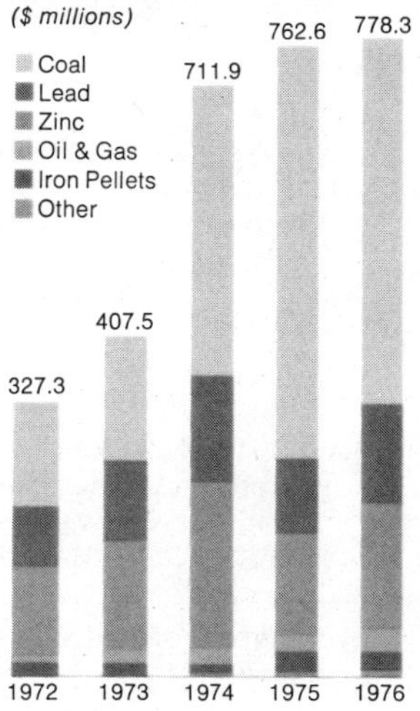

Costs and Expenses

Cost of sales in 1976 increased by 7.0% over the 1975 level due, principally, to lead and zinc. While unit costs of sales of lead and zinc decreased as a result of improved volume, the greater volume, itself, caused total cost of sales to increase. Coal unit production costs increased due to inflation but were offset by lower purchased coal costs.

In 1975 cost of sales rose 10.1% from the previous year. Unit cost increases occurred in coal as a late 1974 labor settlement impacted costs for a full year in 1975 and occurred in metals as very weak lead and zinc demand resulted in production cutbacks and correspondingly high unit costs. Additionally, energy costs were up 84% for lead and 145% for zinc over the 1974 levels.

Depreciation, depletion, and amortization have risen in the 1974-1976 period as capital spending has increased. Capital spending has been concentrated in the areas of expanding and modernizing coal operations and in oil and gas exploration and development.

Increased administrative and selling expenses reflect both inflation and the increased scope and complexity of the Corporation's operations.

Exploration cost increases correspond with the Corporation's expanded mineral exploration program.

Interest expenses increased from $3.6 million in 1975 to $5.2 million in 1976 principally due to a higher level of short term borrowing. Average short term borrowings increased from $8.2 million in 1975 to $26.1 million in 1976.

Operating Profit—Product Line
($ millions)

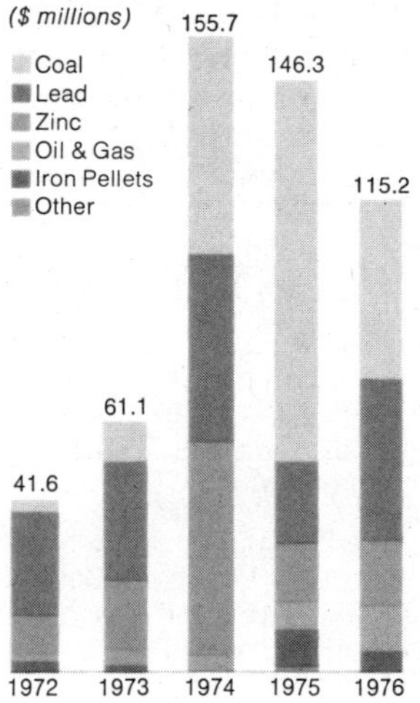

Other Income

Dividends from the Corporation's South American subsidiaries increased from $2,000,000 in 1975 to $7,952,000 in 1976 reflecting, in large measure, a return to profitability of the Corporation's subsidiaries in Argentina. No dividends were received in 1974.

The 1975 gain on sale of assets includes $5,846,000 from the sale by CanDel Ltd. of its Athabasca and Saskatchewan properties. No major assets were sold in 1976 or 1974.

STATEMENT OF CONSOLIDATED FINANCIAL POSITION

St. Joe Minerals Corporation and Consolidated Subsidiaries

December 31, 1976 and 1975	1976 (In thousands)	1975*
Current Assets:		
Cash and marketable securities	**$ 44,623**	$ 45,683
Trade accounts receivable	**85,745**	81,035
Inventories	**80,950**	74,779
Prepaid expenses and other current assets	**17,834**	12,295
Total current assets	**229,152**	213,792
Current Liabilities:		
Notes payable	**30,139**	10,401
Long-term debt—current portion	**8,491**	7,054
Accounts payable	**74,277**	64,204
Accrued income taxes	**16,592**	25,016
Other accrued liabilities	**8,171**	6,567
Total current liabilities	**137,670**	113,242
Working Capital	**91,482**	100,550
Noncurrent Assets:		
Investments	**4,878**	4,849
Property—net	**382,301**	319,118
Deferred mineral exploration	**10,835**	6,237
Goodwill	**27,190**	28,405
Deferred charges and other assets	**4,972**	5,052
Total noncurrent assets	**430,176**	363,661
Total Assets Less Current Liabilities	**521,658**	464,211
Noncurrent Liabilities:		
Long-term debt—less current portion	**43,055**	38,467
Deferred income taxes	**46,490**	39,057
Liability for employee benefits	**5,805**	3,918
Minority interest	**10,535**	10,267
Total noncurrent liabilities	**105,885**	91,709
Excess of Assets Over Liabilities	**$415,773**	$372,502

Shareholders' Equity:

Preferred stock, par value $50 per share, 1,000,000 shares authorized; none issued

Common stock, par value $10 per share:

	Shares 1976	Shares 1975	1976	1975*
Authorized	**25,000,000**	25,000,000		
Issued	**22,165,872**	22,165,872	**$221,659**	$221,659
In Treasury—at cost	**959,572**	1,037,941	**(10,628)**	(11,496)
Outstanding	**21,206,300**	21,127,931		
Other capital			**249**	—
Retained earnings			**204,493**	162,339
Total Shareholders' Equity			**$415,773**	$372,502

**Restated for pooling-of-interests.*
Pages 21, 23 and 25 to 30 are an integral part of these financial statements.

Marketable Securities
Marketable securities are stated at cost which approximates market.

Inventories
Inventories which are stated at the lower of cost (principally LIFO) or market comprise the following:

	1976	1975
	(In thousands)	
Finished metals	**$ 26,591**	$ 12,154
Metals in process and concentrates	**14,809**	25,969
Coal	**7,838**	7,295
Raw materials and supplies	**31,712**	29,361
Total	**$ 80,950**	$ 74,779

The current cost of LIFO inventories at December 31, 1976 and 1975 exceeds the related LIFO values by $33,830,000 and $33,840,000, respectively.

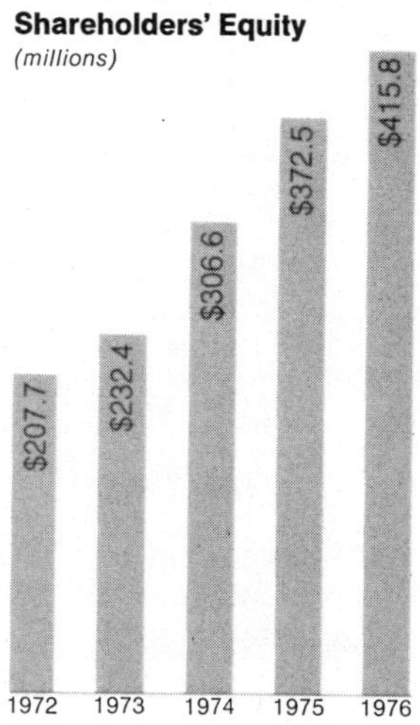

Property
Property (at cost) comprises the following:

	1976	1975
	(In thousands)	
Mining properties and mineral rights	**$ 13,526**	$ 12,580
Mine development	**30,135**	28,831
Oil and gas properties, including exploration and development thereon	**116,415**	83,840
Land, buildings, plant and equipment	**458,141**	393,568
Total	**618,217**	518,819
Less accumulated depletion, depreciation and amortization	**(235,916)**	(199,701)
Property—net	**$382,301**	$319,118

Foreign Operations
The accompanying financial statements for 1976 and 1975 include total assets of $99,854,000 and $83,145,000 and net sales of $21,413,000 and $18,146,000, respectively, attributable to consolidated foreign operations, (principally CanDel Oil Ltd.). Exchange gains and losses are not significant and are included in net income.

The Corporation's subsidiaries operating in Argentina (Compania Minera Aguilar, S.A.) and Peru (Compania Minerales Santander, Inc.) are carried in investments at cost or less, and are excluded from the consolidated financial statements primarily because of unsettled economic conditions and currency exchange restrictions. Dividends from such subsidiaries are recognized in income as they are remitted to the Corporation.

STATEMENT OF CHANGES IN CONSOLIDATED FINANCIAL POSITION

St. Joe Minerals Corporation and Consolidated Subsidiaries

For the years ended December 31, 1976 and 1975	**1976**	1975*
	(In thousands)	
Funds Provided:		
Operations:		
Net income	**$ 68,748**	$ 89,185
Add items not requiring working capital:		
Depletion, depreciation and amortization	**38,391**	32,576
Deferred income taxes	**7,433**	8,876
Amortization of goodwill	**1,552**	1,502
Other	**268**	497
Total From Operations	**116,392**	132,636
Proceeds from long-term debt	**13,704**	6,143
Proceeds from stock options exercised	**1,117**	737
Disposals of property	**2,740**	8,250
Total Funds Provided	**133,953**	147,766
Funds Applied:		
Cash dividends	**26,594**	23,979
Additions to property	**96,487**	91,718
Property of companies acquired	**7,827**	—
Goodwill arising from acquisitions	**337**	269
Reduction of long-term debt	**9,116**	6,580
Other—net	**2,660**	157
Total Funds Applied	**143,021**	122,703
Increase (Decrease) In Working Capital†	**$ (9,068)**	$ 25,063
Analysis of Increase (Decrease) in Working Capital:		
Cash and marketable securities	**$ (1,060)**	$(27,339)
Trade accounts receivable	**4,710**	10,513
Inventories	**6,171**	30,178
Prepaid expenses and other current assets	**5,539**	1,195
Notes payable	**(19,738)**	(6,935)
Long-term debt—current portion	**(1,437)**	1,982
Accounts payable	**(10,073)**	(837)
Accrued income taxes	**8,424**	16,238
Other accrued liabilities	**(1,604)**	68
Increase (Decrease) in Working Capital	**$ (9,068)**	$ 25,063

†The net assets of companies acquired in 1976 included a working capital deficit of $6,682,000.
**Restated for pooling-of-interests.*
Pages 21, 23 and 25 to 30 are an integral part of these financial statements.

FINANCING

Short-Term Debt (Notes Payable)
Information relating to the Corporation's short-term borrowings in 1976 and 1975 follows:

	1976	1975
	(In thousands)	
Balance at end of year	**$30,139**	$10,401
Maximum amount of short-term borrowings outstanding at any month end during the year	**38,502**	16,018
Average short-term borrowings outstanding during the year	**26,141**	8,221
Weighted average interest rate on average short-term borrowings during the year (a)	**6.7%**	8.8%
Weighted average interest rate on short-term borrowings at end of year	**5.9%**	7.6%

(a) Calculated by dividing average short-term borrowings outstanding during the year by related interest expense.

The Corporation has informal arrangements with various banks to maintain average cash balances of approximately 10% of its unused lines of credit. At December 31, 1976 and 1975 such unused lines of credit aggregated $50,000,000 and $38,000,000, respectively.

Long-term Debt
(millions)

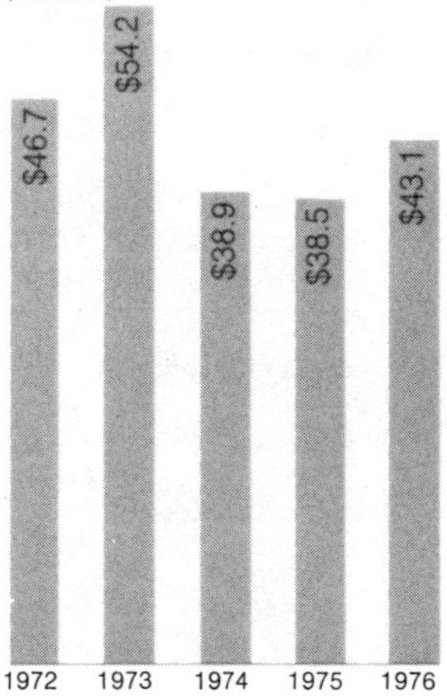

Long-Term Debt
Long-term debt at December 31, 1976 and 1975 was as follows:

	1976	1975
	(In thousands)	
4½% notes payable, due 1984	**$ 6,667**	$ 7,667
Pollution control financing (a)	**28,798**	22,704
Notes payable to bank in monthly installments of $92,000 through 1978 at ½% above the prime rate (6½% at December 31, 1976)	**1,558**	2,657
10% equipment notes payable through 1978	**547**	1,885
6% to 8% notes payable through 1980 to former stockholders of acquired companies	**5,946**	7,101
8% to 8½% notes payable through 1982	**5,517**	585
8½% mortgage note payable through 1983	**2,513**	2,922
Total	**51,546**	45,521
Less current portion	**(8,491)**	(7,054)
Long-term debt	**$43,055**	$38,467

(a) This liability represents the portion of the proceeds from pollution control revenue bonds expended for pollution control facilities at the Corporation's lead and zinc smelters. The Corporation has agreed to make sufficient payments to Trustees in order to pay all amounts due on the following bonds:

State Environmental Improvement Authority (Missouri) 5.75% bonds dated December 15, 1973, due December 15, 1998 .... $ 7,000,000

Beaver County (Pennsylvania) Industrial Development Authority 5.60% bonds dated December 1, 1972, due December 1, 1997 .... $22,500,000

The bonds are subject to optional redemption commencing in 1982 and mandatory redemption in 1988.

The amounts of long-term debt payable in each of the four years subsequent to December 31, 1977 are $6,633,000 in 1978, $2,130,000 in 1979, $1,597,000 in 1980 and $1,538,000 in 1981.

Interest expense relating to long-term debt was $3,145,000 and $2,914,000 for 1976 and 1975, respectively.

For the years ended December 31, 1976 and 1975	Common Stock $10 Par Value Per Share Issued	In Treasury At Cost	Other Capital (In thousands)	Retained Earnings	Total Shareholders' Equity
Balance, December 31, 1974, as previously reported	$105,973	$(12,087)	$5,786	$201,948	$301,620
Adjustment in connection with the pooling-of-interests with Tennessee Consolidated Coal Company (971,300* shares issued)	9,713		(98)	(4,676)	4,939
Balance, December 31, 1974, as adjusted	115,686	(12,087)	5,688	197,272	306,559
Net income				89,185	89,185
Cash dividends:					
St. Joe				(23,493)	(23,493)
TCC				(486)	(486)
Employee stock options exercised (53,381* shares issued from treasury)		591	146		737
Transfer to common stock in connection with two-for-one stock split	105,973		(5,834)	(100,139)	
Balance, December 31, 1975	221,659	(11,496)	—	162,339	372,502
Net income				68,748	68,748
Cash dividends:					
St. Joe				(26,400)	(26,400)
TCC				(194)	(194)
Employee stock options exercised (78,369 shares issued from treasury)		868	249		1,117
Balance, December 31, 1976	$221,659	$(10,628)	$ 249	$204,493	$415,773

**Reflects two-for-one stock split in 1975.*
Pages 21, 23 and 25 to 30 are an integral part of these financial statements.

OTHER FINANCIAL INFORMATION

Stock Split

In May 1975, the Corporation increased the authorized common stock from 12,500,000 shares to 25,000,000 shares and declared a two-for-one stock split.

Stock Option Plans

Under the Corporation's qualified Stock Option Incentive Plan adopted in 1967, key management employees may be granted options to purchase the Corporation's common stock at fair market value on date of grant. Options granted become exercisable one year after date of grant at the rate of 25% each year.

The Corporation also has a non-qualified Stock Option Plan, adopted in 1972, for its key management employees. Options granted under this Plan are exercisable at prices which may be less than fair market value but not less than par value at date of grant; these options expire ten years from date of grant.

A summary of shares issuable under options outstanding during 1976 and 1975 follows:

	1976	1975
	Number of Shares	
Options outstanding at beginning of year	**583,955**	435,680
Granted	**256,200**	206,800
Exercised	**(78,369)**	(53,381)
Cancelled or expired	**(15,280)**	(5,144)
Options outstanding at end of year	**746,506**	583,955

Shares under option at December 31, 1976 are exercisable at prices of $13.00 to $38.63 per share.

The number of shares reserved for the granting of additional options under all plans amounted to 306,824 at December 31, 1976.

The above information for 1975 has been revised to reflect the two-for-one stock split.

CanDel has an Employees' Stock Option Plan whereunder 200,000 shares (approximately equal to 5% of CanDel's oustanding shares) were reserved for purchase by its officers and employees at fair market value on date of grant. As of December 31, 1976, options were outstanding to purchase 118,700 shares at prices of $5.75 to $12.50 per share. Options to purchase 6,850 shares were exercised in 1976. No options were exercised in 1975.

Acquisitions

During 1976 and 1975, in transactions accounted for as poolings-of-interests, the Corporation acquired capital stock of the following companies in exchange for its common stock:

Year	Company	Common Shares Issued
1976	Tennessee Consolidated Coal Company ("TCC")	971,300
1975	Peerless Eagle Coal Company ("Peerless")	284,762

Shareholders' Equity Per Share

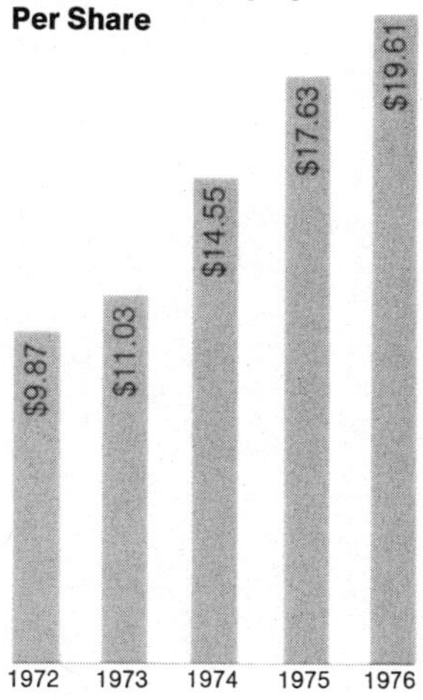

Return on Shareholders' Equity*

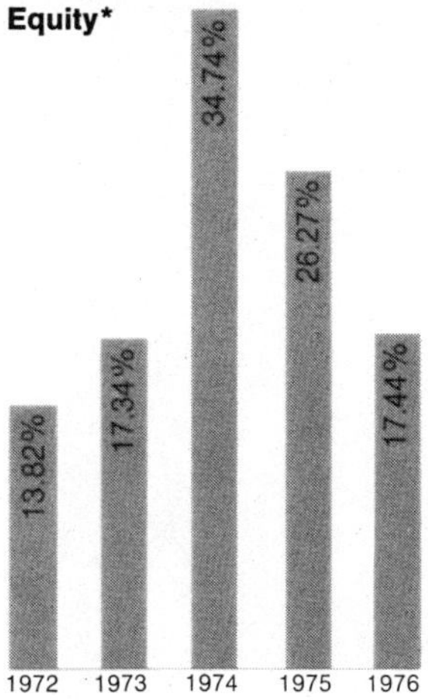

*Based on net income divided by average shareholders' equity.

Dividends Per Share

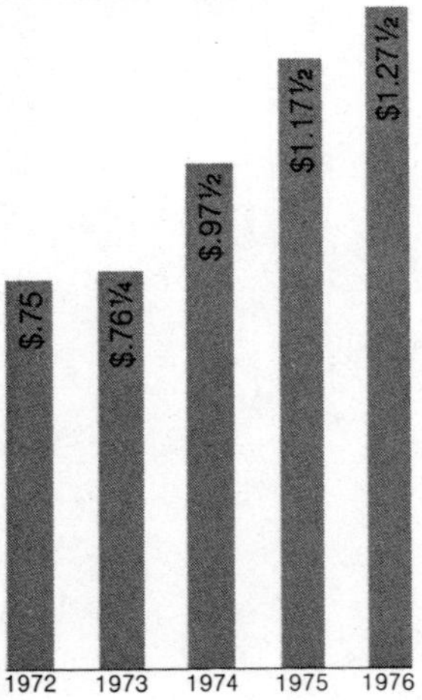

Ten percent of the shares issued in the pooling-of-interests with TCC have been placed in escrow pending resolution of certain contingencies. The accompanying financial statements for the year ended December 31, 1975 have been restated to give effect to the pooling-of-interests with TCC. A reconciliation of net sales and net income previously reported by the Corporation to those appearing in the statement of consolidated income for the year ended December 31, 1975 follows:

	Net Sales	Net Income
	(In thousands)	
As previously reported	$729,380	$81,667
Effect of pooling-of-interests	33,265	7,518
As restated	$762,645	$89,185

The results of operations for TCC in the above reconciliation have been adjusted to give effect to adjustments made to conform TCC's accounting methods to those of the Corporation with respect to accounting for coal mine development and supply inventory costs. The effect of such accounting changes was to decrease excess of assets over liabilities by $1,056,000 at December 31, 1975 and to decrease net income for the year then ended by $127,000.

The pooling-of-interests with TCC increased 1976 net income by approximately $4,600,000 ($.22 per share) for the period in such year prior to acquisition. The pooling-of-interests with Peerless increased 1975 net income by approximately $2,500,000 ($.12 per share) for the period in such year prior to acquisition.

Pension and Profit Sharing Plans

Pension expense for all plans, including amortization of prior service costs over periods of five to thirty years, was $8,532,000 in 1976 and $7,583,000 in 1975. Aggregate unfunded prior service pension costs of the companies was $30,058,000 at December 31, 1976. The actuarially computed values of vested benefits of certain plans exceeded the total market value of the related pension funds by $19,896,000 at December 31, 1976. The Corporation does not anticipate any significant increase in the required contributions to the pension funds as a result of the Employee Retirement Income Security Act of 1974.

The Corporation has a deferred profit sharing plan for salaried employees. Annual contributions to the plan are based on a formula involving consolidated net income and aggregate salaries of eligible employees. Profit sharing expense was $1,913,000 in 1976 and $1,781,000 in 1975.

Minority Interest

Minority interest includes $8,000,000 of 8% cumulative preferred stock of Martin County Coal Corporation, a subsidiary of A.T. Massey Coal Company, Inc. Dividends are paid quarterly and are deducted from other income.

Income Taxes
Income taxes for the years ended December 31, 1976 and 1975 are comprised of:

	1976	1975
	(In thousands)	
Current:		
Federal	**$21,817**	$39,977
Investment tax credits	**(3,819)**	(2,953)
Foreign	**7,390**	5,466
State	**5,941**	5,513
Total current	**31,329**	48,003
Deferred:		
Federal	**7,268**	6,227
Foreign	**165**	1,033
Total deferred	**7,433**	7,260
Total	**$38,762**	$55,263

Deferred income taxes for the years ended December 31, 1976 and 1975 relate to the following timing differences:

	1976	1975
	(In thousands)	
Accelerated depreciation	**$ 3,257**	$ 2,987
Write-off of exploration & development as incurred	**2,938**	6,041
DISC	**3,354**	(1,449)
Other—net	**(2,116)**	(319)
Total	**$ 7,433**	$ 7,260

Closing Year-end Stock Prices*

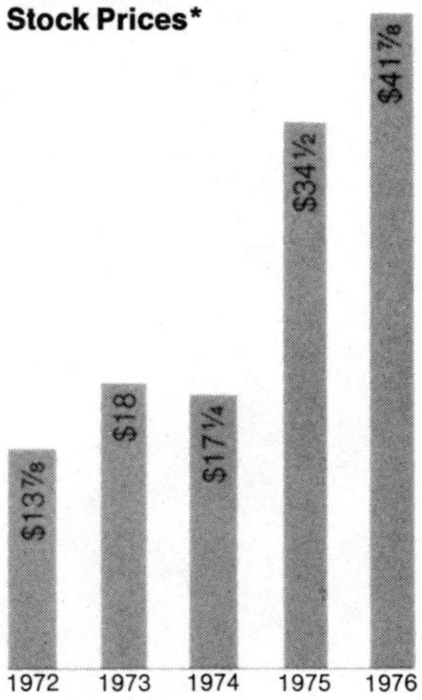

*Adjusted for the two-for-one stock split paid July 15, 1975.

Commitments and Contingent Liabilities
The Corporation is contingently liable as guarantor of leases to Quemetco, Inc. (a company sold in 1972), under which rental payments approximate $315,000 per year for the initial lease term ending in 1997. RSR Corporation, the purchaser of Quemetco, has agreed to indemnify the Corporation against any loss which may be suffered as a result of such contingent liability.

In connection with the acquisition of certain foreign oil exploratory rights, the Corporation is contingently liable for future payments aggregating $6,667,000.

In connection with the acquisition of a joint interest in certain mineral properties, the Corporation is obligated to spend over a period of three years $5,000,000 for exploration and development of such properties.

In October 1976 the Corporation announced an agreement in principle to acquire Coquina Oil Corporation in exchange for approximately 1,100,000 shares of the Corporation's common stock. The Merger was subsequently approved in January 1977 by the Board of Trustees of the Corporation and the Board of Directors of Coquina. Consummation of the Merger is subject to the fulfillment of certain conditions, including approval by the stockholders of Coquina.

Subsequent Event

In January 1977 Massey signed an agreement with Austromineral G.m.b.h. ("Austromineral"), a subsidiary of Voest Alpine A.G., which gives Austromineral an option to buy either 50% of the capital stock of three Massey subsidiaries for $22,000,000 in cash, or all the capital stock for $45,000,000 in cash. If Austromineral elects to purchase only 50%, Massey would continue to operate these subsidiaries. The agreement expires August 1, 1977.

Quarterly Financial Data (Unaudited)

Summarized quarterly financial data for 1976 and 1975 follows:

	Period	Net Sales	Gross Profit	Net Income	Net Income Per Common Share*	Stock Prices*† High	Stock Prices*† Low
		(In thousands)					
1976:	1st Qtr	$176,142	$ 41,394	$17,642	$ .83	45¾	33½
	2nd Qtr	201,410	42,540	17,966	.85	50	40⅜
	3rd Qtr	193,699	40,195	14,831	.70	49	39⅛
	4th Qtr	207,080	42,443	18,309	.87	43⅛	33½
	Year	$778,331	$166,572	$68,748	$3.25	50	33½
1975:	1st Qtr	$189,928	$ 62,568	$30,108	$1.43	24½	17⅛
	2nd Qtr	192,612	42,652	21,102	1.00	34⅛	23⅛
	3rd Qtr	175,386	40,617	17,968	.85	37⅜	27¾
	4th Qtr	204,719	44,989	20,007	.95	39¼	30¼
	Year	$762,645	$190,826	$89,185	$4.23	39¼	17⅛

**First two quarters of 1975 have been adjusted for the two-for-one stock split paid in July 1975.*
†Stock prices as reported on the composite tape by The Wall Street Journal.

During the fourth quarter of 1976 the Corporation received dividend income of $4,952,000 from its South American subsidiaries. In addition, the Corporation decided that it no longer intended to postpone indefinitely the remittance of earnings from its Domestic International Sales Corporation ("DISC") because, in the opinion of management, the benefits of maintaining a DISC have been severely restricted by tax legislation. As a result, the Corporation provided deferred Federal income taxes of approximately $3,456,000 on the accumulated earnings of the DISC as of December 31, 1976. However, the effective Federal income tax rate for the fourth quarter was approximately the same as for the entire year because of other items (principally a tax benefit resulting from the contribution of property to the State of Missouri for use as a public park) which approximated the Federal income taxes provided for the DISC.

SUMMARY OF SIGNIFICANT ACCOUNTING POLICIES

Principles of Consolidation
The consolidated financial statements include the accounts of the Corporation and all subsidiaries except those operating in South America (see foreign operations). All significant intercompany transactions and balances are eliminated.

The statements of consolidated income for the three years ended December 31, 1974 are presented for information only, and, as such, do not include all note information and related statements of changes in consolidated financial position for such years.

Exploration and Development
Oil and Gas
Costs related to the exploration and development of oil and gas properties are capitalized by certain broad areas of interest under the full-cost method of accounting. Such costs include land and lease acquisition costs, geological and geophysical expenditures, rentals on undeveloped properties and costs of drilling productive and non-productive wells. Pending the discovery of commercial reserves in any area of interest, exploration and development expenditures are amortized generally over five years. When commercial reserves are discovered, the unamortized expenditures are depleted on the unit-of-production method based upon estimated recoverable reserves in the area of interest; when areas of interest are abandoned, the unamortized expenditures are charged to expense.

Coal
Development costs of specific coal properties when expected to be significant are capitalized in mine development and depleted on the unit-of-production method. Significant lease acquisition costs are capitalized in mining properties and mineral rights and depleted on the unit-of-production method.

Metals
Costs incurred for exploration of metals are deferred pending decision as to success or abandonment of the projects. If ore bodies are discovered, exploration costs are capitalized as mining properties and mineral rights and subsequently depleted on the unit-of-production method; the costs of exploration projects abandoned are charged to expense. Development expenditures to bring new mineral properties into production, comprising substantially all surface mine development expenditures and initial underground installations, are capitalized and charged to expense on the straight-line method over 20 years. Subsequent maintenance and underground development expenditures are charged to expense.

Depreciation
Buildings, plant and equipment are depreciated essentially by the straight-line method over estimated lives (ranging from 3 to 50 years). Upon disposal of depreciable assets, their cost and related accumulated depreciation are cleared from the accounts and the resultant profit or loss is included in net income. Maintenance and repair expenditures are charged to expense as incurred; major renewals and betterments are capitalized.

Goodwill
Goodwill arising from acquisitions is amortized over appropriate periods not exceeding 40 years.

Pension Plan Costs
The Corporation and its subsidiaries have several pension plans (principally non-contributory) covering substantially all of their employees. Pension costs consist of normal costs and amortization of prior service costs over periods ranging from 5 to 30 years and are generally funded as accrued.

Income Taxes
Deferred Federal and Canadian income taxes are provided for the tax effects of items reported in different periods for financial and income tax reporting purposes relating principally to accelerated depreciation, and write-off for tax purposes of mineral and oil and gas exploration and development expenditures as incurred.

Deferred Federal income taxes ($3,456,000) on the accumulated earnings of a Domestic International Sales Corporation ("DISC") ($7,200,000 at December 31, 1976) were provided in 1976, since the Corporation no longer intends to postpone indefinitely the remittance of such earnings. In 1975 deferred Federal income taxes were provided only on the portion of the income of the DISC considered distributable for income tax purposes.

Deferred Federal income taxes on the accumulated undistributed earnings ($20,526,000 at December 31, 1976) of consolidated foreign subsidiaries are not provided because it is expected that such earnings will be reinvested by such subsidiaries.

Investment tax credits are applied as reductions of Federal income tax provisions in years in which they arise.

Net Income Per Share
Net income per share is computed based on the average number of shares of common stock outstanding during each year after giving retroactive effect to the two-for-one stock split in 1975. The dilution in net income per share which would arise from the assumed exercise of stock options is not material.

Audit Committee
The Corporation's audit committee, which is composed of four outside members of the Board of Trustees, meets a minimum of four times a year. The Committee has unrestricted access to the Corporation's independent auditors.

Replacement Cost (Unaudited)
In compliance with rules and regulations of the Securities and Exchange Commission, the Corporation has calculated information related to the replacement cost of its non-mineral resource productive facilities and the depreciation charges that would correspond with such replacement costs. Inventories and cost of sales have also been calculated on a replacement cost basis. The details of this information are available in the Corporation's 1976 Annual Report on Form 10-K to the SEC.

The Corporation is presently engaged in an effort to develop a meaningful method whereby replacement costs of mineral resource productive facilities may be calculated. This is a new theoretical endeavor in accounting which could produce information that could be helpful to shareholders.

The Corporation establishes the sales prices of its products primarily on the basis of competitive market conditions, rather than directly on costs incurred. Consequently, the impact on the Corporation's earnings of increased costs arising from inflation is not readily determinable.

AUDITORS' OPINION

HASKINS & SELLS
CERTIFIED PUBLIC ACCOUNTANTS

TWO BROADWAY
NEW YORK, NEW YORK 10004

The Shareholders of St. Joe Minerals Corporation:

We have examined the statement of consolidated financial position of St. Joe Minerals Corporation and consolidated subsidiaries as of December 31, 1976 and 1975 and the related statements of income, shareholders' equity and changes in financial position for the years then ended. Our examination was made in accordance with generally accepted auditing standards and, accordingly, included such tests of the accounting records and such other auditing procedures as we considered necessary in the circumstances. We did not examine the financial statements of two consolidated subsidiaries: CanDel Oil Ltd. and subsidiaries for 1976 and 1975 and Tennessee Consolidated Coal Company and subsidiaries for 1975, which statements reflect total assets constituting 12% and 15%, and revenues constituting 3% and 7%, of the respective consolidated totals for 1976 and 1975. These statements were examined by other auditors whose reports thereon have been furnished to us and our opinion expressed herein, insofar as it relates to the amounts included for the two aforementioned consolidated subsidiaries, is based solely upon the reports of the other auditors.

In our opinion, based upon our examination and the reports of other auditors, the aforementioned consolidated financial statements present fairly the financial position of St. Joe Minerals Corporation and consolidated subsidiaries at December 31, 1976 and 1975 and the results of their operations and the changes in their financial position for the years then ended, in conformity with generally accepted accounting principles consistently applied during such years and on a basis consistent with that of the preceding year (1974).

Haskins + Sells

February 4, 1977

ST. JOE MINERALS CORPORATION

Incorporated March 25, 1864, under the laws of the State of New York.
Corporate Office:
250 Park Avenue,
New York, N.Y. 10017
(212) 953-5000

BOARD OF TRUSTEES

D. Broward Craig*
Executive Vice President

Bernard F. Desloge†
Vice President
Killark Electric Manufacturing Co.
Electrical fittings

John C. Duncan*
President and
Chief Executive Officer

Warren E. Fenzi*
President
Phelps Dodge Corporation
Metal mining

William R. Grant*†
Vice Chairman
Smith Barney, Harris Upham & Co., Inc.
Investment banking

Arthur Howe, Jr.†
Educational Consultant

Wing L. Lew
Consultant

Robert V. Lindsay†
Executive Vice President
Morgan Guaranty Trust
Company of New York
Commercial banking

Plato Malozemoff*
Chairman and
Chief Executive Officer
Newmont Mining Corporation
Metal mining

E. Morgan Massey
President and
Chief Executive Officer
A. T. Massey Coal Co., Inc.

Joseph V. McKee, Jr.
Chairman & President
National Union Electric Company
Electrical appliances

Smiley Raborn, Jr.
President and
Chief Executive Officer
CanDel Oil Ltd.

Lawrason Riggs III
Former Chairman

L. Chase Ritts, Jr.
Vice President—Petroleum

CORPORATE OFFICERS

John C. Duncan
President and
Chief Executive Officer

D. Broward Craig
Executive Vice President

James L. Broadhead
Vice President—Development
and Secretary

Charles R. Carlisle
Vice President

R. V. Cronin
Vice President—Finance

John W. Hanselman
Vice President—Administration

Peter B. Nalle
Vice President—Mining

L. Chase Ritts, Jr.
Vice President—Petroleum

Joseph G. Sevick
Vice President—Smelting

Leroy K. Wheelock
Vice President

John A. Wright
Vice President—Sales

Charles E. Barnett
General Counsel

Harold T. Read
Comptroller

Robert A. Sherman
Treasurer

John T. Leyden
Assistant Treasurer and
Director of Taxes

*Member of Executive Committee
†Member of Auditing Committee

DIVISION MANAGERS

Mines

Lawrence W. Casteel, Viburnum, Missouri
Marvin E. Lane, Balmat, New York

Smelters

Charles D. Henderson, Monaca, Pennsylvania
John W. Sherman, Herculaneum, Missouri

CORPORATE EXPLORATION AND DEVELOPMENT

Thomas N. Walthier
Director—Corporate Exploration
Wayne K. Wallace
U.S. Exploration Manager,
Tucson, Arizona
Merwin Bernstein
International Exploration Manager,
Tucson, Arizona
Richard L. Bullock
Director—Corporate Mine Research & Development

CORPORATE RESEARCH AND DEVELOPMENT

Gardner L. Brown
Director—Corporate Research
Michael V. Rose
Director—Commercial Development

CORPORATE COMMUNICATIONS AND SHAREHOLDER INFORMATION

Robert W. Peckham
Director of Corporate Communications

Copies of St. Joe's current Annual Report on Form 10-K to the Securities and Exchange Commission are available to shareholders upon written request to the Director of Corporate Communications, St. Joe Minerals Corporation, 250 Park Avenue, New York, N.Y. 10017

AFFILIATE AND SUBSIDIARY EXECUTIVES

Cia. Minera Aguilar, S.A.—Buenos Aires, Argentina
John E. Loser, Managing Director

Cia. Minerales Santander, Inc.—Lima, Peru
D. M. Wade, Vice President and General Manager

Meramec Mining Company—Sullivan, Missouri
Richard C. Harmon, General Superintendent

CanDel Oil Ltd.—Calgary, Canada
Smiley Raborn, Jr., President and Chief Executive Officer

Energy Research Corporation—Danbury, Connecticut
Bernard S. Baker, President

A. T. Massey Coal Co., Inc.—Richmond, Virginia
E. Morgan Massey, President and Chief Executive Officer

St. Joe Petroleum Corporation—New York, New York
L. Chase Ritts, Jr., President

Placer Service Corp.—New York, New York
William H. Breeding, President

St. Joseph Explorations Limited—Toronto, Canada
Robert M. Ginn, Vice President

Jododex Australia Pty. Ltd.—Sydney, Australia
Desmond F. O'Driscoll, Chairman

Mineracao Sao Jose Ltda.—Rio de Janeiro, Brazil
Jan D. Koene, Manager

St. Joe American Corporation—New York, New York
Thomas N. Walthier, President

Formet Technology Corporation—New York, New York
J. A. Young, President

Annual Meeting

The annual meeting of the Corporation will be held on May 9, 1977 at 10:30 A.M. at the Auditorium of the McGraw-Hill Building, 1221 Avenue of the Americas, New York, N.Y.

Stock Trading

The stock of St. Joe Minerals Corporation is traded on the New York, Midwest, Pacific Coast and Toronto stock exchanges. Its symbol is SJO.

Transfer Agents

Bankers Trust Company
Two Broadway, New York, N.Y. 10004

National Trust Company, Limited
21 King Street East
Toronto, Ontario M5C 1B3

Registrars

Bankers Trust Company
Two Broadway, New York, N.Y. 10004

Crown Trust Company
312 Bay Street
Toronto, Ontario M5H 2P4

Auditors

Haskins & Sells
Two Broadway, New York, N.Y. 10004

St. Joe Minerals Corporation is an equal opportunity employer.

Designed by Len Fury of Corporate Annual Reports, Inc./Major photography by Phil Marco

4

IC Industries, Inc.

Frank J. Allston

At the start of the management message during its 1977 annual meeting of shareholders, the narrator characterized IC Industries as "more than a railroad."

IC Industries, Inc., started in 1851 as a railroad and has grown into a $4-billion international, diversified company. Along the way, it developed a strong identity as a railroad, but railroad operations now produce only about a quarter of sales and revenues.

Today, IC Industries is much more than a railroad, and financial communications activities are geared at conveying the message of diversification through a coordinated program, utilizing a variety of media. The story of IC Industries' past 11 years is one of significantly altering its financial characteristics with substantial sales and earnings growth. In the words of IC Industries' current advertising campaign, it's the story of "Growth by Design."

The design was first conceived in 1963 when the Illinois Central Railroad's management perceived that government regulation and the capital- and labor-intensiveness inherent in the industry forecast a rocky road for a railroad transportation company. Thus was born Illinois Central Industries and the diversification program which was actually launched in 1965, but which really didn't hit its stride until later. In the meantime, in 1966, a new chief executive officer—William B. Johnson, a former railroad lawyer and the head of REA Express at the time—was brought in to oversee an accelerated diversification effort.

In Johnson's own words, "The decision to diversify was not from lack of faith in the essentiality of railroads. Rather, it was management's vision and conviction that there were growth opportunities in selected nontransportation areas. By pursuing these opportunities, we sought to improve the characteristics of our total company."

Although the Company did not have a clear-cut blueprint for diversification when the 1963 decision was made, the direction was clear and, in 1966, a set of objectives, called "Stage I," was established:

Frank J. Allston is Director, Financial Communications, for IC Industries, Inc.

1. To modernize the Illinois Central Railroad.
2. To complete a sound railroad merger.
3. To develop the valuable, long-held railroad real estate.
4. To diversify the business (by far the most important).

At the end of 1968, the diversification program of Illinois Central Industries received a major boost with the acquisition of Abex Corp., the former American Brake Shoe and Foundry Co. A diversified manufacturer and marketer of automotive products, railroad products, specialty castings, and fluid power components and systems, Abex substantially altered the mix of the business. For the first time, IC Industries was no longer solely in the railroad business.

Over the next four years, IC Industries assiduously pursued its diversification program, adding real estate, soft drink, mortgage banking, insurance, and savings and loan companies. In 1972, IC Industries acquired Midas International Corp., the renowned innovator in franchised automotive exhaust systems. In fewer than 10 years, IC Industries had expanded from its original midwestern railroad base to a truly diversified company with international interests. In the last year before the acquisition of Abex, 1967 sales and revenues were $300 million. With the addition of Abex, consolidated sales and revenues nearly doubled to $587 million in 1968, only 48 percent of which derived from railroad operations. Yet the Company was still classified as a railroad, carried a railroad price/earnings multiple in the stock market, and was followed by railroad securities analysts. Clearly, the Company had an identity problem.

In addition to the usual financial publications, IC Industries began to expand its financial program to include its first Fact File in 1972 and its first financial advertising in 1973.

Although its legal name was Illinois Central Industries, the Company was already known unofficially as IC Industries and, in May 1975, shareholders approved an official change in the corporation's name to the shortened form.

A new corporate identification program, complete with new corporate logo, was launched. Its thrust was to link the lesser known corporate name to the better known brand names such as Pepsi-Cola, Midas, and Abex. Corporate advertising in 1975 placed heavy emphasis on operating companies. (Five of these advertisements, covering a period of several years, are shown at the end of this chapter.) The 1975 annual report and the 1975 Fact File stressed the "five thrusts" which represented the diversified operations of IC Industries.

In August 1976, Johnson indicated that Stage I was essentially completed and, in a freewheeling interview with the *Wall Street Transcript,* he laid out the future course of IC Industries, building upon earlier stated objectives of continuing to place emphasis on commercial and consumer products. In the interview, Johnson detailed IC Industries' basic objectives for future diversification and growth:

1. To acquire a large, free-standing consumer products company, probably in food products.
2. To expand or dispose of operating companies in the IC Financial Services Group.
3. To merge or sell the Illinois Central Gulf Railroad.

These objectives came to be known as "Stage II." The year 1978 was the most significant in the Company's history, and there were important developments involving each Stage II objective.

First, in June, IC Industries announced a plan to acquire Pet Inc., a diversified food products and services company. Through a successful cash tender offer, IC Industries acquired 97 percent of Pet common stock in August. Later in the year, IC Industries acquired all of the outstanding Pet common stock, and the two companies were merged.

Meanwhile, agreement was reached to sell the two insurance subsidiaries and three smaller companies in the IC Financial Services Group. The sale of the insurance companies was consummated early in 1979, and sale of the other three companies was completed in April.

In June, 1978, IC Industries and the Southern Railway announced that joint studies would be conducted on the advisability and feasibility of Southern acquiring the Illinois Central Gulf Railroad. In February 1979, the two companies announced that talks had been terminated, despite agreement that there were substantial long-term benefits for both companies from a combination of the two railroads.

Subsequently, Johnson reiterated his belief that the ICG Railroad would inevitably be part of a future wave of railroad mergers, but that no talks had been held with other railroads regarding acquisition of the ICG. In the meantime, he repeated earlier statements that IC Industries was planning to continue to operate the railroad on an efficient and profitable basis.

Acquisition of Pet, a $1.2-billion company, substantially altered the balance of IC Industries operations, so that Consumer Products took over first place in sales. In 1978, Pet results were consolidated with IC Industries results only for the final five months of the year following acquisition. The major contributor to pretax income continued to be IC Commercial Products in 1978, and together, Consumer and Commercial Products contributed more than 85 percent of pretax income in 1978. (With Pet results for the full year, Commercial and Consumer Products accounted for 89 percent of pretax income.)

The new 1979 advertising campaign broke in *The Wall Street Journal* of February 12, emphasizing the Company's successful diversification, with 1978 earnings in excess of $5.20 per share (20 percent better than 1977), and the new tag line, "Growth by Design."

Economic prospects at the start of 1980 were still the subject of debate among economists, but as a result of its highly successful diversification program, IC Industries seemed in a better position to weather any possible downturn. Today IC Industries is a totally different company from that of 16 years ago. It provides substantially improved financial characteristics for its shareholders, and financial communications are oriented toward assuring that the investment community fully appreciates what IC Industries is—"more than a railroad."

Selections from the 1977 annual report are reprinted here. They include presentations about the Company's objectives, its plans for the future, and its posture on disclosure of financial information, as well as a special insert reporting the fourth quarter of the Company's year—something that many annual reports fail to do. Other publications aimed at stimulating investor interest are also shown: the quarterly report of September 1978, which uses a magazine format to provide easy-to-read summaries of the Company's overall operations and more detailed descriptions of particular segments of the business; and a four-page brochure designed to give potential investors and employees a basic idea of what IC Industries is all about. A Fact File from August 1979 helps shareholders and professionals by giving detailed descriptions (aided by charts) of each segment of the Company; by providing profiles of corporate managers; and by keeping the corporate history brief and putting it where most analysts want it—near the end of the booklet, along with the corporate data.

Our Midas Shops now serve customers we used to turn away.

For years Midas dealers looked around under people's cars, and found work for somebody else's repair service! When a Midas dealer spotted something like worn brakes or sagging shocks, all he could do was recommend somebody down the street. Midas used to sell only mufflers.

Now Midas dealers are holding on to those customers. Because, in addition to mufflers, many Midas Shops now offer shock absorber, brake and wheel alignment services.

Besides, with inflation and the energy shortage, people want their cars to last longer, run more efficiently. Midas-International Corp., an IC Industries company, is getting ready—with expanded automotive services coast-to-coast.

In the past few years, IC Industries has diversified into important growth markets. Railroad supply products, soft drinks, life insurance, real estate and more. They've all been carefully chosen to provide balanced sources for growth in sales and earnings.

IC Industries. One Illinois Center.
111 E. Wacker Dr., Chicago, Ill. 60601.

IC INDUSTRIES
The solid growth idea.
Consumer products, commercial products, real estate, financial services, transportation.

Our new name's in all the papers.

We used to be Illinois Central Industries.
Now we're IC Industries.
And it's about time. After all, Illinois Central is a railroad name. And we've been a lot more than that for years.

Since 1967, we've grown from a $300 million regional railroad to a $1.4 billion international multibusiness corporation.

In 1974, most of our earnings came from non-railroad businesses. In fact, the precise figure is 81%, excluding other income (charges) net.

Our Commercial Products Group, lead by Abex Corporation, earned nearly $50 million before taxes in 1974—primarily from sales of automotive and railroad products, castings, and hydraulics.

Our Real Estate Group, through developments such as Chicago's Illinois Center and LaSalle Properties in New Orleans, contributed nearly $14 million before taxes.

Our Consumer Products Group, including Midas-International and three soft drink companies—Pepsi-Cola General Bottlers, Bubble Up and Dad's Root Beer—returned pre-tax income of just under $13 million.

Our Financial Services Group, including Lincoln Liberty Life and Midwest Life Nebraska insurance companies, earned $4 million before taxes.

Our Transportation Group, the Illinois Central Gulf Railroad, contributed $18 million before taxes.

After provision for corporate charges, total IC Industries pre-tax income in 1974 was $92 million.

Our best ever.

So next time you look for IllCent in the stock listings, look for ICInds instead. Our name is finally catching up with us. For more information, write: IC Industries, One Illinois Center, 111 East Wacker Drive, Chicago, Illinois 60601.

New Stock Listing **ICInds.** New Ticker Symbol **ICX**

IC Industries

Diversified in five business groups:
Commercial Products, Consumer Products, Real Estate, Financial Services and Transportation.

The newest member of our family has a family of its own.

In 1894, the Helvetia Milk Company in Highland, Illinois introduced "Our Pet," a baby-size can of evaporated milk.

Today, that 5¢ can of milk has become Pet Incorporated, a billion dollar family of well-known food and food service products, and the newest member of our IC Industries family. It's quite an addition, with fiscal 1978 sales of $1.1 billion and pre-tax earnings of $57.4 million.

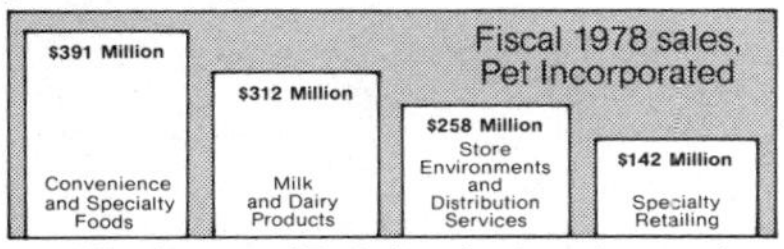

The largest of Pet's four business groups is Convenience and Specialty Foods. It includes Downyflake and Pet-Ritz frozen foods; Funsten Nuts, the world's largest independent processor of tree nuts; Whitman's Chocolates, the 136-year-old brand featuring the best-selling box of chocolates in the world, Whitman's Sampler; Old El Paso, the country's leading brand of Mexican food.

Laura Scudder's, the best-selling snack foods on the Pacific Coast, and Dentler-Facs snack foods in Texas; Musselman's fruit products; Gulf Belle and Orleans brands, the nation's leading processors of canned shrimp and oysters; Reese Finer Foods, a leading importer, manufacturer and distributor of gourmet and specialty food items; and Heartland Cereal products.

The Milk and Dairy Products Group markets Sego diet foods; a full line of Pet fresh dairy products in the Southeast; and of course, Pet Evaporated Milk.

The Store Environments and Distribution Services Group includes Hussmann, for years the world's leader in food store refrigerated display equipment, and now serving nearly every segment of the food distribution system. And Merchants Refrigerated Warehouses, offering 27 million cubic feet of freezer storage in 11 major markets.

Pet's Specialty Retailing and Consumer Service Group includes 312 Stuckey's stores on the nation's interstate highway system and Vendome and 905 party centers in the West and Midwest.

That's the Pet family. The newest member of the IC Industries family. This association marks the beginning of a significant change in the future direction of IC Industries.

We've been more than a railroad for ten years. Now, we're even more. Another billion more.

If you'd like to know about how we've grown, and how we're still growing, write: IC Industries, One Illinois Center, 111 East Wacker Drive, Chicago, Illinois 60601.

IC Industries

Diversified in five business groups: Commercial Products, Consumer Products, Real Estate, Financial Services and Transportation.

The growth of our non-railroad business has put us in glamorous company.

(Ten year sales growth 1968-1977.)

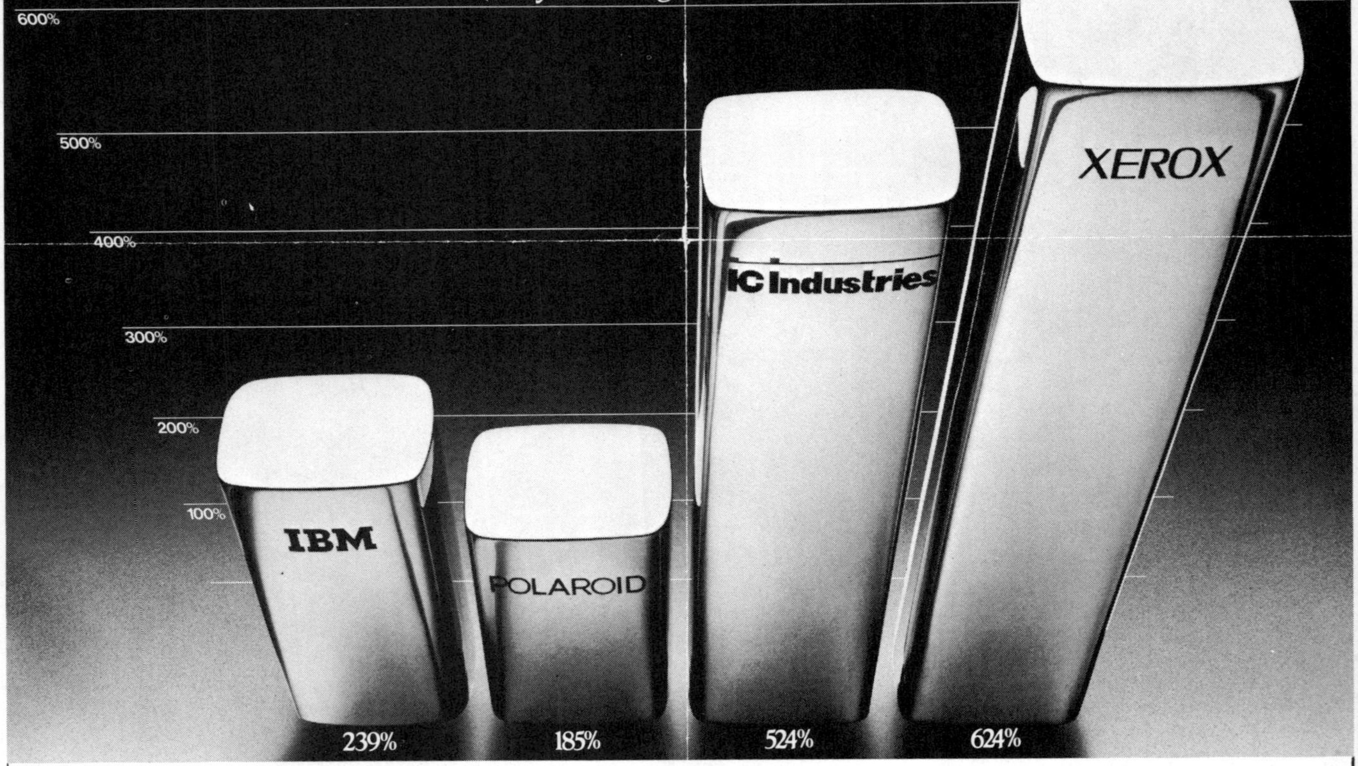

In 1967, we were a $300 million regional railroad. In the last ten years, through diversification and the performance of our operating companies, we've grown a glamorous 524 percent.

Our 1977 sales were a record $1.9 billion. Net income increased 29 percent over 1976, to a record $78.5 million. And net income per common share was up 27 percent to a record $4.55.

Our growth can be attributed to the strength and continuing success of companies like our Abex Corporation. Abex sales have more than doubled since the company joined IC Industries in 1968. In 1977, record Abex sales of $638 million included such diverse products as hydraulics for oil drilling rigs and brake pads for nearly every Volkswagen sold in the world.

And companies like our Midas-International Corporation, with more than 1,000 franchised shops, worldwide. Midas, for years the world's leading specialist in automotive exhaust systems, is also one of the leading builders of commercial and recreational vehicles. Midas sales were a record $264 million in 1977. That's an increase of nearly 240 percent in the six years Midas has been an IC Industries company.

Growth in the soft drink business led to record sales of $174 million for our Pepsi-Cola General Bottlers, Dad's Root Beer and Bubble Up companies in 1977.

The companies in our Financial Services Group produced record 1977 sales of $79 million. In our Real Estate Group, sales reached $39 million.

But growth hasn't been restricted to our non-railroad businesses. Our Illinois Central Gulf Railroad revenues reached $680 million in 1977.

Altogether, we're IC Industries, a $1.9 billion international multibusiness corporation. And while our business may not be as glamorous as some, our ten-year, 524 percent growth certainly puts us in glamorous company.

If you'd like to know more about us, and how we're still growing, write: IC Industries, One Illinois Center, 111 East Wacker Drive, Chicago, Illinois 60601.

IC Industries

Diversified in five business groups: Commercial Products, Consumer Products, Real Estate, Financial Services and Transportation.

1977 annual report

IC Industries is a highly diversified international company marketing a broad range of products and services.

IC Industries

objectives

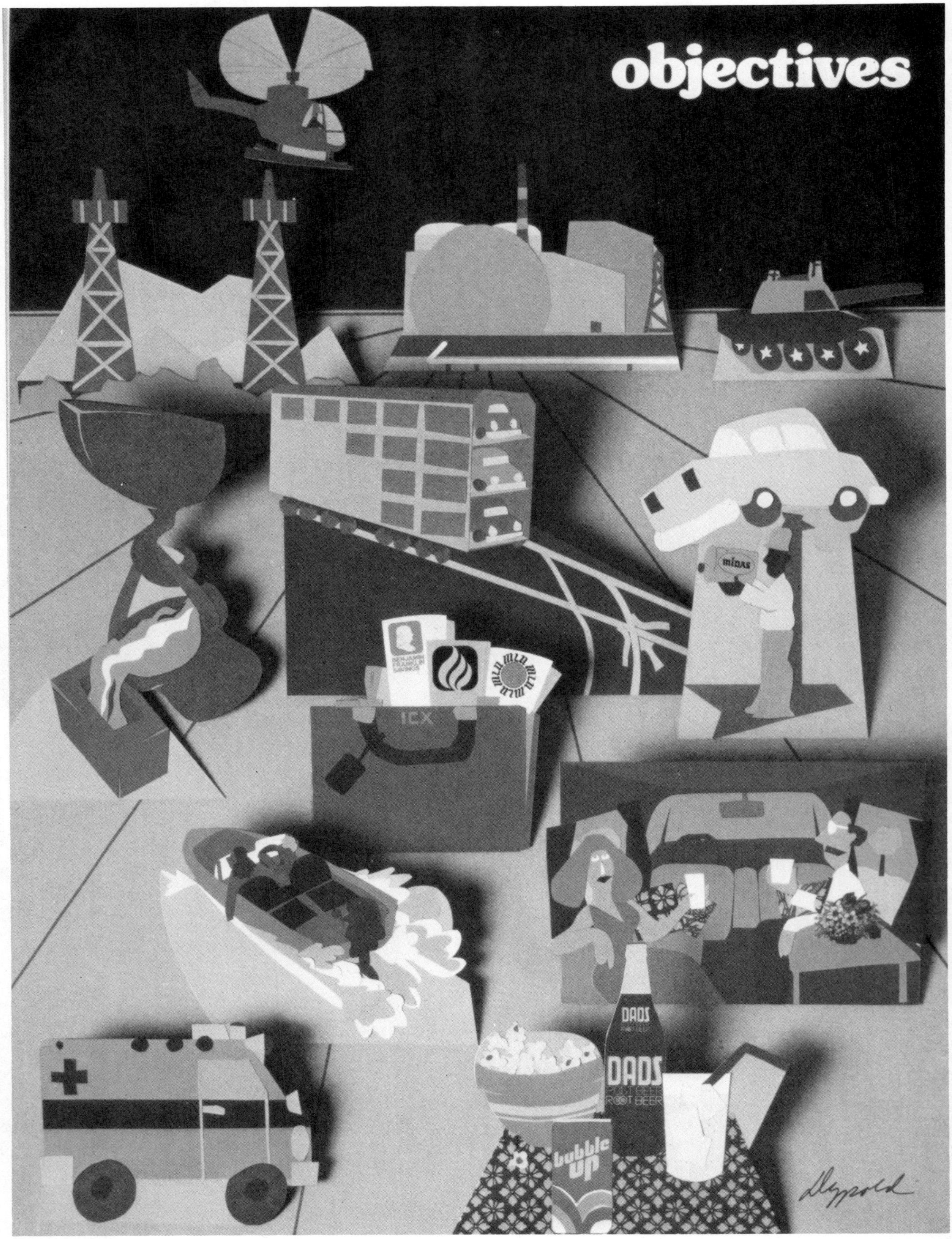

midas
BENJAMIN FRANKLIN SAVINGS
ICX
DADS
DADS
ROOT BEER
bubble up

Managing for the future

The success of any business enterprise is determined by its commitment to challenging objectives and its ability to apply the resources, energy and technology necessary to achieve them. When we say "resources" we mean not only physical resources, but particularly human resources—our people and their talents. The management of IC Industries has a commitment to these objectives:
1. Maintain long-term profitable growth.
2. Improve return-on-investment.
3. Generate and attract adequate capital.
4. Strengthen research and technological capabilities.
5. Emphasize growth primarily in consumer and commercial markets.
6. Strengthen management resources.
7. Demonstrate our concern for the nation's economic vitality, environmental quality and social progress.

Foundation for growth

Our predecessor company, the Illinois Central Railroad, was formed 127 years ago. IC Industries, organized as a holding company to acquire and operate non-rail businesses, was chartered in 1962. Substantial diversification began in 1968.

Since its inception, the Company has built a strong foundation for continued growth and profitability. Our diversity of products and services has created new opportunities for expansion and has provided stability in times of economic stress.

IC Industries is well-positioned to serve growing areas of basic industries in the consumer, power generation, extractive, metals, construction, agricultural, financial services, automotive, aerospace, defense and real estate fields, as well as rail transportation. As a major supplier to many of these fields, the Company enjoys a highly regarded base of capabilities from which to continue expansion — both internally and through additional acquisitions.

The dynamics of our diverse markets, always subject to the natural force of competition and frequently affected by regulations and pressure superimposed on our business, demand a high degree of refinement in strategy, monitoring and control of operations. With that realization, our objectives are focused to create opportunities and minimize risk. And these objectives must not only be defined but constantly reexamined and refined.

Define objectives

1. Maintain long-term profitable growth

As the owners of IC Industries, our shareholders are entitled to benefit from the most productive possible use of their investments. The value of those investments will be enhanced through creative deployment of total assets and management talent.

2. Improve return-on-investment

The investment base supporting each operation must be measured against its contribution to earnings. To strengthen our control system, a senior management task force has been established to review and upgrade standards for acceptable levels of return for all current operations as well as for potential new investments. Under the direction of the President, this task force will identify guidelines and action programs to maximize return and, when necessary, for the redirection of capital to products and markets offering optimum opportunity.

3. Generate and attract adequate capital

Emphasis on return-on-investment creates the need for capital required for additional investments which meet high return standards. The goal is to continue to meet capital requirements through a balance of cash flow from operations and creation of a strong asset base to facilitate favorable borrowing and issuance of new equity.

4. Strengthen research & technological capabilities

IC Industries companies have provided leadership in the development of significant product and service innovations, many of which are proprietary. They are providing benefits of improved utility to the user, lower cost production and higher levels of profitability. Additional emphasis in basic research, product

International sales and revenues — IC Industries

In millions of dollars

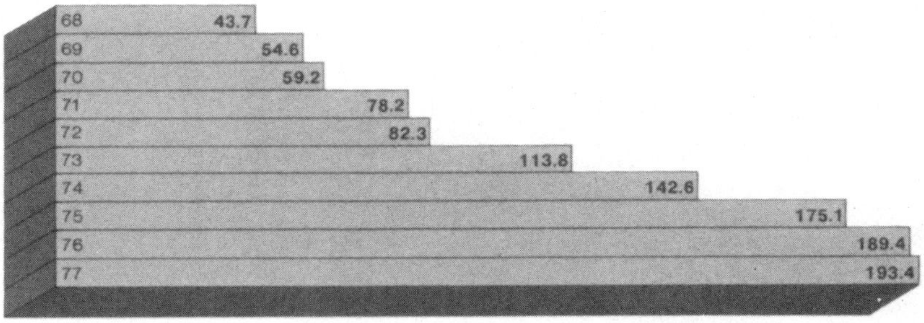

technology, and production efficiencies will continue to have high priority throughout the Corporation. Taking these developments to market will require ongoing programs of improved marketing and selling techniques which, together with scientific advances, will improve profitability for the long term. Of equal long-term importance, this leadership will provide an environment to encourage enterprising young people to seek careers with IC Industries.

5. Emphasize growth primarily in consumer and commercial markets.
IC Industries Consumer and Commercial Product groups direct their products and services to a broad spectrum of markets, each of which is seen to provide average to above-average long-term growth opportunities. IC Industries expansion in Commercial Products anticipates the long-term opportunities of increased productivity and industrial needs in the United States and in other developed and developing nations. Consumer growth in these Products markets will provide us the opportunity to contribute to, and share in, the opportunities provided by increasing consumer leisure time and spending. Competent and experienced managers in our companies are exploring new levels of investment to improve and expand existing product lines, and are planning for further diversification through selective acquisition. Improvement in the strategic planning process is continuing to allow the development and achievement of quantum growth objectives in the near term.

6. Strengthen management resources
The fundamental strength of IC Industries is the quality of its employees — their dedication, productivity and creativity. It is our goal to motivate all employees to seek increased opportunities and responsibilities through initiative, dedication, intercompany promotion, self-improvement and financial rewards with emphasis on developing a continuity of superior skills and highly capable management at all levels.

7. Demonstrate our concern for the nation's economic vitality, environmental quality and social progress
Corporations are licensed to employ assets, people and resources as responsible citizens. As the generator of economic activity, private enterprise is the ultimate source of capital for all institutions in society — public and private. Business must take seriously its responsibility to provide the goods, services and capital to improve the quality of life and the standard of living. IC Industries is committed to produce high-value products and services at reasonable and competitive prices — and at a profit for its shareholders. We shall encourage those within our sphere of influence — employees, shareholders and customers — to participate in worthy causes of public service and to exert their opinions on the process of government.

Achievement of these objectives involves establishment of an interrelated series of operating, financing and human development plans. Implementation of our plans will be accelerated but with the degree of flexibility required for effective and timely problem-solving while simultaneously seeking opportunities and minimizing reasonable risks. We are dedicated to achievement by remaining fully and continuously involved in our businesses and the environment around us. ■■

Sales and revenues— IC Products Company
In billions of dollars

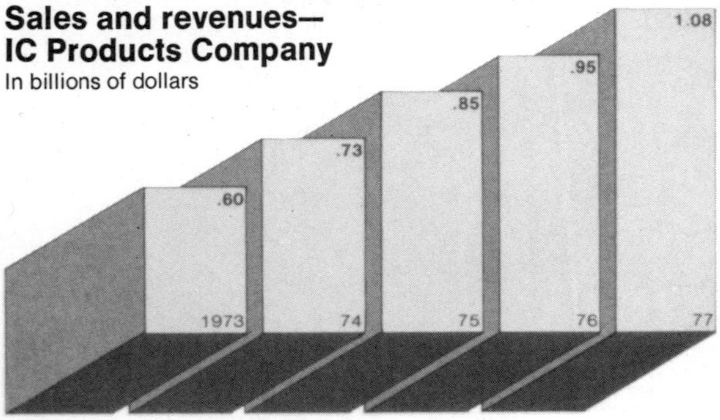

Net income— IC Products Company
In millions of dollars

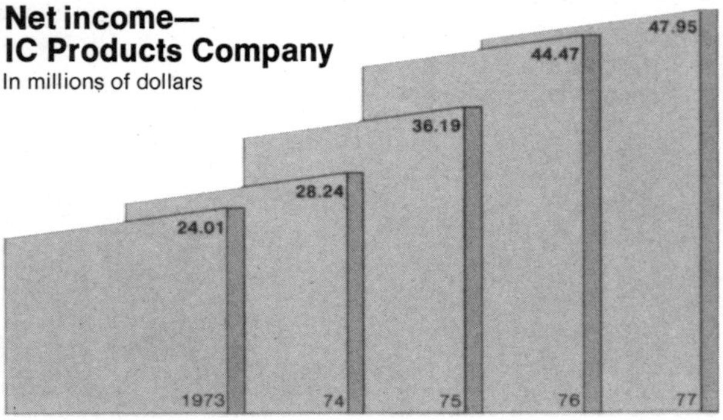

The financial community faces a complex array of considerations in making investment decisions. The IC Industries Investor Relations Program is designed to inform shareholders, investors and those who influence investments of the growth, diversification and long-range objectives of the corporation.

Today, the communications effort utilizes a five-point strategy designed to:

1. Increase awareness of IC Industries as a soundly diversified corporation with above-average prospects for growth in sales and earnings.
2. Increase confidence among current and prospective shareholders that IC Industries is an attractive investment opportunity.
3. Focus primarily on those two operating groups, namely, Commercial Products and Consumer Products, which are achieving the greatest rate of growth and profitability, and which, as the IC Products Company (ICP), are becoming the foundation for the long-range structure of the Company.
4. Communicate management's commitment to selective expansion and diversification.
5. Reinforce management's intention to operate the Illinois Central Gulf Railroad on a profitable basis by fully and adequately maintaining the Railroad, recognizing that in all likelihood it may be merged or sold at some future date.

The IC Industries Investor Relations program has been a comprehensive one and in 1977 employed a number of communications techniques, including:

☐ *Meetings with investment managers, institutional investors, retail brokers, advisory services, and individual shareholders.* Group meetings, largely sponsored by leading investment banking firms, were held in New York, Boston, Chicago, Los Angeles, San Francisco, London, Paris, Geneva, Frankfurt, Brussels, and Amsterdam. At these meetings members of management fully discussed Company operations, problems, opportunities and future prospects. In November, a selected group of investment managers spent three days viewing Company operations in the Chicago area, meeting with Company executives and inspecting ICG Railroad facilities on a two-day rail trip from Chicago to New Orleans.

☐ *Annual Meeting of Shareholders.* In 1977 the informational content of the Annual Meeting was expanded for an in-depth review of diversified operations.

☐ *Continuing communications with shareholders and investment community.* Through the annual report, quarterly reports, report of the Annual Meeting, special reports and news releases shareholders and investors are kept advised of the Company's accomplishments and progress.

☐ *Advertising.* A series of messages about the restructuring of IC Industries from strictly a regional railroad to a highly diversified international enterprise serving multiple markets appeared throughout the year in leading financial publications.

A similar strategy is being employed and expanded in 1978. ■■

Investment managers toured the ICG Railroad for on-train presentations (top) and a visit to Centralia Shops (center). IC Industries management continually meets with institutional and retail investors in European cities (bottom).

opinions

Productivity

Dr. C. Jackson Grayson
Chairman, American Productivity Center;
Director, IC Industries, Inc.

The United States is beyond question the most productive nation in the world. And our productivity is still growing. But an alarming trend has developed in recent years. The productivity growth rate is slowing down. Unless that decline can be halted and the trend reversed, the free enterprise system as we know it today simply will not survive, and we will face a bleak future of lowered living standards and more government control.

A few statistics: From 1947 to 1966, our growth rate was 3.2 percent a year. From 1967 to 1977, it slipped to only 1.5 percent a year. Other nations have done better. Several are achieving growth rates of 4 to 6 percent, and Japan currently tops the list at a whopping 9 percent. It takes no great imagination to foresee the U.S. slipping from its position of economic leadership as other nations catch up and pass us, unless the situation is turned around.

A first step toward a turnaround is to understand what productivity is and what it isn't. Productivity is a much-abused and much-misunderstood word. Some people mistakenly believe that when we talk about increasing productivity we mean merely forcing a speedup, or increasing the work load, perhaps beyond the limit of endurance. But that's not the point. Others assume that greater productivity helps only the rich and slights the poor, which is as far from the truth as you can get.

In simple terms, productivity is the ratio of total output over total input. Or, to phrase it more formally, productivity is "the relationship between resources utilized and results achieved." What this means is that through more efficent use of time, intellect, money and materials, the total output can be made to grow faster than the total input — "increased productivity."

High productivity benefits everyone. It increases employment, increases real wages and creates more wealth to be spread through the entire economy. The only way we are going to get the inflation rate down to a bearable level is to increase productivity. The only way to create the wealth needed to achieve national social goals — such as caring adequately for the very poor, the sick and the elderly — is to increase productivity.

Many factors enter into the measurement of productivity. One is the amount of capital available for investment— the money needed to buy more efficient tools, build more efficient plants. A tax system that severely hampers capital formation, as ours does, contributes to the decline in the productivty growth rate. Government regulations, ever increasing, clamp a power brake on productivity. So do excessive work restrictions put in place by some labor unions — restrictions that are born of a fear of unemployment and a failure to comprehend that growth in productivity always means more jobs, not fewer.

Reversing the downward trend in productivity growth will not be easy, but I am an optimist. I believe it can be done. To help in this effort, the American Productivity Center has been created, with its headquarters in Houston. The Center is engaged in a broad educational and assistance program, to compile data on productivity, study ways to improve it, and help companies review their own particular problems and needs in order to improve their performance.

The Center can assist, but it cannot do the job alone. The effort must eventually reach every individual in every job in every company if it is to succeed. Labor and management must work together on productivity programs, clearly understanding that benefits are mutual. Educational programs are needed, extending to the school, the university, the office, the factory and home. Too many misconceptions go unchallanged as to the crucial role productivity plays in a free enterprise

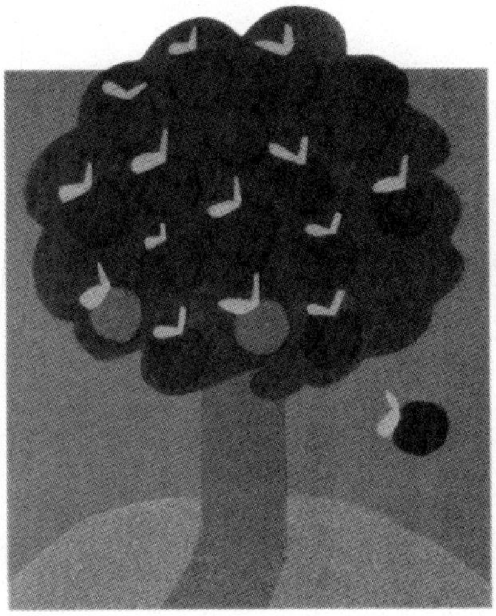

system and its corrollary, a free society.

The public, through elected representatives, will ultimately decide if we are to remain on a course of prosperous growth or fall into decline and let our economic and personal freedoms slip away. An informed public will choose wisely, but too many misinformed voices now are clamoring for more regulations, more restrictions.

It is up to all of us to counteract those voices by hammering home the message that growth in productivity is absolutely vital. It is the key to more jobs, better pay in real terms without inflation, a better return for the shareholder, and a rising standard of living for everyone in America. This message must be impressed on management, on labor and—most emphatically—on our lawmakers in Washington. ■■

Dr. Grayson was elected to the IC Industries Board in 1974. He served as Dean of the Schools of Business Administration, Tulane University, 1963 to 1968, and Southern Methodist University, 1968 to 1975. He was Chairman of the U.S. Price Commission from 1971 to 1973. Dr. Grayson activated the American Productivity Center, a private sector center for research, education and training in 1977.

Overregulation— its impact on economic growth

William J. Taylor
President and Chief Executive Officer, Illinois Central Gulf Railroad Co.

Regulation by government is an old story to the Illinois Central Gulf Railroad and to the railroad industry in general. The nature and degree of this regulation, however, are matters of growing concern as the railroads are denied the flexibility they need to cope with rapidly changing conditions and to compete with other means of transportation which are less fettered. There is growing concern, too, over the ways in which government is extending its regulatory powers to embrace—in some cases smother—nearly the entire range of private enterprise. This trend affects other segments of your company, as well as the Railroad. If the total cost to IC Industries of regulation of all types could be computed, the amount would be staggering.

Plainly, something is radically wrong with the transportation policies of this country when so many railroads, so vital to the economic health of the nation, are in so much trouble. Illinois Central Gulf, I am pleased to report, is in far better shape than many of the nation's railroads, but its earnings are less than they should be, and less than they would be were it not for the uneven hand of the government applied through regulation.

Hardly a move can be made without permission from the Interstate Commerce Commission and/or one or more of the regulatory agencies of the 13 states in which the Railroad operates. Requests for needed adjustments in rates or in routes are subject to lengthy delays for the production of volumes of data and the perusal of the data by the commissions. Often, by the time the agencies render their decisions, the cost pressures that prompted a request in the first place have increased intolerably and the decision comes too late to give the relief that was sought. This condition was at least tolerable in the days when railroads represented the only feasible means of moving the bulk of America's goods, but in the competitive marketplace of today, the burdens have become unconscionable. This nation's transportation policy must be changed to permit railroads to compete on terms at least as favorable as their competitors.

Railroads spend millions on maintaining and improving the rights-of-way they own (and on which they also pay local taxes) while trucks benefit from government-built highways toward which they contribute only nominal user taxes. Barge lines that compete directly with the rails pay nothing for the use of waterways maintained by the federal government, and can change their rates quickly while the railroads cannot. Coal slurry pipeline operators can make a long-term contract with users to insure the recovery of the capital investment plus a reasonable return over the life of the assets. Railroads must make like investments to serve new customers, but are prohibited by law from making contracts which will insure the return of their committed capital.

Overregulation has meant a wholly inadequate rate of return for the railroads, and not even the lesson of the eastern railroad failures, which resulted in the formation of Conrail under government guarantees and subsidies, has brought the reform that is needed to keep the rail networks healthy. Money-losing lines cannot be closed down, as a losing manufacturing plant might be, without permission that may be long in coming — or stalled indefinitely by political considerations — while the companies and their shareholders bear the loss.

Bad as the situation is for the railroads, other industries and businesses also feel the effects of overregulation, and the urge to regulate is spreading. The proliferation of regulatory bodies in the last few years is nothing short of alarming — all of them with good purposes in mind, of course, but all grasping for more power and using that power in

Mr. Taylor joined IC Industries in 1969 as Vice President of Governmental Affairs. He became Vice President of Legal Affairs in 1974. In April 1976 he became President and Chief Operating Officer of the Illinois Central Gulf Railroad, a wholly-owned subsidiary of IC Industries, and in February 1978, was elected President and Chief Executive Officer of the ICG.

ways that add up to an enormous drag on the economy.

For example, everyone is in favor of safety, but some of the rules promulgated by the Occupational Safety and Health Administration (OSHA) are stifling beyond belief, and go so far beyond the the intent of Congress that measures are now being taken to trim its sails. A proper concern for the purity of the environment has brought into being Federal and state agencies that compete to see which can formulate the most stringent — and the most costly — rules for protecting the environment. In the food and drug field, the floods of regulations on testing and labeling (again with the best of intentions) bring delays and confusion and force up the price of products. In every direction, the mood of the country, reflected in Congress, seems to be one that demands a new law, a new regulatory agency, to "cure" every single flaw in American life, be it real or imagined.

That there is need for regulation in an increasingly complex society is beyond question. No one could logically argue otherwise. But when regulation comes to mean blizzards of paperwork that discourage or bankrupt small businesses, an unfair competitive climate that threatens the very life of many railroads, and a system so time-consuming and so costly that it applies a brake to economic growth, the entire regulatory mechanism is overdue for an overhaul.

Private enterprise is by now so overburdened with regulations of all varieties that management is frustrated and oftentimes defeated in its attempts to carry out its responsibilities to its shareholders. A system in which an ostensibly all-knowing, all-wise government suppresses, compromises and delays the working of all business and impedes economic growth is grossly out of balance and destructive of freedom. The next step in regulation ought to be to regulate the regulators and restore the balance between the public and the private sectors. Otherwise, the whole structure of private enterprise that has served this nation so well stands in jeopardy. ■■

The importance of capital formation

John P. Fagan, Vice President, Finance and Treasurer, IC Industries, Inc.

Every growing company, including IC Industries, requires sizable infusions of capital to maintain its own healthy growth and contribute to the necessary growth of the free world's economy. Only through steady, well-managed expansion can prosperity be insured, and capital formation is the lifeblood of that expansion.

Capital is generated in two ways — internally through profitable sales and operations; and externally through the placement of securities in the capital markets. IC Industries is currently looking to the capital markets, as well as internally generated funds, to fuel its own expansion by capital expenditures of about $200 million a year.

Timing is vital in making the decisions as to how and where to seek the needed funds. The ups and downs of the business cycle, the shifting nature of the capital markets, and the uncertainties of government tax and other regulatory policies from year to year all play a part in the decisions that must be made, and affect the degree of risk that is involved in planning for years ahead.

Some risk is inevitable. The money committed today for a new plant will create new jobs and new products, but that does not happen overnight. It normally takes up to three or four years to bring a new plant into profitable operation. Meanwhile, the cost of the borrowed capital mounts up, particularly in periods of high interest rates and serious inflation such as we have now and even greater inflation in the recent past. Every decision to commit capital, a decision that is made by the board of directors on the recommendation of management,

Mr. Fagan joined IC Industries in April 1968, as Assistant Vice President in the Secretary-Treasurer Department and in July 1969, was named Treasurer of both IC Industries and its railroad subsidiary. He was elected a Vice President of IC Industries in 1972 and Vice President—Finance in 1975. Mr. Fagan is President of IC Leasing, Inc.

must rest on painstaking analysis of dozens of factors. These range from the probable mood of the consumer a few years hence to the possibility — or, rather, the probability — that the government will change its fiscal and tax policies in the middle of the game. Above all, the timing must be right to fit the curves of the business cycle.

A major concern at present is the shift that has taken place in the capital markets in recent years. The small, individual investors have withdrawn from the stock market in large numbers, leaving more of the field to the big, institutional investors — pension funds, banks and the like. Some institutions can shift rapidly from equities (stocks) into the debt market (bonds), in pursuit of higher yields, and to a degree this shift has occurred. The changing pattern has had a serious negative effect on the stock market, with the result that companies seeking capital through new stock issues have found an atmosphere that is generally less than favorable. Yet the ratio of debt (borrowed funds) to equities (shareholders' investment) must be carefully balanced in a company's balance sheet, and not overloaded on the debt side, if the company is to attract investor favor. The decision as to which road to take in raising new capital also becomes a matter of precise timing.

The debt market's behavior is influenced to a great and troubling extent by actions of the Federal government, which must finance its huge deficits through the sale of bonds and notes which compete with corporate issues for the investor's dollar. The capital requirements of state and local governments, which can issue bonds with the interest exempt from Federal taxes, also play a large part in this picture.

The present instability in the capital markets could be overcome in large part by bringing back to the marketplace the individual investors who have deserted it. But for that to happen, a shift must come in the anti-business bias than runs through the tax structure. It's no wonder investors shy away when they see dividends doubly taxed and hear politicians threatening to tax capital gains on the same basis as ordinary income. In some quarters, "profit" is even considered a dirty word, although it should be plain to everyone that without earnings there would be no jobs.

Shareholders should raise their voices against anti-business laws in our society. In their own interest, they should write to their elected representatives and demand specific measures to assure fair and equitable treatment of business.

Labor is entitled to fair compensation for its services, but must be willing to contribute to the success of the enterprises which employ them by contributing to productivity improvement.

Government, at all levels, should enact policies and procedures which stress fair trade, and elimination of trade and tariff barriers in order to assure that U.S. corporations may compete effectively in world markets. If other governments unfairly support corporations within their borders, the U.S. government should not hesitate to enact legislation to insure the competitiveness of American firms.

Consumers should demand quality products at a fair price while, at the same time, insisting that the U.S. government develop a trade approach which will permit consumer access to all goods and services, no matter what their origin, at a fair, competitive price.

Corporate management, as the coordinator of American capital formation efforts, has the responsibility to blend the parts in the most productive and economic manner so that government, labor, the consumer and the shareholder can all achieve the maximum benefits from their endeavors.

Educators, at every level from high school through the university graduate level, have an obligation to assure that their students understand, and have an appreciation for the private enterprise system and how it operates.■■

IC Industries

Report of operations

4

Soft drink consumption is increasing rapidly and is benefitting IC Industries three soft-drink companies—Pepsi-Cola General Bottlers, Dad's Root Beer Company and Bubble Up Company. Story on Page 16.

1977 —another record year for the IC Industries

As consumption of soft drinks continues its rapid growth, IC Industries three soft drinks companies—Pepsi-Cola General Bottlers, Dad's Root Beer Company and Bubble Up Company—are experiencing increased demand for their products. New, larger packages are providing greater convenience for consumers. Fountain sales through restaurants and "fast food" outlets have also increased significantly as more people are "eating out" instead of at home.

As a result, the IC Industries soft drink business produced record sales of $173 million in 1977, an 18 percent increase over the $147 million recorded in 1976.

Anticipated increase

As people throughout the world have more leisure time available, soft drink consumption is expected to continue its growth. IC Industries three soft drink companies are engaged in marketing products which account for more than 80 percent of U.S. soft drink sales and are positioned to serve the anticipated increase in demand. In 1977 cola drinks accounted for 63 percent of industry sales, lemon-lime 13 percent and root beer 5 percent. Pepsi-Cola General Bottlers is the second largest Pepsi-Cola franchise in North America. Early in 1978, Pepsi-Cola Bottling Company of Cincinnati, Ohio, which had sales of $38 million in 1977, was acquired through merger.

Throughout the world soft drink consumption is increasing.

"IC" Pepsi-land

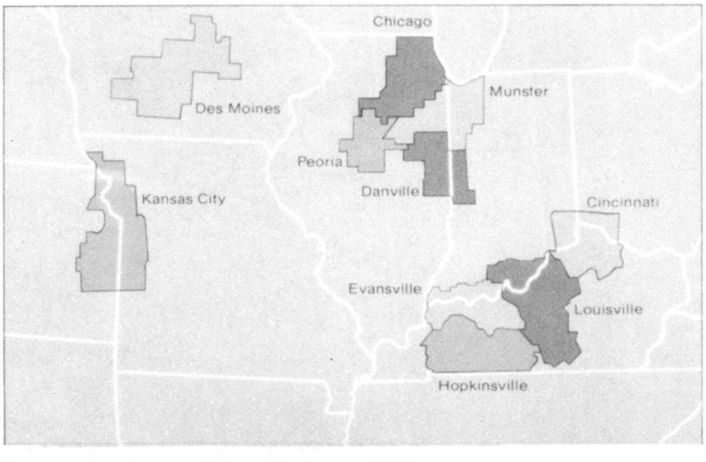

Pepsi-Cola General Bottlers

Pepsi-Cola General Bottlers serves major markets in seven midwestern states—Illinois, Indiana, Iowa, Kansas, Kentucky, Missouri and Ohio.

With the addition of facilities in Cincinnati, Pepsi General now operates 10 bottling and canning plants. Completion of additional canning facilities is expected in 1978.

In addition to products of the Pepsi-Cola Company, including Pepsi-Cola, Diet Pepsi, Pepsi Light and Mountain Dew, other soft drink brands marketed by one or more Pepsi General divisions include Dad's, Bubble Up, Dr. Pepper, 7-Up, Orange Crush, Country Time Lemonade, Hawaiian Punch, Welch's Sparkling Grape Soda and other flavors.

2-Liter shatterproof plastic bottle

One of the key developments in 1977 was introduction of Pepsi-Cola in the new 2-liter polyester shatterproof plastic bottle. U.S. Pepsi-Cola franchises secured an early sales advantage when the Pepsi plastic bottle was approved by the Food & Drug Administration.

This new package is enjoying good consumer acceptance in the three Pepsi General markets—Chicago, Munster and Cincinnati—where it is presently marketed.

In 1978 Pepsi General plans to make this new convenience package available in all of its markets for Pepsi-Cola and other major brands, including Dad's and Bubble Up.

Pepsi-Cola had food store sales leadership and registered 1977 sales gains in all the Company's markets, including the recently acquired Cincinnati market.

Pepsi challenge

As part of a new, more aggressive marketing program, Pepsi General launched the Pepsi Challenge in Metropolitan Chicago during 1977. Consumers who expressed a brand

16

soft drink business

Robert W. Selleck, Pepsi-Cola General Bottlers

Jules Klapman, Dad's and Bubble Up

loyalty for Coca Cola were invited to make a taste comparison of their brand with Pepsi-Cola and 63 percent of those tested expressed a preference for Pepsi in direct "blind" taste tests. The success of these tests was vigorously communicated in a heavy advertising schedule and contributed to the 1977 sales increase.

IC Consumer Products sales
In millions of dollars

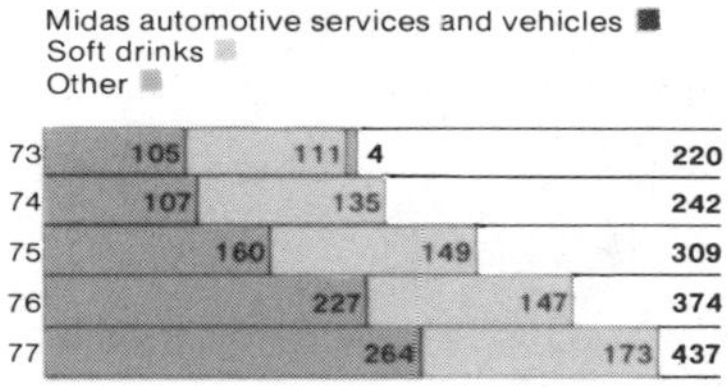

Dad's Root Beer
The sale of soft drink concentrate by Dad's Root Beer Company continues to expand in the face of the growing root beer segment of the U.S. soft drink market and growing competition. This segment now accounts for between five and eight percent of all soft drink sales in the United States. Dad's has more than 170 franchised bottlers in the U.S., including eight new franchises added in 1977.

Bubble Up
Bubble Up Company in 1977 continued to build its base from the low point which existed just prior to acquisition in 1973. During this past year another 21 bottlers were franchised to serve the highly competitive lemon-lime beverage market. Bubble Up has more than 180 bottlers in the U.S., and 16 other nations.

Newly designed packaging, intended to present a stronger appearance in the marketplace, have been adopted by both Dad's and Bubble Up. Marketing efforts in 1978 will be concentrated on strengthening existing bottlers, stronger brand identity through the new graphic designs, and introduction of new, larger packages, including the two-liter shatterproof plastic bottle.■■

Consumer acceptance of the Pepsi-Cola 2-liter polyester shatterproof plastic bottle has been good. Other Pepsi General brands will soon be available in this container. New Dad's and Bubble Up packaging has been re-designed to enhance product appearance in the marketplace.

The IC Commercial Products Group (Abex Corporation) established new sales and pre-tax income records in 1977. Sales of $638 million exceeded 1976 by 11 percent and pre-tax income of $64 million was up 6 percent.

The sales increase resulted from both internal growth and through acquisition of the former Stanray Corporation, whose operations were integrated into those of Abex.

Sales of three of the four product groupings—automotive products, hydraulics and railroad products—increased over 1976. Castings sales lagged behind the prior year, but this was more than compensated by increases in the other three product groupings.

Automotive products

Abex Automotive Products, retaining its worldwide leadership position in automotive friction braking materials, again experienced a record year in 1977 with sales of $180 million, up 13 percent over 1976.

Highlighting achievements last year was specification of the new Abex non-asbestos, resin-bonded disc brake pad for all Volkswagen Rabbits, with automatic transmissions, sold in the U.S. Later in the year, this product was also specified for the new Dodge Omni and Plymouth Horizon sub-compact automobiles.

A new Abex facility was opened in late 1977 at Berkley Township, New Jersey, to expand the Company's capability for road-testing truck and passenger car braking materials.

Hydraulics

The new Abex Denison Gold Cup transmission, featuring an improved piston pump and motor, moved from field testing to substantial sales during the year and was a factor in hydraulics sales reaching a record $122 million, up 36 percent.

The broadening of the Abex hydraulics line in 1977 with addition of Remco hydraulics, Meade fluid power products and Jetway aircraft loading bridges has greatly enhanced the Abex competitive position.

Abex continues to maintain its leadership in aircraft hydraulics sales with specification of its equipment on several new fixed and rotary wing military and civilian aircraft. The U.S. Army recently announced plans to acquire up to 7,000 XM-1 main battle tanks which utilize Abex hydraulic pumps. Abex also has a contract to supply air-cooled noise suppressors for ground testing of U.S. Air Force F-16 fighter planes.

Railroad products

The addition of Standard Railway Equipment (Stanray) to Abex Railroad Products, was a factor contributing to new record sales of $173 million in 1977, a 15 percent increase.

Stanray brought a market leading

Abex hydraulic pumps provide control power on Sikorsky UH-60A Army (bottom) and S-76 commercial helicopters.

Addition of Standard Railway Equipment (Stanray) broadened the Abex line of railroad products in 1977, including coil steel covers for flat cars shown at the right. Other products added to the Abex line are freight car roofs and ends and uncoupling devices, complementing the existing line of brake shoes, steel wheels, bearings, trackwork and switching equipment.

Abex casts specialty parts used in General Electric gas turbines for peaking power.

position in railroad car roofs and ends, coil steel covers for flat cars, and uncoupling devices to the existing Abex line of trackwork, steel wheels, locomotive bearings, brake shoes and switching equipment.

The new Abex plant for the assembly of mounted railroad wheel sets at Corsicana, Texas, is expected to be in operation later this year. This facility is designed primarily to service unit trains which normally require new wheels every two years. An initial order for 2,000 wheel sets to be utilized on 500 new 100-ton tank cars was received in 1977.

Castings

A lengthy strike on the U.S. iron range, a severe decline in the metal processing industry, particularly steel, and a slackening of capital investment to increase productive capacity, were among factors in the 1977 decline in sales of Abex castings to $163 million, off 7 percent, primarily in manganese steel castings. Other types of Abex specialty castings were not as severely affected. One particularly strong area of sales has been castings for gas turbines used in stationary and supplemental peaking power generation.

The first alloy Abex castings for turbine engines in the new XM-1 main battle tank were delivered in 1977. Also last year field testing was begun on castings utilizing the new Abex proprietary THERMAX metallurgical process which permits strengthening of the entire family of heat-resistant alloys by as much as 80 percent. ■■

IC Commercial Products Sales In millions of dollars

Automotive products ■ Castings ■ Hydraulics ■ Railroad products ■

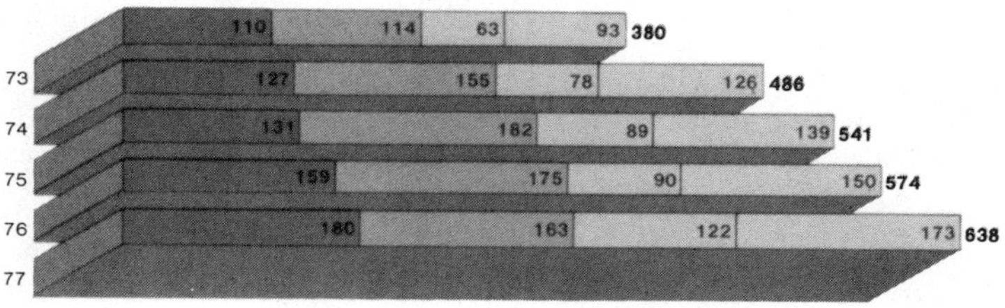

In 1977 Abex introduced a new line of non-asbestos, resin-bonded disc brake pads. The new Dodge Omni (right) and Plymouth Horizon subcompact automobiles were the first U.S. automobiles to utilize this exclusive new technological breakthrough. The new Abex disc brake pads were also specified for Volkswagen Rabbits with automatic transmissions sold in the U.S.

Grand opening ceremonies for the 1,000th Midas automotive service shop worldwide were conducted in December at Gaithersburg, Maryland.

On December 1, 1977, Midas opened its 1,000th Muffler Shop in the Washington suburb of Gaithersburg, Maryland, as the culmination of a week-long series of new shop openings in Melbourne, Australia; London, England; Brussels, Belgium; Paris, France; Hamilton, Ontario, and five U.S. locations coast-to-coast.

During this series of openings Midas, supported by the Alexander Graham Bell Association for the Deaf, conducted a program to emphasize the need to control noise pollution. Through such civic efforts, Midas has demonstrated to consumers its social consciousness as a good citizen, both at the corporate level and locally through its franchised operations.

With subsequent openings, Midas had 1,003 shops in operation worldwide at the end of the year, an increase of 100 shops for the second successive year.

Midas automotive shops—worldwide

New shops added each year ■
Net shops at year end ■

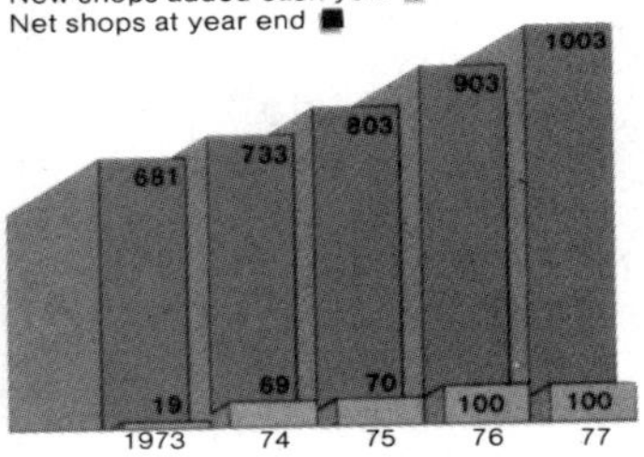

Sales total $264 million

Midas sales in 1977 from its muffler shops and its recreational and commercial vehicle business grew to $264 million, 16 percent over the previous year.

A major factor influencing the continuing growth in Midas sales has been the strength of the automotive aftermarket in the United States. This increased consumer demand for quality automotive replacement parts and services is a major factor in Midas plans for addition of new shops at the rate of 100 per year for the foreseeable future.

Midas is the leader in successfully extending the modern franchising method of distribution to the automotive field, as demonstrated by Midas' growth over the past five years.

Broadest vehicle line in industries

With its line of Midas Mini and Class A motor homes, commercial and delivery vans, recreational trailers, Black Diamond heavy-duty trailers and customized van conversions, Midas now offers the broadest line in the vehicle industry.

Midas achieved its third successive year of substantial sales growth in 1977 when nearly 18,000 vehicles were sold, a 21 percent increase.

Last year Midas participation in the leisure-time market was enhanced with the acquisition of the Sea Nymph line of boats and canoes. ■■

Sales of Midas vehicles continued to increase in 1977. Shown at right is a Black Diamond highway trailer.

Midas vehicles sold

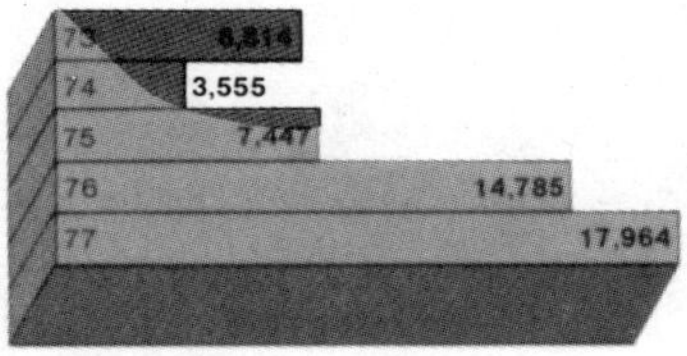

IC Real Estate Group and IC Financial Services Group

Lincoln Liberty Life Insurance Co. and Midwest Life Nebraska both experienced record sales of insurance products in 1977, highlighting a record sales and earnings year for Financial Services.

New Illinois Center construction activity in 1977 marked the resurgence of commercial real estate development by IC Real Estate Group companies.

Ground was broken last year for an addition which will more than double the size of the Hyatt Regency Chicago Hotel and construction commenced early in January, 1978, on the Three Illinois Center office building. Plans have been announced for beginning construction in 1978 on the Four Illinois Center office building and an apartment building.

These development activities, coupled with sales and lease of ICG Railroad real estate and sales by LaSalle Properties at Elmwood Industrial Park, near New Orleans, produced sales and revenues of $39 million for the IC Real Estate Group in 1977. Pre-tax income of $17.1 million was 9.2 percent greater than 1976.

Financial Services

Sales and revenues of the IC Financial Services Group were a record $79 million with pre-tax income of 9.5 million, five times increased over 1976.

□ *Lincoln Financial, Inc.*

Lincoln Liberty Life Insurance Company benefitted from investment income which was improved over 1976, and significant strides made in expanding its agency force to position the Company for future growth. Premium income was a record $33 million.

Benjamin Franklin Savings Association experienced a 21 percent growth in savings and a 20 percent growth in the number of accounts. Top Check, a bill-paying system from savings accounts, was introduced during the year.

Life Insurance in force—IC Industries

In billions of dollars

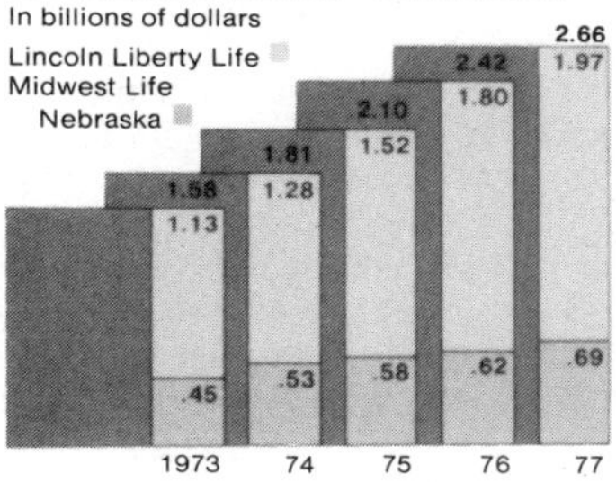

□ *Midwest Life Nebraska*

Midwest Life Nebraska also experienced a good year with increased return on invested assets and premium income up 14 percent to $12 million. For the ninth consecutive year, Midwest Life Nebraska increased its return on invested assets at a greater rate than the industry as a whole.

□ *IC Leasing, H. F. Philipsborn*

IC Leasing Co. had another successful year including the financing of 42 shops for Midas in 1977. The total backlog of committed loans by H. F. Philipsborn & Co. grew to $65 million at year-end, a 12 percent increase. ■■

Illinois Center planned and existing streets and buildings are: 1. One Illinois Center; 2. Two Illinois Center; 3. Hyatt Regency Chicago Hotel; 4. Hyatt Regency addition; 5. Three Illinois Center; 6. 48-story apartment bldg.; 7. Four Illinois Center; 8. Prudential Bldg.; 9. Standard Oil (Indiana) Bldg.; 10. Outer Drive East condominium; 11. Harbor Point condominium.

existing ■
under construction or announced

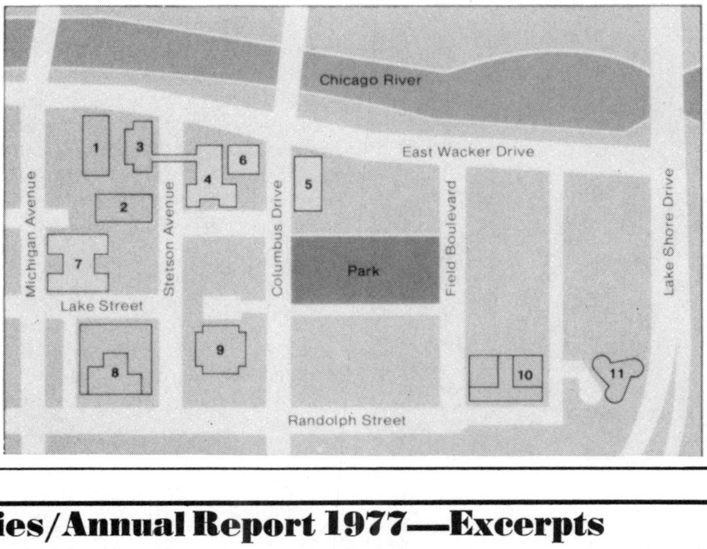

21

IC Transportation Group

Rebounding from two difficult years, the IC Transportation Group had pretax income of $5.1 million in 1977. Illinois Central Gulf Railroad, the Group's primary operating company, and its subsidiaries, on a generally accepted accounting principles basis and including railroad real estate, had consolidated net income of $30.3 million, up 36 percent.

This turnaround was accomplished while the ICG continued its program of substantially increased capital and operating expenditures for maintenance-of-way and equipment totaling $367 million. Included was $12 million of proceeds from sale of preference shares in 1977 to the Federal government under the 4-R Act.

Improved track conditions resulted in a reduction in slow orders, which allowed cars to reach their destinations sooner and be returned to service faster for an improvement in overall utilization. In addition, there was a 14 percent improvement in loss and damage claim experience.

Above: Piggyback (left) and coal continue to be important sources of revenue for the Illinois Central Gulf Railroad. Below: The ICG expended record sums in 1977 on right-of-way improvements and is continuing to install continuous welded rail on important freight routes.

Abandonment program advances

By the end of 1977, the ICG had abandoned or filed with the Interstate Commerce Commission applications to abandon approximately 1,800 miles of uneconomic trackage. Of this total the ICG has received final or conditional authority to abandon 854 miles. The ICG will continue the progressing of its line abandonment program in 1978, including the filing of additional abandonment petitions with the Commission. The abandonment program is designed to rationalize the system and increase traffic density, thereby achieving greater operating efficiency and providing better service.

An aggressive marketing program, new customer services, and substantially improved track conditions resulted in improved overall service to shippers and an increase in system density from 6.7 to 7.1 million gross ton miles per route mile. A continuing increase in system density is a prime objective in the ICG's profit improvement program.

Although carloadings were slightly behind 1976, net freight revenue ton miles improved by 4.6 percent, reaching 30.197 billion. Continued growth of such coordinated services as the Link, Delta Cannonball, and the Soo Connection; popular Slingshot and Minibridge container piggyback services; and the start-up of a new run-through with the Cotton Belt all contributed to 1977 revenue growth.

Net freight revenue ton miles—ICG Railroad In billions

Impact of coal strike

The nationwide coal strike which commenced in December adversely affected ICG revenue and earnings in December and continued into 1978.

The ICG plans to acquire a total of 1,050 new and rehabilitated freight cars (including 200 new 100-ton coal hopper cars), 1,243 piggyback vans and 100 fully-enclosed tri-level autoracks in 1978. At year-end there were 1,060 units in the ICG's locomotive fleet, including 113 diesel-electric units remanufactured and upgraded at ICG's Paducah, Kentucky shop in 1977. A new locomotive service and maintenance facility will be constructed at Vicksburg, Mississippi.

Long recognized as an industry leader in safety programs, the ICG was instrumental in a successful railroad-state safety program, Operation Lifesaver, which contributed to a 23 percent reduction of Illinois grade crossing fatalities.■■

1977 freight revenue contribution—ICG Railroad In percent

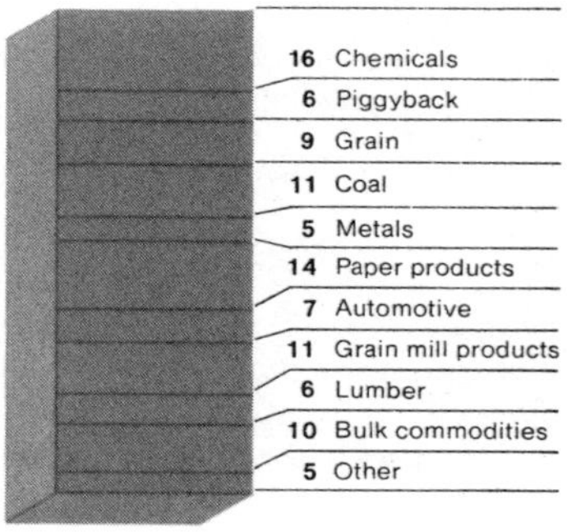

IC Industries

Interim report for the third quarter and the nine-month period ending September 30, 1978

3

The newest IC Industries company is Pet Incorporated, a diversified food products and services firm.
Story on Page 3.

To our shareholders:

Third quarter—
sales and revenues
In millions of dollars

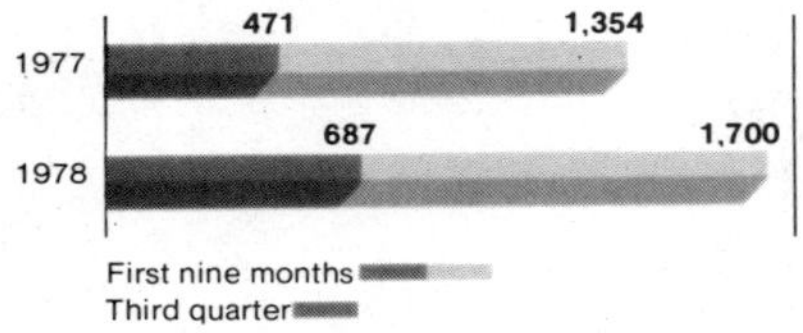

net income
In millions of dollars

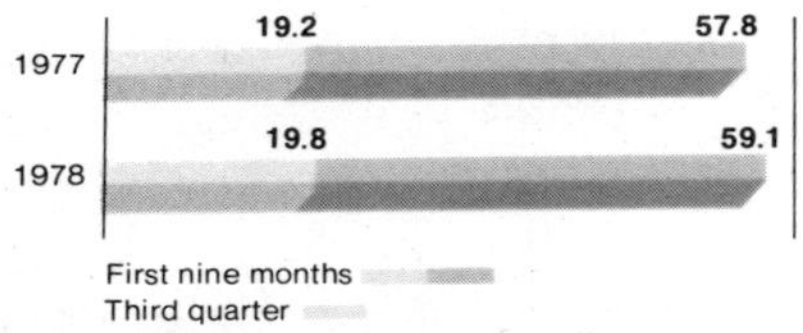

Third quarter net income was $19.8 million, or $1.03 per common share, a 3 percent increase over the restated $19.2 million, or $1.00 per common share for 1977. Sales and revenues from continuing operations were a record $687.2 million, nearly 46 percent above 1977.

We are quite satisfied with our third quarter results when we consider the substantial impact of non-recurring costs during this unusual period. These include Illinois Central Gulf Railroad strike insurance payments to the Norfolk and Western and the resulting work stoppage on our own railroad, as well as substantial transitional adjustments and costs associated with the purchase of Pet.

Sales and revenues for the nine-month period from continuing operations were a record $1.7 billion, a 25.6 percent increase over 1977. Net income of $59.1 million represented a 2.2 percent improvement over the restated $57.8 million last year. However, as a result of an increase in average common shares outstanding from 14.7 million to 15.7 million, net income per common share of $3.06 compares with a restated $3.15 in 1977.

Outlook

The continuing high level of business activity in all our operating groups and the continuing impressive growth in the backlog of unfilled orders at Abex and the Hussmann Group of Pet Inc. reinforce our earlier judgement that we shall have an outstanding fourth quarter and that IC Industries net income per common share for the year will be materially improved over the record restated $4.31 for 1977.

The third quarter was particularly significant in the accomplishment of certain long-range objectives. First, the Company acquired Pet Inc. which positioned IC Industries solidly in the consumer products market with a wide range of nationally distributed brands of food and food-related products. Second, definitive agreements were signed to sell five operating companies—Lincoln Liberty Life, Midwest Life Nebraska, Benjamin Franklin Savings and two smaller companies—in the IC Financial Services Group in early 1979. Third, the Company agreed to cooperate in the Southern Railway's study on the advisability and feasibility of the Southern acquiring the ICG Railroad with such studies continuing satisfactorily. Hence, with decreased dependence upon the cyclicalities of railroad transportation, this "new" IC Industries will now operate from a substantially stronger base, both financially and in the various markets we serve worldwide.

Foreign currency translation losses

Foreign currency translations for the Corporation resulted in a loss of $2.2 million, or 14 cents per common share, compared with a loss of $474,000, or 3 cents per common share, in the third quarter of 1977. For the year-to-date foreign currency losses amount to $3.0 million, or 19 cents per common share, while they totaled $1.1 million, or 7 cents per common share, a year ago.

William B. Johnson
Chairman and Chief Executive Officer

Robert F. Schnoes
President and Chief Operating Officer

On the cover:
The Pet Incorporated headquarters building is shown against a backdrop of the St. Louis Gateway Arch and the Mississippi River.

Contents

Message from Management, inside front cover

Consolidated statement of income, page 1

Pet... the new $1 billion member of the IC Industries Family, page 2

Group operating highlights, page 7

Special Christmas offer for IC Industries shareholders, inside back cover

Form 10-Q

A copy of IC Industries Quarterly Report to the Securities and Exchange Commission (Form 10-Q) may be obtained, without charge, by writing to Vice President of Corporate and Investor Relations, IC Industries, Inc., One Illinois Center, 111 East Wacker Drive, Chicago, Illinois 60601.

IC Industries, Inc. and Subsidiaries Consolidated statement of income

For the quarter and nine months ended September 30, 1978 compared with the same periods for 1977

	Quarter ended September 30,			Nine months ended September 30,		
	1978	1977	% change	**1978**	1977	% change
	(Dollars in thousands except per common share amounts)					
Sales and revenues from						
Continuing operations	**$687,169**	471,345	45.8	**$1,700,317**	$1,353,835	25.6
Commercial Products	**180,946**	159,718	13.3	**544,480**	468,665	16.2
Consumer Products	**313,077**	131,429	138.2	**568,853**	348,217	63.4
Real Estate	**9,447**	15,253	(38.1)	**33,866**	25,897	30.8
Transportation	**183,699**	164,945	11.4	**553,118**	511,056	8.2
Income before taxes from						
Continuing operations	**31,212**	25,053	24.6	**89,732**	82,948	8.2
Commercial Products	**15,988**	13,104	22.0	**50,667**	46,226	9.6
Percent	**51.2**	52.3		**56.5**	55.7	
Consumer Products	**26,278**	16,728	57.1	**47,877**	37,692	27.0
Percent	**84.2**	66.8		**53.3**	45.5	
Real Estate	**3,408**	6,312	(46.0)	**13,783**	8,791	56.8
Percent	**10.9**	25.2		**15.4**	10.6	
Transportation	**(3,310)**	(4,402)	24.8	**(5,087)**	2,166	NM
Percent	**(10.6)**	(17.6)		**(5.7)**	2.6	
Other (charges) income, net	**(11,152)**	(6,689)	(66.7)	**(17,508)**	(11,927)	(46.8)
Percent	**(35.7)**	(26.7)		**(19.5)**	(14.4)	
Taxes on income	**13,200**	7,293	81.0	**35,156**	28,724	22.4
Income from continuing operations	**18,012**	17,760	1.4	**54,576**	54,224	0.6
Companies being sold:						
Income before taxes	**2,791**	2,237	24.8	**7,072**	5,751	23.0
Taxes on income	**979**	816	20.0	**2,557**	2,170	17.8
Income after taxes	**1,812**	1,421	27.5	**4,515**	3,581	26.1
Net income	**19,824**	19,181	3.4	**59,091**	57,805	2.2
Preferred dividend requirement	**3,719**	3,877	(4.1)	**11,157**	11,526	(3.2)
Available for common shares	**16,105**	15,304	5.2	**47,934**	46,279	3.6
Per common share:						
From continuing operations	**.91**	.91	0.0	**2.77**	2.91	(4.8)
From companies being sold	**.12**	.09	33.3	**.29**	.24	20.8
Net income	**1.03**	1.00	3.0	**3.06**	3.15	(2.9)
Average common shares outstanding (in thousands)	**15,673**	15,250	2.8	**15,673**	14,670	6.8

Notes: **1** Earnings are reported on the basis of generally accepted accounting principles, are subject to year-end audit and in management's opinion are a fair statement of the results for the interim periods.
2 Pet Incorporated was acquired in August 1978 in a cash tender offer. The business combination was accounted for as a purchase and the 1978 results include Pet subsequent to the purchase as part of the Consumer Products Group.
3 The third quarter and nine months of 1977 have been restated: (a) to include the results of Security Investment Company, the owner of the Pepsi-Cola Bottling Company of Cincinnati, which was acquired on February 8, 1978 in a business combination accounted for as a pooling of interests; (b) to give effect to retroactive car hire billing adjustments directed by the Association of American Railroads in 1978; (c) and to give effect to the adoption of FASB Statement No. 13 "Accounting for Leases."
4 In September 1978 an agreement was reached to sell the principal companies comprising the Financial Services Group. Accordingly, the consolidated statement of income has been reclassified.
5 Fully diluted net income per share is $.89 and $.87 for the third quarters of 1978 and 1977, respectively, and $2.67 and $2.66 for the respective nine-month periods.
6 Foreign currency translations resulted in a loss of $2,176,000 ($.14 per common share) and a loss of $474,000 ($.03 per common share) for the third quarters of 1978 and 1977, respectively, and losses of $2,983,000 ($.19 per common share) and $1,071,000 ($.07 per common share) for the respective nine-month periods.

Pet...the new $1 billion member of the

Pet Dairy markets a full line of high quality fresh dairy products in 10 Southeastern states. In addition to traditional milk and ice cream products, Pet Dairy markets flavored and frozen yogurts, low fat, protein fortified skim and cultured milk items.

Pet nine-month sales
In millions of dollars

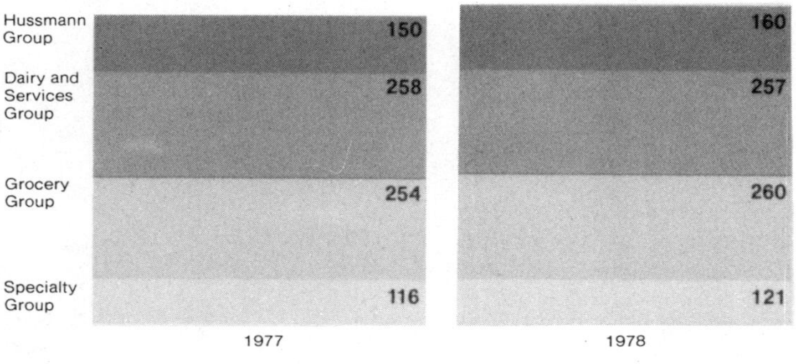

The acquisition of Pet Incorporated in August 1978 brings a new dimension to IC Industries and gives the Company a broad base for growth in the food and food-related fields.

Pet's heritage dates back over 90 years. Until the 1950s, Pet's fortunes were built primarily on one product —evaporated milk. By 1967 the company had diversified and today sales are over $1 billion with some of the best known brand names in the country. Pet's earnings in the past five years have grown at a compound rate of approximately eight percent per year.

The common denominator of Pet is that each of its products and services is in some way related to the U.S. Food System. This food system provides Americans with a vast selection year-round of convenient, nutritious and safe food at the lowest percentage of family income in the world. The complex, efficient food system moves produce from the farm through processing, production, warehousing, distribution and marketing into food stores and restaurants, and to consumer.

Numerous external factors continually influence the food system—food purchases and eating patterns —including government regulation, changing lifestyles and social trends. For example, the increasing number of working women has created a demand for convenience foods which offer value as well as save time. Today's consumers are concerned with nutrition, weight control. food safety and naturalness. All of these must be considered in the planning and marketing of food products and each offers varying opportunities for Pet businesses.

These Pet businesses are divided into four groups—Grocery, Dairy and Services, Hussmann and Specialty. In total, Pet markets approximately 2,000 products, operates 410 retail stores and employs approximately 19,000 people.

Grocery group

The Grocery Group consists of manufactured food products sold primarily through supermarkets. These include such household brand names as Old El Paso Mexican

IC Industries family

foods, Sego diet foods, Musselman's apple products, Laura Scudder's snack products, Orleans and Gulf Belle canned shrimp and oysters and Pet evaporated milk.

Today, Old El Paso is the leading brand in Mexican food, one of the fastest growing markets in the food industry, and has the most extensive product line and widest distribution in the country. Within the Old El Paso line, taco products are the most popular and most widely promoted items. Mexican products are well known and widely used in the Southwest where they long have been a family staple. Old El Paso has successfully promoted the convenience and ease of making tacos in Eastern and Midwestern markets where demand has increased significantly. Growth prospects for this Mexican food line are excellent.

Consumer interest in fitness and weight control in recent years has created new opportunities in the diet food market. Sego capitalized on this with a marketing campaign that helped boost the Sego liquid food diet market share. A promising new product is Sego powder in a popular canister package.

Musselman is well known for apple products, particularly apple sauce. The fastest growing, however, is apple juice. Sales jumped 21 percent last year reflecting a trend toward nutritious drinks and natural foods.

Another growing product line is Orleans and Gulf Belle canned shrimp and oysters. This operation recently expanded by adding freezing capabilities and is now marketing frozen shrimp to the food service industry.

Boyd F. Schenk, President, Pet Incorporated

On the West Coast, Laura Scudder's markets a full line of snack products. Its principal product, Laura Scudder's potato chips, is the leading seller in the California market. Corn and tortilla chips are growing in importance, and in the past few years Laura Scudder's natural peanut butter has experienced remarkable growth.

The Group's senior citizen, Pet evaporated milk, continues to be a consistent profit producer by increasing its market share, even though the evaporated milk market has declined slowly for about 30 years. The Grocery Group also markets the Heartland cereal line and the Reese line of specialty and gourmet foods.

In 1975 Pet formed an International Division from export activities and several small foreign

From its original heritage as the first producer of canned evaporated milk, Pet has grown into a highly diversified company with a broad line of products and services. Shown here displayed in the Pet test kitchens are some of the many products and labels which Pet markets to meet the growing demand for quality foods. Major brand marketing is supported by extensive advertising and promotion.

Home delivery of milk products is an important Pet Dairy tradition and highly popular with consumers.

operations. Last year, the Black Body Company, a manufacturer and marketer of equipment and systems using infra-red heat transfer, was acquired. Black Body's technology opens new markets for Pet in the food service equipment business worldwide with the introduction of the fully automated conveyorized CTX 70 cooking system.

Pet is also expanding sales to the food service market. With the increasing trend of Americans eating one out of three meals away from home, the food service market is growing at twice the rate of the grocery industry. Pet's food service sales are centralized in this group.

Dairy and Services Group

Five profit centers—Pet Dairy, Merchants Refrigerating, 905 and Vendome party centers, and Stuckey's Stores comprise the Dairy and Services Group.

Pet's dairy operation is a major factor in 10 Southeastern states where it markets a full line of fresh dairy products. With a reputation for quality products and customer service, new growth records have been set annually with doubled sales in the past 10 years.

For the past two years extremely competitive pricing adversely affected margins and hurt sales volume. In the new competitive environment, marketing efforts have been intensified and increased emphasis has been placed on such items as fruit drinks and yogurt. New products recently introduced include premium ice cream and modified milk products, such as low fat milk and protein fortified skim milk. Pet Dairy's marketing area has one of the fastest growing populations in the nation.

Merchants Refrigerating provides more than 27 million cubic feet of cold storage space in 11 plants strategically located across the country, supplying cold storage and transportation for the products of various customers. Merchants is considered one of the industry leaders because of its innovative services, including computerized inventory control, order selection, consolidated shipments and blast freezing.

Stuckey's provides "one-stop service" to travelers with its 312 company-owned and franchised stores along interstate highways. Travel continues to be part of the American lifestyle and Stuckey's is uniquely positioned to meet travelers' needs. In recent years Stuckey's has been steadily expanding food service in its stores and recently opened a newly designed prototype store with separate restaurant facilities, large rest rooms, warm decor and a new logo. Expansion of the successful concept is under

Customers find shopping for gifts more convenient in this new prototype Stuckey's store along Interstate highways.

Self-service 905 party centers in Missouri and Vendome party centers in the Los Angeles area cater to the growing leisure time and home entertainment markets. These Pet operations sell wines, liquors, beer, party supplies and holiday gifts. This 905 store is located in St. Peter's, Missouri, near St. Louis.

4

way in new and remodeled stores.

Two of Pet's retailing businesses, 905 and Vendome, cater to the growing leisure and home-entertainment market.

905 operates 40 stores in Missouri, primarily in metropolitan St. Louis. Considered the largest specialty liquor retailer in the country, 905's self-service stores offer extensive wine selections and carry all types of liquor and soft drinks, plus a variety of snack items and imported cheese.

Vendome's 28 party centers are in Southern California, where wine consumption outpaces the rest of the country. As the largest independent wine and spirits retailer in that area, Vendome is noted for its fine selection of imported and domestic wines and holiday gifts.

Hussmann Group

A decade ago, Hussmann, long a leader in refrigeration and refrigerated display cases in supermarkets, initiated a total service program aimed to serve the supermarket industry. Through internal expansion and an active acquisition program. Hussmann's role has expanded to serve almost every segment of the food distribution system. During this period, Hussmann's sales grew from $68 million in 1968 to $207 million in fiscal 1978.

Hussmann is the world's leader and holds the No. 1 market share in food store display equipment, and is the only manufacturer with a complete line of refrigerators,

Pet's Hussmann Group is the world's leader in food store refrigerated display equipment and today serves almost every segment of the food distribution chain. Other Hussmann products include shelves and insulated doors and building panels.

Right: Contech Laboratories, Pet's research division, develops new products and conducts quality control testing for Pet operating divisions. A Contech product development was Sego liquid diet foods (far right) which are growing in popularity among weight-conscious Americans.

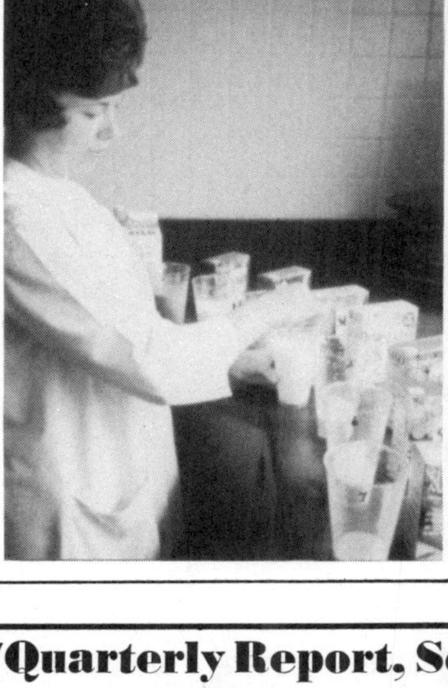

5

Consumers like the convenience of Pet-Ritz pie crust shells, the nation's leading brand.

refrigeration, shelving, coolers, and checkouts for new and remodeled stores. This strong market position is built on quality products and readily available service provided by Hussmann branches and distributors.

Hussmann's industrial products include refrigeration units, insulated doors and insulated building panels—products used extensively in the construction of food processing plants. Hussmann also manufactures panels and refrigerated cooling systems for refrigerated and freezer warehouses.

High energy costs required dramatic changes in the supermarket industry, and new lifestyles and increased leisure of consumers resulted in changes in stores themselves. Hussmann has maintained its leadership position by staying abreast of market trends.

Hussmann's new Power Management System utilizes a microcomputer which controls energy usage in food stores and cuts energy costs as much as 25 to 30 percent. A new Mini Power Management System controls energy usage and costs in plants, office buildings and banks.

The growth of convenience stores and boutique supermarket departments has created an expanded market for Hussmann fixtures, such as deli cases, flower cases, bakery displays and ice cream-dipping cabinets. The newest addition to the Hussmann group, Star Cooler, opens up new growth markets for ice makers and ice merchandisers.

Specialty Group

The diverse Specialty Group includes the businesses of Frozen Foods, Whitman's Chocolates, Funsten Nuts, Pet Bakery and two smaller operations, Mr. Panel and St. Louis Lithographing.

In Frozen Foods, Pet was the innovator of frozen piecrust shells and the Pet-Ritz brand remains No. 1 with more than 50 percent of the market. Downyflake is a leading brand of waffles, pancakes and French toast. Other frozen products include pies, cobblers and non-dairy topping.

New products are vital to Frozen Foods' growth. In recent years the Frozen Foods operation has expanded from the traditional dessert and breakfast market into main dish categories. Promising new products include Toaster French Fries and Toaster Hash Browns.

The company's oldest business—founded in 1843—and probably the best known candy brand is Whitman's Chocolates. Whitman's Sampler is still the world's largest selling box of chocolates. Whitman's produces a broad line of boxed chocolates, candies and holiday specialties, resulting in a large proportion of Whitman's business occurring between Halloween and Mother's Day.

Funsten today is the largest independent processor of tree nuts in the world. Most of Funsten's nuts are purchased by commercial customers for use in ice creams, candies and bakery items containing pecans, walnuts and almonds.

Pet Bakery's two plants produce a wide variety of fresh bakery products for both retail and commercial sale throughout the country. Aunt Fanny's pecan twirls is the company's most popular label; however, a majority of its products are sold under various private labels.

Bright future

The addition of Pet to the IC Industries family of companies has produced a partnership which promises substantially improved earnings potential for shareholders.■■

During recent years the number of specialty frozen food items available has increased significantly. Pet's Downyflake is a leading brand of waffles, pancakes and French toast. A recent addition to the Downyflake line is French-fried potatoes for heating in the family toaster.

Group operating highlights

The addition of operating results for Pet Incorporated following acquisition in early August produced a marked increase in sales and revenues and pre-tax income for the **IC Consumer Products Group.** Pretax income of $47.9 million for the first nine months was 27 percent greater than 1977 on sales and revenues of $568.9 million, a 63 percent increase over the prior year.

Midas-International year-to-date sales increased by 24.5 percent to $245 million. Revenues from the Automotive Group's 1,071 shops worldwide and associated operations set all-time records in September. Extension of the famous Midas lifetime guarantee on mufflers to foreign automobiles, effective October 1, 1978, is expected to result in further sales increases for Midas automotive service shops. Midas Vehicle Group revenues continue strongly ahead of last year.

Sales of IC Industries three soft drink companies—Pepsi-Cola General Bottlers, Dad's Root Beer and Bubble Up companies—for the first nine months were 12.4 percent ahead of 1977 for a new record $170 million.

Included in the consolidated total are Pet sales of $153 million, approximately 62 percent of Pet's total sales for the quarter. The Hussmann Group reported substantially increased shipments in September, and the backlog of unfilled orders increased to $66 million at the end of September, a

Top: Midas Silencers Limited currently operates 17 automotive service shops in the United Kingdom, including this new shop which was recently opened in Glasgow, Scotland.

Center: The crane on this West German Army Leopard I recovery tank is one of 600 such units which utilize Abex Denison hydraulics for crane functions, accessories and winches.

Chicago Mayor Michael A. Bilandic is shown in front of new construction currently underway in Illinois Center, the world's largest privately financed urban redevelopment project, in which Illinois Center Corporation is a joint venture partner. Construction activities in Illinois Center currently involve three buildings with at least one more scheduled for start in 1978.

IC Industries three soft drink companies are benefiting from increased soft drink consumption.

20 percent increase over last year. Sego Liquid Diet products continue their strong growth, reflecting Americans' growing weight consciousness. The Vendome party center stores in Southern California have experienced greatly increased sales following the recent expiration of California's fair trade laws covering alcoholic beverages.

IC Commercial Products Group (Abex Corporation) experienced a strong third quarter, resulting in year-to-date pre-tax income of $50.7 million, a 9.6 percent increase over 1977, on sales of $544 million. Incoming orders continued strong in September and exceeded sales by $6.6 million, resulting in an increase in orders backlog to $314 million, compared with $219 million a year ago and $225 million at the end of December. Orders for all four market groups—automotive, castings, fluid power and railroad products—are well ahead of 1977. Especially encouraging was the September incoming orders rate for manganese steel castings which was the best in three years. The new Abex railroad wheel mounting plant at Corsicana, Texas, will go into operation about November 1 to serve the growing Southwest unit coal train market.

The Abex Jetway Division recently was awarded an order by Delta Airlines for 44 aircraft loading bridges to be installed at the new Midfield Atlanta Airport. Previously Jetway had been awarded a 41-unit order from Eastern Airlines and an order for 11 from Piedmont Airlines, making a total of 96 of the planned 127 bridges at Atlanta for a combined contract total of $15 million. Jetway is currently negotiating with four airlines for the remaining 31 Atlanta bridges.

The **IC Real Estate Group** reported nine-month pre-tax income of $13.8 million, a 57 percent increase over 1977. During the quarter sale of land in Illinois Center for a rental apartment building, on which construction has now commenced, favorably affected Group sales and earnings.

Pre-tax income from **IC Financial Services Group** "companies being sold" was $7.1 million, a 23 percent increase over the first nine months of 1977.

Following a strong second quarter performance, the **IC Transportation Group** experienced excellent operations during the third quarter, but the final result was a $3.3 million pre-tax loss because of the recent railroad clerks' strike. The Illinois Central Gulf Railroad disbursed $3.2 million to the Norfolk & Western Railroad under terms of a railroad industry mutual benefit insurance plan against struck carriers. In addition, the third quarter results reflect a further estimated pre-tax loss of approximately $4.0 million because of the four-day strike of such clerks against the ICG in September. Without this $7.2 million adverse effect, the IC Transportation Group would have produced good earnings and remained profitable for the nine-month period in spite of the severe weather and long coal strike during the first quarter.

Despite lost traffic in September, the ICG reported increased revenues for both the third quarter and nine months. Year-to-date Transportation revenues were $553 million, 8.2 percent over the comparable period in 1977. Major increases in September, compared with the prior year, were realized in corn and grain and other food products, but strike results produced negative comparisons in most other major commodities.

The ICG is continuing its program of significantly increased capital and operating expenses for maintenance of way and equipment. The combined total in the third quarter was $124 million, up 39.3 percent over 1977, and for the nine months, was $328 million, an increase of 23.8 percent.■■

"Run-through" services make operating efficiencies and cost savings possible for connecting railroads. This Illinois Central Gulf-Cotton Belt (Southern Pacific) run-through saves at least a day's time on through freight movements from the West, South and Mexico to points in the North, East and Canada, eliminating costly switching delays.

IC Industries is a highly diversified international company marketing a broad range of products and services.

IC Industries

	Marketing categories	Operating units
IC COMMERCIAL PRODUCTS GROUP	Automotive products	Abex Corporation Friction Products Group Signal-Stat Division A. L. Hansen Manufacturing Division Kokomo Spring John Gillen Manufacturing
	Railroad products	Railroad Products Group
	Castings	Amsco Division Engineered Products Division Waukesha Foundry Division
	Hydraulics	Denison Division Aerospace Division Jetway Division Remco Hydraulics Mead Fluid Dynamics
IC CONSUMER PRODUCTS GROUP	Automotive services and vehicles	Midas-International Corporation Automotive Group Vehicle Group
	Soft drinks	Pepsi-Cola General Bottlers, Inc. Dad's Root Beer Company Bubble Up Company, Inc.
	Food products, store equipment and associated services	Pet Incorporated Grocery Group
		Dairy and Services Group
		Hussmann Group
		Specialty Group
IC REAL ESTATE GROUP	Real estate	Seay & Thomas, Inc. Philipsborn Equities, Inc. Illinois Center Corporation LaSalle Properties, Inc.
IC FINANCIAL SERVICES GROUP	Financial services	Lincoln Financial, Inc. Lincoln Liberty Life Insurance Company Benjamin Franklin Savings Association H. F. Philipsborn & Company Midwest Life Nebraska IC Leasing, Inc.
IC TRANSPORTATION GROUP	Railroad transportation	Illinois Central Gulf Railroad Chicago & Illinois Western Railroad

Notes:
(1) Results for 1977 have been restated to include the results of Security Investment Company, the owner of the Pepsi-Cola Bottling Company of Cincinnati, which was acquired on February 8, 1978, in a business combination accounted for as a pooling of interests.
(2) Pet Incorporated results reflect reporting on a fiscal year ending March 31, 1978.
(3) Definitive agreements have been reached to sell all stock of Lincoln Liberty Life Insurance Company, Benjamin Franklin Savings Association, Midwest Holding Corporation (including Midwest Life Nebraska) and two smaller IC Financial Services Group subsidiaries. It is anticipated that the sales will be completed in early 1979.

Products and services	1977 Sales and revenues (See Notes)		
Automotive and aircraft disc brake lining, clutch material. Vehicle lighting, signal and safety devices, tire hardware. Locks, hinges, latches, window regulators. Compression, extension and torsion springs. Machine keys, pins, other high volume small parts.	$180,000,000		
Trackwork, switch stands, wheels, brake shoes, braking systems, bearings, car roofs and ends, locomotive and car wheel truing machines. Remanufactured electric motors and generators.	$173,000,000		
Heavy-duty castings, welding alloys, dredging pumps. High-temperature alloy castings, copper- and iron-based castings. Precision castings, pumps and blending systems.	$163,000,000		
Hydraulic pumps, motors, valves, bench and floor presses. Hydraulic equipment for aircraft and space vehicles. Aircraft passenger loading bridges, jet aircraft noise suppressors. Hydraulic cylinders, motion compensators, shock suppressors. Pneumatic control valves and cylinders, air presses, air-driven work feeders	$122,000,000		
1,071 automotive service shops worldwide. Recreational and commercial vehicle manufacture, aluminum boats.	$264,000,000		
Independent bottler of Pepsi-Cola and other soft drinks in seven states. 171 franchised Dad's and 181 franchised Bubble Up bottlers serving 225 markets worldwide.	$211,000,000	**IC PRODUCTS COMPANY**	**$1,113,000,000**
Evaporated and powdered milk, diet food products, grocery and specialty items, Mexican foods, fruit products, snack foods.	$354,000,000		
Fresh milk, ice cream and fresh dairy specialties, refrigerated warehouses, roadside stores, party centers.	$351,000,000		
Freezer and refrigerated display cases, refrigeration and environmental control systems, storage coolers, checkout counters, shelving and general merchandise fixtures.	$207,000,000		
Frozen foods, confections, bakery products, nuts, lithographing, panel centers.	$191,000,000	**PET INCORPORATED**	**$1,103,000,000**
Planning, joint venture development, marketing, property management. Funding, land and development loans, construction loans, standby commitments. Joint venture partner in development of Illinois Center, Chicago. Developer of Elmwood Industrial Park, New Orleans; partner in Poydras Plaza, New Orleans.	$ 39,000,000		
Financial holding company. Life, health, accident insurance in 42 states. Savings and loan services in Houston area, financing, funding of home building. Mortgage banking services and construction lending. Life, health, accident insurance in 26 states. Financing for leasing of equipment, franchise locations.	$ 79,000,000	**REAL ESTATE AND FINANCIAL SERVICES**	**$118,000,000**
Common carrier rail services over 8,948 miles of line in 13 states from the Great Lakes to the Gulf of Mexico. Switching services in Chicago and construction of transportation equipment.	$680,000,000	**TRANSPORTATION**	**$680,000,000**
		TOTAL SALES AND REVENUES	$3,014,000,000

The newest member of our family has a family of its own.

In 1894, the Helvetia Milk Company in Highland, Illinois introduced "Our Pet," a baby-size can of evaporated milk.

Today, that 5¢ can of milk has become Pet Incorporated, a billion dollar family of well-known food and food service products, and the newest member of our IC Industries family. It's quite an addition, with fiscal 1978 sales of $1.1 billion and pre-tax earnings of $57.4 million.

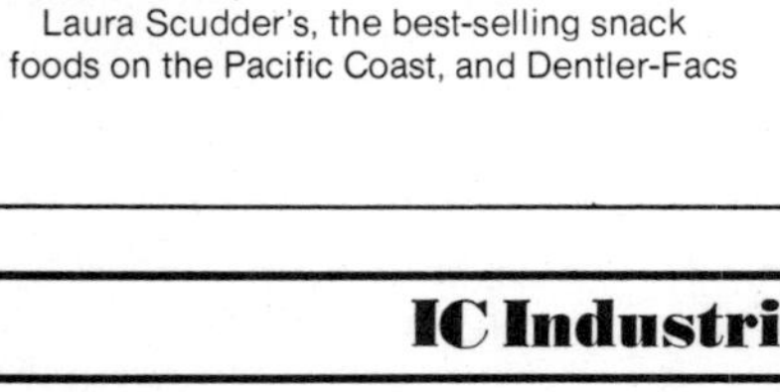

The largest of Pet's four business groups is the Grocery Group. It includes Pet evaporated and powdered milks; Sego diet foods; Old El Paso, the country's leading brand of Mexican food;

Laura Scudder's, the best-selling snack foods on the Pacific Coast, and Dentler-Facs snack foods in Texas; Musselman's fruit products; Gulf Belle and Orleans brands, the nation's leading processors of canned shrimp and oysters; Reese Finer Foods, a leading importer, manufacturer and distributor of gourmet and specialty food items; and Heartland Cereal products.

The Dairy and Services Group includes a full line of Pet fresh dairy products in the Southeast; Merchants Refrigerated Warehouses, offering 27 million cubic feet of freezer storage in 11 major markets; 312 Stuckey's stores on the nation's interstate highway system; Vendome and 905 party centers in the West and Midwest.

The Hussmann Group features the Hussmann brand name, for years the world's leader in food store refrigerated display equipment, now serving nearly every segment of the food distribution system.

Pet's Specialty Group includes Downyflake and Pet-Ritz frozen foods; Funsten Nuts, the world's largest independent processor of tree nuts; and Whitman's Chocolates, the 136-year old brand featuring the best-selling box of chocolates in the world, Whitman's Sampler.

That's the Pet family. The newest member of the IC Industries family.This association marks the beginning of a significant change in the future direction of IC Industries.

We've been more than a railroad for ten years. Now, we're even more. Another billion more.

If you'd like to know about how we've grown, and how we're still growing, please write to us.

IC Industries

CR-14-10/78

IC Industries, Inc.
Corporate Offices
One Illinois Center
111 East Wacker Drive
Chicago, IL 60601
(312) 565 3000

IC Industries, Inc.
European Office
55, ch. Moise-Duboule
1209 Geneva. Switzerland
Tel. (41.22) 98.23.11
Telex 22884

IC Industries
Growth by design.

Fact File
August 1979

IC Industries is a highly diversified international company marketing a broad range of products and services.

Contents

Company profile
page 2

The IC Industries family of companies
page 4

IC Products Company
page 5

IC Commercial Products Group
page 5

Abex Corporation
page 6

IC Consumer Products Group
page 11

Pet Incorporated
page 12

Soft Drinks
page 15

Midas-International
page 19

IC Real Estate Group
page 21

IC Transportation Group
page 22

Other operations
page 24

Recent financial highlights
page 26

Financial information
page 27

Shareholder profile
page 28

Financial charts
page 29

Chronology of growth
page 36

Corporate management
page 37

Corporate data
page 40

1978 sales and revenues
(see note)
in billions of dollars

Percent of 1978 pre-tax income
(see note)
by product group, excluding other income (charges), net

The orderly planned future growth of IC Industries lies in its program of selective diversification in Commercial Products and Consumer Products.

Note: The statement of income has been reclassified to reflect continuing operations. The financial service companies being sold are included in a separate caption in the Consolidated Summary of Income with the remaining companies in the Financial Services Group included in the other (charges) income net in the Consolidated Summary of Income.

1

Company subsidiaries

IC Commercial Products Group
(IC Products Company)
Abex Corporation
Abex Industries Ltd. (Canada)
Abex Industrial, S.A. (Mexico)
Amsco Mexicana, S.A. (Mexico)
Denison Hydraulics, Japan, Ltd. (60%)
Abex Mead Limited (England)
Abex International S.A. (Switzerland)
Abex A/S (Denmark)
Abex Denison Limited (England)
Abex Engineered Products Limited (England)
Abex Ges.m.b.H. (Austria)
Abex GmbH (Germany)
Abex Industries Aktiebolag (Sweden)
Abex Industries S.A. (France) (99.9%)
Abex International Holdings Limited (Bahamas)
Abex Pagid Equipement S.A. (France) (66.6%)
Abex Pagid Reibbelag GmbH (West Germany) (66.6%)
Frendo Abex S.p.A. (Italy) (66.6%)
Societa Italiana per l'Amianto S.p.A. (Italy) (97.6%)

IC Consumer Products Group
(IC Products Company)
Midas-International Corporation
Frolic Homes, Inc.
Huth Manufacturing Corporation
Indiana Trailer Supply, Inc.
International Parts (Canada) Limited
International Stamping Co., Inc.
Ken-Craft Products, Inc.
Midas Automotive Limited (Canada)
Midas Realty Corporation
Midas S.A. (Belgium)
Midas Silencers Limited (England)
Muffler Corporation of America
Muffler Corporation of Canada Ltd.
Norris Homes Incorporated

Pepsi-Cola General Bottlers, Inc.
Danville Pepsi-Cola Bottling Co.
Genadco Advertising Agency, Inc.
Kolmar Products Corporation
Pepsi-Cola Peoria Bottling Co.
Pepsi-Cola Bottling Company of Kenosha and Racine, Inc.

Dad's Root Beer Company

Bubble Up Company, Inc.

Pet Incorporated—
Principal Operations
Dairy and Services Group
Pet Dairy
905 International Stores
Public Warehousing and Distribution
Stuckey Stores
Vendome Stores
Grocery Group
Grocery Products
International Food Sales
Mountain Pass Canning
Musselman Fruit Products
Reese Finer Foods
Snack Foods
Southland Canning & Packing
Hussmann Group
Food Service Equipment
Food Store Equipment
Hussmann-Canada
Hussmann-Mexico
Industrial
International
Specialty Group
Pet Bakery
Frozen Foods
Funsten Nut
St. Louis Lithographing
Whitman's Chocolates

IC Real Estate Group
Illinois Center Corporation
LaSalle Properties, Inc.
Philipsborn Equities, Inc.
South Properties, Inc.

IC Transportation Group
Illinois Central Gulf Railroad Company
Mississippi Valley Corporation
Waterloo Railroad Company
GM&O Land Company
Gulf Transport Company

Chicago & Illinois Western Railroad

Other
IC Leasing, Inc.
H. F. Philipsborn & Company

Corporate data

Executive Offices
One Illinois Center
111 East Wacker Drive
Chicago, IL 60601
(312) 565 3000

European Corporate Finance Office
55, ch. Moise-Duboule
1209 Geneva, Switzerland
Tel. (41.22) 98.23.11
Telex 22884
Cable ABEXINTER GENEVA

European Office
55, ch. Moise-Duboule
1209 Geneva, Switzerland
Tel. (41.22) 98.23.11
Telex 22884

State of Incorporation—Delaware

Listed—
(Common and Series 1 Preferred Stock)
New York Stock Exchange
Midwest Stock Exchange
Pacific Stock Exchange
(Common Stock Only)
The Stock Exchange in London
Amsterdam Stock Exchange

Stock symbol—ICX

Stock transfer office and registrar of stock—
The Northern Trust Company, Chicago

Secretary and General Counsel—
Robert S. Kirby

Public accountants—
Peat, Marwick, Mitchell & Co.

Consulting accountants—
Price Waterhouse & Co.

Corporate calendar
Fiscal year ends—December 31

Annual meeting—second Thursday in May

Annual report published—late March

Quarterly income statement—
twenty days after calendar quarter

Directors meet for dividend action—
February, May, August and November

Dividend payment dates—January 1, April 1, July 1, October 1

5

Corporate Communications—A Comprehensive Plan

Marvin L. Krasnansky

Editor's Note:

What follows is the five-year plan developed for B-D by Marvin L. Krasnansky, one of the most able professionals in the corporate communications and investor relations area. The plan he developed during his tenure there is comprehensive, fitting investor relations in with other aspects of corporate communications, such as press relations, which many corporations tend to overlook or ignore.

The plan itself provides one of the best available insights into the workings of a modern investor relations program. In most cases, cost figures have been removed from this plan, at the request of Mr. Krasnansky.

The external environment for the Company over the next five years will become increasingly difficult, making it more important than ever to maintain "open" communications with the public. To communicate effectively in this environment will require greater coordination of all of the Company's efforts in this area. How well we do in this endeavor will have a real impact on profitability.

To serve the needs of a corporation that will be approaching the $1 billion-a-year sales level toward the end of this planning period will also require an increase in communications expenditures for additional manpower, a corporate advertising program, and a corporate identification system. This last point is especially important if we are to achieve greater visibility, particularly with investors.

With regard to the latter, it is a reasonably safe assumption that institutionalization of the market will continue, and although we must be responsive to the

Marvin L. Krasnansky was Vice President, Corporate Communications, of Becton Dickinson & Co.

special needs of professional investors, we must also increase our efforts to keep and attract individual investors. In the area of public affairs, increasing antibusiness government regulation requires that we develop formal Company positions on critical issues and that we work more effectively with legislators, regulators, and business and trade groups to bring our views to bear on these issues.

EXTERNAL ENVIRONMENT

In broad terms, the external environment for B-D over the next five years will be marked by ferment, change, and hostility rising from growing public skepticism about established institutions, including both government and business. This will require increased efforts on the part of the Company to impart its message more effectively to its key audiences—the general public, the media, health care professionals, shareholders, investors, the investment community, public officials, employees, customers, and suppliers. At the same time, the cost of communications (advertising, printing, and so forth) continues to rise, and communications channels are becoming increasingly crowded with competing and often conflicting messages.

To achieve an effective dialog with these publics will require an increasingly "open" communications policy to preserve and enhance the Company's credibility. The degree to which we are able to maintain a high level of credibility with our publics will have a significant impact on the Company's freedom of action, profitability, labor relations, reputation for quality and efficiency, evaluation in the stock market and capital markets, and our ability to affect the legislative and regulatory climate. Viewed, then, from this perspective, how well we respond to this external environment will have a real, if difficult to measure, effect on the bottom line.

In the investor relations area, while it is axiomatic that nothing is ever permanent, it is a reasonably safe assumption that the next five years will see a continuation of the trend toward institutionalization of the stock market. To be sure, interest in the market on the part of individuals will probably increase from the depressed levels of recent years; in fact, this revival may already be underway. Nonetheless, the trend toward institutionalization will continue, even if at a slower pace.

Similarly, it appears likely that institutional investors will continue to focus on a rather narrow list of major companies whose industry position, capitalization, and growth rate qualify them as "institutional grade" stocks. As a result, the so-called "two-tier" market is like to continue.

In the area of public affairs, the major external factor that will affect our industry will be the degree of government control of quality and cost of health care. The energy crisis and its impact on operating costs and availability of raw materials will also continue to have a major impact on operations. In addition, the degree to which government extends its control over the operation of the economy will restrict the freedom of management to operate and alter the decision-making process. At the moment, the indications are that there will be continued efforts to expand government regulation and control, although in the past two years there has been some movement in the other direction.

The role of the multinational company and its relations to host countries are being reexamined, and new regulations and rules are being considered at an increasingly rapid rate. Also, on a local level, state legislative bodies continue to increase their involvement in issues affecting the economy, business, and the environment. This increases the possibility of diversity of regulations and variations in the cost of doing business from one state to another. Also, younger, better educated, and more socially conscious legislators are likely to enlarge the range of legislative involvement on the state level.

INTERNAL ENVIRONMENT

With the inclusion of the director of corporate communications as a member of the corporate operating committee, considerable progress has been achieved during the past year in more fully integrating the corporate communications department as an element of corporate management. This has permitted the department to be kept abreast of developments, has provided an opportunity for departmental input in the management process, and has enabled the department to anticipate events rather than simply react to them. In order to bring this process full circle, we must expand the level of communication with the divisions, working through the group vice presidents.

The inclusion of the public affairs function in the framework of a total communications effort enhances the effectiveness of the function by combining the information-gathering and -dissemination capacity of the department. The legislative response capability has been improved by the addition of the state legislative monitoring service. Greater exchange of information between corporate communications and the other divisions has also increased effectiveness. Further improvement in this area will yield even greater benefits. The new public affairs advisory committee will also increase the effectiveness of the program.

OPPORTUNITIES AND PROBLEMS

In assessing the Company's communications opportunities and prospects over the next five years, it is fair to say that the base from which we start has more assets than liabilities. We enjoy a high reputation for the quality of our products; we are a leading company in an industry which is well regarded by the investment community; we are achieving increasing recognition for our management skills; we are among a relatively small number of companies that enjoy reasonably liquid markets for their securities; we have avoided the snarls that have entangled many major companies in recent years (such as illegal political contributions, environmental controversy, questionable accounting and financial practices, and shareholder discontent); we enjoy good labor and community relations; and we have taken a position of leadership in the health care industry in providing the investment community with detailed information on our business, as well as in the accessibility of our senior management. On the other side of the coin, there remains the lingering question on the Street as to the quality and depth of B-D management and the concern over our ability to develop significant new products.

In a broader vein, the growing institutionalization of the market and the continuation of the "two-tier" market pose a double concern for the Company. On the one hand, with institutional money managers focusing on a narrowing band of companies (about 200, on average, according to a recent study), it is critical for B-D to maintain its status in this select group. On the other hand, with B-D already a highly institutionalized stock, continuation of this trend would bring greater volatility. At the same time, our relatively high multiple and low payout make the stock difficult for stockbrokers to sell to individual investors. However, despite these obstacles, we must make the effort to keep the individual shareholders we now have and to attract others. To this end, senior management must focus on the need to effect an alliance with a major retail brokerage firm as a co-manager of future financings, and major inside stockholders should consider utilizing this firm in effecting diversification of their B-D holdings.

To help achieve this and other objectives, it is important for the Company to attain greater visibility with its key audiences. To do this, we must do a better job of coordinating our communication efforts. The Company's growth through acquisition and internal diversification has brought about a proliferation of communications to the publics and markets we serve. At the same time, the rising cost of advertising and promotional activity has made it extremely expensive and difficult for individual divisions to create strong identities of their own. As a consequence, B-D often lacks a clear identity and image in its primary market, health care.

To overcome this, we must develop a cohesive corporate identification system, based on sound research and analysis of our communications problems and needs. This will provide a strong link between the divisions and the parent. An element in this overall communication effort should be a corporate advertising program directed at investors, in which health care professionals will be a special target audience, as both customers and potential investors.

Toward the conclusion of the time period covered by this five-year plan, B-D sales will be in the area of $1 billion a year. To service the communications needs of a company of this size will require additional professional staffing in such areas as public relations, investor relations, internal communications, editorial services (speeches, position papers, and executive correspondence), and public affairs. It may also be desirable to coordinate the Company's advertising and promotional activities under either the corporate communications department or a corporate marketing function, if such a corporate department is established.

While recognizing the necessary budget restrictions resulting from the present external business and economic environment, the Company must be prepared to commit greater manpower and financial resources to corporate communications over the next five years if the objectives recommended in this plan are to be achieved.

In the public affairs area, the effective involvement of our industry in the development of a financially sound, well-organized, and efficient health care delivery system for the United States should be our primary consideration. Our attention should also focus on assuring access to adequate supplies of energy and raw materials for the Company and the health care industry.

The antibusiness bias of a large segment of the media, many educators, legislators, and a substantial segment of the public poses substantial problems. Programs to increase the credibility of business and to improve the effectiveness of communicating the role of profits in meeting national objectives offers substantial opportunities for business.

On the following pages are several important objectives from the B-D five-year plan, along with proposed strategies, action plans, and estimated costs of achieving those objectives. They can serve as models for other companies that are making a concerted effort to improve investor relations.

OBJECTIVE:

To establish the quality and depth of B-D management in the investment community.

STRATEGY:

Management ranks second only to a company's earnings record in the minds of investment professionals. As the ORC study shows, there is a direct correlation between these two key factors and P/E ratios. Considerable progress has been made in this over the past year toward establishing the leadership roles of Jack Howe and Marvin Asnes as well as the qualities of the group vice presidents and other senior officers. The basis for this progress is the continued good earnings performance of B-D and the greater exposure of management to the investment community.

ACTION PROGRAMS:

1. A tour of major financial cities by senior management should be scheduled annually, supported by similar presentations by other officers in other cities. Cities covered should include New York, Boston, Philadelphia, Atlanta, Chicago, San Francisco, Los Angeles, Dallas, and Houston in the United States (the New York appearance should be before one of the two specialty groups covering the health care industry); abroad, we should cover London, Paris, Brussels, Zurich (or Geneva), and Frankfurt on a less frequent basis.

As a general rule, these presentations should be bunched together in order to maximize the effort involved in preparing the presentation, graphics, and information packages. COST: Travel, hotels, meals, etc., to be determined.

2. Senior management should continue to make itself accessible to visits by analysts at corporate headquarters. This affords an opportunity to reinforce positive attitudes through the vehicle of one-on-one encounters—again with Messrs. Howe, Asnes, Harter, the Group VPs, and other senior officers. Cost: Minimal.

3. Two days after the issuance of each quarterly report, we should have a luncheon meeting with key analysts in New York to review the results and answer any questions they might have. Cost: Minimal.

Objective:

To achieve greater recognition in the financial community for the Company's growth record.

Strategy:

Since the earnings record of a company ranks even slightly ahead of management capability in the minds of analysts, emphasis on this long-term record should be given special stress in all written and verbal communications.

Action Program:

The Company's historic growth record in sales and earnings should be a focal point of presentations to and discussions with analysts. This growth record should become a major theme of all our verbal and written communications.

Cost: Nil.

Objective:

To focus greater attention on the Company's long-term growth objectives.

Strategy:

While the Company has publicly stated that its long-term growth goal is 15 percent a year compounded over the next five years, this is too rigid a goal on a year-to-year and quarter-to-quarter basis.

Instead, I believe our emphasis should be on achieving 15 percent *compounded* growth over the next five years, while acknowledging that in any given year or quarter, results may vary somewhat above or below that target. Obviously, the narrower the range, the higher the degree of credibility.

In support of this approach, we should delineate in more specific terms how we plan to achieve this growth.

Action Program:

This should be a major theme of our overall communications effort.

COST: Nil.

OBJECTIVE:

To position B-D as a medical/hospital/laboratory supply company which manufactures a diverse mix of products.

STRATEGY:

To overcome the idea that B-D is primarily a "needle and syringe" business, we must increasingly focus on how the Company has evolved over the past decade as a broad-based medical science and technology company that is placing its investment and management emphasis on new and emerging products and markets. We should stress that this diversity has been achieved both from within the Company and through acquisitions.

In addition, we should develop a comprehensive corporate identification system designed to link all the divisions more clearly to the parent company.

ACTION PROGRAMS:

1. Our communications should continue to stress the diversity of our products, a major theme of our basic presentation to analysts.

In addition, we should plan to take groups of key analysts, who follow the Company closely, to the research center and major production facilities in order to provide them with greater insight into our capabilities. Such a program would be most effective if it were tied to specific newsworthy developments. Such visits would do more than anything we say to demonstrate the range of our abilities and the quality of our people. COST: Per seminar.

2. We should expose our research people to key medical and science writers through private off-the-record luncheons. The objective is to establish our people as a source of information on developments in health care technology. This should result in increasing reference to B-D people as "expert" sources and an increase in stories about B-D's accomplishments in medicine and science. COST: Minimal.

3. A consulting firm should be retained to provide experienced guidance in the development of a corporate identification system that will serve the Company for at least the next 10 years. The consultants would be charged with studying the Company's identification problems and needs, designing and developing a graphics system and manual, and assisting the Company in implementing the program. COST: To be determined.

OBJECTIVE:

To increase the number of individual B-D shareholders.

STRATEGY:

Ownership of B-D stock continues to be highly concentrated. After eliminating family and other insider holdings, institutions would appear to hold approximately 50 percent of the shares.

This represents a dangerous degree of concentration in institutional hands. Although the current economic and market climate makes it extremely difficult to attract individuals, it is important that we start to make the effort.

Even taking into consideration that the Company has been publicly owned only since 1962, our ratio of shareholders per million shares is well below the norm. A study of 34 NYSE companies with 10 to 20 million shares outstanding (including 15 companies with 15 to 20 million shares outstanding) shows that these groups of companies averaged 2,500 and 2,600 shareholders per million shares. This compares with B-D's average of 887 per million shares. Putting it another way, B-D would have 43,000 stockholders if it had the average ratio of stockholders:shares as the companies in the study. So, even considering the difficulties of the present market climate, there is considerable room for improvement in this area.

ACTION PROGRAMS:

1. The task of attracting additional individual investors should be approached as a marketing problem. To do this, we must first have sophisticated marketing data on which to base the program. Therefore, I recommend a three-pronged research effort:
   (a) A telephone survey of 100 new shareholders to determine the specific factors that influenced their decision to acquire B-D shares and to measure their characteristics and investment objectives. In addition, we should develop a questionnaire to be sent to new shareholders on a continuing basis. COST: To be determined.

   (b) A mail survey of former shareholders to determine their reasons for selling B-D shares and a continuing survey for the same purpose. COST: To be determined.

   (c) A telephone survey of 50 retail stockbrokers (including some identified by new and old shareholders as an important influence in their decision to buy or sell B-D shares) to obtain some understanding of the reasons that brokers recommend buying B-D stock. COST: To be determined.

(The information gathered from this research could also be used in merchandising the stock to retail brokers by informing them of what we have learned about the principal reasons investors buy the stock and the most effective approaches other brokers have employed in placing the stock with their clients.)

2. With this information, we should make a major effort to get the research and sales support of major retail brokerage firms. As part of this effort, we should offer to provide a senior official to follow up any favorable research reports by talking to the firms' registered representatives (RRs). A number of firms have telephone "hotlines" linking all of their offices, and frequently have analysts interview key officials of subject companies. In addition, as we travel around the country on our presentations, we should arrange to visit the local offices of these retail firms to talk to the brokers.

This kind of follow-up to research reports is a key factor in merchandising the stock on a retail basis. It is axiomatic that "stocks are sold, not bought." The impetus comes from the RR, who in effect is his own "analyst," weeding through the 100 or so research reports the typical major firm publishes annually and selecting those stocks with the best prospects. At any given time, a successful RR will have his clients in 10 to 15 issues. Our job is to get B-D on his list.

As a means of staying in contact with interested brokers, we should offer to put them on a special mailing list to receive our quarterly and annual reports and other pertinent information. COST: Nil, other than mailing material.

3. With the heavy concentration of high-income stockholders in central and northern New Jersey, we should make a special effort with the branch offices of major retail firms in the area, exploiting the fact that B-D is well-known in the region. Many firms sponsor investment seminars and provide display areas for company products and literature. We should take full advantage of these opportunities. COST: Nil.

4. We should send a letter of welcome to all new shareholders, containing the annual and latest quarterly reports. (The new shareholder survey should be included in this mailing.) As difficult as it is to attract new shareholders, we should go out of our way to make them welcome and keep them informed.

   The mailing should also include a stuffer illustrating the Company's consumer products. COST: To be determined.

5. We should advertise the availability of our annual report in the special annual report sections of various business and financial publications. These ads draw excellent responses, and with an improved shareholder monitoring system we should be able to measure the conversion rate of inquiries to new shareholders. COST: To be determined.

6. We should consider implementing an automatic dividend reinvestment program. To gauge the interest, I suggest that we survey shareholders through the use of an insert in the annual report mailing. COST: To be determined.

7. We should develop a basic presentation on B-D for use by divisional people with local business, civic, and service organizations. The talk would be accompanied by appropriate slides developed from existing files and the upcoming annual report. (The existing analyst presentation could readily be adapted for this purpose.) COST: Nil.

8. As part of our effort to create a greater awareness of B-D among our various publics, we should employ corporate advertising, primarily in media aimed at investors and health care professionals. The latter group is composed of customers for our products, and is an affluent group, many of whom are potential investors. COST: Depends on size of program and the media used.

OBJECTIVE:

To improve the quality and scope of the quarterly report.

STRATEGY:

In addition to the annual report, the Company normally has only five other opportunities a year to address its shareholders directly. These opportunities should be exploited to the fullest in an effort to provide shareholders with meaningful information about current developments throughout the year, not just once a year.

ACTION PROGRAM:

We have made a good start in this direction, but should take the process one step further by expanding the quarterly report to include other "feature material," such as new products, close-ups on various divisions, key personnel, and acquisitions.

(A number of major companies use a "magazine" format for their quarterly reports, featuring the financial results for the period and other important developments during the quarter, plus feature stories. Such an approach could permit us to combine the quarterly report and the in-house publication, *B-D World,* and could help save money.)

COST: Sufficient amount to design a new "magazine" format for the quarterly report; budget for four quarterly reports to shareholders.

OBJECTIVE:

To provide close surveillance over shifts in stockholders, particularly institutions.

STRATEGY:

Given our objective of seeking to increase the number of individual shareholders and recognizing our heavy institutional holdings, it is critical that we develop the capability to measure trends in our shareholder list.

Action Program:

Working with our transfer agent, we should develop detailed information on the breakdown between individual and institutional holdings. The information should be available on a monthly basis. All holders of 1,000 or more shares should be identified on a master list. All institutional shareholders of 10,000 or more shares should be identified and their holdings tracked. With this information, we should be able to identify trends, contact the institutions involved, and determine the reasons for their buy/sell decisions. On occasion, where we see a large institutional holder start to sell, we might be able to fill the role of a "middleman" by suggesting another institution which may be interested in acquiring its share.

Cost: Details have been provided in previous memos.

Objective:

To provide securities analysts with detailed statistical and background information on B-D and the health care industry.

Strategy:

In order to assist analysts in their understanding of B-D and the health care industry, it is desirable to provide them with a variety of statistical and background information which goes beyond the scope of the annual report. In effect, we should help them do their homework and thereby increase the likelihood that they will follow B-D rather than some other company where they must dig for such information. In addition, this approach will help us posture the company and the industry as we think it should be.

Action Program:

We should publish a B-D fact book, which would be updated annually, as a supplement to the annual report. The book would include a section on management. (Such fact books are especially effective with smaller banks and trusts which do not have extensive research capabilities and use the fact book as an indication that they are fulfilling their fiduciary responsibility.)

Objective:

To resume publication of B-D World *and put it on a regular publication schedule (alternative to combining* B-D World *and quarterly reports).*

Strategy:

Just as the annual report is a key to the effective communication of B-D's objectives, *B-D World* offers the best opportunity to address all our employees. Since we are competing with so many other demands for our employees' time, *B-D World* must be well-written, interesting, and attractive if our message is to get through.

Action Program:

Before publication was suspended, *B-D World* was redesigned to make it more attractive, and its content was upgraded to include more meaningful articles on our products and markets. It should be used more frequently to tell the Company's story. For example, one issue should be used as an annual report to employees. In addition, we should put the magazine on a regular schedule of four issues a year.

Objective:

To increase the level of exposure for B-D in major business and financial publications and key trade and professional media.

Strategy:

All other things being equal, the better a company is known, the higher its multiple will be. Among other considerations, it is easier for an RR to sell a client a well-known company such as Johnson & Johnson (J&J) than a lesser known company such as B-D. (A factor, of course, is J&J's high visibility as a result of its consumer products.) In order to achieve greater visibility with the investing public, we must increase our efforts to obtain exposure in major media.

Action Programs:

1. Exploitation of B-D technical and scientific capabilities, as discussed earlier.
2. Establishing public relations liaison people in the operating division who can be trained to alert the corporate PR staff to story possibilities. (This has been delayed by the manpower reduction in the department.)
3. Increased awareness on the part of group vice presidents and divisional officers of the PR potential arising from their operations.
4. Accepting requests for interviews from financial media such as Barron's and Dow Jones. One widely used technique is to grant Dow Jones an interview a day or two before quarterly or annual earnings are reported. The thrust of these stories is to say that the Company expects earnings of about $X and to review the results and examine the outlook. These interviews are carried at some length on the DJ ticker and in abbreviated form in *The Wall Street Journal* on the following day.
5. Schedule interviews for top corporate officers with financial editors in conjunction with the analyst presentation programs as well as their other travels. (This is another way of getting the most bang for the buck out of the time, money, and effort involved in these programs.)

Cost: Nil.

Objective:

To improve communications with people who make unsolicited product suggestions.

STRATEGY:

Each year, about 1,000 people send unsolicited ideas and suggestions for new products or existing line improvements to our operating divisions. Many of those contacting us are customers and other friends of the Company who simply want to share an idea. Others are interested in a business transaction involving remuneration in some form. It is in our best interest that such unsolicited ideas be acknowledged in a prompt and friendly manner that protects the rights of both parties.

ACTION PROGRAM:

To assure that every submitter of an unsolicited idea is treated uniformly as an important individual to the Company, we are developing, in conjunction with the law department, a personalized letter and a brochure that will explain corporate policy to the recipient and offer him an agreement form to be signed and returned in a postage-paid envelope. The text and format would be used by each division, and copies of the letters would be sent monthly to the law department.

OBJECTIVE:

To provide immediate access to pertinent competitive information.

STRATEGY:

Several corporate and divisional staff departments have a continuing need for financial, marketing, and product information concerning competitors. Such resources are invaluable in planning our own short-term and long-range programs. Currently, there is a paucity of the materials needed, and what is available is located in different sections of the Company.

ACTION PROGRAM:

Establish a corporate competitive information center and devise an instant retrieval system available on a need-to-know basis. Communications, planning, and law departments would be responsible for planning the program, and the system may be maintained by the corporate library.

Implementation of this program would be one of the responsibilities of the manager of investor relations, a new position in the department.

COST: Minimal.

OBJECTIVE:

To develop an all-purpose brochure for a wide variety of uses.

STRATEGY:

As part of our efforts to foster a clearer identity of B-D as a broad-based leader in health care, this brochure would present a comprehensive overview of the Company's business and history, with the latter stressing the Company's innovations in health care technology. The brochure would be used for recruiting, sales, customer relations, corporate relations, public affairs, community relations, trade shows and exhibits, and so forth.

COST: Amortized over the expected three-year shelf life, with the cost to be shared by the corporate departments and the divisions on a per-copy basis.

OBJECTIVE:

To improve communications with the company's middle and senior management.

STRATEGY AND ACTION PROGRAM:

To provide improved communications with widely scattered management, we should publish a monthly management newsletter. This would cover all material presently communicated via B-D announcements as well as such subjects as cost-saving ideas, energy, materials, and fuel conservation ideas of a general managerial nature, a new product summary, brief digests of Wall Street research reports, safety ideas, security practices, and special messages from management on matters of timely interest.

COST: Minimal.

OBJECTIVE:

To keep management advised on trends and developments in corporate social responsibility issues and to assist it in ensuring adequate corporate responses.

STRATEGY:

The Company must maintain channels of communication to management and the community to provide continued understanding of its viewpoints. In addition, there should be a periodic review of Company operations and programs to advise management of appropriate actions to enhance the effectiveness of the Company as a responsible corporate citizen. Corporate and divisional contributions programs should be monitored to recommend actions that will maximize effectiveness. The Company should also assist in developing communications between management and the community leaders, and it should advise local and corporate management on issues of social responsibility.

OBJECTIVE:

Assure adequate involvement of the Company in corporate headquarters community.

STRATEGY:

The Company should be represented to major community organizations where cooperation of business with other groups will produce solutions to major community problems. It should solicit the cooperation of other business representatives and community leaders in identifying and solving the problems. Another important task is to provide management expertise to community betterment projects, either directly or through encouraging the participation of other management employees.

The major differences between this plan and B-D's previous one is the greater emphasis on investor relations activity. From a budget standpoint, the most significant increases are attributable to the need for additional staffing, a corporate advertising program, and a corporate identification system.

6

Investor Relations at Medtronic

Robert A. Gaertner

What follows is an attempt to communicate a sense of whatever personality, individuality, or uniqueness the investor relations program at Medtronic possesses. The method chosen is a montage of bits and pieces on the program's genealogy, environment, motivation, and performance, in contrast with other possible methods, such as the highly detailed "studio portrait."

Analogies for the quality of investor relations at Medtronic come more readily from nature than from mechanics. In a plant-like way, there has been a rhythm of growth and pruning and adaptation to the environment, as opposed to careful design and construction. The program's "horticulture," though entrusted now to the public relations department, has been a favorite activity of Medtronic's top executives, particularly its presidents. They chose to be neither absentee landlords nor putterers, but active, full-time gardeners. For Medtronic, both the nature of its investor relations program and the program's high level of visibility seem appropriate. Some history should help explain this.

On April 30, 1961, at the end of the fiscal year, Medtronic's sales were $298,000. It was during that year that the Company began the manufacture of what was to prove to be the world's first widely used, implantable electronic medical device: the heart pacemaker. Over the next five years, sales grew at an annual rate of 63 percent, to $3.4 million; they grew at 55 percent for the next five years, to $30.6 million; and at 33 percent for the five years ending April 30, 1976, when annual sales reached $130 million. Those growth rates created a voracious appetite for capital: working capital plus fixed and other assets totaled more than $1 million in 1966 and almost $87 million ten years later.

The heart pacemaker, with its high-technology basis and health care setting, was found highly desirable by investors, particularly of the institutional kind.

Medtronic's need for capital and its attractiveness to investors led to a series of equity offerings, some very high price/earnings multiples, and the holding of the majority of its stock by a number of institutions. It also meant a large following of analysts on Wall Street, on both the "sell" and "buy" sides.

Robert A. Gaertner is Director of Corporate Administration at Medtronic, Inc.

By 1978, some things changed and some stayed the same. Medtronic continued to grow—to $182 million in sales and $121 million in working capital, plus fixed and other assets. The following of analysts had contracted a bit on the sell side, and the company was still owned primarily by institutions. The price/earnings multiple, however, had changed sharply. From a high of 100 times the trailing year's earnings in winter 1972–1973, it moved to a low of 8 times the previous year's earnings in the fall of 1977, and was around 16 times that of the previous year in fall 1978.

Obviously, general market conditions had something to do with the drop in evaluation. In Medtronic's case, there was also a series of events that fed into the market trend. Without discussing them in great detail, these were the announcement in June 1974 of a "down" fourth quarter, following the announcement of an intention to raise much-needed working capital with an equity offering and the subsequent delay of that financing; going ahead with the primary stock offering in December 1974 in a tough market; the unexpected resignation, in December 1975, of a president who was highly regarded in the investing community; and a series of four advisory communications to physicians involving product performance, beginning in December 1975 and ending in October 1977. (Some of these matters are covered in the press releases shown in the back of this chapter, along with other information that may be of interest to investors.) Except for the 1974 stock offering, each of the events violated that cardinal rule of investor relations: "Avoid surprises."

The picture was not all bleak. During the same 1974–1978 period, Medtronic continued its record of annual sales and earnings increases, became largely self-financing, initiated a cash dividend, and was listed on the New York Stock Exchange.

In its eventful history, Medtronic has had three presidents. Each has been close to the investor relations function. The first, one of the Company's co-founders and its current chairman of the board, Earl E. Bakken, had to execute one of the main feats of the entrepreneur: no matter what the individual's personality or background, he must take the story to the people with the money and sell them on it. Known more for his sincerity and brain power than for his slick, polished image, he would go forth with slide projector in hand and products stuffed in his pockets. He did it not because he wanted to, but because it was required.

The Company's second president, Thomas E. Holloran, served as one of its top executives from one critical benchmark in corporate size ($10 million in sales) to another ($100 million in sales). Already legal counsel and a board member before joining the Company as executive vice president in 1967, he provided leadership for Medtronic's major financings. These ranged from $1.5 million in convertible debentures in 1968 to about $14 million for 670,000 new shares in 1974. He was highly articulate, accessible, and informed on every aspect of the business. Professional investors liked him and he was comfortable with them. It is not surprising that for most of the time he was with the Company, the investor relations actively existed largely in his office.

Medtronic's third president, Dale R. Olseth, elected in early 1976, had been an outside board member and president of another, similar-size manufacturing company based in the Minneapolis-St. Paul area. Prior to that, he had been an officer of a major regional brokerage firm and had had experience as a securities analyst for this firm. In fact, he had worked on some of Medtronic's initial security offerings from the investment banker side. For two reasons—the investors' need to get to know him and his own securities industry background—his involvement in investor relations has been extensive.

High-speed growth, heavy institutional ownership, a recent history of surprises, and a broad role played by the company's top executives—all help to explain investor relations at Medtronic. Its communications philosophy, habits, policies, and procedures also played an important role.

The Company is old enough to have its traditions and young enough to remember where they originated. A sharing, candid communications habit, in large part independent of organizational structure, began in the 1950s when the entire workforce was gathered around a single table at lunch. Size (3,600 employees in 1978) and geographic dispersion (worldwide) have had their effect on what at first came naturally, so the habits have been formulated into statements of philosophy and policy, in the hope of retaining the tradition.

One such document is entitled, "Corporate Statement on Communications." It is quoted as follows, with minor deletions:

> It is imperative that all of us who work for Medtronic remain fully committed to open and frank communication. If we desire to make better decisions related to our jobs, if we expect a high level of motivation and commitment from ourselves and others, if we seek a greater sense of self-realization, we must communicate in this manner. Though there are risks involved, our posture will continue to be to take those risks—convinced they are far outweighed by the risk of losing our individual and corporate sense of direction.
>
> This posture means we make a considered effort to inform others of what they need to know, that we give our attention to the messages being delivered, that we express the questions that come to our mind, and that all questions are answered as completely and promptly as possible.
>
> This communications posture further means that at times all of us will be privy to information not generally available to the world outside Medtronic. Such information could be of importance to others, particularly those who are competing with Medtronic and who are making decisions related to trading in our company's common stock. There are sanctions, unwritten in the marketplace and written in securities regulations, if we do not handle this kind of information properly.
>
> There are no handy, all-purpose roadmaps in this regard. As with most issues, common sense and a healthy sensitivity to potential problems must provide most of the guidelines.

This philosophy within Medtronic does have deep roots, and it is alive. When this creed is neglected, it is usually because of inattention rather than out of intention; and, instead of trusting wholly to self-determination, some structure has been put in place. On the subject of investor communications, the Company states: "It is the policy of Medtronic, Inc., to communicate openly with the investment community . . . and, at the same time, meet timely disclosure requirements, protect intellectual property, and not counteract operating strategies."

Taking the policy a step further, Medtronic states, in a procedure for communicating with securities analysts:

> The public communications department has responsibility for day-to-day contact with securities analysts, as well as arranging for visits and meetings, reviewing analysts' reports, and keeping management apprised of developments in this area.
>
> The chief executive officer and certain corporate officers have the authority to determine the content and tone of communications with securities analysts. They have the authority to occasionally initiate or respond directly to such contacts, but should advise the public communications department of these conversations.
>
> The law and finance officers have the authority to influence these communications to assure their consistency with legal and accounting reporting requirements.
>
> All other employees, as a rule, should refer all contacts from securities analysts to the public communications department.

There is an inner tension in the communications habit, philosophy, policy, and procedure affecting investor communications at Medtronic, created by the understandable fear that openness leads to susceptibility—to an inability to resist the press for information and to the possibility of giving away something of value. The tension has been left unresolved: the Company wants to go perceptibly beyond minimum requirements for disclosure without providing aid and comfort to its competitors.

Setting issues of a potentially material nature aside (on the premise that they undergo formal and rigorous review), the tests for deciding when to talk or not to talk include the following:

1. Does the information have value, strategically or otherwise?
2. Is it readily available from other sources?
3. What is the understanding sought, and can it be obtained by dealing in general concepts rather than sharing specifics, or by putting together already available information?

4. What is the gut reaction of more than one executive: quite literally, does the prospect of giving away the information cause the gut to tighten and stay tight?
5. Does talking about it suit Medtronic's objectives?

A good example of this kind of issue, which was current at the time of this writing, dealt with questions from securities analysts regarding Medtronic's new product plans for pacemakers. Portions of the information were already available, either in the Company's own statements or in observations made by spokespeople for competitors, and some parts of these statements were inaccurate. The understanding sought was the answer to the question: will Medtronic's product line be competitive, ahead, or behind? Gut reactions to discussing the subject were unanimously tight for two reasons: a detailed plan covering an 18-month time frame was highly proprietary, and correcting the inaccuracies without the detailed plan could lead to negative conclusions. It was clear that Medtronic's objectives would be served by attempting to respond to the underlying question.

The strategy adopted was to affirm what was generally known to be accurate; to deal with what was inaccurate by conspicuously failing to comment on those details; to comment on the three general areas of interest where the Company has been focusing development efforts, and to offer equally general views of the market impact and time frame for each; and to point to the history of new product introductions in pacemaking as a good guide for timing the availability of major new families of products and subsequent family extensions.

The strategy was made part of briefing documents prepared for the annual meeting of shareholders. Some elements were included in presentations made at the meeting and at a follow-up session for analysts, and all elements were touched on in responses to the anticipated questions on the subject.

Subsequent reports and feedback indicated a positive perception that Medtronic's pacemaker product line would remain adequately competitive for the following 12 months and could then move into a clear leadership position. In the ensuing weeks, questions on the subject became far less persistent and much of the inaccurate information faded from view. Without giving up key marketing information, the Company served its own objectives and communications philosophy, and apparently served the needs of the analysts as well.

The investor relations program at Medtronic has two understood, if not regularly articulated, objectives: the first is to assure that communications meet the Company's disclosure requirements and are responsive to the investors' need to understand; the second, which flows from the first, is to communicate to the investment community in a manner that enhances and certainly does not inhibit the ability of the market to establish a value on the Company not unlike the value the Company puts on itself.

The tools selected to achieve these objectives are modestly customized, off-the-shelf items, used with a dedication to developing the professional skills and talents demanded. Innovative, expansive techniques have been precluded by preexisting high levels of interest and periodic bursts of activity precipitated by internal developments.

Two examples of efforts to meet program objectives can be found in Medtronic annual reports. The first example is a series of special features that began appearing in the Company's annual reports in 1974. Aimed at expanding shareholders' understanding of Medtronic and its industry, they use a general-circulation-magazine writing style and graphics. A seven-page section in the 1977 report focused on the Company's products, describing what they are, what they do, and something about their history. The section was the result of three basic considerations. First was a self-imposed requirement to always give prominence to products in the annual reports. A second input came from watching investors in individual and group meetings fascinated by the hardware, asking basic questions, and very often mentioning a close relative or friend with a similar device. The third factor was the realization that the subject matter had not been covered at length in shareholder communications, although it was popular with professional investors.

Another effort to meet program objectives was introduced in the 1977 report and was repeated in 1978. It was a listing of business and financial goals. They represent an attempt to help the securities analyst deal with elements of the future that will strongly affect his calculation of Medtronic's present value. (Still another feature of Medtronic's annual report is the one-page summary reproduced here. It is much better than the usual table of contents and in fact can serve alone as a means of keeping investors informed about corporate developments.)

As they appeared in 1978, the *business* goals included the following:

1. The bulk of our resources and energies—financial, technological, and management—will be directed toward our basic business: heart pacemakers and closely related products.
2. We must ensure that our position in this business is one of product and market leadership.
3. Compound annual revenue growth from our present businesses should be approximately 20 percent. Earnings should grow at a rate equal to or greater than our revenue growth, based on maintaining or improving historical after-tax margins of 10 percent.
4. A growing part of revenues will come from international operations in markets that are in earlier development stages than in the U.S. and Western Europe.
5. Diversification will be a major area of attention, and opportunities will be pursued through internal development and acquisitions, but limited to the health care field.
6. We will continue to invest, through work on new technologies, in phases of implantology other than pacemakers, but only after a careful evaluation of long-term commercial feasibility.

The *financial* goals, as stated in 1978, were the following:

1. The return on average equity is targeted to reach 20 percent over the next several years.

2. Growth in investment should approach 25 percent per year.
3. New investment opportunities will be sought, but they must show a strong potential for providing returns consistent with the overall corporate target.
4. The capital structure will consist primarily of equity, with interest-bearing debt available as a financing option within a limit of 20 percent of total capital.
5. Dividends will be equal to approximately 20 percent of the previous year's earnings after taxes, and should reflect the longer-term expectations of the Company.

These goals are not only an example of a way to address the objectives of the investor relations program. Whatever credibility they have is in the Company's history, and their very articulation is evidence of top management's deep involvement. The content of these goals far exceeds the minimum requirements for communications with the investing public. As such, they reflect the bits and pieces of the montage assembled here to communicate a sense of what is different about investor relations at Medtronic.

NEWS RELEASE

Medtronic

Medtronic, Inc.
3055 Old Highway Eight
Minneapolis, Minnesota 55418 USA
Telephone 612 781-6061

June 23, 1977

FOR IMMEDIATE RELEASE

Contact:

Bob Gaertner, Financial
Gary Strumpfer, Media
(new #612/574-3023, 3037)

MINNEAPOLIS -- The board of directors of Medtronic today (Thursday) declared the company's first cash dividend, setting a quarterly dividend of 10 cents per common share that is payable on July 31, 1977, to shareholders of record July 11, 1977.

Speaking for Medtronic's board, Dale R. Olseth, president and chief executive officer, said the action followed adoption of a new corporate policy on dividends. "As an objective," Olseth explained, "the policy suggests a dividend payout rate of approximately 20 percent of the preceding fiscal year's after-tax earnings."

Olseth said that, according to the policy, the payout rate would change "only in relation to changes in long-term expectations regarding investment needs and opportunities. Our board will review the dividend policy annually.

"While Medtronic continues to have aggressive growth objectives," Olseth said, "the company has reached a stage in its development where it can provide shareholders a modest dividend payout without affecting its ability to achieve those objectives."

Medtronic recently reported earnings of $1.95 per share for its fiscal year ended April 30, 1977.

\- 30 -

NEWS RELEASE

Medtronic, Inc.
3055 Old Highway Eight
Minneapolis, Minnesota 55418 USA
Telephone 612/574-4000

Contact:

October 27, 1977

FOR IMMEDIATE RELEASE

Bob Gaertner, Financial
Gary Strumpfer, Media
(new #612/574-3023, 3037)

MINNEAPOLIS -- Medtronic said it is preparing communications to expand the group of pacemakers involved in an advisory letter sent to physicians in August 1976.

Bob Gaertner, the company's public communications director, said, "It will take several days for us to complete the process of advisory-related communications with government officials and physicians. Pacemaker patients who might be affected will be informed as a result of this process."

Gaertner explained that the August 1976 advisory action and an initial expansion in November 1976 involved about 20,000 Xytron® model pacemakers, all manufactured prior to August 1975. "The underlying problem was the possibility of moisture penetration into the circuit container, the development of a short-circuit and then an accelerated draining of the units' battery-supplied power.

"The advisory expansion now in process involves approximately 17,000 additional Xytron® units from the same manufacturing period," Gaertner said, "and is initiated by us because of the same moisture-penetration problem."

"Most of these pacemakers have been implanted for periods of two to three years," Gaertner said. "A very high percentage will continue to perform properly, with our analysis indicating that

- more -

virtually all units have better than a 95 percent probability of normal operation over the next six months. Most patients, moreover, have a natural cardiac rhythm that sustained them before they received a pacemaker and would sustain them again if their pacemaker stopped functioning."

No pacemaker units manufactured by Medtronic after August 1975 are involved.

The company is providing physicians with information on the units involved. Medtronic recommends that doctors evaluate individual patients on the basis of this information to determine whether their condition warrants a closer follow-up schedule or replacement.

- 30 -

NEWS RELEASE

Medtronic

Medtronic, Inc.
3055 Old Highway Eight
Minneapolis, Minnesota 55418 USA
Telephone 612/574-4000

Contact:

Bob Gaertner, Financial
Gary Strumpfer, Media
(612) 574-3023, 3037

April 13, 1978

FOR IMMEDIATE RELEASE

MINNEAPOLIS -- Medtronic announced today (Thursday) a warranty program it calls "Pacing for Life" that departs from standard warranties in the industry and offers, on its leading models in the U.S., to replace pacemakers with comparable units at no charge whenever replacement becomes necessary.

Consequently, patients with Medtronic Xyrel®-VL and Xyrel®-VP lithium pacemakers purchased beginning April 15 will not have to pay for another pacemaker again in their lifetimes, subject to the conditions of the new warranty.

Because of advances in technology, particularly involving power sources, the projected longevity of pacemakers has increased in recent years. While it was not unusual in the past for patients to have two or more replacements in addition to their initial pacemaker implant, the typical patient today will most likely need only one replacement.

Warranties on pacemakers sold in the U.S. have stretched in the past three years from 30 months to seven years and higher. A replacement for a pacemaker still under warranty usually is provided at no cost, while one for a unit out of warranty is sold at full price.

According to Lawrence Perlman, Medtronic executive vice president and head of its pacemaker operations in the U.S., the change in warranty policy is "important in a number of ways."

Perlman said, "There are benefits to the patient in the form of

- more -

a reduced financial risk and the expression of product confidence implicit in the policy.

"The impact on the issue of the cost of health care delivery should be positive in the years ahead," Perlman stated, "as we assume most of the risk and future costs for pacemaker replacement units.

"In addition to increasing future costs, the new warranty removes a part of potential future pacemaker sales. To reflect the added value of the warranty and to reduce our economic risk," he continued, "we are increasing the price of the models covered by approximately nine percent -- our first price increase on pacemakers in the U.S. since August 1976.

"We believe that 'Pacing for Life' is a significant development," Perlman added, "one that underscores our leadership position in the industry and commitment to stay in that position."

Dale R. Olseth, Medtronic president and chief executive officer, said the move to change the warranty and prices on leading pacemaker products in the U.S. "should have a meaningful positive impact on earnings in the short-term and therefore on funds available for new investment."

- 30 -

NEWS RELEASE

Medtronic

Medtronic, Inc.
3055 Old Highway Eight
Minneapolis, Minnesota 55418 USA
Telephone 612/574-4000

June 28, 1978

FOR IMMEDIATE RELEASE

Contact:
Bob Gaertner, Financial
Gary Strumpfer, Media
(#612/574-3023, 3037)

MINNEAPOLIS -- Directors of Medtronic, Inc. today (Wednesday) increased the company's quarterly dividend to 12 cents per share, up from 10 cents in each of the previous four quarters.

The increase was in line with the corporate policy on dividends, which suggests an annual payout rate of approximately 20 percent of the previous year's after-tax earnings. Medtronic earnings for the fiscal year ended April 30 were $2.29 per share.

The dividend is payable July 31, 1978 to shareholders of record July 10, 1978.

- 30 -

NEWS RELEASE

Medtronic

Medtronic, Inc.
3055 Old Highway Eight
Minneapolis, Minnesota 55418 USA
Telephone 612/574-4000

August 21, 1978

FOR IMMEDIATE RELEASE

Contact:
Bob Gaertner, Financial
Gary Strumpfer, Media
(#612/574-3023, 3037)

MINNEAPOLIS -- Medtronic today (Monday) reported an 18.8 percent sales increase for its first quarter ended July 31.

Sales were $50,847,000 compared with $42,786,000 for the same quarter a year ago. Earnings were $5,989,000, up 27.3 percent from $4,706,000; and earnings were 11.8 percent of sales versus 11.0 percent last year. Earnings per share for the first quarter were 79 cents compared with 63 cents, a 25.4 percent increase.

Dale R. Olseth, Medtronic president and chief executive officer, said the quarter's results were due mostly to "broad acceptance of our new Xyrel® programmable pacemaker, the Tenax™ family of positive-anchoring pacemaker leads and the 'Pacing For Life' warranty program.

"U.S. pacemaker operations were particularly strong," Olseth stated, "although certain of our European markets did not achieve the growth anticipated." He added that "pacemaker unit volume increased slightly over the immediately preceding quarter and was the highest it has been in the last five quarters."

Olseth concluded that Medtronic's fiscal year was "off to a very good start" and that the company "should have another year of uninterrupted sales and earnings growth."

- more -

MEDTRONIC, INC.
CONSOLIDATED STATEMENT OF EARNINGS

(Unaudited)

	Three Months ended July 31, 1978	1977
	(In Thousands)	
NET SALES	$50,847	$42,786
Interest and other income	791	458
	51,638	43,244
Cost of products sold	19,160	16,639
Research and development expenses	4,422	3,764
Selling, general and administrative expenses	17,390	14,441
Interest	603	546
	41,575	35,390
Earnings before income taxes	10,063	7,854
Provision for taxes on earnings	4,074	3,148
NET EARNINGS	$ 5,989	$ 4,706
Weighted average shares outstanding	7,579	7,517
EARNINGS PER SHARE	$ .79	$ .63

Medtronic 1978: A Capsule Review

Page 3 — Letter to shareholders cites strong operating results in a year that tested the company's ability to face adversity, continued good sales and earnings growth in the current year, exceptionally strong financial position, and a 20 percent increase in the quarterly dividend.

Page 6 — Operating highlights include the sale of about 80,000 pacemakers in Fiscal 1978, most of them lithium-powered units. Leads, the wires that connect the pacemaker to the heart, are of growing importance to Medtronic; we are the world leaders in the development and sales of these products. Throughout the world, some 200,000 patients received pacemakers last year.

Page 7 — International sales increased 23 percent to $75 million and continue to represent 41 percent of Medtronic's total worldwide revenues.

Page 9 — Medtronic added substantially to its product line during the year; leading the way were a rate-programmable lithium product and a new generation of Tenax™ pacing leads, a family of positive anchoring products.

Page 11 — The company's research and development investment topped $16 million during the year, an increase of nearly 40 percent. That money went primarily for development of new pacemakers and related products.

Page 12 — Social Responsibility — Medtronic has contributed over $1 million to community organizations over the past five years, reaching about $400,000 last year.

Page 13 — The worldwide Medtronic workforce numbers 3,550, an increase of 4.3 percent during the past year; most additions came in diversified, non-pacemaker businesses.

Page 14 — What is medical nuclear imaging and why is it important? This in-depth look at dynamic studies of the heart reveals them to be an accurate, simple, non-invasive way to find out if patients have some of the early stages of heart disease. What's more, nuclear imaging may help expand the use of pacemakers and other cardiac prosthetic devices — and that spells synergy for Medtronic.

Page 16 — Diversified Operations — a look at several non-pacemaker Medtronic businesses: medical nuclear imaging; devices for moving blood such as a circulatory support blood pump; neurological products for pain control and rehabilitation; and heart valves.

Page 21 — Investor information includes details on the 1978 annual meeting (August 23) and other sources of news and data about the company that are generally available to shareholders.

Page 22 — A discussion of business targets reviews the company's performance vis à vis our mainline business, heart pacemakers, and the attainment of goals for revenue, earnings, international revenues and diversification. The review of financial goals highlights return on average equity, growth in investment, new investment opportunities, capital structure and dividends.

Page 24 — Management discusses and analyzes the company's performance in sales (up 23 percent), cost of products sold (increased 27 percent), research and development investment (up 39 percent), overhead (a 17 percent increase), and a tax rate that dipped slightly.

Page 26 — The nine-year summary of the company's performance is followed by statement of earnings, changes in financial position, the balance sheet and notes.

Page 35 — Listing of Medtronic corporate officers.

7

What's a Castle & Cooke?

N. John Douglas

The long-range objective of Castle & Cooke's investor relations program is to raise the Company's profile in the investment community. Target audiences consist of professionals in the banking, brokerage, and investment advisory world. They include current owners of Castle & Cooke stock and debentures and prospective individual and institutional investors, as well as employees, who are reached through stockholder materials (if they are shareowners) and through *The Castle & Cooke Report,* a newsletter published every other week.

Over the years, security analysts have known the brand name Dole, for pineapple and bananas, and the brand name Bumble Bee, for tuna and salmon. But few recognized the name of the parent—Castle & Cooke—or much else about the Company, except that it owned some valuable real estate.

That, basically, was the problem Doremus & Co., the Company's public relations counsel, uncovered in 1973, when it conducted an in-depth nationwide survey of investment community opinion about Castle & Cooke. Only 40 of 117 security analysts contacted then believed themselves to be well enough acquainted with the Company to discuss it. Of the 40, only seven considered themselves well informed about Castle & Cooke; only nine said they had had regular direct contact with management.

That 1973 survey clearly demonstrated the need to broaden and intensify the Company's communications with prospective investors. Senior management itself recognized that Castle & Cooke had to be better understood. Its goals were:

1. To stimulate increased interest in, and support of, the Company by the investment community, including both present and potential shareowners.
2. To identify the Company more closely with its well-known brand names—Dole, Bumble Bee, and Bud of California.
3. To underscore that Castle & Cooke is primarily a balanced food company which, through sound management, has achieved stability and growth.

N. John Douglas is Director of Investor Relations for Castle & Cooke, Inc.

4. To emphasize the Company's strengths—in management, brand names, aggressive marketing, quality production, and timely distribution, as well as strong financial control.

5. To underscore the value of the Company's stock-and-cash dividend policy—that is, the distribution of eight stock dividends in the last eight years and an increased per share cash dividend rate in 1974.

6. To point out some of the "hidden assets" in Castle & Cooke as an investment vehicle—for example, the 151,500 acres of prime lands which the Company owns in Hawaii and California, more than an acre behind about every 150 shares of stock.

The Company implemented an aggressive communications program based on direct contact with the investment community and indirect contact through the business press. It initiated regular management presentations to security analyst groups in selected cities throughout the United States. From 1973 (immediately following completion of the opinion survey) through 1979, Castle & Cooke management teams have made a total of 30 presentations to analyst groups ranging in attendance from 20 to more than 150. The Company has also cultivated the European investment community.

Management also talked to stockbroker associations in a number of key areas throughout the country and developed a direct mail program for this audience. In addition, analysts have participated in field trips to the Company's piers and ships in New York City and Long Beach, California; to its mushroom farms in Soquel, California, and East Windsor, Connecticut; to its MountainGate real estate operations outside Los Angeles; to its Sea Ranch residential development north of San Francisco; and to its fruit plantations and processing facilities in Honduras.

Since 1976, Castle & Cooke has held annual, two-day, in-depth seminars, providing analysts with opportunities to meet, question, and assess the Company's operating managers in "shirt-sleeve" sessions. (An agenda for one such meeting is reprinted at the end of this chapter.) One of the many benefits of such sessions has been the analysts' appreciation of the breadth and depth of managerial expertise in Castle & Cooke. In addition, the Company has had group discussions with analysts on important specialized subjects, such as taxes and their influence on the Company's operations.

Following each major meeting, attendees and other analysts on Castle & Cooke's mailing list received a printed report of the presentation, including a transcription of the question-and-answer session and charts containing industry data and the Company's relative position in various categories. Excerpts from an 80-page presentation made to analysts by the Company are reprinted at the end of this chapter. (The rest of the presentation included in-depth information about the financial position of the Company, per capita consumption of different food lines, and selling prices of different foods over a 10-year period, as well as analyses of different product lines, marketing strategies, foreign competition, problems, production facilities, sales capabilities, and R&D activities.)

After each major group session, post-meeting surveys were conducted by Doremus & Co. (Castle & Cooke's public relations consultants) to measure analysts' reactions and to obtain suggestions for future presentations. The response has been increasingly positive. The analysts continue to ask for personal contact with management. As a supplement to the group meetings, the director of investor relations met individually and in small groups with key analysts in cities across the country. In connection with annual meetings of stockholders, the Company has conducted field trips for stockholders and analyst-attendees.

In addition to providing analysts and brokers with the corporate information they want, Castle & Cooke also seeks to make the meetings memorable in other ways. For example, luncheon and dinner menus feature the Company's food products (Dole, Bumble Bee, and Bud of California), thus clearly linking those well-known brands with the corporate name. As another example, attendants at some meetings are told that a banana tree has been planted for them in Central America—and nine months later, the fruit from that tree is delivered to the analysts at their homes!

In the area of publicity, Castle & Cooke has made its annual and quarterly reports and other printed materials more informative. Its printed materials have won awards from a number of professional groups. The Company also distributed news releases about significant corporate developments (some of these are reprinted at the end of the chapter), and it communicated with shareholders and employees about legislative and economic issues affecting business.

Other programs are designed to keep the Company name constantly before analysts. For example, the Company distributed a Cooke & Castle desk diary/time planner to each analyst, subtly reminding him or her of the Company on a daily basis. (The Company has plans to provide each analyst with desk-top information or fact kits on Castle & Cooke.) It has also sponsored exhibits and information booths at investment shows in Atlanta, Los Angeles, and New York City.

In addition to direct contact with the investment community, the Company and Doremus developed feature articles with the business and financial press. These ranged from a *Nation's Business* "Lessons of Leadership" profile of D. J. Kirchhoff, president and CEO (the article is reprinted here), to a *Business Week* story about Castle & Cooke's corporate strategy. Other publications discussing developments in the Company included *Barron's, Forbes, Dun's Review, Journal of Commerce, Financier, Financial World, California Business,* and the *Los Angeles Times.* Radio and TV interviews were also developed. In connection with many analyst meetings, Doremus arranged interviews for management with local newspaper editors and radio and TV reporters. This was particularly successful in New York, Chicago, Dallas, Houston, Seattle, Portland, San Diego, and Florida.

Castle & Cooke also began a limited program of corporate advertising directed to the national investment community. The ads focus on the Company's brand names—Dole, Bumble Bee, and Bud of California—as well as on the Company's financial record. They have appeared in *The Wall Street Journal, Barron's,* stockbroker and security analyst trade journals, and investment club magazines. (Some of these ads are shown here.) By advertising the annual report in special publications, the Company received more than 20,000 reader requests for it in one year. The Company is also planning an investor awareness program for publication in suburban and weekly newspapers.

The Company has evidence that the program has been well worth the investment of time, effort, and money. Comprehensive follow-up surveys conducted by Doremus for Castle & Cooke in 1976 and 1979 show clearly that more analysts are following the Company and now understand it better. Also, market letters and research reports by investment firms have been generally supportive of the Company, even though in the past year its growth has been impeded by conditions outside its control. In addition, meetings with analysts and brokers are well attended. The in-depth seminars and field trips are popular with analysts and have added greatly to investment community knowledge about the Company and appreciation for the expertise of its management and operating personnel. Company officers are being "visited," personally or via phone, by an increasing number of analysts.

The cost of this successful program probably could be expected to run about $150,000 a year, plus consultants' fees of about $100,000. The staff consists of two professionals, who also are responsible for corporate communications, public relations, and community affairs.

CASTLE & COOKE, INC.
SECOND ANNUAL SECURITY ANALYSTS' MEETING
AT QUAIL LODGE, SEPTEMBER 20-21

Tuesday, September 20:

9:00 AM	Leave 50 California Street, via Chartered Bus (via US 101 to State Highway 1, along Coast route)	
11:00 AM	Arrive at Mushroom Farm Soquel	
11:00-11:10 AM	Coffee Break	
11:10-11:15 AM	Brief Welcome *M. MacNaughton	
	SECURITY ANALYSTS' PROGRAM	SPOUSES' PROGRAM
	Presentation by Mushroom Group (Garbini Inn, 3820 Soquel Drive--next to the Mushroom Farm) *C. E. Mumaw *W. W. Chalkley	Presentation on Mushroom Production, Selection, Storage and Usage
12:00-12:45 PM	Tour of Spawn Facility Mushroom Houses and Packing Operation	Tour of Mushroom Farm; Browsing Cooper House Boutiques (Santa Cruz)
12:45 PM	Leave Soquel	
2:00 PM	Arrive at Quail Lodge, Carmel Valley (Clubhouse)	
2:00-3:00 PM	Registration (pre-assigned) and Lunch	
3:00 PM	Presentations (Fairway Room)	Tour of Cannery Row and 17-mile Drive; Afternoon Tea at Del Monte Lodge
3:05-3:15 PM	Introduction-Positioning Castle & Cooke for Future Growth *D. J. Kirchhoff	
3:15-3:35 PM	Long-Range and Strategic Planning *C. J. Patterson	
3:35-3:55 PM	Financials *L. Marks, Jr.	
3:55-4:10 PM	Questions & Answers	
4:10-4:30 PM	Other Activities *H. B. Clark, Jr. *R. S. Gordon	

4:30-5:35 PM	Processed Pineapple *A. J. Vangelos *D. L. Jocelyn *D. G. Sjostrom	
5:35-5:45 PM	Questions & Answers	
7:00-8:00 PM	Open Bar (Clubhouse Terrace--Poolside)	
8:00 PM	Dinner (Clubhouse Dining Room)	
9:10 PM	Open Bar	

Wednesday, September 21:

7:30-8:25 AM	Breakfast--Clubhouse Dining Room	
8:25 AM	Presentations (Fairway Room)	Presentation by Castle & Cooke Consumer Services/ Quality Control Departments
8:30-9:45 AM	Seafood *J. S. McGowan *W. S. Kamin *R. Jensen	Visit to Carmel Mission; Two hours of touring and/or shopping on Ocean Blvd., Carmel
9:45-9:55 AM	Questions & Answers	
9:55-10:05 AM	Coffee Break	
10:05-11:10 AM	Bananas and Fresh Pineapple *R. W. Fisher *W. J. Crum *R. V. Igleheart	
11:10-11:30 AM	Production Services *J. V. Scibetta *W. Henry *J. D. DeMent	
11:30-11:40 AM	Questions & Answers	
11:40-12 noon	Real Estate *H. B. Clark, Jr. *W. G. Haight	
12:00-12:20 PM	Marketing *E. L. DelBeccaro	
12:20-12:25 PM	Round-Up *D. J. Kirchhoff	
12:25-12:35 PM	General Questions & Answers	
12:35-1:00 PM	Check-Out	
1:00 PM	Cocktails & Lunch (Carmel by-the-Sea Beach)	
2:00 PM	Bus leaves for San Francisco	

Long-Range and Strategic Planning

Castle & Cooke--a portfolio of diversified but related businesses that lend themselves to individual measurable performance and operating management, but interacting parts of a unified executive management and financial control.

Primary corporate financial objectives:

- o 10% compound growth in earnings per share as an average over a moving five-year span.
- o Annual increase in actual dollar profits.
- o Minimum annual return on average equity of 15%.
- o Minimum annual return on assets of 7.5%.

Within each of our operating entities, we seek to evaluate current performance and longer term strategies in terms of these corporate financial objectives. In instances where there is little likelihood of achieving or maintaining a reasonable level of contribution to these goals, we may make the always difficult decision of divestiture or wind-down to permit redeployment of the assets. The sale of our Value Giant merchandising activities and our recent announcement concerning our Hawaiian Trucking operations are examples.

One of the strongest characteristics of a diversified company is its ability to allocate financial resources to the most productive areas. Within our portfolio are activities strongly positioned in near mature businesses, as well as real estate assets, that provide us with cash flow to exploit opportunities in other elements of our current businesses, as well as entry into attractive new-but-related growth activities.

We are principally a food company--and it is with food products, or products distributed currently or potentially through food industry channels, that we look for our long-term growth and profitability.

Our first priority is to evaluate the position of our cash generators--those products and market areas where we are already the leader and low-cost producer. The maintenance or protection, but not expansion, of this position is generally the lowest risk and highest return on investment available to us.

We assess such factors as production locations and market position, as well as vertical considerations relating to insuring our competitive cost position, supply availability, or hedging our logistic capability. Obviously these are not headline grabbers--and could even be considered defensive--but they are the essence of good management.

Second, we evaluate opportunities to expand our current businesses or proudcts in present markets, or into new geographic or functional markets. This can be accomplished by market expansion, acquisition, or construction--or by a combination of these. Our mushroom business is a clear example of this approach.

Third, we look for opportunities for line or product extensions in markets or distribution channels in which we are already involved. These can be accomplished with internally generated new products, marketing agreements, or through the acquisition of businesses in closely related product categories.

Fourth, we look for opportunities for entry, through acquisition, into areas within the food industry that have above-average growth and profit potential. In recent years, our entry into mushrooms and Alaskan shellfish products, and much of the additional expansion in these areas as well as in other seafood activities, has been accomplished through acquisition.

We feel strongly that we should bring something to the marriage besides capital and an allocation of corporate overhead. So we look for opportunities for operating synergism--or, at the very least, some degree of relationship to the philosophy, knowledge, and experience of our management. Because of our management style, and time, effort, and expense involved in any acquisition regardless of size, we look for businesses that are at least $50 million in sales--or that have the potential to attain that size in a relatively short time through internal growth or perhaps consolidation with other businesses having a high degree of fit.

After a cursory look at the food industry--particularly in the United States--you might conclude that "belly capacity" has been reached, and that the future growth of any individual food item is directly dependent on population expansion. This conclusion is probably pretty accurate in terms of total pounds of food consumed. However, within this apparently static situation, rather dramatic shifts and changes are taking place. It accurately identified and evaluated, they can represent attractive growth opportunities. Among these, we are particularly looking for fit with our relatively wide-ranging strengths in agricultural production, perishable products, processed products, logistics, and marketing.

We recently reached an agreement in principle to acquire Bud Antle, Inc., the largest lettuce and celery grower-shipper with sales in excess of $80 million. At first glance, the iceberg lettuce industry might be viewed as unattractive for entry. The product has been readily available for a long time--and therefore it would appear to be mature. Shipper prices for head lettuce seem overly sensitive to small variations in supply. On an overall basis, industry returns have not been compensatory. However, in reality, lettuce consumption has been growing steadily during the last decade, despite increasing prices. Similar to bananas, this is counter to the long-term decline of many fresh fruits and vegetables. In the past few years, the rate of growth as accelerated and U.S. consumption is now almost 25 pounds per person--one of the highest of any single food item. Consumer use patterns and attitudes toward informal, lighter meals, weight control, and foods perceived as good for health--all of these bode well for salads in general and lettuce in particular--for both at-home and away-from-home eating.

In fact, much of the growth in lettuce consumption is traceable to the food service industry--an area in which many of our current products have limited application, and one that we've identified as particularly attractive for broader entry by Castle & Cooke. Lettuce is a major item in virtually all discretionary or captive food service operations. The frequency of use in fast food products, such as hamburgers and tacos, is obvioius. Add to this the rapidly growing popularity of medium-priced theme restaurants built around a limited menu and a salad bar. But, food service operators are confronted with rapidly escalating costs in labor, construction, and energy--plus availability of productive labor and various government regulations. Many feel that convenient, prepared products are already an economic necessity for a viable operation.

Lettuce--trimmed, cut, washed, and pre-cooled--packed in the field in California can be attractive from a cost, convenience, and quality standpoint when compared with product prepared at restaurant level, provided it is combined with an effective distribution and delivery system. A value-added product of this type also reflects improved margins and stable pricing. Antle has been a leader in developing the processing, packaging, and distribution techniques for this potentially important segment of the lettuce business. Progressive and large users such as McDonald's are already using the product in several U.S. divisions as well as in their new operations in Sweden and Germany. The future for this new segment of the lettuce industry appears bright.

newsrelease

Castle & Cooke, Inc.

A worldwide food company using primarily the DOLE, BUMBLE BEE, ROYAL ALASKAN, and BUD OF CALIFORNIA brand names
. . . also engaged in Real Estate and Other Activities

For Immediate Release

CASTLE & COOKE ELECTS TWO WOMEN DIRECTORS

HONOLULU, May 4--Mary E. Lanigar of Palo Alto, Calif., retired partner of Arthur Young & Co., certified public accountants, and Betty F. Hirozawa of Honolulu, vice president-administration of the Hawaii Employers Council, were elected directors of Castle & Cooke, Inc.

They became the first women on Castle & Cooke's board of directors since the late Wilhelmina Tenney, who served from 1940 until her death in 1951.

Miss Lanigar retired in 1976 as a partner of Arthur Young & Co. after 34 years as a CPA. She is a director of Wells Fargo & Co.; Wells Fargo Bank, N.A.; Lucky Stores, Inc.; Transamerica Corp., and the Pacific Lumber Co. She also is a governor of the Pacific Stock Exchange, Inc.

Mrs. Hirozawa has been with the Hawaii Employers Council since 1951. She became vice president-director of research in 1975 and vice president-administration in 1978.

Miss Lanigar and Mrs. Hirozawa succeed W. M. Bush and James J. Finch, who did not stand for re-election. Mr. Bush, a retired executive vice president of Castle & Cooke, had been a director of the company since 1957. Mr. Finch, a California citrus and avocado rancher and a retired executive vice president of Newhall Land & Farming Co., had been a director of Castle & Cooke since 1966. Messrs. Bush and Finch become advisory directors of Castle & Cooke.

* * *

May 4, 1979
(0605)

Released through Doremus & Company · 120 Broadway · New York, New York 10005 · (212) 964-0700
Contact: Emil A. Schneider, Public Relations · Castle & Cooke, Inc. · Financial Plaza of the Pacific · Honolulu, HI 96802 · (808) 548-6611
or N. John Douglas, Investor & Public Relations · Castle & Cooke, Inc. · 50 California Street · San Francisco, CA 94111 · (415) 986-3000

newsrelease

Castle & Cooke, Inc.

A worldwide food company using primarily the DOLE, BUMBLE BEE, ROYAL ALASKAN, and BUD OF CALIFORNIA brand names
. . . also engaged in Real Estate and Other Activities

For Immediate Release

HALF OF CASTLE & COOKE'S $314 MILLION EXPENDITURES
ARE INVESTED IN FRESH FOODS, TO MEET CHANGING TRENDS
IN EATING HABITS, KIRCHHOFF TELLS N. Y. SECURITY ANALYSTS

NEW YORK, May 10--Market research by Castle & Cooke, Inc. indicates that the company is "in tune with the changes that are impacting the food industry," D. J. Kirchhoff, president and chief executive, told the New York Society of Security Analysts at a luncheon meeting here today.

"These trends fall principally into two categories," he said. "One is the increasing emphasis on nutrition and natural foods, plus the shift to lighter meals. The other key trend is the expansion of meals consumed away from home - the food service industry."

To meet consumer needs resulting from these trends, Castle & Cooke has made capital expenditures of $314 million in the past five years, Mr. Kirchhoff reported. More than half the total was invested in the fresh foods area and about one-third in processed foods.

Castle & Cooke produces and markets Dole bananas, pineapple and mushrooms; Bumble Bee and Royal Alaskan seafoods, and Bud of California lettuce, celery, cauliflower and cabbage.

Mr. Kirchhoff said that the new trends in consumer eating habits were taking place not only in North America, but also in the company's principal overseas markets, Europe and Japan. As a

Released through Doremus & Company ; 120 Broadway · New York, New York 10005 · (212) 964-0700
Contact: Emil A. Schneider, Public Relations · Castle & Cooke, Inc. · Financial Plaza of the Pacific · Honolulu, HI 96802 · (808) 548-6611
or N. John Douglas, Investor & Public Relations · Castle & Cooke, Inc. · 50 California Street · San Francisco, CA 94111 · (415) 986-3000

result, international sales now account for about 30 percent of the company's total corporate revenue, contrasted with 27 percent in 1977 and 20 percent in 1974, he reported. Sales to European and Middle East markets rose 50 percent last year over 1977, and sales in the Far East soared 78 percent, he added. This compared with a 25 percent revenue increase in the North American market, he pointed out.

Mr. Kirchhoff discussed several product lines whose market shares had improved. "Though an aggressive expansion program in select U. S. markets, Bumble Bee lightmeat tuna has climbed to third place from fifth in the past two years in major brand sales," he reported.

In lettuce and celery, the company's Bud of California subsidiary (acquired by Castle & Cooke early in 1978) is the nation's leading producer on a year-round basis, he said. Spurring sales, he added, was the recent introduction to the retail market of a 1-pound bag of pre-cut lettuce and cabbage, for use in salads and coleslaw. "The trimming, coring, washing and cutting are already done for the buyer, so that there's no waste and it arrives field fresh," Mr. Kirchhoff explained.

The food service market has been "a significant factor" in Castle & Cooke's growth, he continued. "From virtually nothing two years ago, the institutional portion of our lettuce business now represents more than one-sixth of our total lettuce sales. The fastest growing part of the institutional business is in pre-cut lettuce, where our market share has grown rapidly to about 30 percent. We are a major supplier of McDonald's domestic lettuce requirements, and ship products as well to Kentucky Fried Chicken and Burger King."

Overseas sales have also moved up strongly, he reported. Bud of California products account for more than 50 percent of the celery and 40 percent of the lettuce shipped into Hong Kong. Its share of lettuce exports to Europe has climbed to 59 percent from 7 percent in the past three years.

Continuing, Mr. Kirchhoff said that Dole fresh pineapple sales have been increasing at about 25 percent compounded annually over the past few years. The company's banana business, he said, "appears to be set to enter a transitional stage, going from a high investment and low return situation to a lower investment and improved return level, because we've achieved the world market penetration level we sought."

Commenting on prospects for the company's food lines, Mr. Kirchhoff said: "Five of the fresh food product lines in which we compete -- bananas, lettuce, celery, cabbage and fresh mushrooms -- rank among the top 20 food items in the U.S. supermarket produce departments. The combined market for these five items is more than $2 billion annually in the U.S. alone, and the volume is growing."

* * *

May 10, 1979
(0649)

LESSONS OF LEADERSHIP

Keeping a Venerable Company Up-to-Date

Under Donald J. Kirchhoff, managers at 126-year-old Castle & Cooke are shifted from division to division, providing what he calls a cross-pollination that works well

At one point during World War II Navy service in the Pacific, Donald J. Kirchhoff ended up functioning as a commissary officer.

Was this experience the trigger that later propelled him from Harvard, with a mint-new, master-in-business-administration degree, into the business world of food?

"You've got to be kidding," says Mr. Kirchhoff in one of his two principal offices, this one high in a San Francisco financial district skyscraper (the other is in Hawaii).

"I went to work for a food-store chain, the Kroger Co., as an accountant because that was the best job I could get and I had a family to support."

But all of Mr. Kirchhoff's business career has been spent in facets of the food industry. He is now president and chief executive officer of Castle & Cooke, Inc., the 126-year-old Hawaiian-based food products company.

Turning point in career

If you had to choose a single event in his career as being a turning point, it would have to be one that was of the build-a-better-mousetrap variety.

In this instance, the mousetrap was the banana. What was developed was a disease-resistant variety and a new marketing concept: Box the bananas at the growing site, ship them that way to the ripening rooms, then on to the retailer in the same container.

This is the reason why you no longer see those big stems of bananas being unloaded from ships at ports and why the bananas you buy in supermarkets are not bruised or discolored.

It is also why there now are fewer spoilage problems for banana shippers, with consequent favorable impact on profits.

Mr. Kirchhoff was manager of the Honduras division of Standard Fruit and Steamship Co. at the time the banana—an existing variety—was improved through implementation of Standard Fruit research suggestions, changing the way an industry markets. That was 11 years after he got that M. B. A. degree at Harvard in 1949.

Training discipline

A lot of M. B. A.'s are working for Castle & Cooke. Mr. Kirchhoff believes getting an M. B. A. is a good route to take for any young person who wants a business career.

"You don't have to have an M. B. A.," he says, "but if you get one, you will have received the training discipline you need in managing."

A good manager is a good manager, he believes, and it doesn't matter whether what is managed is the manufacturing of bolts or the growing and marketing of bananas.

He has instituted a sharp reversal of historic management practice at Castle & Cooke.

"It used to be that a manager might spend his whole career in pineapples, for instance," says Mr. Kirchhoff. "Now we have pineapple people running operations in seafood, seafood people running operations in sugar, and so on. It gives you the cross-pollination you need so that you don't produce just experts in one segment of company business."

Castle & Cooke's world, as the company terms it, ranges over the mainland U. S., Europe, and from Hawaii to Latin America, from Alaska to the Philippines and Thailand.

From sugar to steel pipe

The company's products include bananas and fresh and processed pineapple, all under the Dole label; sugar; Bumble Bee-brand tuna and salmon; Dole and Shady Oak mushrooms; Alaska king and snow crab; lettuce; and canned vegetables.

Castle & Cooke owns and operates an eight-vessel refrigerated fleet; has real estate operations in California and Hawaii (where, with its plantations, it is the islands' fourth largest landowner, holding approximately 150,000 acres); and has a variety of subsidiaries.

The subsidiaries include a swimming pool equipment manufacturer, a steel pipe producer in Thailand, a rock-quarrying operation in Malaysia, and a heavy equipment distributorship and several small transportation-related subsidiaries in Hawaii.

Mr. Kirchhoff was president of Standard Fruit in 1964 when Castle &

Reprinted from Nation's Business

Cooke acquired a majority interest in Standard.

He had joined Standard after three years at Kroger and three years as controller of another grocery chain, National Food Stores, of Michigan. He turned down a job with Standard in 1954, but two years later joined the company as manager of the operations analysis department. He was assistant to the president when he was made general manager of the Honduras division and given the assignment to turn the banana operation around.

He was elected executive vice president and a director of Castle & Cooke in 1970, president in 1973, and president and chief executive officer in 1975.

Home for Mr. Kirchhoff is a house in Hawaii, where he gardens and raises tropical fish. He and Mrs. Kirchhoff have three grown daughters.

Thrives on traveling

Mr. Kirchhoff, 52, spends about 60 percent of his time on the job traveling to various operations of Castle & Cooke. He divides the other 40 percent between the company's corporate headquarters in Honolulu and the foods division headquarters in San Francisco.

"I'm able to sleep in anything that moves," he says, so he doesn't mind the traveling. In fact, he thrives on it.

Is he a workaholic?

"No, but I enjoy my work. I always have."

An executive who believes in tight, centralized financial controls, Mr. Kirchhoff also feels that a business organization should enable decisions to be made at the lowest level possible.

Revenues on the rise

Castle & Cooke has paid a dividend every year since 1896, and it has shown a steady surge in revenues. In the period 1968-1976 they increased from $341.7 million to $850.3 million. Last year—the final figures are not yet in—revenues came close to $1 billion.

The company was founded in 1851 by Samuel Northrup Castle and Amos Starr Cooke, two lay missionaries who came to Hawaii in 1837 with the seventh group of missionaries sent to the islands. When their mission board decided the missionaries had to become self-supporting, the two men started a general store.

Over the years C & C's history has been intertwined with that of Hawaii and its chief industries: sugar, pineapple, ships, and tourists.

While C & C began as a mercantile company, it now primarily is a food company which raises or buys from others the foods it sells. That, basically, is where Mr. Kirchhoff believes its future growth will come.

"We'll grow within our product line," he says. "With products we will either develop or acquire."

An executive who likes competition, Mr. Kirchhoff also believes that business must have a keen social responsibility.

In an interview with NATION'S BUSINESS, he talked about this, as well as about his career.

When you decided to box bananas, why did you settle on a weight of 40 pounds?

Tradition was the deciding factor. Bananas at that point were shipped on the stem. Then they went into ripening rooms, were picked off in bunches, and sent to the retailer in 40-pound boxes.

The concept of selling prepackaged bananas from the tropics was difficult enough for retailers to accept, so we decided the easiest way was to go along with what a retailer had been receiving. We ship other weights—15 kilos, for example, to Italy. In Japan, the magic number is 12 kilos. These are weights that retailers there had grown accustomed to receiving.

The big change was that you packed the bananas at the source, and they weren't unpacked until they actually reached the retail level.

How many different types of boxes did you try?

We tried returnable wooden boxes, plastic, almost every feasible type. The problem was having a container that would be conducive to the ripening process. It turned out the corrugated cardboard box was the answer.

Was there any compelling reason behind the push to box bananas?

You could say it was the survival of Standard Fruit.

The company did not control the same quantity of plantable lands as did its competitors. And the primary banana at that time was the Gros Michel. It was susceptible to Panama disease. The industry was a sort of migrant one. If the disease wiped out an area, you'd move on to another one.

Because of limited lands, Standard had to try to find a better banana, so to speak. We planted the Giant Cavendish, which is resistant to Panama disease, but which has a thinner skin. When you shipped it on the stem, it was susceptible to bruising, and you ended having to sell it at a discount.

So we had solved the problem of growing a good, new banana. But we also had to solve the problem of getting it to the market in good shape. Now everybody is growing the Cavendish-type banana and shipping it in boxes.

The whole process was more difficult than it sounds.

Did you ever just blow up and get mad at the banana?

I don't think so. I don't think I'm the type who blows up when there is a problem to be faced.

Besides, when you are growing bananas, nothing is ever really settled. A windstorm might knock you out of business, for instance. The business makes you become adaptable to change. You have to have a modus operandi which enables you to make plans with an awful lot of options and to switch in a hurry.

E. L. Del Beccaro, vice president of marketing services (left), checks an idea with Castle & Cooke's president.

Reprinted from Nation's Business

Mr. Kirchhoff likes to visit with company executives in their own offices.

Senior Castle & Cooke executives include (left to right) Leonard Marks, Jr., executive vice president-chief financial officer; Henry B. Clark, Jr., executive vice president; Robert S. Gordon, senior vice president; Mr. Kirchhoff; and Malcolm MacNaughton, chairman.

In other words, flexibility is an asset?

Yes. I believe it is for any manager. I suspect that one of the problems government has is inflexibility in its bureaucracy. Inflexibility makes it difficult to cope.

Technology and a change in management style have both played important roles in your company's upsurge in recent years. Which is most important?

Technology is terribly important to our company, and the continued advancement of technology is our management style, in effect.

Reprinted from Nation's Business

You have been termed a centrist, one who believes in tight centralized controls. Is that a fair description?

No, I wouldn't classify myself as a centrist. But I do believe in strong financial controls. We are so scattered around the world that, if you don't have tight control, some things will get out of whack somewhere, somehow.

We are centralized in terms of technology, in terms of research, in our environmental efforts. But we are pretty decentralized when it comes to management. We have six operating groups with complete staffs of their own. They have full profit and loss responsibility, and they make decisions. But we at headquarters do exercise financial control.

You certainly did institute one major change in management for Castle & Cooke, didn't you?

Yes, we made a major change in that managers would no longer spend their entire career with just one division. It has worked very well.

What was the primary reason for changing managers from division to division?

I suppose it was the realization that we weren't realizing our full potential with personnel.

Since this was quite a change from a historic policy, did you ever fret about the decision once it was made?

I'm not a worrier, and I have a favorite saying, "It doesn't pay to look back." I don't try to rehash what has been done. I like an organization where the decisions can be made at the lowest level possible.

That's why I like the idea of tight controls and a fairly centralized staff. They give some assurance that you're going to get various types of views into a decision, although the decision itself can be made at a low level.

What is your basic business philosophy?

I guess my basic philosophy is that I want to leave the world better than it was when I entered it.

Some would say that's a "motherhood" answer.

No, it isn't a motherhood answer. I feel that very deeply. I'm very proud of some of Castle & Cooke's accomplishments around the world. I've seen the way we changed the landscape when we started some of our operations, and the way we changed the people. We provided education for kids, and we made little peasants entrepreneurs—successful people.

So you believe business has a social responsibility?

Yes, I do. Business has many responsibilities—to give the people who put up the capital as good a return as possible, to provide the best product it can—and certainly it has a social responsibility, too.

Where will your future growth come from? Acquisitions?

Pineapples grown in Hawaii, Honduras, and the Philippines are one of the basic products of Castle & Cooke. A portable conveyor belt speeds the harvesting.

Plastic shrouds have protected growing bananas from insects and dirt. The cable line carries the big stems of fruit from the plantation to the packing shed.

We are a food company, and we will keep expanding in terms of product lines, not only by acquisition, but by internal development. We have had great success in developing the fresh pineapple market, and it hasn't hurt our processed pineapple product. We are experimenting with a number of products that we grow.

You know, there is a situation today where people are somewhat frightened by additives to foods, preservatives. I see the company growing in the area of natural foods—if you want to call them that—or just plain fresh produce.

Also, we will be expanding our seafood operations. For example, all of our crab is now sold in institutional channels and ends up in restaurants or with similar buyers.

Crab is still a relatively expensive item, and that makes it difficult to sell in the retail trade right now. But we are constantly looking at this situation. It could change in the future.

How were you affected by the squabble over the porpoise catch in the course of tuna fishing?

Our fleet was laid up for several months in the spring of 1977 as a result of it, so it hurt us to some extent profitwise. The dispute is now somewhat resolved, but it was really an unfortunate thing. We try to do the best we can to protect the porpoises.

Incidentally, the number of porpoises in the sea is increasing rapidly, despite the tuna fishing.

How do you view the relations of business with government?

I think business has a definite responsibility to point out the pitfalls of some government actions. Once you get a law, it's a law, and you're stuck with it, good, bad, or indifferent.

We certainly need to bring to bear all the knowledge, all the data, that we can possibly bring on any suggested government action.

I feel government has a shortsighted attitude toward the fundamental laws of economics. Too often, ideas turn into rules without much thought about what they are going to do to the goose that lays the golden egg, the economy.

Are you optimistic or pessimistic about business today?

Optimistic. I'm a competitor. If you're a competitor, you're always optimistic. □

REPRINTED FROM NATION'S BUSINESS, JANUARY 1978

©, 1978, by Nation's Business

8167

SHOP FOR GROWTH

Are you a person who likes to shop around—to find that unique combination of both quality and price? It's usually worth the effort whether it's at the supermarket or in the stock market.

Castle & Cooke, the company that grows and markets such popular and respected brands as Dole, Bumble Bee and Bud of California, also offers an outstanding long-term record of financial growth. Castle & Cooke's natural products are favorites in the home as well as in the growing food service market. And its stock is held by an increasing number of investors.

Shop around. Then check out Castle & Cooke.

CASTLE & COOKE

CASTLE & COOKE, INC., HONOLULU AND SAN FRANCISCO

Stock up on a growing company

Castle & Cooke. Growing is our business: providing some of the healthy, natural foods that are so important in today's, and tomorrow's, nutrition- and calorie-conscious world. You probably already know our brand names: Dole pineapple, bananas and fresh mushrooms, Bumble Bee and Royal Alaskan seafood, and Bud of California fresh vegetables. Growing is also our history. You'll discover a company with a remarkable financial record—an aggressive company alert to future trends, nation-wide and world-wide.

Growth isn't just another buzz-word at Castle & Cooke. It's our stock in trade.

CASTLE & COOKE

CASTLE & COOKE, INC., HONOLULU AND SAN FRANCISCO

8

Investor Relations at FMC Corporation

William R. Baker

In large publicly held companies, there are several possible organizational homes for the investor relations function: the office of the financial vice president, the public relations department, or the treasurer's department, for example. At FMC we have elected to make it a financial function and have organized it within the treasurer's department.

Although the primary function of investor relations is communications, the specialized nature of those communications provides a strong reason to organize investor relations separately from the traditional communications or public relations functions. Because we are communicating primarily with investors, we believe that the individuals responsible for those communications should understand and be familiar with the specialized information requirements of that audience. In brief, we believe it is easier to find financial people who can communicate well than to find a communications person who understands finance, accounting, and economics.

Having financially trained investor relations people is especially important in communicating with institutional investors. Since institutions account for more than 70 percent of the volume on the New York Stock Exchange, no serious investor relations program can afford to ignore them. Companies without large institutional followings should be eager to influence institutions, and companies such as FMC that already have a large institutional following should be careful to preserve it. Because the most effective method of communications with these institutions is face-to-face contact, the investor relations person (IRP) must be able to communicate with institutional analysts or portfolio managers using the same concepts and terminology that they use.

The IRP should be the initial and primary point of contact within his company for any analyst, portfolio manager, or other investor. Other company executives should be made available, but only with the approval, coordination, and participation of the IRP. The reasons are threefold:

William R. Baker is Director of Investor Relations for FMC Corporation.

1. The IRP should be an expert on SEC disclosure rules, and as such, he should participate in all discussions with investors to ensure that the regulations are being followed.
2. Because he coordinates the data that flow to investors, the IRP should be present to moderate the discussions of other executives to ensure that an appropriate level of data is provided.
3. To ensure consistency, the IRP should not provide analysts with unsupervised sources of information from within his company. To do so would give them an opportunity to play one contact off against another to obtain more information than the IRP would normally volunteer.

SHAREHOLDER COMMUNICATIONS

Perhaps the single most important element of shareholder communications is the annual report. We at FMC believe that the annual report serves a much broader purpose than simply to report the previous year's activities; it is also an important means of communication with customers, suppliers, employees, potential new employees, and others. To appeal to a broad range of audiences, the report must maintain its value throughout the year. Consequently, we try to write a report that will appeal to all segments of our public, from analysts and individual shareholders to non-shareholders.

We write the annual report operating review and financial review for those who want detailed information about the previous year's results (and also to meet SEC requirements). In addition, for financially less sophisticated audiences, we prepare a lengthy photoessay that conveys what we most want them to know about FMC during that year. A two-page organization spread explains to both insiders and outsiders how the various parts of the Company fit together. This spread is important in clearly portraying a complex, diversified company such as FMC. We also rely on heavy use of graphs and photographs to make the annual report more appealing to all audiences, especially those who are not professional investors. (Our success is indicated by the fact that our 1977 and 1978 reports won Best of Industry Awards from the National Association of Investment Clubs, which cited them as being best from the viewpoint of the individual investor.)

The quarterly report is certainly the next most valuable vehicle in shareholder communications, because it provides a frequent opportunity to update the Company's story. Rather than being merely recitations of the business activities of the quarter, FMC's quarterly reports utilize a feature article format to highlight particular divisions or products that we want our readers to know about. We believe that this approach is more appealing to a broader range of audiences. The chairman's letter is used to report the results of the quarter, followed by feature articles of two or three pages each. The criteria for selecting subjects for the feature articles are heavily influenced by what we perceive to be of interest to investors; however, we also write about the less glamorous parts of our business in order to present a balanced picture of the Company.

A third element in our regular communications with shareholders is our company magazine, *Progress,* an internal/external quarterly publication that is made available to shareholders. Over 50 percent of FMC's shareholders have asked to receive it on a regular basis, but it is also designed to inform potential shareholders and others about corporate developments. Written in magazine style and heavily illustrated, *Progress* is easy to read while being informative about aspects of the Company not covered in the annual and quarterly reports. *Progress* focuses on individual product lines and typically covers either their production or end use. (A sample issue of the magazine is reproduced at the end of this chapter.)

But face-to-face communication provides the most effective means of conveying a company's financial message. The IRP should be responsible for scheduling, planning, and executing all management meetings with investors, such as the ones outlined below.

Annual meeting of shareholders. We view the annual meeting as a prime opportunity for management to communicate with shareholders. Because our annual meeting is usually not scheduled at a time when earnings are announced, we believe the annual meeting can be a forum to discuss topics other than the Company's operations. This gives us an opportunity to show the shareholders a facet of management that they do not often see. In 1978, for example, FMC's chairman followed up on a major speech he had made and talked about the need for a national export policy to help correct the nation's balance of payments deficit. His comments received much wider press attention than a report on operations alone would have gotten. Because the audience attending an annual meeting is only a fraction of the Company's total shareholder population, we also reprint an edited transcript of the meeting, including the questions and answers, for distribution to our shareholders.

The most demanding task of the annual meeting is to prepare management for the hundreds of possible questions that might come up at the meeting. To this end, we prepare an extensive question-and-answer book based on booklets of potential questions prepared by several of the major accounting firms (such as Peat Marwick Mitchell & Co.; Ernst & Whinney; and Haskins & Sells), our culling of the business press for "hot issues," and our own experience with questions from shareholders and special interest groups.

Most managements are extremely concerned about the possibility of disruption or embarrassment at the annual meeting. As a result, those charged with its preparation must be ready for any eventuality. At FMC, we have a carefully prepared alternative meeting plan for use in the event of disruption. The alternative plan discharges the minimal legal obligations of the meeting and brings it to a quick conclusion.

Analyst social meetings. Our experience with analyst societies in most cities, with the notable exceptions of New York and Boston, has been that a high proportion of those who attend analyst society meetings have little real interest in the Company or have interests other than those that prompted the Company to make the presentation. Nonetheless, we try to schedule one or two analyst society meetings a year. We invite the business press to attend these meetings, and will also arrange press interviews with management. In addition, an analyst society appearance gives us the opportunity to reprint our presentation for distribution to a much broader audience. The press coverage and secondary distribution of the presentation are, in our estimation, important reasons for analyst society presentations.

Meetings with institutional investors. We have found that private, by-invitation meetings with small groups of interested institutional investors are our most effective meeting format. The groups are large enough to maximize the use of top executive time but small enough to be informal and personal. We rely on brokers to sponsor most of these meetings: the brokers normally get a better turnout (with appropriate direction) because of their broad range of contacts, and they also turn up new contacts with whom the Company may not have been acquainted. Being associated with a broker in this way enhances the Company's investment image by demonstrating its institutional support. The broker also benefits, of course, since he gets credit for bringing his clients—or potential clients—together with companies' top management.

We favor sponsors who follow and support FMC with research, although nonresearch sponsors can be helpful in secondary financial centers where they have established programs. Whenever possible, however, choosing sponsors who provide ongoing support makes the most sense. It is desirable to cultivate a number of sponsors rather than to become too closely associated with any one, in order to minimize the loss of support if a favored sponsor should cool. Also, sole reliance on only one sponsor can overtax a relationship.

Analysts' briefings. In order to give the financial community an opportunity to review the Company in depth, it is important periodically to schedule a meeting for a full day or longer. Extended meetings provide an opportunity to expose a broad cross section of management to investors in a controlled environment. Such meetings also indicate the Company's interest and willingness to communicate fully with the financial community.

Ensuring sufficient attendance to justify the effort of such a meeting is a critical consideration. An easy solution is to hold the meeting in New York City, although there is certain to be a part of the audience that will come for only a portion of the program and be absent for the rest. We always try to select locations that keep the audience relatively captive and offer few distractions—airport hotels and off-season resort areas are good choices in this regard. To encourage attendance, we try to make our meetings as convenient as possible by picking locations where good transportation minimizes the need for staying overnight and by keeping the meeting on schedule so that departing flights are not missed.

In order to get the right audience, we use four techniques. First, the meeting is by invitation only. This means that the IRP strictly controls attendance and will not allow individuals with marginal interest to attend. Second, notice of the date and location is sent out at least four months in advance. Third, invitations are made by personal letter only, each typed individually and personally signed by the IRP. Fourth, a month before the meeting, the unanswered invitations are followed up by telephone, using whatever leverage is available to maximize attendance.

In preparing speeches and presentations for analyst meetings, there are a few important rules to follow. First, keep it brief. No speaker should talk more than 15 minutes, unless he is a genuine spellbinder. If a presentation will last longer than 15 minutes, we try to use two or more speakers. Second, whenever possible, slides or other visual aids should be used to highlight and amplify important points. Visual aids can also be very helpful to speakers who rely heavily on a written text. Third, content should be factual and straightforward, without either fluff or omissions. A candid discussion of problems will do more to build credibility for management than a glowing report of higher earnings. Fourth, the IRP should participate in the preparation of every investor-oriented presentation to ensure its appropriateness, maximize its appeal to investors, and avoid disclosure problems.

ADVERTISING CAMPAIGNS

Unless they are specifically aimed at financial audiences, most corporate advertising campaigns are not suitable for use in the financial media. The message carried to a financial audience should be different from the message conveyed in general corporate image advertising to a broader cross section of the population. FMC has a highly acclaimed corporate image campaign running in the general business media; we have recently launched a separate financial advertising campaign to run in specific financial media.

Whether the benefits of financial advertising justify the costs is a question that each company must consider in the context of its own circumstances. FMC has documented a need for this type of advertising through attitude research studies. FMC has a relatively low level of recognition in the financial community compared with its major competitors. As a result, the Company is generally not as well regarded as it should be. Increased recognition has been shown to result in more favorable opinions, and advertising is a powerful tool for increasing recognition.

We want to create name recognition that will help make financial audiences receptive to our other communications. Our new campaign is designed to have a distinctive look that is as important as the copy itself in establishing recognition. This campaign will run entirely in print media. Television is by far the most effective advertising medium, but it is too expensive for a campaign aimed at the relatively narrow financial audience.

Although advertising is important in creating awareness of the Company, some types of advertising are of little value, in our opinion. For example, we do not believe in advertising quarterly earnings results. Competition for advertising readership is extremely keen, and something more exciting than a statistical summary is necessary to win attention. Furthermore, those investors who are really interested in quarterly results do not rely on advertising as a source of statistical information.

Similarly, FMC does not conduct annual report advertising. Despite the follow-up surveys produced by all the publications that seek annual report advertising, we still regard the quality of response as extremely poor and the cost of fulfilling the requests as extremely high.

Every IRP should maintain a personal mailing list of his most important contacts. We maintain such a list and use it to mail a wide variety of information that is of interest to close followers of the Company but is unsuitable for broad, general distribution. We also maintain a general interest financial mailing list, and we purchase several selective analyst and portfolio manager lists to ensure that our annual and quarterly reports are getting full distribution to the institutional investors in whom we are interested.

THE ROLE OF SURVEYS

It is often difficult to judge the effectiveness of communications programs and to justify the funds committed to them. One of the most important but often overlooked tools that can answer such questions is research into the attitudes and awareness of the target audience. Surveys provide not only the basis for establishing programs, but also the benchmark for assessing the programs' success. Before any major new program is launched, a benchmark survey should be conducted to determine present attitudes or perceptions. Periodic follow-up surveys then provide a measure of the level of achievement of program goals.

A variety of surveys can be used, depending on individual requirements. Simple shareholder surveys can be done inexpensively in-house, although the validity of the results may be questionable if the responses are heavily weighted by retired people who have ample time to reply. Normally, the added cost of retaining an outside firm to survey a statistically valid sample is well worthwhile.

More elaborate and costly surveys are useful in certain circumstances. For instance, when FMC first began to accelerate its investor relations program, an extensive survey of attitudes among both individual shareholders and institutional investors was conducted by a major research firm. This survey is being used as the benchmark against which we will measure the effectiveness of our investor relations programs and financial advertising campaigns.

It is also useful to have informal surveys conducted after important meetings to test the appropriateness of the message, the impact of delivery, and the level of recall. Such surveys are relatively inexpensive when purchased, or they can be done in-house. They are a valuable aid in refining subsequent presentations.

COMMUNICATION WITH BROKERS AND HANDLING STOCK TRANSFERS

Recently, there has been a great deal of interest in communicating with registered representatives, and FMC is currently developing a program tailored specifically for them. The potential audience is large, probably close to

50,000. With such a large audience, we will rely primarily on space advertising and direct mail as the most efficient means of communication.

In preparation for our program, we have been building a mailing list from brokers' responses to cooperative mass mailings. In addition to sending regular mailings of annual and quarterly reports to people on this list, we intend to develop special mailing pieces targeted to appeal to brokers. These communications to brokers will be structured differently from the institutional communications that are the backbone of most investor relations programs. For brokers, the message must be kept brief and uncomplicated, and it must be more directly promotional (although without touting) than institutional communications. The broker must be given the selling points that he can use to sell the company to his clients. Brokers do not have time to make elaborate presentations; they must sell quickly. Tailoring a message to meet that need in a manner satisfactory to both the Company and the SEC is a real challenge.

Because of the large broker population, meetings with brokers are not usually a cost-effective means of communication. At FMC, we avoid the so-called stockbroker societies, as they tend to be more social than business-oriented. IRPs may want to visit brokerage offices to talk with brokers, as we do, but it is not recommended for any of the top management of major companies to invest the time in such visits.

FMC is one of a number of corporations that serves as its own stock transfer agent. We have found that we can perform the stock transfer function at a lower cost than outside contractors, while providing better service to our stockholders. The stock transfer function's primary service to management is maintaining and analyzing shareholder records, as well as reporting on changes in ownership in which we are keenly interested. The timeliness of our transfer information is far superior to that of any outside firm, and by performing the function in-house, we are able to carry out special analyses of shareholders and trading patterns that outsiders would not undertake on a timely basis or at a reasonable cost. Furthermore, manual adjustments to the data can be made to account for special situations such as tracing a nominee to its beneficial or aggregating family groups of holders.

GOALS AND OBJECTIVES

IRPs are often quoted as saying that the objective of investor relations is to provide investors with sufficient timely information so that a fair price for a company's securities can be established based on full and fair disclosure. We do not sanction touting a company's stock, or any other form of manipulation, but certainly the effort put into communicating with investors can only be intended to enhance the image of a company and widen the market for its stock.

How do we go about assisting the market in establishing a "fair price"? We try to establish long-term personal relationships with as many institutional investors as possible. An IRP should never lose a contact: if the contact sells the stock or switches to a different job, he should not be crossed off the list. It is amazing how old friends can come back to help you after years of separation.

These contacts are established by providing a service that consists of making available accurate and timely information that investors can rely on. Investors are extremely hesitant to invest in companies that are perceived to provide unreliable or incomplete information about their affairs. Companies, as well as IRPs personally, must establish credibility before investors will rely on them. Credibility for an IRP comes from knowing the company inside out and being able to answer questions fully and accurately. Answers must be straight: the IRP has to tell a company's story as it is *all* the time, even when the news is bad. Talking straight about problems is more important to build credibility than boasting about successes. Investors *expect* a company to do a good job and be successful; failures and mistakes are what really interest them, and neglecting to communicate about failures or mistakes will do severe damage to a company's credibility.

As a matter of policy, the IRP should tell as much as possible about his company without causing either competitive damage or SEC disclosure problems. This often runs counter to the desires of a company's operating management, but it is difficult to be credible without being open. To be fully effective, a good IRP should be able to represent the company's CEO. He must know the details of the company's operations, market conditions, accounting and financial policies, and economic outlook; he must have an understanding of legislation affecting the company, and he must be able to interpret a wide range of company policies.

Over time, he should become the most favored contact in the company because he will have the greatest grasp of current detail and can put it in terms that investors understand. The IRP can achieve his preferential status not because he is smarter than everyone else, but because he is in constant contact with the questions that are being asked. Anyone who has the questions in advance should certainly know most of the answers.

Progress

NUMBER 4/1978

MC in Spain

pening new worlds
or our chemicals–p. 14

FMC

Progress

NUMBER 4/1978

FMC Progress is published four times a year and is available at no charge.
Attention editors. *We welcome the use of articles and pictures found in this magazine as long as permission is received from FMC Public Relations.*
Information: *Write, or call FMC's national toll free telephone information service: 800-621-4500 (in Illinois only, 312-861-5900)*

cover

Exquisite Eva Gallego, 5, daughter of an employee of FMC's Foret, S.A. plant in La Zaida, Spain who attends a company-built school, is one of the 35 million Spaniards who enjoy a lifestyle as modern as any. Special report on the role FMC expects to play in providing the chemical building blocks for the good life in all of Europe begins on page 14.

contents

Material handling:

A "pig-um" that won't poke for NASA 1

Power transmission:

Those absolutely basic, always busy bearings 4

Food:

Powder power in the kitchen 9

Agarose — fingerprinting the blood 10

Chemicals:

Foret — a foothold for industrial chemicals in Europe 14

What Foret makes for whom 16

Brace for space. A 40-ton beam, largest component in the FMC-designed Payload Ground Handling Mechanism built for the National Aeronautics and Space Administration, moves into place more than 100 feet above ground at the Kennedy Space Center in Florida. The special mechanism will move huge payloads into NASA's space shuttle, the workhorse spaceship of the 1980's. See page 1.

FMC Progress Staff

Norm Bezane, Editor
Publications Manager

Margo Parsons
Staff Writer

Albert H. Campbell
Advertising/Public Relations Director

Richard Johnston
Media Relations Manager

Fred E. Rosewater, Jr., San Jose
Western Public Relations Manager

Frank Malkwitz, Brussels
Public Relations/Advertising Manager

Robertz Design Company, Chicago
Design and production

PRINTED IN U.S.A.

A "pig-um" that won't poke for NASA

With all systems go at the Kennedy Space Center some day, a kind of space freightliner called the Orbiter shaped and sized somewhat like a DC-9 jet will carry a 60-foot-tall package of space satellites into earth orbit, rising from Pad 39-A with a mighty roar. Seven days later, the Orbiter will return and 160 hours after that rise with another payload for another trip. Some day is almost here thanks in part to two FMC divisions that have teamed up to design and build a key system that helps make the whole concept work.

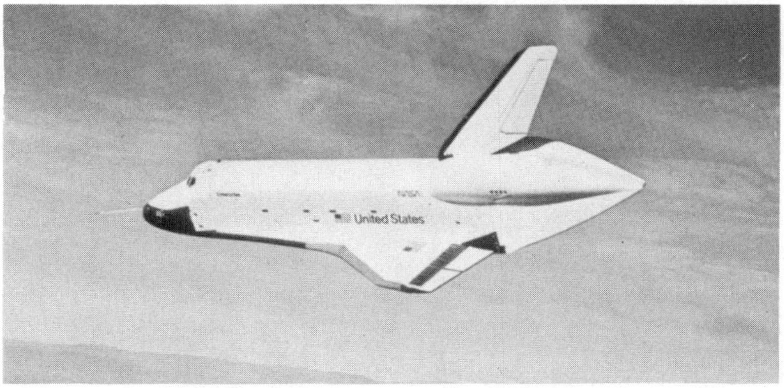

NASA's reusable space shuttle loaded with the help of an FMC system will soon carry payloads into earth orbit, then return to land for another trip.

The reusable space shuttle will carry more than 200 payloads into orbit. FMC's PGHM plays a key role.

To be launched sometime next fall, the National Aeronautics and Space Administration (NASA) reusable space shuttle and fleet of sister ships will, in the next decade, carry more than 200 huge payloads into earth orbit. Most of the satellites and building blocks for space stations will be loaded aboard the Orbiter launch vehicle by means of the FMC system.

Nicknamed "pig-um," FMC's Payload Ground Handling Mechanism (PGHM) is designed to complete the simple-looking yet tricky feat of moving a 65,000-pound payload as tall as a four-story building and 15 feet in diameter into the Orbiter payload cargo bay. The PGHM and payload can't poke or bump anything in the process.

FMC's Engineered Systems Division, creator, designer, and builder of one-of-a-kind machines for industry and government, developed the PGHM after submitting an ingenious plan that won it the NASA contract in competition with several top aerospace contractors. FMC's Material Handling Systems Division has built many of the components for the giant handling device.

The $4 million PGHM is actually a framework of 350,000 pounds of steel installed 130 feet above ground within a payload change-out room in a rotating service structure. But it is also a carefully designed superstructure designed to lift and carry the payload without damaging its sophisticated and delicate innards.

The system goes to work when the payload is delivered in a vertical position to the launch site in a protective canister. Eased from the canister, the tall payload is grasped by a PGHM mechanism that transfers it into the service tower's clean room.

Transfer from the canister to the PGHM takes about four hours and is carried out for the most part with manual power assist controls.

The PGHM and Orbiter can handle one 60-foot-tall payload or five 12-foot-tall separate ones, individual space satellites, for example, stacked carefully on top of one another but each removable individually for last-minute servicing.

Five-inch-long, handle-like prongs on the various payloads are grasped by specially designed FMC retention fittings. Since the payload is so tall and bulky, special provision had to be made to allow for raising or lowering it slightly or tilting it at top or bottom to keep the payload in a perfect vertical position during transfer into the Orbiter.

Once the payload is inside the clean room, doors close and the PGHM and payload are ready to move up to the waiting Orbiter. It's simpler said than done. The entire Rotating Service Structure moves in a giant semicircle along steel tracks to the launch pad and the Orbiter.

Doors enclosing the PGHM open and the payload moves horizontally into the Orbiter payload bay at two inches a minute, gliding on wheels that ride on an overhead bridge at the top of the structure. Before the payload enters, the

(continued)

Towering above the Engineered Systems Division's Harold Young and Andy Rado and the Material Handling Systems Division's Sam Byrd, the huge Rotating Service Structure at the Kennedy Space Center awaits installation of the FMC-designed and built PGHM. The 60-foot-tall mechanism fits within the large cavity in the structure at the top of the photo. ▶

A new era in space

Strapped to booster rockets, the Orbiter will look like this when it leaves Pad 39-A.

Within 200 milliseconds, NASA's space shuttle Orbiter and auxiliary boosters will reach 6.5 million pounds of full thrust, setting off a mighty roar which will be heard miles away. The shuttle's significance, however, will reach around the globe. The space shuttle opens the door to the economical and routine use of space, NASA says.

Carrying as many as five satellites at once in its payload bay, the Orbiter will also be able to retrieve malfunctioning satellites from space for repair on earth and serve as a space bus for non-astronaut scientists visiting space stations. The combination of features is expected to sharply reduce the cost of putting useful objects up in space, accelerating and improving the use of satellites for mapping weather, finding minerals, providing communications, measuring pollution, studying ocean currents, spotting forest fires and a host of other purposes.

The Orbiter will also be the prime launch vehicle for the European Space Agency's $500 million space lab, a working space laboratory sponsored by 11 nations that itself could make as many as 50 round trips into space in the 1980's.

The landing of the first Orbiter is not an end but a beginning. A spectacular beginning it will be. The space vehicle will land on a 15,000-foot Cape Kennedy runway. Its skin will be so hot special vehicles will race to its side to pump in coolant as soon as it glides to a stop.

PGHM is stopped several inches from the cargo bay door of the Orbiter by an automatic system. Engineers can then make sure it is properly aligned for entry and activate a specially designed motion-controlling system.

The handling task is even more complicated than it seems. During transfer no portion of the PGHM or payload can touch the Orbiter, protecting both the payload and the Orbiter from damage. The biggest complication of all is that strong winds that often buffet the Cape can cause the Orbiter to sway up to three

FMC won the NASA contract in competition with top aerospace contractors.

inches. During transfer, both PGHM and payload have to move precisely with the Orbiter when there is wind sway, accomplished by a common connecting beam floating within a main support beam.

"Making this transfer," Engineered Systems Project Manager Andy Rado sums up, "is a little bit like moving a heavy bulk cargo from ship to ship on a rough sea, with the two ships side by side."

Engineered Systems built a working mock-up of the PGHM at its Santa Clara, California shop last year, began assembling the PGHM at the Cape in June, and expects to turn a working system over to NASA before year end. Sometime next fall, if all goes well, the first Orbiter will be launched carrying its first PGHM-placed payload.

FMC
FMC
FMC

Those absolutely basic, always busy bearings

Spinning merrily along, a rotating shaft transmits the power that runs just about every machine or mechanical device from the tiniest precision watch to the most powerful industrial machine and awesome supertanker. Few would spin at all without the support of the simplest of devices that spends most of its time going around in circles. It's the absolutely basic, always busy bearing.

Bearings — known to many but understood by few — are one of industry's most sought after products, generating

Bearings generate a whopping $7.5 billion in sales. FMC makes millions of them.

a surprising, whopping $7.5 billion in worldwide sales for the people who manufacture them. Among prime contenders for a specialized portion of the business: FMC's Bearing Division, Indianapolis, Indiana, maker of millions of bearings each year.

Fighting friction and supporting rotating shafts that keep machines in motion, the division's Link-Belt® bearings help business produce the essentials of modern life. Machines that till the soil, pump oil, harvest food, carry freight, cool the office, print publications, mine coal, make paper and steel and do much more all rely on Link-Belt bearings to keep them going.

Simply described, the anti-friction bearing is a kind of metal doughnut. Two bearings support the weight of a rotating shaft. The shaft rests on the doughnut hole. Without the use of bearings, the shaft would produce heat through friction hot enough to damage machines, cause moving parts to wear out, or require the equipment to do more work to overcome resistance.

Inside the doughnut are well-lubricated metal balls or rollers. They roll and turn smoothly in a groove called a raceway as fast as the shaft wants to go. The shaft can then rotate for the life of the bearing.

Simple. But considering the many different machine applications, the job is immense. FMC makes four major bearing types in 9600 different sizes and variations, including some that work in Arctic temperatures and others that run in industrial kilns in temperatures over 650 degrees F.

FMC specializes in certain types of bearings that account for a sizable portion of the total bearing market and may have up to six million parts going through one stage of production or another at any one time.

Even lubricants can be complicated. Bearings rotate smoothly only if they're lubricated properly. A significant percentage of those FMC makes have the lubricants sealed in, meaning they don't have to be lubricated during the life of the bearing. Others have special openings for lubricating. Some 76 lubricants are supplied by FMC for specific applications, including one with a price tag of $600 a pound.

Ball bearings, the biggest seller, have a number of metal balls as rolling contact surfaces, are available at low cost, and operate at high speed. Tractors, harvesting machines including hay balers, small fans and blowers all rely on them to keep operating.

Spherical roller bearings, capable of carrying heavy loads, have a number

(continued)

◀ *Precision is the goal of these new employees, seen making and assembling bearings—basic products for all of industry—at FMC plants in Clinton, Tennessee and Indianapolis.*

Assemblers swiftly select interchangeable rings and roller elements to put together the final product, checked before and after assembly.

Spherical bearings are a popular line.

Bearing parts await final assembly.

Cylindrical roller bearings have become a big seller since introduction in the 1970's.

of barrel-shaped rollers to roll with the shaft. Their biggest uses are in steel mills, heavy construction equipment and giant vibrating screens.

Collar-mounted bearings, so called because of the way they are secured to a shaft, find application in conveyors, mining and trenching machines, debarking logs, industrial furnaces and other heavy duty applications.

Cylindrical bearings, the division's newest product line, weren't made in quantity until the opening of a new plant constructed four years ago to

The bearing is a kind of doughnut. Inside are well-lubricated metal balls that roll and turn smoothly.

manufacture them exclusively in Clinton, Tennessee. "In the late sixties," explains Sales Manager Bill Weber, "we weren't in the business at all. But we saw that potential customers for this type of bearing were having trouble getting product and were in a good growth market."

Now seven models of cylindrical roller bearings made in over 100 sizes make up a large percentage of total division sales. A good portion of the plant's output is used by makers of tractor trailer trucks — the 18 wheelers of CB radio fame — for their transmissions and axles. Manufacturers of earth moving machines such as crawler tractors and front-end loaders and oil field pumps are other good customers.

"We're specialists," stresses Marketing Manager Dick Bergmann. "We don't manufacture bearings for the huge, domestic, automobile companies. The bearing business is so big and there are so many opportunities, we select our customers to capitalize on our strengths: production capability, engineering know-how and application experience."

Adds Indianapolis Works Manager Jim Mitchell: "We manufacture high volume standard bearings by the thousands here, but we also produce low volume special application bearings designed to solve a customer's specific problems."

What's the lowest volume the plant manufactures? "One," he says, matter-of-factly.

Making one or many, the emphasis is on quality. "This is a tough, competitive business," says Jim Franklin, eastern regional sales manager. "Quality may be a cliché, but this is one business where it really is the first rule. If you don't have quality, you don't compete."

A tomato harvester, Franklin notes, could cost more than $100,000 but can't function without $700 worth of FMC bearings deep within its power transmission components. If the bearings perform, there's no problem. But if a

Cylindrical roller bearings are used by the makers of 18 wheelers of CB radio fame.

bearing fails and can't be replaced immediately, acres of crop could be lost.

Quality often means precision. Bearings routinely are ground to tolerances of two-ten-thousandths of an inch — the difference between high and low spots no greater than the breadth of a human hair.

It's not uncommon, though, for

FMC's skilled work force to achieve tolerances of twenty-five-millionths of an inch (a width equal to a human hair cut into more than 100 thin strips, with the width equal to just one strip).

Precision begins with the raw materials and is an integral part of every manufacturing step. Bearing steels, for example, must be the finest available and rigid quality control standards throughout manufacturing assure their strength, stability and freedom from internal defects.

Steel is used to form the three load-supporting elements common to most bearings: the outer ring, the inner ring and the rolling elements, either balls or rollers. The fourth element, a retainer or separator, may be made of bronze alloys, iron, polymers, steel or composites.

The rings are formed from seamless steel tubes or solid steel cylinders; gracefully powerful automatic bar machines and numerically controlled machines cut and shave the steel to precise configurations.

Rollers are cut from wire-like stock or compressed into pellet-shaped pieces of steel and then machined into precisely finished and shaped rolling elements.

Once formed, the rings and rolling elements are heat treated in a precise combination of controlled atmosphere furnaces, cooling liquids and tempering processes to make the hardened steel required for building a reliable bearing.

The last step in the forming process, grinding, produces the precision finish specified by the division's engineers or customers.

Before assembly, every component of every bearing is inspected; every inner ring and outer ring is measured for tolerance acceptability and each rolling element is examined for individual quality and uniformity. A final check assures that all the components fit precisely together.

Some large bearings are placed in massive cast iron and steel housings called pillow blocks that must be formed to an exact fit. That may not sound like much—except that a 1717-pound pillow block is more than a yard wide and almost two feet high and thick.

Much of this manufacturing technology isn't taught in a classroom, says

FMC's skilled work force achieves tolerances of twenty-five millionths of an inch.

Engineering Manager Bill Derner. "It's developed by our engineers, working in our research and development lab and in helping our customers solve their problems."

"This is often called a mature business, and it is in a sense, but there is still a lot of room for creativity — in selling, service and product innovation," sums up Division Manager Bob Rogers.

Bearings are absolutely basic for industry. And they're a basic part of a power transmission products group that makes a solid contribution to FMC too.

This is the third in a series of articles on FMC's power transmission divisions.

Photos by Tony Kelly.

Bearing Division

Principal products: Collar mounted roller bearings; ball bearings and ball bearing units; cylindrical roller bearings; self-aligning spherical roller bearings and spherical roller bearing units; sleeve bearing units.

Customers: Original equipment manufacturers (OEM's) in construction, mining, agricultural, petroleum, transportation, materials handling and industrial machinery businesses; worldwide network of independent distributors who serve replacement, or aftermarket, business.

Sales: Continuing to increase.

Sales force: Both direct and indirect sale force with over 900 distributors worldwide.

Industry position: In upper fourth of all U.S. manufacturers ranked by annual sales.

History: Predecessor Link-Belt Company, Indianapolis, Indiana, manufactured bearings under contract to Shafer Bearing Company, Chicago, from 1934-1947. Continued to produce bearings under the Link-Belt trade name; acquired by FMC in 1967.

Employees: Over 1000.

Plants: Manufacturing facilities in Indianapolis, Indiana, and Clinton, Tennessee.

The bearing builders—a sensitive touch

The people who grind, machine, assemble and ship bearings from Indianapolis are a special group. Many have devoted decades of service to the company and their experience is behind every bearing built.

Bud Medenwald came to work for the Link-Belt Company in 1936 for what he describes as "good wages then — 30¢ an hour." He was one of the first three men to work in the division's bearing assembly, "and I can remember sitting on a nail keg separating assembly housings," he recalls. Medenwald takes great pride in the workmanship he learned as a young man and in its enduring quality. A massive bearing he helped construct for a Ford Motor Company plant decades ago is still being used, he said.

Buren "Pinky" Gentry started with Link-Belt in 1950 and since then he's been a trucker, a drill press operator, a utility worker, a supervisor and a split housing machine operator.

"I went back to production," he says, "because it's sort of like you're your own boss, like you're running your own business."

He operates a split housing machine on the incentive program; the more productive he is, the more he earns. The machine accepts bearing housings as heavy as 1400 pounds and turns, or bores, an interior cavity to a tolerance of .003 inch. A bearing will be positioned inside the housing. Gentry's attitude toward his work: "Every part must be a good part. If you can't make money for the company," he says, "I just don't see that your work is of much value. But if you're making good parts for the company, you're making money for yourself, too."

Paul Harmon joined Link-Belt in 1947. At one point in his career as a machinist, he contributed to solving a complicated cutting problem with bronze retainers.

After watching the cutting machine carefully, he noticed that moving a certain small lever "made the machine do what we wanted it to." With that problem solved, the division rapidly increased its production of retainers. Harmon's reaction? "I used to hear people say automation will kill jobs. I believed it. But it isn't so. We put more men to work here when we figured out how to make the machines do more."

While he's quick to admit that things have changed — and to acknowledge the company's growth — some things, he says, haven't changed. "It's still a good, friendly place to work."

He can rotate a bearing with 22 rollers and tell if one of the rollers has a one-sixty-fourth-inch flatness.

Ed Hicks started at Link-Belt in 1942; one of his first jobs was grinding bearings to be used in amphibious vehicles being built by FMC to storm the beaches in World War II.

Today he is a bearing assembler. "We have inspectors," he says, "and some people may think that what we do isn't required — but we do it anyway. We give the bearing one more check to make sure it's in perfect working order."

Quality control has a special place with him. "If you take the time," he says, "you can feel if there's something wrong, like some grit inside the bearing. Or you can feel if there's a flat side to one of the bearings." That means his sense of touch is so sensitive he can rotate a bearing with 22 rollers in it — and tell if one of the rollers has as little as a one-sixty-fourth of an inch flatness to it. No wonder Hicks believes "there's no reason why a bearing shouldn't be perfect when it leaves our line."

Bert Yeager, who came to work at Link-Belt in 1940, is an inner ring grinder. "It's a challenge," he says, "to try to make it good — but when it works, you know you've had something to do with it."

As part of his job, Yeager operates a grinding machine which turns surfaces of precision bearings to tolerances of fifty-millionths of an inch. "I just try to make the machine do what it can — and what it was built to do," he says.

George Albrecht, who began with Link-Belt in 1959 and works today as a centerless grinder operator, grinding the diameter of bearing inner or outer rings.

"Everybody locates off what I grind," he says, "so if I'm consistent, they can keep their raceways consistent."

He grinds to tolerances that range from one-thousandth to four-ten-thousandths of an inch, and it's important to keep your grinding on size and to keep roundness. I can hear a ring that's out of round." And what makes the job satisfying? "When you have things you have to figure out yourself. Like today, I had a setup I'd never done before — and I've been running this machine a long time. I got it figured out, though, and I was right."

Everett "Heavy" Gilles came to work for the Chain Division in 1945 and transferred to the Bearing Division ten years later to work in the shipping department. "People," he says, "can really make a difference. Like here in shipping, our paychecks are based on the weight we ship each week. That makes for a good group effort — to get the materials out to our customers. Something else we have here is people who give recognition. When the boss gives me recognition, he's telling me that my job is important, and when people recognize that, why, you do a better job. That helps the company — and it helps me, too."

Powder power in the kitchen

As the day begins, miles of toothpaste flow in ribbons onto millions of brushes wielded throughout Central America, as far away as Japan and India, even in Fiji. Without minute amounts of carrageenan mixed in, the ingredients would be so runny, they couldn't be squeezed out of the tube.

Soaking up water like a sponge to form a bulky but smooth gel in any liquid, the pure and powdery white natural product called carrageenan thickens, stabilizes, provides texture and body, and prevents ingredients from separating in everything from foods to fresheners. FMC's Marine Colloids Division, the world's largest producer, has helped make its use almost as prevalent worldwide as the seaweed from which it is extracted.

Soaking up water like a sponge, carrageenan thickens, stabilizes, provides texture.

In the dawn's early light in the U.S. sleepy parents are opening up Similac or Enfamil, convenience baby formulas that may be poured directly from cans to baby bottles without resterilization. Carrageenan prevents the cream in them from separating.

The family mascot chomping on a meaty breakfast of canned dog food can thank carrageenan for helping to keep his food moist and appetizing.

The bathroom is kept fresh with stick-type air fresheners like Airwick Solid, Glade, Renuzit, and Wizard made up of

(continued)

This is the second of two articles. The first appeared in the last issue.

Shopping List

golden egg custard	no-cholesterol replacement for eggs
Jello or Royal pudding	makes cooking easier
chocolate milk	keeps cocoa suspended
lo-fat milks	provides richness
ice cream	prevents separation during melting
Carnation instant breakfast	provides thickening
olives with pimentos	gels pimentos
Similac or Enfamil	prevents ingredients separation
Wyler's lemonade mix	provides body
Reddi Wip instant	stabilizes whip
frozen coffee whitener	provides stabilization
air freshener	provides gelation
chocolate syrup	provides thickening, suspension
Open Pit barbecue sauce	provides thickening, suspension
canned dog food	provides thickening, gelling
prepared gravy	provides thickening
Smucker's lo-cal jelly	produces gelation
Italian salad dressing	imparts mouthfeel
lasagna dinner	gives freeze-thaw stability
shampoo	thickens, stabilizes
Milk of Magnesia	suspends ingredients
Carnation or Pet milk	prevents fat separation
Toothpaste	solidifies toothpaste
Borden egg nog	thickening and stabilizing
Ovaltine hot cocoa mix	thickening
Borden's frosted shake	stabilizers

fragrance and emulsifier and water. Carrageenan turns the mix into a rigid gel and controls the release of the fragrance over several weeks.

If the children should be getting chocolate milk in their lunch bag, carrageenan is there to keep the chocolate in suspension by trapping it in its complex gel structure. Otherwise it would rapidly settle to the bottom of the Thermos, forming a hard cake that could not be dislodged by simple shaking or stirring.

Low-fat milk substitutes also rely on carrageenan to impart richness lost when the butterfat is removed. Powdered instant breakfasts such as those reconstituted with milk would be too watery if they did not also contain carrageenan.

Smucker's low-calorie jellies that go on toast are solidified by carrageenan instead of the sugar that normally makes the jelly gel. Last but not least, the coffee whitener has carrageenan to give it a rich mouthfeel, and if it happened to be the frozen type, to give it freeze-thaw stability.

When sweet tooth satisfaction is a priority, carrageenan is at work again. Along with vegetable gums, it keeps ice crystals from forming in ice cream and ice milk, prevents the ingredients from separating when the ice cream melts, or adds body and homogeneity to chocolate and other toppings for ice cream sundaes.

The set in puddings and custards once could be achieved only through precise and prolonged cooking. Now with carrageenan added to instant pudding mixes, a more rapid set is obtained, scorching is minimized and the pastiness of an all-starch pudding is softened. A cold pre-

Carrageenan keeps the chocolate in suspension. Otherwise it would rapidly settle to the bottom.

pared pudding which requires no cooking is a high priority project at Marine Colloids and should be available in a few years.

Gelatin with carrageenan doesn't require refrigeration, is popular with institutional feeders who prefer it over the kind available in the home that goes in the refrigerator.

Especially in Europe, carrageenan adds body to popular flan desserts. Many of the European pastry glazes which contain fruit pieces and look so much more appetizing than those made in America include carrageenan to gel the glaze and make the fruit shine.

Carrageenan contributes to beauty and health as well. It has at various times been used in hand lotions, bath gels and bath salts. In the hospital it serves to suspend the particles in those tasty barium cocktails used in radiology to diagnose ulcers.

(continued)

Agarose — fingerprinting the blood

Which proteins are present in the blood and in what quantity? The crucial answers can help diagnose whether a certain cancer is present in a specific organ of the body, check for fatty substances, determine whether someone has had a heart attack and perform scores of diagnostic or clinical tests. Agarose, another Marine Colloids seaweed product, has an important role to play.

Agarose powders form testing media that technicians use to make a kind of fingerprint of blood. Mixed with water and heated, agarose forms a thick gel on a thin sheet of plastic film or glass plate. Applying an electric current moves human proteins through the gel at different rates.

Using this technique, up to 100 different molecules in blood are separated out and show up in bands on the plate for identification and measuring. This electrophoresis technique is in use in virtually every major hospital and research lab in the U.S. and in Europe.

Agarose may one day contribute to a cure for cancer and help solve the deepest mysteries of life. Researchers use it to analyze the molecules that form cancer cells and separate out DNA, the genetic code substances that allow cells to duplicate themselves.

Marine Colloids' fastest-growing product line, agarose and a complement of related products under development, has a very long way to go to catch up with carrageenan. But in contributing to human welfare, they are clearly number one.

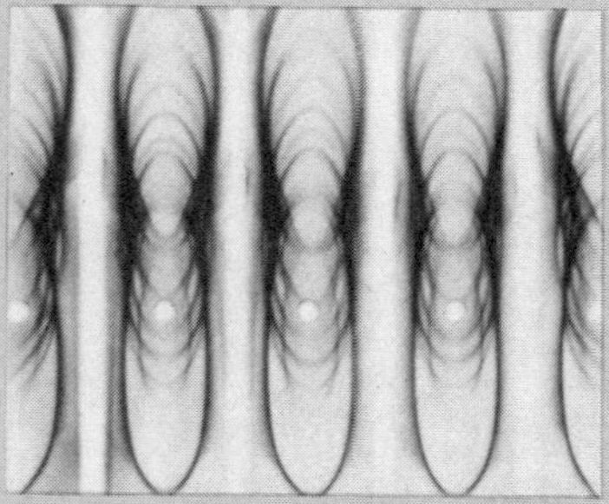

Blood molecules separate on test medium.

When everything is added up, more than three-fourths of the carrageenan Marine Colloids makes for hundreds of purposes goes into foods. Three out of five times carrageenan is mentioned on labels it is likely to be from Marine Colloids, one of two U.S. producers and one of four major producers in the world.

When sweet tooth satisfaction is a priority, carrageenan is at work again.

A natural rather than artificial product because of its seaweed origin, carrageenan is also GRAS – generally recognized as safe by the Food and Drug Administration.

Carrageenan complements FMC's Avicel® microcrystalline cellulose, and they are even found together in some foods such as ice cream. Avicel is there to prevent loss of texture when the ice cream is removed repeatedly from the refrigerator.

Avicel swells in water, remains apart from, and does not combine with liquids. Carrageenan dissolves like a sugar cube in water, combining with it to form a gel sometimes described as a jungle gym-like network of extremely large molecules. Both are colloids invisible to the naked eye.

Carrageenan, like Avicel, is used as an ingredient in very small quantities – as little as 50 parts per million. One pound of carrageenan is enough to stabilize the cream in 20,000 pints of condensed milk. Here the similarity of the two products ends.

Together, Avicel and carrageenan are projected to have attractive growth potential pursuing different functional roles

Seaweed is harvested or gathered on shore.

Carrageenan extract looks like soup.

Carrageenan concentrate is crushed into powder, blended to make 125 product types.

in both foods and pharmaceuticals.

"From a growth standpoint," says Harris (Pete) Bixler of Marine Colloids, "we're on a bit of a plateau after the 15 percent growth days of the sixties. The reason is the slowdown in the introduction of new convenience foods. But the days of rapid growth should return."

Bixler sees a so-called fabricated foods era ahead – imitation milk, meats, cheeses and other products. The new foods would be less costly than their genuine counterparts and better in the sense that they would contain less saturated fats and cholesterols. Carrageenan's ability to react with non-meat proteins could make it a key ingredient in these "fab foods."

Growth potential outside the U.S. is also considered excellent even though Marine Colloids already has a hefty export business equal to 50 percent of total sales.

Carrageenan's future isn't necessarily restricted to food and pharmaceuticals. Marine Colloid's aggressive new enterprises department is actively looking at scores of opportunities in the biomedical field for agarose and related products (see box). Its research department is also constantly looking into industrial applications in addition to developing methods to artificially cultivate seaweed supported in part by a grant from Canada's National Research Council.

Carrageenan may one day be used in large amounts to solidify water-based explosives, aid in plating metal, help seeds retain moisture under drought conditions and improve oil drilling muds. Carrageenan, like the slippery seaweed it comes from, also has lubricating properties with a variety of uses that may include moving coal in slurry pipelines.

Wide-ranging research is also looking into a great variety of other marine-related activities including growing shrimp, salmon and other food material capitalizing on the technology developed in cultivating seaweed under controlled conditions. One of the most intriguing projects is a special test of growing algae in wastewater treatment ponds at the Industrial Chemical Group's Green River, Wyoming plant.

It thickens shampoos and lotions, and those tasty barium cocktails used to diagnose ulcers.

Tests appear to show that minute algae added to the water thrives, consuming the wastes to solve a problem while growing a commercially valuable algae crop that Marine Colloids could make into other products. Marine Colloids already is working with half a dozen other FMC divisions.

Whether carrageenan is used by industry or in food, all of it is made in Rockland, Maine (population 10,000) in a sprawling plant appropriately located right on the seacoast.

Producing the fine white carrageenan particles is a two- to three-day process. The seaweed moss is dumped into big pasting tanks and cooked for many hours in a bath of water and chemicals that digest the carrageenan and release it into solution.

A pea soup-like carrageenan extract is then filtered to remove impurities, and dewatered and concentrated using one of two processes. The dried carrageenan flake or fiber is then ground into the fine powder that then flows into drums.

Since carrageenan is a product of a living raw material, it's not surprising that its character changes depending on the region of the world where it originated and even from season to season delivered from the same seacoast. "We do nature one better by upgrading it all along the process through blending," says Production Manager Bill Blakemore. Analysis of seaweed and carrageenan before and after production, creates some 25 basic product types, each the result of careful seaweed blending. Over 100 blended finished products go to customers, the result of complex blending.

One of the best blends of the year has happened not in the plant but across the negotiating table—the merger of Marine Colloids with FMC.

"Before, our growth was limited by lack of capital and limited seaweed raw materials. FMC can now provide the capital and resources and financial controls to help us grow and profit," says Bixler.

FMC for its part has acquired a complementary product line and a high-powered creative research team oriented toward growth.

"There's a real spirit here, a real desire to get this company moving to help it grow," says an enthusiastic researcher. "All of us are rolling up our sleeves."

Marine Colloids Division

Main products: 175 varieties of kappa, iota, lambda and other carrageenan for food, cosmetics and pharmaceuticals; complementary products including locust bean and guar gum powders extracted from seeds; agarose powder and beads made from agar, a derivative of seaweed, for medical applications.

Customers: 100 food manufacturers, stabilization houses that produce blended components for foods, pharmaceutical and cosmetics companies, others.

Sales: Growing modestly but expected to return to the high rate of the 1960's.

Sales Force: 11 salespeople at four sales offices.

Industry position: World's largest producer of carrageenan.

History: Founded 1937 as Algin Corporation of America, later combined with Seaplant Corporation, Bedford, Mass., to become Marine Colloids, Inc., merged and became Marine Colloids Division of FMC Corporation in 1977.

Employees: 280

Plants: A 180,000 square foot manufacturing facility in Rockland, Maine; seaweed drying plants in Yarmouth and Pictou, Nova Scotia; Miminegash, Prince Edward Island.

Foret—a foothold for industrial chemicals in Europe

Two blocks from the tree-lined Paseo de Gracia in Barcelona, Spain, a few miles from the spot where Ferdinand and Isabella greeted Christopher Columbus on his return from the New World, is a modern high-rise office building, headquarters for FMC's Spanish subsidiary, Foret, S.A. There its 250 managers, technicians, and staff are opening up another new world for FMC — the industrial chemical market of Europe.

In Barcelona, Spain, where Columbus returned FMC is opening up a new world for FMC.

From bustling Barcelona, a city of three million as diverse as New York and colorful as San Francisco, Foret manages a network of eight plants throughout Spain. Its 1347 employees have built the nation's third largest producer of industrial chemicals.

Since 1960, Foret has grown with Spain, participating in the so-called "Spanish miracle"— rapid industrialization that has given it all the things of modern life and boosted its economy to number 12 in the world.

Already larger than many FMC divisions, Foret is expected to become much larger in the future, says Managing Director Alfredo Bernad.

"FMC has in Foret an excellent base from which to expand its chemical activities in Europe," Bernad says. "Spain is a good country on the way up. It's also good geographically because we are close to the rest of Europe and Africa and we have excellent links to the other countries of South America."

Foret produces scores of chemicals in six major categories, five of them also made by FMC's Industrial Chemical Group in the U.S. (See page 16.) It also has a small but growing agricultural chemical business.

☐ **Silicates.** Hundreds of thousands of tons of silicates are produced at four

(continued)

From this high rise office building in Barcelona, Spain, the 250-person headquarters staff of Foret, S.A. manages a network of eight plants. A motor-scooterist-manager prepares to leave for lunch. ▶

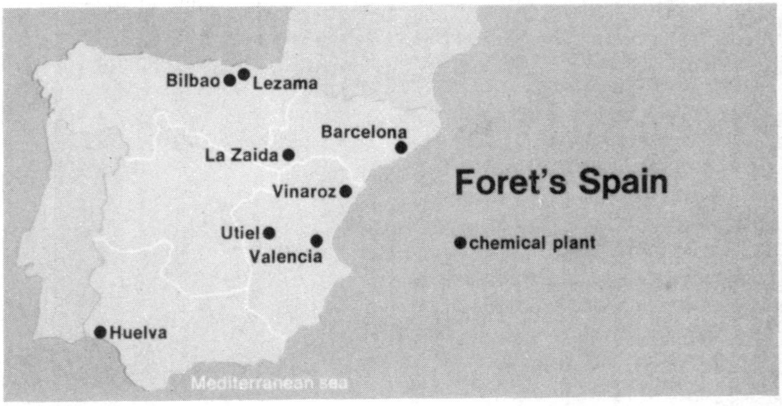

FORET
S.A.
RENAULT

What Foret makes for whom

Sulfides (sulfuros)

Carbon disulfide: reacts with another chemical to form rayon fibers, cellophane.
Sodium sulfide: removes the hair from hides for leather making; producing kraft paper; flotation agent in mining.
Carbon tetrachloride: for aerosol propellants, refrigerants, fire extinguisher fluid.

Sulfide products are made in Barcelona and Vinaroz.

Peroxides and persalts (peroxidos y persales)

Sodium perborate: bleaching agent or whitener in detergents and toothpaste.
Hydrogen peroxide: for bleaching white paper or removing the color from cotton, wool, fur, silk, straw, while adding brilliance to textile colors; bleaching cane furniture; making other chemicals, plastics and polyester fibers; preserving cheese; making hair colorants.
Persulfates: three types, for making plastics, etching copper; textile processing and bleaching.

La Zaida, a modern new plant, is the manufacturing point.

Spanish leather tempts Inmaculada Trabal, daughter of Foret's Enrique Trabal. Sodium sulfide made by Foret removes hair from hides.

locations from soda ash and pure sand utilizing new, sophisticated Foret-developed technology. Four basic silicates offered in a variety of formulations are used in everything from paints, paper, foundry sands and white fillers to TV tubes.

☐ **Phosphates.** Foret gets 200,000 metric tons of phosphate rock a year from mines in the North African desert and transports them to its big plant on the Mediterranean coast at Huelva for processing into an array of phosphate products.

With Foret, FMC has become the world's largest producer of STPP (sodium tripolyphosphate) for detergents. Foret pioneered a wet process that is different from the U.S. method of burning elemental phosphorus and is applying it in projects outside Spain.

☐ **Sulfides.** Carbon disulfide made from natural gas shipped over on tankers from Libya and fused with sulfur from France at Foret's integrated chemical complex in Barcelona is sold mostly to rayon and cellophane manufacturers. It's also used to make carbon tetrachloride and sodium sulfide needed by tanners to remove hair from animal hides.

☐ **Peroxides.** Peroxygen chemicals, including hydrogen peroxide made organically at La Zaida and sodium perborate produced from a mineral called rasorite imported from Death Valley, California, are the main sellers. They're used for everything from bleaching fabrics, pulp and paper to serving as a brightener in detergents.

☐ **Barium and zinc salts.** Starting with native baryte ores, Foret makes a variety of chemicals used as pigments and reinforcers in paint, printing inks and linoleum.

☐ **Sulfur derivatives** are produced from sulfur and serve as fixing agents in

Flamenco dancer doesn't work for Foret, but she benefits anyway. Dress fabric most certainly was bleached with hydrogen peroxide.

developing film and preserving beverages and shellfish.

☐ **Agrochemicals.** Foret provides an array of fungicides and insecticides that protect everything from tomatoes, sugar beets and bananas to corn, peaches, peppers and potatoes. One of the main products is Furadan® insecticide-nematicide, manufactured by FMC in the U.S. but made into granules by Foret in Spain. Foret hopes to expand this business dramatically in the future.

Though many of these products and plants date back 50 years or more, Foret

(continued)

Sulfide products are made from sulphur.

Final silica will be reliquified for shipment.

Phosphorus (fosfatos) chemicals

Sodium tripolyphosphate: for detergents (making up about one-third of the bulk of the final product); industrial bottle washing; water softening.
Phosphoric acid: brightening aluminum; rust-proofing metal for automobiles, appliances, other products.
Others: trisodium phosphate for industrial cleaners, household cleansers; tetrasodium pyrophosphate for detergents, soaps, and textile processing.
Foret makes phosphates at Huelva.

Silicates (silicatos)

Sodium silicate: a filler material in tires, paper, paints, feed supplements; a binder in detergents; an adhesive to glue corrugated cardboard; for foundry cores and molds to make the sand retain its shape; textile and pulp bleaching.
Sodium metasilicate: aid in compacting soil to prevent roof falls in tunnel construction; making paper and cement; textile finishing and bleaching; printing.
Potassium silicate: thickener for ceramics; catalyst for cracking petroleum; coating for cathode ray TV tubes to improve picture quality.
Silicate products are produced in Barcelona, Lezama, Valencia, Bilbao, Utiel and Huelva.

Barium and zinc salts (sales de bario y zinc)

Lithopone: providing white pigment for paints, printing inks.
Zinc oxide: reinforcement for rubber.
Barium carbonate: glassmaking; filler and extender in making printing inks.
Barium and zinc oxides are made in Barcelona and Vinaroz.

Sulfur (sulfurous) derivatives

Potassium pyrosulfite: preservative for wine, beer, shellfish.
Ammonium thiosulfate: fixing agent in photography.
Sodium hydrosulfite: wool bleaching.
Sodium sulfite and sodium thiosulfate: anti-chlorine agent; leather tanning; rayon processing.
These products are produced in Barcelona and Vinaroz.

Agrochemicals (agroquimicos)

Metham-na: fungicide for tomatoes, peppers, bananas.
Furadan® insecticide-nematicide: for corn, sugar beets, potatoes, bananas.
Dizineb: for grapes.
Ethion: imported from FMC in the United States, for citrus.
Others: tiuram dasa, micronized sulfur, coloidal sulfur dasa, nabam, for peaches, almonds, pears, apples.
Agricultural chemicals are produced in Vinaroz.

Foret phosphates, perborate and silicates go into detergents made by five leading makers.

has constantly updated its technology. The company has always been willing to change, even in 1890 when two Frenchmen came to Spain to start a champagne business, produced vinegar, and switched to chemicals.

Don Jorge Foret joined the fledgling organization seven years later and subsequently lent his name to it.

When FMC entered into partnership with Foret in 1966, the company launched a massive expansion program, replacing its antiquated Barcelona plant with a large Zona Franca chemical complex in an industrial park near the airport.

Foret-built village has school for worker's children. Plant Manager Ricardo Pueyo visits.

◀ *Spanish ceramics use potassium silicate and other forms of silicate as a thickening agent. Silicates have many applications.*

Visiting market in the old section of Barcelona, Foret telephone operator Dolores Cantarell buys vegetables protected by agricultural chemicals.

It also expanded the important Huelva plant to begin producing phosphates there.

Foret Business Development Director Dan O'Brien, a long-time FMC employee who was assigned to Spain shortly after FMC made its first investment, says the Foret-FMC partnership has long been a productive one and is almost unlimited in terms of opportunities. "We are in the right place with the right people at the right time," he says. Thinking ahead to Spain's imminent membership in the Common Market, the development director talks of Foret in terms of its European presence rather than just as one of Spain's top companies.

Poised to go after new business in the rest of Europe, Foret expects to capitalize on its own and FMC's strength in mining and mineral development as the basis for new products and will build new plants (not necessarily just in Spain) as the market dictates.

Courtly, soft-spoken Alfredo Bernad, who became managing director of Foret earlier this year, considers it to be "one of the most progressive companies in Spain." He also gives credit for much of Foret's forward thinking to his two predecessors, including Ricardo Ancira who, after nine years at Foret, has returned to his native Mexico for FMC's Industrial Chemical Group.

Bernad is streamlining Foret still further. "We're not without our problems, but we're taking steps to correct them," he says. Foret has strong engineering and technical departments which design plants, expand facilities, improve processes, and help customers with product applications. Technology has flowed both ways and it is more than likely that the

(continued)

Multinational team including visitors from Philadelphia huddle at Foret's Barcelona headquarters to plan a new plant. Foret managers (left to right) Len Erickson (finance), Jose Sanz (specialty chemicals), Enrique Trabal (marketing), Managing Director Alfredo Bernad, and Dan O'Brien (business development, on telephone) meet with the Industrial Chemical Group's Ford Wilson and Greg Edwards (right).

applications and techniques which have been jointly developed in Spain will eventually bear fruit in the Americas.

The new head of technical services is Ramon Olin from the northeastern region of Spain whose capital is Barcelona. Olin returns to Spain after many years at FMC's Research & Development Center at Princeton, New Jersey.

Foret has a separate marketing organization, Coproqui, for resale products and maintains delagaciones (regional sales offices) in Spanish cities. Coproqui also handles some FMC machinery lines.

"We emphasize prompt delivery and good service," says Division Director Enrique Trabal.

More than one-fourth of Foret's sales consist of exports to Portugal, Chile, Venezuela, Colombia, Thailand, Libya, Greece, Syria, Lebanon and North Africa. Foret also has affiliates in Venezuela for the production of phosphates and in Greece and Lebanon for making silicates. Each of these ventures is based on Foret technology.

Despite the economic difficulties that have generally plagued Europe these past

Plants use sophisticated technology.

One of many new plants dwarfs workers.

Meticulous inspection is given to every shipment.

few years and seem to have descended on Spain in particular in 1978, Bernad says the year has been a relatively good one for Foret both at home and abroad.

Looking ahead, Bernad tempers optimism with caution but looks upon the changing times as an opportunity for Foret to progress even further. With a penchant for hard work and ambitious plans, the almost entirely Spanish-staffed company operates like its American counterpart but with one difference.

Most managers arrive before nine, work until two, dine with their families until four, and are back at the office until well into the night. The lunch "hour" is still a sacred institution in Spain, but the long break restores energy levels. And that energy Foret will need to meet its ambitious goals.

Produced by Norm Bezane, Chicago and Frank Malkwitz, Brussels; photos by Manfred Ehrich.

Major Markets and Operations

Food and Agricultural Machinery and Chemicals
Agricultural Chemical Group
Food Machinery Group
Agricultural Machinery Division
Citrus Machinery Division
Food Machinery International Division
Food Processing Machinery Division
Packaging Machinery Division
Food and Pharmaceutical Products
Marine Colloids Division

Industrial Chemicals
Industrial Chemical Group
Alkali Chemical Division
Phosphorus Chemical Division
Specialty Chemical Division

Material and Natural Resource Handling Equipment
Material Handling Group
Airline Equipment Division
Engineered Systems Division
Environmental Equipment Division
Marine and Rail Equipment Division
Material Handling Equipment Division
Material Handling Systems Division
Mining Equipment Division
Semiconductor Products Division
Petroleum Equipment Group
Fluid Control Division
Wellhead Equipment Division

Construction and Power Transmission Products
Construction Equipment Group
Cable Crane and Excavator Division
Construction Equipment International Division
Hydraulic Crane Division
Woodlands Equipment Division
Power Transmission Group
Bearing Division
Chain Division
Drive Division
Power Control Division

Government and Municipal Equipment
Defense Equipment Group
Northern Ordnance Division
Ordnance Division
Steel Products Division
Sweeper Division
Fire Apparatus Operation

Special Products
Special Products Group
Automotive Service Equipment Division
Industrial Packaging Operation
Outdoor Power Equipment Division
Turbo Pump Operation

FMC Corporation
200 East Randolph Drive
Chicago, Illinois 60601

FMC

RETURN POSTAGE GUARANTEED

Hungry giants. Each capable of devouring two acres of peas an hour, a pair of FMC's new self-propelled pea harvesters, built by FMC Food Machinery Europe, St. Niklaas, Belgium, swiftly harvest a field near the sea in Great Britain. In this revolutionary machine, the pods are stripped from the vine by a picking head prior to entering the threshing system where the peas are gently separated from the pods.

9

Investor Relations in an Adverse Environment

Gerald A. Parsons

"How do you run a successful investor relations program when your company has just come to the brink of financial disaster?"

This was the question Evans Products Company faced in the summer of 1974. Until then, Evans, a company whose revenues had grown from $100 million to $1 billion in ten years, had been something of an institutional darling. The Company was diversified but was predominantly engaged in the building products business. Its stock was in a cyclical decline, along with a lot of other companies at that time. Having sold at a high of around $28 in 1972, it had dropped to as low as $10 during the first quarter of 1974. Management had decided to try to do something about this by bringing in a full-time investor relations professional. In so doing, they gave him full responsibility not only for the Company's relationships with the investment community but for its total corporate public relations and advertising activities as well. Unfortunately, his program never got off the ground before things began to come apart at the seams.

Evans was a highly leveraged company, with heavy borrowings to support customer financings of the purchase of its single-family homes. Its railcar leasing subsidiary, although essentially independent from the parent, put a further strain on the Company's resources whenever there was a lag between delivery of completed railcars from the manufacturing division to the subsidiary and the subsidiary's permanent outside financing of these cars. Such a lag in financing railcars occurred in 1974.

Nevertheless, Evans' lenders, comprising over a dozen blue-ribbon banks spread throughout the country plus a major insurance company, had routinely met with management in June for a detailed review of operating plans and had come away with a generally favorable attitude toward the Company's near-term prospects.

Early in 1974, Evans had already begun to suffer from rising interest rates. New housing construction fell off sharply in the summer, unexpectedly plunging its lumber, plywood, and wood paneling operations into the red.

Gerald A. Parsons is Vice President, Corporate Relations, of Evans Products Co.

When money tightened further during the summer, Evans' lenders began to delay additional credit for home financing on which they were only informally committed. Rumors of the company's uncertain financial condition began to surface, and soon there were widespread rumors of impending bankruptcy. Institutional shareowners began to dump their stock.

In the panic selling that took place during the late summer and that continued into the fall, the stock price dropped to $2. In the process, institutional ownership went from over 60 percent to just over 20 percent. Analyst coverage of the company dropped to near zero.

During the late summer, management moved quickly to halt the rapid deterioration in the Company's financial condition. This involved shutting down losing or low-margin operations, determining to sell assets to pay down debt, strengthening the remaining operations, and improving managerial planning and controls.

The first part of the new investor relations program involved publicly laying out the problems with which the Company was confronted and making a full explanation of what management intended to do constructively to solve them.

This was accomplished in a detailed letter to shareholders which included a balance sheet showing that the Company's financial condition was not as serious as was widely suspected. This was the first time the Company had published an interim balance sheet. The letter was condensed and was put in the form of a news release that resulted in broad press coverage. It also formed the basis for discussions with worried investors and analysts.

Ultimately, management was able to negotiate new loan agreements with an expanded group of banks, which gave the Company time to put its plans to work. Furthermore, although major write-downs added significantly to the already heavy operating losses reported for 1974, the Company returned to a profitable level, and debt was reduced substantially in 1975.

However, bad times can generate unfavorable publicity. During 1974 and 1975, the financial press had a heyday with the news of "financially troubled Evans Products Company." Nevertheless, management was determined to keep a low profile and to "let the facts speak for themselves."

For some time, Evans had been openly communicative. While pursuing a conservative communications program and avoiding the flamboyance that had been somewhat characteristic of the past, management considered it essential to continue to provide detailed information to all who were interested in the Company from an investment viewpoint. This policy included issuing balance sheets and product line breakdowns of revenues and earnings in all interim statements. (This, incidentally, was before these items were a reporting requirement.) The annual report, once written primarily for "Aunt Jane," was restructured to provide as much information as possible to the professional investor, and at the same time to be understandable to the average individual investor. The annual report was supplemented by an expanded industry fact book written primarily for analysts.

To take advantage of the larger shareholder base and to help maintain this broadened ownership, emphasis was placed on contact with the retail-oriented brokerage firms. Most institutions were considered to have only a passive interest in the Company, if any. Furthermore, most institutionally oriented brokerage firms would not have anything to do with Evans.

For some time, the low-profile approach didn't seem to be effective. If no one is interested in listening, the facts will not "speak for themselves." The 1975–1976 period called for a great deal of missionary work, making cold calls on individual research managers or industry specialists, trying on a low-pressure basis to interest them in following the Company, and letting them know about the information the Company was willing to provide. At the same time, a continuing attempt was made to meet periodically with old friends and acquaintances among the institutional investors. The point of such contacts was to keep them informed of recovery plans and performance progress even though these people probably could not seriously consider investing in the Company until a performance record could be reestablished. Emphasis was also placed on reestablishing credibility with those who had been burned while Evans' stock price plummeted in 1974.

Most of the direct contact with brokerage people and individual institutional investors was made by the vice president–corporate relations. To ensure consistency of response, all communications with the financial community were funneled through him. In this way, access to top management was kept open but controlled. Since analysts who had once followed Evans seldom visited the Company's Portland, Oregon headquarters anymore, regular monthly trips to New York and periodic visits to other major financial centers were set up to facilitate contact.

The Company shunned public appearances before analysts until late in 1976. By then, it had begun to recover rapidly both operationally and financially. By November 1976, management was ready to stand before an assembled group of analysts, portfolio managers, and a few substantial individual investors to discuss what had been accomplished. This meeting was held in a private club in New York. It was organized internally, and invitations were sent only to individuals who had expressed interest in the Company. A representative group of operating and corporate staff management was dispersed strategically among the dinner guests. There was no formal presentation, but a lengthy, open question-and-answer session followed dinner, featuring participation by several members of management. Although these people expressed confidence, no forecasts or bold promises about the future were made. The meeting was well attended, and generated substantial interest among others who later heard about it and asked to be invited to any similar meetings scheduled for the future.

In the spring of 1977, after reporting substantial earnings progress in 1976, Evans sought and was granted an invitation to make a formal presentation before the New York Society of Security Analysts, the Company's first such appearance there since late 1972. The purpose of this meeting was to reach a broader, more general audience than the industry specialists who would normally be expected to follow the Company. It also provided a forum for reviewing the company's long-term performance goals, which, by this time, management considered appropriate to publicize. These goals covered expected return on invested capital, debt/total-capitalization ratio, anticipated capital expenditures, and dividend payout ratio. *The Wall Street Journal*'s coverage of the meeting provided broad dissemination of this information.

During the recovery period, there were two notable exceptions to the dearth of coverage of the Company by major brokerage firms. After careful analysis, one firm recommended the stock as a good speculative buy for aggressive retail accounts at around $4 a share, beginning in the spring of 1975. The other, after allowing a bit more time for improvement in results, began to recommend the stock in early 1976 at $6 a share, both to its aggressive retail clients and to institutions.

Meanwhile, most other major brokerage firms either refused to cover the stock in their research programs altogether, or carried out only "maintenance research," i.e., they kept abreast of developments, but wrote no reports and remained more or less passive in their opinions.

The prime example of a lack of brokerage coverage was Merrill Lynch, which withdrew its opinion on the Company in September 1974, stating, "We conclude that there is such a degree of uncertainty as to the future nature of the Company and its financial position that we cannot offer an investment opinion until the outlook is clarified." After the major crisis had passed with the Company's completion of new loan agreements in early 1975, and with speculative interest among individual investors picking up, it was only natural that the largest brokerage firm in the country would begin to receive a great many client inquiries on Evans. Since its own research department maintained "no opinion," Merrill Lynch brokers began calling the Company directly from all over the country. Despite repeatedly bringing this to the attention of the head of research and the industry specialists who might be involved, and despite otherwise good personal relationships between the people involved and Evans' vice president–corporate relations, Merrill Lynch specifically refused to follow the Company formally until its opinion was finally reinstated in December 1977.

By the end of 1976, however, a combination of demonstrated performance, gradual but fairly steady stock-price improvement, and rekindled investment interest among institutions had led a few brokerage firms to take a more active interest in following the Company.

During this period, brokerage research in general was going through great upheaval and consolidation, because of the abolition of fixed rates on brokerage commissions. As an example, part of Merrill Lynch's reluctance to reinstate coverage of the Company was the result of a policy decision to limit dramatically the number of companies the firm would follow. This led to an almost frantic attempt by some companies to bypass traditional communications lines and to get directly to the brokers or registered representatives. Evans took a more limited approach to this problem with a specially designed annual direct mailing of a summary of operations, results, and financial highlights, which fit into a no. 10 envelope and was sent to thousands of registered reps, using the Technimetrics mailing list. The mailing piece was suitable for redistribution to clients, and additional quantities were made available upon request. A few meetings were held with local offices of national brokerage firms to discuss the Company's performance and prospects. However, no further attempt was made to stimulate broker interest, since it was considered too promotional and inconsistent with the Company's low-key approach.

Evans' management had prided itself on its close relationships with its lenders. The Company's 1975 loan agreements were with an expanded group of 25 major banks. While Evans' top financial officers had built up strong personal relationships with their banking counterparts, the chairman and chief executive officer had not significantly involved himself at a comparable level. It was determined that he should build a closer personal relationship with the top officers of all the Company's lending banks.

To ensure that this would be done on a neutral, strictly goodwill basis, arrangements for periodic visits were made by the vice president–corporate relations. The financial people assisted in some of the intitial contacts, but did not become involved in the meetings themselves. This facilitated participation by a number of top officers on the investment side of the banks who might otherwise have shied away from becoming involved in commercial banking relationships and, thus, potential conflicts of interest.

Although most bank research departments adhere strictly to their independence, especially from their commercial banking partners, it has proved in a number of cases to be particularly valuable to have a good acquaintance with the Company at the top levels of its banks. Periodic individual meetings with the presidents and chairmen of the Company's banks have become routine, and they are believed to have enhanced relationships and built greater confidence at all levels.

Clearly, one of the prime objectives of a corporate communications program is to make the Company as understandable as possible. This is not always easy, especially if business operations do not all fall neatly into specific industry categories, or if circumstances are such that financial reporting is complicated by special items.

In consolidating the Company, management eliminated certain operations, helping to narrow the diversity of businesses in which it was engaged. The Company's purchase in the open market and the ultimate call of its remaining outstanding convertible debentures eliminated their potentially dilutive effect, and eliminated the need to report both primary and diluted earnings.

By purchasing the Company's common stock on the open market when the price was below book value, management made prudent use of available funds. A successful exchange offer of a higher-yield junior preferred stock for common stock not only solidified the ownership position of many investors who had first purchased their stock on a speculative basis, but by reducing the number of common shares outstanding, both actions enhanced per share earnings for the common stock.

Certainly, a key part of any total corporate communications program must be the building of awareness of the Company among potential investors in the first place. People tend to be more interested in investing in companies they recognize and know something about. As a majority of the readers of this case history would probably attest, few among the total investing public would be apt to know much about Evans Products Co. Yet a number of its operations are well known throughout the country, and especially in the industries they serve, under their various trade names. With some of the primary investor relations objectives well on their way toward accomplishment, major emphasis was put on building upon the public awareness of some of its component parts to enhance the awareness of the Company as a whole. This encompassed building, vehicle, and product identification, including signage, product promotion, and advertising. Finally, planning was begun on an overall corporate advertising program directed at increasing the investing public's awareness of the Company rather than at mounting a frontal attack on security analysts.

In conclusion, managing a successful investor relations program is often a difficult assignment, even when most things are going well, because of the variety of uncontrollable and unpredictable outside factors which bear on the results. Managing a successful program under adverse circumstances may sometimes seem almost impossible. Sticking to basics, however, can have most rewarding results, especially when the investor relations manager is made a full-fledged member of the management team, and when each of the other members of the team does his job superbly.

Such has been the case at Evans at the time of this writing. Evans' management turned the Company around both operationally and financially in a remarkably short period of time. 1977 and 1978 were successive record years for earnings, and in 1978 and 1979, Evans' revenues and earnings reached all-time highs. The Company became a prime borrower in 1978, with a rock-solid balance sheet. During the same period, the Company was cited on a number of occasions for its excellence in corporate reporting and in its overall relations with the financial community.

The Company's stock has generally outperformed the market, reaching a peak selling price of over $25 during the summer of 1978, and trading at around that level in the volatile market of 1979. In terms of client holdings, the stock has become one of the most successful recommendations of each of the two major brokerage firms that recommended Evans during the recovery stage. While relatively broad share ownership has been maintained, a significant number of extremely high-quality institutions have once again taken substantial positions in the stock.

Management has been cohesive, consistent, and conservative in its communications with investors. Current thrust is now focused on planning for the future to maintain and enhance long-range results. For the investor relations professional, this is a far more comfortable atmosphere in which to operate.

10

The Next Ten Years in Investor Relations

Charles D. Kuehner

Prophecy is a hazardous exercise. Nevertheless, I'll stick my neck out and say that the next decade's challenge in corporate investor relations is largely predictable on the basis of what *is* happening now—the problems already confronting us. In discussing that future, I'll focus on two broad aspects:

1. The investment environment of the next ten years.
2. New tasks of corporate investor relations.

Before looking ahead, however, it is necessary to see where we stand today.

As all people involved in investor relations know, in the past half-dozen years, the nation's shareowner population has declined by about 6 million: one out of every five shareowners has "voted with his or her feet." For each of the last ten years, individuals have been net sellers of stock. Individuals today own only 54 percent of all corporate stock vs. 67 percent ten years ago.

Since "May Day" of 1975, some 70 brokerage firms have closed. The registered rep population has dropped some 12,000 in the past ten years. The flight of security analysts from brokerage firms to jobs with institutional investors points up that fewer and fewer security analysts are available to service *individual* investor needs. This has significant implications for all corporations.

Another way to measure investor confidence is to relate market prices to book values. In 1970, the Dow Jones Industrial Average of 30 companies was at 839—well above its book value of 573. As of early March 1980, the Dow was selling at about 870—well below its book of about 950.

In addition, book value is stated in *nominal dollars* of far more purchasing power than today's *market-price dollars.* When inflation is taken into account, book value of the Dow jumps to 1900. With the Dow selling at 870, American industry is selling at 46 cents on the dollar. This is hardly evidence of investor enthusiasm.

But the market doesn't go up or down without a reason. Let me suggest one factor that is often overlooked: when we adjust for current costs of depreciation

Charles D. Kuehner is Director, Investor Relations, for American Telephone & Telegraph Co.

and equipment and for inventory profits, American industry is earning less than 4 percent on its investment. This is substantially less than an investor can obtain in top-quality AAA tax-free bonds.

Similarly, what do we find when we look at the situation from the standpoint of the investor? On the basis of the Standard & Poor's 500, since 1970, an investor's realized return from both cash dividends and market appreciation has averaged only 5½ percent per year. This, too, suggests that improved earnings are needed if the stock market is to come back to life again.

To sum up, the nation's 25 million investors, in the words of the marathon runner, have "gone up against the wall," and the task in investor relations is to help assure that we have no more dropouts.

Now, let's turn to the future. I will cover just three areas important to investors—capital demand, capital supply, and the inflationary economic environment.

Demand for capital. Forecasts of the demand for capital, especially equity capital, call for an increase far above anything experienced in our lifetimes. One fact alone suggests a large latent demand for capital: some two thirds of America's industrial capacity is now over ten years old, and modernizing the obsolescent facilities will require massive capital investments. High debt ratios also point up the need for heavy infusions of new equity. Since the mid-1960s, debt ratios of the nation's leading industrial companies have doubled from the 15 percent range to almost 30 percent. Consequently, many companies have had their credit ratings downgraded because of excessive debt.

One other key point with respect to capital demand must be mentioned: There will be some 12 million *more* people in the labor force by 1985, and each new worker will require an investment by industry of at least $40,000. That's almost $500 billion for the 12 million additional workers alone!

Supply of capital. If the demand outlook is serious, the supply side looks positively grim. We have already noted the flight of individual shareowners from the market. An additional fact is that the number of traditional savers—those between 50 and 65 years old—is hardly increasing at all. Who, then, will put up the money?

Not private pension funds! Apart from the new investment to compensate the impact of inflation, the period of explosive growth in private pension funds is past. Most workers are now covered, and press reports say that some 7,000 smaller firms have abandoned their pension plans because of too much paperwork, as well as problems related to the provisions of the Employee Retirement Income Security Act (ERISA).

Insurance funds may make some contribution to the capital supply, but insurance companies are legally restricted to mortgages and bonds. Mutual funds are also unlikely to play a major role: they are still experiencing net redemptions and are getting smaller every year.

State and local pension funds, however, have been increasing equity ownership at a fast clip and may well continue if government payrolls keep growing. But they can't begin to do the whole job; somewhere, somehow, individuals will have to be brought back into the market. This all adds up to one inescapable fact: to meet our nation's economic and social goals, we simply *must* increase the number of individual shareowners by several million people.

Economic environment. Now let's turn briefly to the matter of inflation. This word was hardly in anyone's vocabulary 15 years ago. Today, however, Americans view inflation as their number one problem, and it is also the number one problem of people in the investor relations arena. What is the inflation outlook? Unfortunately, virtually all economists envision continued high rates of inflation into the indefinite future. Instead of buying stock, individuals are putting their savings into nonproductive assets such as gold, diamonds, stamps, art, and real estate.

And this is not being done without reason, as the numbers indicate. In the past dozen years, the price of gold has increased at a compound rate of 29 percent a year, diamonds at 15 percent a year, and housing at an annual rate of 10 percent. But the "product" of investor relations—common stocks—has gone up less than 3 percent a year in average market value during the same period.

For all of us in the investor relations field, it's quite obvious that the external environment promises to be essentially hostile. Peter Drucker, perhaps the most creative business philosopher of this century, has addressed that condition in his landmark book, *The Practice of Management.* In Drucker's words, "Managing goes way beyond passive reaction and adaptation. It implies responsibility for attempting to shape the economic environment."

Doesn't that mean that all American business must become more active and outspoken in helping to build an understanding of how the private enterprise system works? Some companies are doing precisely that. A recent *Harvard Business Review* article entitled "Taking on the Hostile Media" cited Mobil Corporation and its public issue ads as a fine example of what can be done. Mobil has elected to put itself into the "marketplace of ideas" by hitting many burning public issues head on in the press. What is most striking about the Mobil campaign is the forthrightness of the company as a bold spokesman for our business system.

There are other companies, of course, that have targeted important public and economic issues. W. R. Grace, for one, targeted the crying need to eliminate the "disincentivization" of our nation's tax policy. General Electric has been a pioneer and long-time champion of increased capital formation, and has actively participated in congressional hearings to further political and public understanding of that neglected national need. In its quarterly and annual reports, as well as in the media, U.S. Steel has conducted a vigorous program for its shareowners, centering on the vital need to increase our nation's productivity.

However, in the hostile environment in which American business operates today, it will take the efforts of many additional companies, each using its own approaches and expertise, to turn public opinion around. It's a job that needs doing, and investor relations practitioners can lead the way to better understanding of the critical issues facing American business and our nation. After all, we communicate with an audience of 25 million vitally interested readers at least once a quarter.

One example of what can be done is the recently legislated cut in capital gains taxes. Much of the success of that endeavor must be attributed to the vigorous efforts of business leaders and investors in taking the message to Congress. However, we still have double taxation of dividends and we still tax capital gains at rates far above the two other leading industrial nations of the Free World—West Germany and Japan.

If the United States is going to compete in domestic markets and in world markets, we've simply got to compete in national tax policies with those nations. For all practical purposes, that would require cutting taxes on capital gains to zero. It would also require pervasive cutbacks in government overregulation of business.

As I noted, Wall Street has been doing less than in the past to serve the individual shareowner and to stimulate growth of the shareowner population. Who will take up the slack? Shouldn't a basic objective of corporate investor relations be to increase the number of individual shareowners? It seems to me that people involved in investor relations have the primary responsibility of informing investors on these issues. In short, we must make the external environment less hostile to individual investors. If we don't, who will?

Gaining more individual shareowners would clearly serve to make any company's stock less vulnerable to the block-trade penchant of many institutional investors. Should there be any doubts on that score, just talk to some of the "top-tier" companies of some five years ago: they have seen what happens when institutions decide to dispose of large blocks of shares. Why not establish a basic goal of increasing corporate shareowners by 5 percent or even 10 percent this year? Here is a "laundry list" of ideas that might serve that objective.

Employee stock plans. Employee stock plans have been around for a long time, especially for management people. However, most companies seem to overlook nonmanagement employees as a source of additional shareowners. Recently, I conducted a survey of some 200 American companies and found that only one third even had a stock purchase plan for nonmanagement employees.

But the "kicker" is that only 1 percent of those 200 companies had 90 percent or more of their nonmanagement employees actually enrolled! Last year, in talking with a visiting delegation of Japanese businessmen, I found that almost every Japanese firm had 90 percent or more of its employees enrolled in a stock purchase plan. Here's another arena in which American industry is going to have to meet the competition.

Now, I must confess that my own company has not been in this select group. However, effective January 1, 1979, under AT&T's labor contract, a new savings plan commenced: under the plan, each dollar saved by an employee in either fixed income securities or company stock will be matched by a 50 cent company contribution—in company stock. This should serve to increase our number of shareowners substantially over the years.

Dividend reinvestment. Dividend reinvestment plans can be a great help in expanding your company's shareowner list. The opportunity to reinvest conveniently and at low cost is an incentive for a non-shareowner to buy your stock. On the other side of the coin, it is also a disincentive for a current participant to sell your company's shares. Considering the need for new equity capital, it's evident that many more companies will be joining the dividend reinvestment parade in future years.

Annual meetings. Another way to enhance shareowner loyalty is to demonstrate that your company really cares for the shareowner as an individual. One effective way to do this is to put your annual meeting "on the road." By moving it each year to the various regions where your shareowners live, you demonstrate that you really do care about them.

Mini-meetings. Another concept—which has been used successfully by G.E., U.S. Steel, AT&T, and other companies—is to hold several regional shareholder meetings, perhaps three or four a year. These take place after the official annual meeting, and are effective vehicles for top management to meet with shareowners and to conduct a constructive dialog.

Open houses. It's a well-established principle of shareownership that people will buy stock in companies they know and can see. What better way is there to explain a company to existing shareowners—as well as to members of the community—than to hold open houses at plants, offices, and in the community?

Registered rep program. How about mounting a registered rep program? In military parlance, RRs are the soldiers in the trenches. Surveys indicate that RRs need pertinent information about your company tailored to their own orientation. As one RR in Denver told me: "We have only 60 seconds to close the sale." For this reason, information must be brief and matter-of-fact.

In conclusion, I see the following problems in the years ahead. First of all, the national economy will be in continuing deep trouble from inflation and from the lack of adequate capital formation. Second, there will be an overriding need to attract massive amounts of new equity capital, and that means *individual* investors. Third, the securities industry will continue to be in a state of flux. But, above all else, it will be a challenge and an opportunity for corporate management to take stronger command of its own destiny by means of innovative investor relations.

In short, there are problems out there, but I'm optimistic that solutions are also at hand. To quote once more from Peter Drucker: "Man is happiest when he faces a challenge." On that basis, all of us involved with investor relations should really enjoy the years ahead!

Index

advertisements
  financial, 235–236
  national, 8
  use of, 213
American Stock Exchange, listing on, versus over-the-counter, 3
American Telephone & Telegraph Co.
  employee stock plan, 272
  use of mini-meetings, 273
analysts
  briefings, 234–235
  see also securities analysts, security analysts
analyst society meetings, presentations at, 8–9, 233–234
annual direct mailing, for recognition, 266
annual meetings
  Borg-Warner approach to, 9
  to enhance shareowner loyalty, 273
  management message at, 135
  as prime means of communication, 233
annual report
  advertising availability of, 187, 213
  aimed at professional investor, 264
  to attract investors, 6–7
  changing approach to, 96
  desired qualities of, 95
  financial review in, 232
  graphs and photos in, 232
  inclusion of fourth quarter report in, 137
  insert in, 187
  legal questions concerning, 95
  listing of goals in, 200
  meeting SEC requirements, 95–96
  no advertising of, 237
  one-page summary in, 200
  operating review in, 232
  time spent reading, 96
  timing in, 98
  use of general-circulation magazine features in, 200
antibusiness bias of media, 183
automatic dividend reinvestment program, 187

balance sheets, issuance of, 264
bank officers, management relationship with, 167
Baruch, Bernard, on short selling, 4
Becton Dickinson & Co., 179–193
Beta coefficient, used to define market risk, 2
block sales, 4
book value, of Dow Jones Industrial Average, 269
Borg-Warner
  annual meeting of, 9
  annual report of, 6–7
  Annual Report 1979, 13–39
  attracting security analysts, 5–6
  Financial Bulletin 1979, 70
  Investor Fact Book 1979, 40–61
  investor relations and disclosures policy, 12
  national advertisement of, 82–83
  photo book, 7
  presentation by, to security analysts, 84–94
  "Sets Record" card, 81
  Shareholder Report, 3rd Quarter 1979, 62–69
  special interim report, 71–80
brand names, use of, for recognition of company, 136, 211, 213
brochure, as communications plan tool, 191–192

brokerage firms
closing of, 269
use of, for research and sales support, 187
brokerage industry
effect of negotiated brokerage commission rates on, 5

capital
demand for, 270
supply of, 270–271
capital gain taxes, as compared to West Germany and Japan, 271–272
capitalization of earnings, 2
cash dividend policy, as statement to investors, 3
Castle & Cooke
advertisements of, 228–229
direct mail program of, 212
investor relations program's long-range objective of, 211
Lessons of Leadership, 224–227
management presentation of, 212
news releases of, 213, 220–223
security analysts meeting agenda, 215–216
security analysts presentations, 212–213, 217–219
stockbroker association presentations, 212
The Castle & Cooke Report, 211
clientele effect, 3
collective buy-sell decisions, interpretation of, 4
commissions
effect on Wall Street research of, 4
negotiated brokerage rates, 5
communications
openness in, fear of susceptibility due to, 198
policy, open, 180
presentation, for regional use, 188
program, limits of, 5
tools for investor relations, 6, 186
company magazine
B-D World, 179–180
Progress, 233, 239–262
consulting firm, use of, 185
corporate advertising, use of, for recognition, 188
corporate communications plan, 179–193
corporate head-quarters community, company involvement in, 192–193
"Corporate Statement of Communications," of Medtronic, 197
credibility risk, 2

direct mail program, 212
disclosure
appropriate, 6
minimum requirements of, 5
policy, 2
quality, 6
dividend
announcements, 3
policy, 3
dividend reinvestment, to expand shareowner list, 272
Doremus & Co., public relations counsel, 211, 212
Dow Jones Industrial Average, 269
Drexel Burnham, study of Wall Street research, 5
Drucker, Peter *(The Practice of Management),* 271, 273

economic environment, 271
efficient market theory, and investor relations, 1–2
Employee Retirement Income Security Act (ERISA), 270
employee stock plans, for nonmanagement people, 272
Ernst & Whinney, 233
Evans Products Company, 263–268
external environment
as consideration of communications plans, 180–181
of the future, 271
external image, as consideration of investor relations program, 181–182

fact book
aimed at analysts, 264
as supplemental investor publication, 7–8, 189
Fact File, of IC Industries, 136, 138
financial bulletin, as investor publication, 8
financially-trained IR people, value of, 231
Financial World Silver Oscar of Industry, 98
FMC
annual report of, 236–237
company magazine *Progress,* 239–262
investor relations program of, as part of financial program, 231
name recognition problem of, 235
use of advertising, 235–236
use of surveys, 236

General Electric
champion of increased capital formation, 271
regional shareholder meetings of, 273

generally accepted accounting principles (GAAP), 2

Harvard Business Review, 271
Haskins & Sells, 233

IC Industries
advertisements of, 139–142
annual report of, 136
Annual Report 1977, excerpts from, 143–160
brochure for potential investors of, 171–174
diversification effort of, 135–136
Fact File, 136, 138
Fact File, August 1979, 175–178
Quarterly Report, September 1978, 161–170
incremental tax rate, 3
individual investors, programs to attract, 185–187, 273
individual shareowners, to reduce vulnerability to blocktrade, 272
individual stocks
effect of short selling on, 4
variation in price of, 2
industry fact book, *see* fact book
industry influences, on price of individual stocks, 2
inflation, 271
in-house publication, use of, in communications plan, 188, 189–190
Institutional Investor magazine, 98
institutional investors meetings, 234
institutionalization of the stock market, effect on investor relations, 180, 182
insurance funds, contribution to capital supply of, 270
interim balance sheet, 264
interim reports, use of, 97
internal environment, as a consideration of communications plan, 180–181
investment shows, use of exhibits and booths at, 213
Investor Fact Book, 6, 7–8
investor relations and disclosure policy, 6
investor relations person (IRP), financial training of, 231–232
investor relations programs
Castle & Cooke's long-range objective for, 211
dealing with recognition problems, 136
goals of, 237–238
low-profile approach in, 264–267
Medtronic's objectives of, 199
as part of financial program, 231
reactive versus initiative, 5
tools of, 199
investor relations staff, 9

Japan
compared to America, in capital gains taxation, 272
employee stock plans of, 272

King, Benjamin, study of pricing of individual stock, 2

Lessons of Leadership, 224–227
listing, effects of, on sales, 3
long-term growth objectives, as object of attention in investor relations plan, 184–185
low-profile approach, to investor relations, 264–267

mail survey, as tool in communications plan, 186
management
accessibility of, to analysts, 184
advising of social responsibility, 192
consistency of, value in, 268
establishing quality and depth of, 183–184
fiduciary task of, 2
improving communications with middle and senior, 192
meetings with investors, 233
presentations by, 212
stock valuation control by, 2
tour of financial cities by, 183
market influences, on price of individual stock, 2
market price dollars, 269
market risk, 2
Medtronic
Annual Report 1978, summary page, 210
background information on, 195
business goals of, 200
"Corporate Statement on Communications," 197
financial goals of, 200–201
investor relations program objectives of, 199
need for capital of, 195
recognition program of, 197
sample press releases of, 202–209
merchandising stock, on retail basis, 187
Merrill Lynch, withdrawal of opinion, 266
mini-meetings, as regional shareholder meetings, 273

minimum disclosure requirements, 5
Mobil Corporation, 271
modern portfolio theory, assisting the investor relations manager, 1–2
multiple colinearity, affecting individual stock prices, 4

negotiated brokerage commission rates, 5
news releases
  Castle & Cooke's, 220–223
  see also press releases
New York Society of Security Analysts, 3, 265
New York Stock Exchange
  listing on, versus over-the-counter, 3
  Medtronic's listing on, 196
nominal dollars, 269

open houses, for recognition, 273
Opinion Research Corporation, study of security analysts by, 10
over-the-counter market versus listing, 3

Peat Marwick Mitchell & Co., 233
pension funds, 270–271
photo book, Borg-Warner's, 7
press releases
  Medtronic's, to physicians, 196
  see also news releases
product line breakdown, 264
Progress, FMC company magazine, 233, 239–262

quarterly report,
  feature article format of, 232
  improving, 188
  magazine format for, 137–138
  value of, 8

recognition of company
  action programs for, 190
  among potential investors, 267–268
  importance of, 182, 185–186, 235
  through products, 211
regional shareholder information meetings, 9
registered representatives (RRs), 187
  communications with, 236–237
  population, drop in, 269
  program, value of, 273
reinvestment
  high rate of, 3
risk, 2

St. Joe Minerals Corp.
  annual report of, 95–98
  Annual Report 1976, 99–133
  background information on, 95
  investor communications program of, 95
secondary distributions, 4
securities analysts
  providing detailed information for, 189
  see also analysts, security analysts
Securities and Exchange Commission
  and brokers communications, 237
  meeting annual report requirements of, 95, 96, 232
  study, on investor decisions, 7
security analysts
  attracting, 5–6
  meeting agenda, 215–216
  meetings of, presentations to, 212, 217–219
  Opinion Research Corporation study of, 10
  requirements of, for investor relations program, 10
  see also analysts, securities analysts
shareholder meetings, 9
shareholder populations, decline in, 269
shareholder representative, 9
shareholders, new
  letter of welcome to, 187
  telephone survey of, 186
short selling, effect on price movement of, 4
special interim reports, 8
Standard & Poor's 500, 270
stockbroker associations, 212
stock dividends, 3
stockholders, surveillance of shifts in, 188–189
stock splits, 3
surveys
  to judge effectiveness of program, 236
  telephone, use of, 186

test for deciding whether to talk, 198–199

unsolicited ideas, acknowledgement of, 190–191
U.S. Steel
  on productivity, 271
  use of mini-meetings, 272

visibility of management, establishing, 183–184
volume, effect on prices, 3–4

The Wall Street Journal, 137, 213, 266
Wall Street research
  and commissions, 4
  after negotiated brokerage commission rates, 5